Que's Guide to Data Recovery

Scott Mueller

with Alan C. Elliott

Que's Guide to Data Recovery

Library of Congress Catalog No.: 90-62953

ISBN 0-88022-541-6

94 93 92 91 4 3 2

Interpretation of the printing code: the rightmost double-digit number is the year of the book's printing; the rightmost single-digit number, the number of the book's printing. For example, a printing code of 91-1 shows that the first printing of the book occurred in 1991.

Publisher: Lloyd J. Short

Associate Publisher: Karen A. Bluestein

Acquisitions Editor: Tim Ryan

Product Development Manager: Mary Bednarek

Managing Editor: Paul Boger

Book Designer: Scott Cook

Production Team: Jill D. Bomaster, Scott Boucher, Jeanne Clark, Martin Coleman; Sandy Grieshop, Betty Kish, Bob LaRoche, Sarah Leatherman, Howard Peirce, Tad Ringo, Christine Young

To Emerson and Amanda,
my personal drivetrain

Product Director
Shelley O'Hara

Senior Editor
Sandra Blackthorn

Editors
Sara Allaei
Sharon Boller
Kelly Currie
Beth Hoger
Mike La Bonne
Lori A. Lyons
Gregory Robertson
Heidi Weas Muller

Technical Editor
Bruce Morse

Composed in Garamond and Macmillan
by Que Corporation

Scott Mueller

Scott Mueller is the president of Mueller Business Systems, an international personal computer consulting and seminar training firm. His company specializes in technical seminars and documentation covering the upgrade, repair, maintenance, and troubleshooting of microcomputer hardware, operating systems software, and local area network systems, as well as data recovery from damaged or corrupted disks, operating system file structures, and data files. Mr. Mueller is an expert in data recovery techniques and has extensive experience with floppy and hard drives, interfaces, and disks.

Since 1982, Mr. Mueller also has developed and presented seminars and training courses with the American Institute, an internationally recognized seminar company. He has designed, written, and taught comprehensive seminars in all areas of microcomputer hardware and software. These seminars are presented throughout America, Canada, Europe, and Australia.

Mr. Mueller is the author of several books and training manuals, including the best-selling *Upgrading and Repairing PCs*, published by Que Corporation.

Trademark Acknowledgments

Que Corporation has made every effort to supply trademark information about company names, products, and services mentioned in this book. Trademarks indicated below were derived from various sources. Que Corporation cannot attest to the accuracy of this information.

Apple and Macintosh are registered trademarks of Apple Computer, Inc.

COMPAQ and DESKPRO are registered trademarks of COMPAQ Computer Corporation.

CopyWrite is a trademark of Quaid Software, Ltd.

dBASE is a registered trademark of Ashton-Tate Corporation.

DS Backup is a trademark of Design Software.

FastBack is a registered trademark of Fifth Generation Software.

IBM is a registered trademark and Micro Channel and PS/2 are trademarks of International Business Machines Corporation.

Microsoft is a registered trademark of Microsoft Corporation.

Norton Utilities and Norton BackUp are registered trademarks and Norton DiskEdit is a trademark of Symantec Corporation.

Novell and NetWare are trademarks of Novell, Inc.

PC Tools Deluxe and Copy II PC are trademarks of Central Point Software.

Speedstor is a trademark of Storage Dimensions, Inc.

SpinRite is a trademark of Gibson Research Corporation.

UNIX is a registered trademark of AT&T.

Wang is a registered trademark of Wang Laboratories, Inc.

WordPerfect is a registered trademark of WordPerfect Corporation.

WordStar is a registered trademark of WordStar International, Inc.

Contents at a Glance

II Recovering Data

Introduction

Welcome to *Que's Guide to Data Recovery*. This book provides the information necessary for you to restore disk-based information that has become lost, damaged, or completely inaccessible.

In my work in personal computer service and repair, I cannot limit my knowledge to either hardware *or* software problems. I continually find hardware problems that actually are software problems in disguise. Many service calls turn out to be cases in which the hardware functions perfectly according to diagnostics tests but the system still doesn't boot and run correctly. I have discovered that no matter how great your background and knowledge of hardware, you cannot effectively troubleshoot and correct PC problems if you don't understand the operating system and software running on the PC.

As an example, I have found that many technicians use the brute-force method of *reformatting* a disk to correct a problem when all that's actually required is a small software patch applied in the correct place. Users are much happier when you can repair a system quickly and efficiently—without replacing a disk needlessly—and restore access to their original data.

Anyone with control of an IBM or compatible system needs to know about data recovery, which is the primary reason that I wrote this book.

Another reason that I wrote this book relates to the cost of repairing PCs. Repairing most IBM and compatible systems today is easy and relatively inexpensive due to the modularity of the systems' designs and the relatively low cost of the replacement parts. In most cases, however, the information stored on a particular PC or the actual job that it performs is far more valuable than the system itself.

Suppose, for example, that a problem occurs with a system that functions as a file server on a network with 100 users (all of whom are salespersons taking orders from customers). The job function of the system and its data are extremely important to the company using the system. If it fails, the system can be replaced instantly with a duplicate or equivalent one, but every minute that the system doesn't allow the salespersons to take orders, the company loses money. For this reason, many companies offer service contracts guaranteeing that a system can be made functional or a backup system can be installed within a certain time period.

You cannot buy new copies of your data at the local store or buy "equivalent" data to replace that which is lost. Unless a backup exists, you must re-create the data from scratch. Therefore, the data stored on most business users' systems is priceless. You can buy a new 20M hard disk today for $200, but it doesn't come preformatted with the data that was on the one that failed. If the information on a system is priceless, then so is the knowledge of how to recover and restore that information in case of disaster.

This point leads to the last reason that I wrote this book: the lack of backups of users' data. Nearly all that has been stated about the importance and value of data recovery knowledge and skill is meaningless if you have complete backups of all your data and program files. If all users had perfect backups of their data, a book such as this wouldn't be needed, and data recovery knowledge and skills would be relatively worthless. Unfortunately, the reality is that many users don't have recent backups, and the less frequently backups are made, the more valuable data recovery knowledge and skill become.

Who Should Read This Book?

If you are more than just a user of your system and want to be more involved in the design, organization, maintenance, and troubleshooting of the system, this book is designed for you. If you want to eliminate all the mysteries of how the system operates—especially regarding your data—read this book. To accomplish these goals, you need a level of knowledge that is probably uncharacteristic for many other tools of your business, but the state of the current microcomputer industry demands such knowledge. You must be the craftsman who knows exactly which tool to use for the task and how to use that tool correctly.

Que's Guide to Data Recovery is designed for users who want a good understanding of why things work the way they do. Each chapter gives detailed explanations and reasons for each problem or situation you may encounter so that you will be better able to handle tough problems. You will attain a "feel" for what is going on in your system so you can rely on your own judgment and observations—not just a table of canned troubleshooting steps.

With the knowledge and skills gained from this book, you will be the master of your system. With a full understanding of how information is stored on your system's disks and knowledge of how to recover that information if a problem occurs, you will be able to troubleshoot problems and judge the differences between hardware and software problems more effectively. Finally, you will gain skills that may become extremely valuable when a catastrophic data loss occurs and no backup is available. This level of knowledge and skill will make your use of an IBM or compatible system much more productive and trouble free.

What Is in This Book?

In Part I of this book, you examine disk drives and DOS.

A major cause of data recovery problems stems from improper use of disk drives. Chapters 1 through 4 examine floppy and hard disk drive characteristics that are most often misunderstood and result in the need for data recovery. These chapters include simple steps for properly formatting and using floppy and hard disk drives.

Chapters 5 and 6 cover in detail the more advanced and hard to understand areas of DOS. These chapters aren't intended to be a complete discussion of all aspects of DOS but instead focus on the operational characteristics and mechanics as they relate to disk storage and data recovery.

In Chapter 7, you examine in detail the way disks are organized under DOS and gain a complete understanding of what is stored on a disk, where it is stored, and why it is there. This chapter includes an examination of boot sectors, file allocation tables, directories, and more. You learn to look at a disk just as DOS does, to gain insight into problems with disk corruption.

Part II of this book focuses on data recovery.

In Chapters 8, 9, and 10, you examine tools, techniques, and procedures to use in order to solve the various problems you may encounter with files and disks. The tools vary from the DOS DEBUG program to the popular Norton and Mace Utilities.

Chapter 11 examines virus programs and other related types of malicious or destructive software. You learn what a virus program is and what variant types of programs exist. You learn procedures for protecting your system from this type of software and which software utilities and tools make this protection possible. You examine some techniques and tools for detecting whether your system has been invaded before the damage occurs, and you examine how to correct the damage after it occurs.

Chapter 12 covers preventive maintenance procedures that make future data recovery operations easier (and maybe even unnecessary). You examine the backup process from both a hardware and software perspective. Although this chapter doesn't cover the hardware directly, it does give some hardware information and tips so you can properly identify whether the problem is hardware or software related; then this chapter explains how to solve the problem regardless of its cause. (For detailed information on the hardware, see *Upgrading and Repairing PCs*, published by Que Corporation.)

Six appendixes contain concise information on statistics for floppy disk drives, hard disk parameter tables, sector formats, disk maps, ASCII character codes, and memory maps.

Que's Guide to Data Recovery is a valuable reference tool, containing many charts and tables of information needed for data recovery operations. Many pieces of information have been gathered from various reference sources, but most of the information and techniques have been culled from actual experience and work in the field. I sincerely hope that you enjoy this book.

Part I

Examining Disk Drives and DOS

Includes

Disk Drive Fundamentals
Floppy Disk Drive Operation
Hark Disk Basics
Hard Disk Formatting
DOS Background
DOS Versions
Disk Format and Structure

1

Disk Drive Fundamentals

To become a surgeon, you must take courses in human anatomy. That way, when you're performing an operation, you don't wonder about the functions of all the little tubes in your patient's chest. In the same way, you should know about the anatomy of disk storage before you try to diagnose and cure problems related to your disk drives.

Before you can begin using data recovery concepts, you must understand how disk drives store and read information. This chapter provides details about how disk drives operate and discusses how information is written to and read from a disk. This chapter defines many terms used throughout the book, including *cylinders*, *tracks*, and *sectors*. Finally, the chapter introduces you to the logic of how the *formatting* process prepares a disk to receive information.

Understanding How Data Is Stored

Because this book discusses the recovery of data from damaged disks, you should know exactly how data is stored on the disk in the first place. Understanding the magnetic data storage process will help you develop a feel for how your disk drives operate and an understanding of why disks and disk drives act or react in certain ways. Knowing what is going on "under the hood" certainly can improve how you work with disk drives and disks.

Almost all disk drives used in personal computer systems today operate on magnetic principles. Although several forms of optical disk drives are available, they usually are used only as secondary peripheral devices. The computer to which an optical disk drive is connected probably still uses a magnetic storage medium as the primary disk system. Optical disk drives are a completely new type of technology and have a long way to go before they completely replace magnetic storage in computer systems.

Magnetic drives, such as floppy disk drives and hard disk drives, operate using a basic principle of physics known as *electromagnetism*. The principle of electromagnetism states that as an electric current flows through a conductor, a magnetic field is generated around that conductor. This magnetic field then can influence any magnetic material within the field. For example, you probably have noticed that when you bring a magnet near a ferrous metal object (into the magnetic field), the magnet "reaches out" and attracts the object even before touching it. You also may have observed how two magnets attract or repel each other according to which ends of the magnets are brought close to each other. This phenomenon occurs because a magnet has "north" and "south" poles, just like the Earth. If you have two magnets, opposite poles attract and like poles repel.

On most magnets, you cannot change which pole is north and which pole is south. However, electromagnetics are created by the passing of an electric current through a conductor. By reversing the direction of the electrical current flow, the magnetic field polarity also is reversed. An electric motor operates using the principle of electromagnetism to exert pushing and pulling (attracting and repelling) forces on magnets attached to a rotating shaft. By creating magnetic energy in this manner, you can write or store information on a floppy or hard disk.

Another effect of the electromagnetic principle is that if a conductor is passed through a magnetic field, an electrical current is generated. As the polarity of the magnetic field changes, the direction of current flow changes. An electrical generator or alternator (such as the one on your car) operates by rotating electromagnets past coils of wire conductors in which large amounts of electrical current can be induced. This operation of electromagnetism is how data is read back later.

The read/write heads in your disk drives (both floppy and hard disk) basically are constructed as U-shaped pieces of magnetic material, much like a horseshoe magnet (see fig. 1.1). Because of the shape, any magnetic fields generated are concentrated in the gap between the ends of the U. The drive head is not a magnet itself but instead consists of material in which a magnetic field can be generated. The drive head has coils of wire wrapped around it through which a current can flow. When the disk drive passes a current through these coils, a magnetic field is generated in the head. This field has a polarity based on the direction of the flow of current through the coils. The magnetic field is concentrated in the head gap area (the area between the points on the U) that is resting on or very close to the surface of the disk.

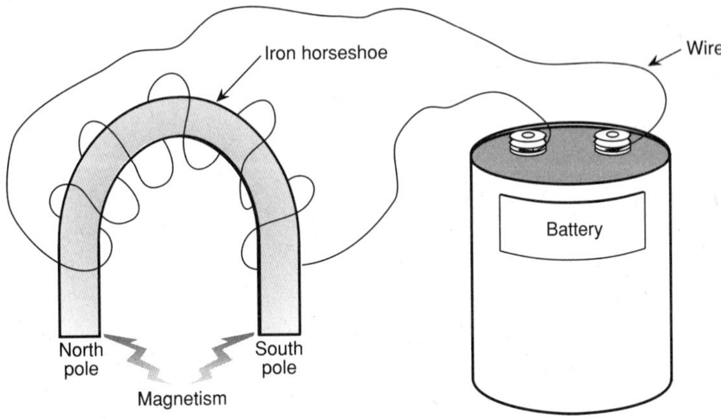

Fig. 1.1. *Passing an electrical current through a wire surrounding an iron horseshoe, turning it into a magnet.*

A disk consists of some form of substrate material (such as mylar for floppy disks or aluminum for hard disks) on which a layer of magnetizable material has been deposited. This material usually is some form of iron oxide to which various other elements have been added. In a disk, the polarity of each particle's magnetic field normally is in a state of disarray. Because none of the individual particles' fields are pointing in the same direction, each tiny individual magnetic field is canceled by some other field pointing in the opposite direction, which means that the information on the disk is random and of no real use in its present state.

At some point during your academic career, you may have performed an experiment that involved placing metal shavings on a piece of paper and a magnet on the other side of the paper. As you moved the magnet under the paper, you observed how the metal filings moved and lined up to the poles of the magnet. A disk contains similar metal particles that can be influenced by a magnetic field.

As the magnetic field generated by the drive head is focused in the head gap area, and as the head gap is touching or in very close proximity to the surface of the disk, the strong magnetic field causes the particles in the disk surface near the head to become polarized in the direction the field in the head gap is pointing. All particles in the area near the head gap are aligned in the same direction. This process of aligning the particles "writes" information to the disk. These particles remain aligned until the read/write head changes them again. This semipermanent state enables a disk to retain or store information even when the computer is turned off. The individual metal particles no longer are situated randomly on the disk; instead, all particles are aligned in the same direction, which creates a specific meaningful magnetic pattern (a *field*) that can be read (by the head, as will be discussed later) in that region of the disk. This local field is generated by the many magnetic particles operating as a team to produce a detectable field with a unified direction. The term *flux* describes a magnetic field with a given direction. A disk can store information in two states only: as a strong aligned flux in one direction—referred to as a logic 1—or a strong aligned flux in the other direction—a logic 0. Chapters 2 and 3 provide more information on how the head reads information from disk.

As the disk surface rotates under the drive head, the head can lay down a magnetic flux over a region of the disk. When the electrical flow through the coils in the head is reversed, the magnetic field polarity in the head gap also is reversed. This process causes the flux being placed on the disk to reverse as well. The flux reversal simply is a change in polarity of the alignment of magnetic particles in the disk surface. A drive head uses these flux reversals to write (record data) on a disk.

In a computer, data is stored as a series of 0s and 1s. Each piece of 0/1 information is called a *bit*. To store bits from the computer's memory, the computer must be capable of writing and reading a binary pattern (a two-state pattern—in this case, 0 and 1) similar to the computer's 0/1 memory. In the case of magnetic storage, you can create a binary pattern on disk by causing the magnetic particles for one polarity to mean 0 and the reverse polarity to mean 1. In this way, each 0/1 bit written to disk is represented by the magnetic particles' alignment on disk.

For each data bit that is written to disk, a pattern of flux reversals is placed on the disk in specific areas known as *bit cells*. A bit cell simply is an area of the disk controlled by time and rotational speed in which flux reversals are placed by a drive head. The particular pattern of flux reversals used for storing a given data bit is the *encoding method*. The drive logic or controller circuitry encodes the data to be stored as a series of flux reversals over a period of time according to the encoding method used. Popular encoding methods include modified frequency modulation (MFM) and run length limited (RLL) encoding. All floppy disk drives use the MFM scheme, but hard disks may use either MFM, RLL, or modifications of these two popular methods. Encoding methods are described in more detail in Chapter 3.

When a drive head passes over a disk surface in which a magnetic flux previously has been placed, a current of a given direction is generated in the head coils. The direction of the current flow depends on the direction of the flux. When the head passes over an area where the flux direction reverses, the current flow being generated in the head coils also reverses. The currents generated in the head while the head is passing over a disk in read mode are virtually identical to (although much weaker than) the currents passed through the heads during the recording of the disk. Sensitive electronics in the drive and controller assembly then can amplify and decode these weak electrical currents back into data that is (theoretically) identical to the data recorded originally.

Figures 1.2 and 1.3 illustrate the processes by which information is written to and read from a disk. Stated simply, a disk is recorded on by the passing of electrical currents through an electromagnet (the drive head), which generates a magnetic field that is stored on a disk. The computer sends memory patterns (such as 10110) to the drive head. Electrical pulses cause the drive head to reverse polarity in patterns that match the 0/1 bits of the computer's memory. The polarity of the drive head causes the metal particles to align north-south or south-north.

A disk is read by the passing of the head back over the surface of the disk. The magnetized particles on the disk cause a weak signal in the head. Each signal matches the polarity of the information on disk. Amplifier circuitry in the head converts the signals into 0s and 1s and sends them to the computer's memory. This process enables your computer to read back the same information that was recorded.

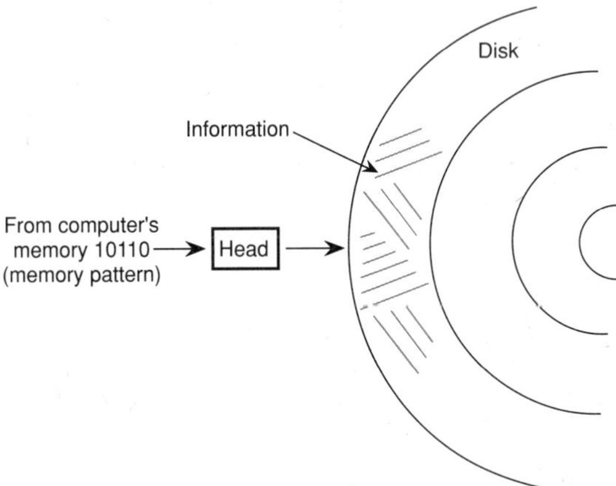

Fig. 1.2. *Writing information to disk.*

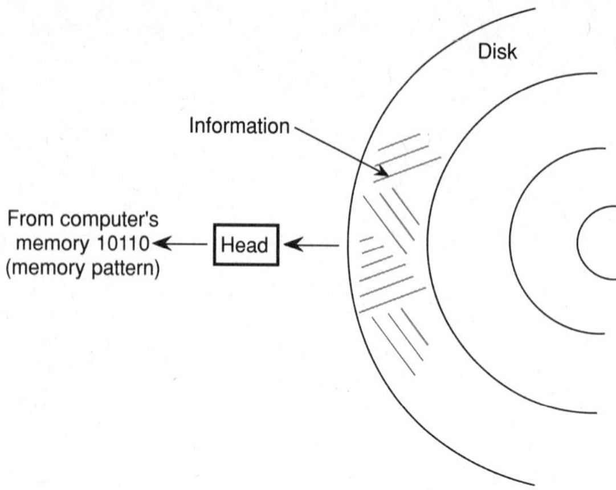

Fig. 1.3. Reading information from disk.

Defining Elements and Terms

Before data can be placed on a disk, the disk must be divided into numbered areas so that stored information can be retrieved accurately. This process is known as *formatting* (see the section "Formatting a Disk" later in this chapter). A disk that has not been formatted has no such numbered bins for data storage.

The act of formatting a disk can be likened to building numbered shelves or storage bins in a warehouse so that items stored in the warehouse can be located accurately. In the terminology of disks and disk drives, these numbered storage areas are referred to as *tracks* and *sectors*. This section explains how disks are formatted and defines the terms involved. In addition, this section examines the creation of tracks and sectors and the contents of each of these fields.

Tracks

Tracks are concentric rings on which data can be written or from which data can be read. Floppy disks usually contain 40 or 80 tracks on each side, and hard disks contain from 100 to several thousand tracks on each side.

When a disk drive is constructed, the drive is designed so that the heads can move in and out across the surface of the disk as it rotates. The head assembly can stop at given places along the path of movement. The head assembly remains stationary over a particular point on the disk during reading and writing operations, and the disk itself rotates constantly. As the disk surface rotates under the head, the head follows a circular path—a track—on the disk. As the disk rotates and the head remains stationary, the head can read from or write to this single track area on the disk. Accessing more of the disk's recording surface requires that the heads move inward toward the center of the disk or outward toward the outside of the disk until another stopping point or track is encountered.

Each drive is designed with a head assembly that can stop only at predetermined places. This drive feature limits and defines the total number of tracks that a disk can have. A 5 1/4-inch, 360K disk drive, for example, is designed to permit only 40 stopping points in the head's travel. These 40 stopping points (40 tracks) are spaced 1/48 inch apart and are numbered from 0 to 39. The track at the outer portion of the disk's recording area is assigned the number 0, and the track nearest the center of the disk is assigned the number 39 (see fig. 1.4).

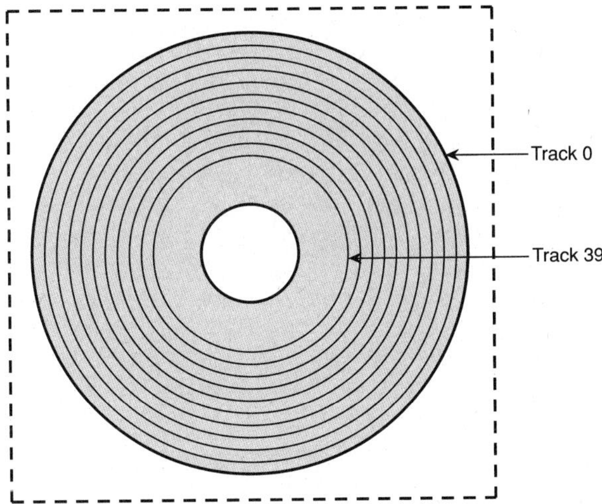

Fig. 1.4. Tracks on a 5 1/4-inch, 360K disk.

These tracks are circular, concentric, and not connected in any way. A disk is not like a phonograph record, which has a single groove that follows a spiral path from the outside to the inside of the record. In a disk, the tracks are perfectly circular and do not touch each other.

Cylinders

A standard floppy disk drive has two heads: one head reads and writes to the top of a disk, and the other head reads and writes to the bottom of the disk. Each head is mounted on the same movement mechanism, the *head actuator*. The head actuator can move the heads to any given track position for reading and writing. The heads move together. When the top head is over the 35th track, the bottom head is over the 35th track on the other side of the disk.

This dual head movement causes confusion in discussing the term *track,* because track 35 exists on the bottom as well as on the top of the disk. In fact, a 360K disk has 40 tracks on *each side*—a total of 80 tracks. Consequently, a so-called 80-track floppy disk really has 160 tracks, because 80 tracks are on the bottom and 80 tracks are on the top. The term *cylinder* describes both tracks at a given position on the top and bottom of the disk. For example, cylinder 25 refers to the top and the bottom surface of the track at the 26th position from the outside of the disk. Instead of saying that two track 25s exist, you can say more accurately that one cylinder 25 exists.

To minimize head movement during reading and writing operations, both tracks (on the top and bottom of the disk) are written to or read from before the heads move on to the next pair. Single-headed drives (which are obsolete) could use only the tracks available on one side of the disk. A two-headed drive writes first to the bottom surface and then to the top surface before moving on to the next cylinder or track pair.

The bottom track is on side 0, and the top track is on side 1. At head position 0, cylinder 0 consists of track 1 on side 0 and track 1 on side 1. Cylinder 1 consists of track 2 on side 0 and track 2 on side 1. The disk tracks are numbered from the outside to the inside cylinders in this manner. During data recovery, this knowledge of how information is written to disk can help you understand where to look for "lost" information.

In summary, cylinders are concentric tracks that line up vertically through all sides of a disk.

Sectors

A single disk track's area is too large to be managed effectively as a single storage unit. Most disk tracks can store 8,000 or more bytes of data—a capacity that would be too large (and therefore inefficient) for storing small files. For this reason, a disk track is divided into several numbered divisions known as *sectors*. These sectors can be described as slices of a track (see fig. 1.5).

Different types of disks and disk drives split a track into different numbers of sectors depending on the density of the tracks. Floppy disk formats, for example, currently use between 8 and 18 sectors per track. Hard disks usually store data at a higher density and can use between 17 and 64 sectors per track. Sectors created by standard formatting procedures always have had a 512-byte capacity, but this number may change in the future.

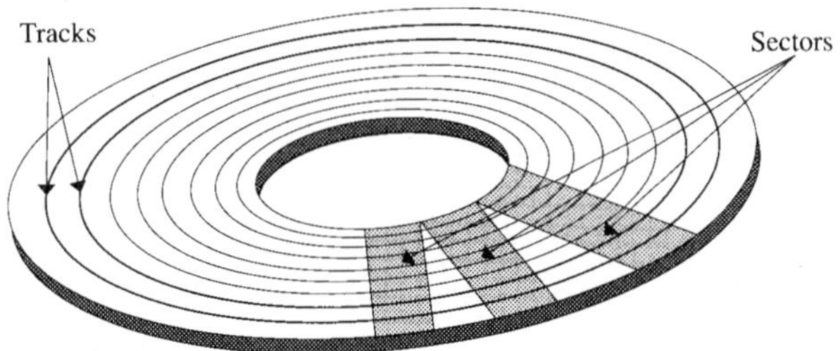

Fig. 1.5. A disk's tracks and sectors.

Track sectors are numbered beginning with 1, unlike the tracks or cylinders themselves, which begin with 0. A 1.2M floppy disk, for example, contains 80 cylinders numbered from 0 to 79, and each track on each cylinder has 15 sectors numbered from 1 to 15. (Why sector numbering starts with 1 is a mystery, but that numbering is the standard.) Sectors are numbered sequentially on floppies, but on hard disks sectors often are *interleaved* at some preset value. Interleaved sectors are not numbered in sequential order but instead are numbered in an intertwining fashion. (The term *interleaved* is explained in much more detail in Chapter 4.) The interleave usually is required because the disk spins so fast that after reading a sector, the disk controller is not ready to read the sector that immediately follows. Therefore, the next sector desired is spaced several sectors away to enable the controller to catch up.

When a disk is formatted, additional areas are created on the disk so that the disk controller can number sectors and identify the beginning and the end of each sector. These areas precede and trail each sector's data area. This process accounts for the difference between a disk's unformatted and formatted capacities. A 2M, 3 1/2-inch floppy disk, for example, has a capacity of only 1.44M when formatted, and a 38M hard disk has a capacity of only 32M when formatted. Reserved areas exist for all kinds of disks.

Many people say that each sector on a disk is 512 bytes in size. Technically, this statement is incorrect! Each sector can store 512 bytes of data, but the data area is only a portion of the sector. Each disk sector typically occupies 571 bytes on a disk, of which only 512 bytes are available for user data.

You can think of each sector as a page in a book. Each page contains text, but the entire page cannot be filled with text. Each page must have top, bottom, left, and right margins. The margins contain information such as chapter titles (track and cylinder numbers) and page numbers (sector numbers). These areas are created and written to during the formatting process for the disk (see the section "Formatting a Disk" later in this chapter). The formatting process fills the data area of each sector with a dummy value as a result of testing the disk's surface for usable spots. After the disk is formatted, the data area can be altered by normal writing to the disk. The sector header and trailer information (the area in the sector before and after the 512-byte data area) cannot be altered. This information is changed only when the disk is formatted.

Each sector has a prefix portion that identifies the start of the sector and the sector number, as well as a suffix portion that contains a ***checksum*** code used for ensuring the integrity of the data (see fig. 1.6). As the name implies, a checksum is a number that should match the value calculated by creating a sum from the data stored in the sector.

For example, suppose that you assign a number value to each letter of the alphabet. You can calculate a code for a particular sentence by adding up the numbers associated with each character. That sentence then has a "checksum" value that can be checked against the value of the original sentence. If, for some reason, one letter in the new sentence is changed, you get a different total when you add up the letter values and the checksum does not match. The checksum found in each sector's suffix portion is used in a similar manner to check the integrity of the data contained in that sector.

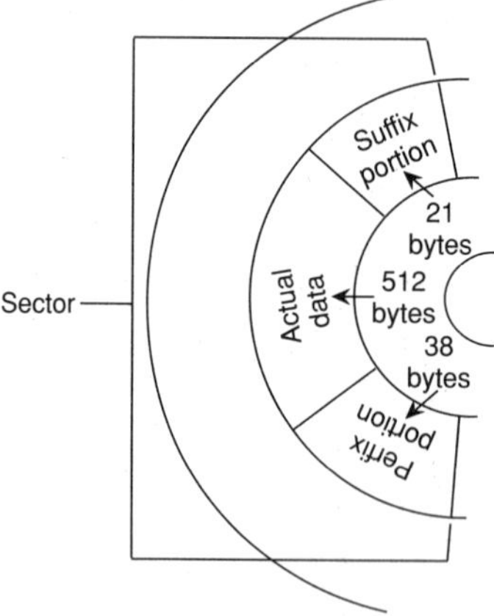

Fig. 1.6. Division of a sector.

In addition to a sector's prefix and suffix portions, gaps that don't contain usable data space exist between tracks and between each track's sectors. The prefix, suffix, and gaps account for the space that is lost between the unformatted capacity of a disk and the actual formatted capacity.

Formatting a Disk

Now that you know how disks can be segmented into tracks and sectors, you are ready to learn the basics of formatting. Usually, you must consider two types of formats: the *physical* (or *low-level*) format and the *logical* (or *high-level*) format. When a floppy disk is formatted, the DOS FORMAT command performs both processes simultaneously. When formatting a hard disk, however, you must perform each operation separately. In addition, a hard disk requires a third step between the two formats in which *partitioning* information is written to the disk. To format a hard disk, then, you must perform three steps: the low-level format, the partitioning, and the high-level format. These processes are examined in detail in Chapter 4. This section provides an overview.

A hard disk is designed to hold more than one operating system. In order for the hard disk to hold more than one operating system, a separation of the levels of format must exist. The physical (low-level) format always remains the same, regardless of which operating system is used, but the high-level format must be different for each operating system. The partitioning step enables more than one type of DOS to use a single hard disk or a single type of DOS to use the disk as several logical drives.

During the low-level format, the disk's tracks are divided into a specific number of sectors. The sector header and trailer information is recorded, as are intersector and intertrack gaps. Each sector's data area also is filled with a 512 dummy value—usually the value F6 (in hexadecimal); however, other values or even patterns of bytes can be used. For floppy disks, the actual number of sectors recorded on each track depends on the type of disk and drive. For hard disks, the number of sectors per track depends on the drive interface and the controller used. (The specifics of interfaces and controllers are covered in Chapter 3.)

The following listing provides examples of hard disk sectoring for different types of interfaces:

Interface	*Sectors/Track*
ST-506/412 MFM	17
ST-506/412 RLL	25 or 26
ESDI or SCSI	32 through 64

After performing a low-level format, and prior to performing a high-level format, you must use the DOS FDISK program to partition the hard disk. This program prepares the hard disk to hold information concerning one or more operating systems (see Chapter 4 for more information on FDISK).

During the high-level format, DOS places on the disk the structure necessary for managing files and data. During this step, DOS places a volume boot sector, a file allocation table (FAT), and a root directory on each logical drive that is formatted. (These items are discussed in detail in Chapter 4.) These data structures enable DOS to manage accurately the space on the disk, keep track of files, and manage defective areas so that they do not cause problems.

High-level formatting really isn't formatting at all; high-level formatting involves creating the table of contents for the disk. The low-level format is the real format in which tracks and sectors are written on the disk. The single DOS FORMAT command performs both low-level and high-level format operations on a floppy disk but only high-level format operations for a hard disk. Hard disk low-level formats require a special utility usually supplied by the system or controller manufacturer. These formats are discussed in detail in later chapters.

Chapter Summary

You now understand the basics of disk operation. You are familiar with the basic terms that describe areas of the disk, and you understand how formatting divides a disk into usable areas. This chapter provides a foundation of knowledge that will be built on throughout the rest of the book. The following chapters explain floppy disk drives and hard disk drives in greater detail.

2

Floppy Disk Drive Operation

As a user, you can prevent most data recovery situations by knowing a little about computer hardware. In this chapter, you examine floppy disk drives and floppy disks in great detail. More than 75 percent of all floppy disk and drive problems are caused by improper system operation. Although examining the ins and outs of floppy disks and drives takes time and may seem complicated at first, doing so will enable you to grasp and understand the technology completely.

By knowing how a drive works physically, you can eliminate "pilot error" problems, and you can distinguish between easily solvable problems and serious hardware problems. You can be a much better system user if you understand fully how the system works.

Understanding Floppy Disk Drive Operation

The physical operation of a floppy disk drive is fairly simple. The operations of a 5 1/4-inch disk drive and a 3 1/2-inch disk drive are similar. When the disk is inserted into the drive, one head is positioned above the disk and the other head is positioned below the disk. With the disk loaded, both heads clasp and ride on the disk as the disk spins. The disk itself rotates at 300 rpm or 360 rpm. (Only high-density 1.2M drives rotate disks at 360 rpm.) With the disk spinning, the heads can move in and out approximately 1 inch, writing 40 or 80 cylinders. A single cylinder is comprised of the track on the top and the track on the bottom of a disk (see Chapter 1 for more information on cylinders).

The heads actually record using a "tunnel erase" procedure in which a track is written to a specified width, and then the edges of the track are erased to prevent interference with any adjacent tracks. This "tunnel erase" procedure magnetically clips the tracks' edges, resulting in clearly defined tracks that do not blend into adjacent tracks. A problem that results from using the same disk in different size drives is that the tracks can be recorded at different widths for different drives, which can cause incompatibilities between some drives. Drives record at different widths because as new (technically advanced) drives are introduced, they require smaller widths to record the same material, which results in different recording widths for various drives. This situation is examined in more detail later in the section "Recording Problems with 1.2M and 360K Drives."

Each floppy drive has two motors: the spindle motor and the head actuator. The *spindle motor* spins the disk in the drive at 300 or 360 rpm. In all but the oldest floppy drives, these motors are a direct-drive, pancake type of motor. The older full-height and some older half-height drives used a motor with a belt driving the spindle. Belt-driven floppy drives have not been produced for many years; however, you may see belt-driven motors in old (early to mid-80s) drives. This motor or spindle assembly often has strobe marks that radiate outward from the center and are used for making speed adjustments to the drives. Speed adjustments are required periodically because a drive operating off-speed can cause the computer to read data incorrectly from a disk. Because many diagnostic software tools for testing drive speed are available and because the drive bottom must be visible for strobe marks to be useful, strobe marks are used less frequently today. Most modern half-height floppy drives have automatic speed adjustment circuits that sense and correct drive speed continuously. These drives need not be (and cannot be) adjusted.

The *head actuator* is the motor that moves the read/write heads in and out across the surface of the disk as it spins. Head actuator motors usually are called *stepper motors*—a name that reflects the special type of motor that head actuators use. The stepper motor coils and uncoils a split steel band around the motor shaft. As the band wraps and unwraps, the rotary motion of the shaft is converted into linear head movement. Each increment or "step" in the motor's travel usually results in a single track movement for the heads.

The rotation of the stepper motor varies with different drive types. The stepper motor rotates 1.8 degrees per step for the 80-cylinder drives and 3.6 degrees per step for the 40-cylinder drives. When an 80-cylinder drive is used for recording on 40-cylinder disks, the heads are double-stepped to write on the appropriate tracks.

Another operational characteristic that differs with floppy drive type is the use of low- and high-density disks. High-density disks are written on differently than low-density disks. To optimize recording, low-density disks use a lower write current signal at the heads during recording. You can wreak havoc when using low-density disks formatted as high-density disks or when using high-density disks formatted as low-density disks. In each case, the improper format causes problems. These problems and the precise differences between high- and low-density disks are discussed later in the sections "Recording Problems with 1.44M 3 1/2-Inch Drives" and "Recording Problems with 1.2M and 360K Drives."

Reviewing the Types of Floppy Drives

Four basic types of floppy drives are available for any IBM-compatible system. Table 2.1 summarizes the four drive types according to their formatting specifications. Note that low-density is the same as double-density, and such disks usually are labeled DS/DD (for double-sided/double-density). High-density disks usually are labeled DS/HD (for double-sided/high-density).

Table 2.1
IBM-Compatible Floppy Disk Drive Formats

5 1/4-Inch	*Low-Density*	*High-Density*
Bytes per sector	512	512
Sectors per track	9	15
Tracks per side	40	80
Sides	2	2
Capacity	360K	1,200K

3 1/2-Inch	*Low-Density*	*High-Density*
Bytes per sector	512	512
Sectors per track	9	18

continues

Table 2.1 *(continued)*

3 1/2-Inch	*Low-Density*	*High-Density*
Tracks per side	80	80
Sides	2	2
Capacity	720K	1,440K

Actually, table 2.1 shows only the formatting characteristics for each drive's standard format. If correctly installed and operated, some drives can format other capacities. If you use the correct format software and command parameters, for example, you can use a 1.44M drive to format a 720K disk. The 5 1/4-inch drives also can format several other types of disks, including single-sided and 8-sector-per-track disks. Formatting is covered in detail in the "Formatting Disks" section later in this chapter.

The capabilities of each type of drive often are discussed in terms of the data rate, controller, and ROM BIOS. The *data rate* is the speed at which the information is placed on or read from the disk. The *controller* is the electronic circuitry that "controls" the tasks of placing the information on the disk and reading it from the disk, including controlling the movement of the head to the right location on the disk. The *ROM BIOS* (read-only memory basic input/output system) is the software built into the device at the factory that logically controls the movement of information to and from the disk.

Tip: You can use several methods to determine drive size. First, check your computer's original specifications. If looking at the specifications does not help, check the drive's faceplate, which sometimes indicates the drive's size. On many 1.44M 3 1/2-inch drives, for example, the button used to eject the disk is stamped with "1.44." If you still are unable to determine the size, place a high-density disk in the drive and use the FORMAT command, not specifying a drive size. If the disk drive is high density, a 3 1/2-inch drive will attempt to format your disk at 1.44M. A 5 1/4-inch drive will attempt to format your disk at 1.2M. If you get many `BAD SECTOR` errors or a `TRACK 0 BAD` error during the format, you may assume that your drive is low density and is having problems trying to format a high-density disk. If the disk formats at high density with no bad sectors, then you know your drive is high density. In addition to these methods, several programs have commands that can determine drive size; the SYSINFO command in Norton Utilities Version 5.0 is one example.

As you can see in table 2.1, disk capacities are determined by several parameters, some of which remain constant on all drives. For example, all drives use 512-byte sectors. (This condition holds true for hard disks as well as floppy disks, as you will learn later in Chapter 4.) Although DOS never has changed from 512 bytes on any fully compatible drives, DOS seems to treat sector size as a changeable parameter. DOS has the capability of using sector sizes other than 512K, a fact that may be important on future drive sizes.

You also may note that all standard disks and drives today are double-sided. IBM has not shipped PC systems with single-sided drives since 1982, and most people consider these drives to be obsolete. In addition, IBM never has used any form of single-sided 3 1/2-inch drives (although that type of drive did appear in the first Apple Macintosh systems in 1984). IBM officially adopted 3 1/2-inch drives in 1986 and has used only double-sided versions of these drives.

360K 5 1/4-Inch Drive

The 5 1/4-inch low-density drive is designed to create a standard format disk with 360K capacity. The industry term for low-density drives is *double-density* drives. *Low density* is used throughout this book because the term *double density* is somewhat misleading—especially when juxtaposed with *high density*.

The term *double density* arose after manufacturers used the term *single density* to indicate a type of drive that used frequency modulation (FM) encoding to store approximately 90K on a disk. This now-obsolete drive actually never was used in any IBM-compatible systems. When the manufacturers began producing drives that used modified frequency modulation (MFM) encoding, the term *double density* was adopted to indicate the new encoding process and the increase (approximately twofold) in recording capacity. All modern floppy disk drives, including all the types listed in this section, use MFM encoding. Encoding methods such as FM, MFM, and RLL are discussed in the next chapter.

A low-density drive normally records and numbers 40 cylinders with two tracks each, starting with 0 at the outer edge of the disk. Head position (or side) 0 is recorded on the underside of the disk, and head position (or side) 1 is recorded on the top of the disk. A low-density drive normally divides each track into 9 sectors but can format 8 sectors per track to create a disk compatible with DOS Version 1.1 or earlier. An 8-sector-per-track format is rarely (if ever) used today.

In the first IBM systems, low-density drives were all full-height units, which means that they were 3 1/4 inches tall. Full-height drives are obsolete today and have not been manufactured by any companies since 1986. Later units manufactured by IBM and most compatible vendors have been half-height units, which are only 1.6 inches tall (see fig. 2.1). You can install two half-height drives in the place of a single full-height unit. Half-height drives are produced by several manufacturers and do not differ substantially. A third kind of drive now common on PCs is the 3 1/2-inch drive, which is discussed later in the sections on 720K and 1.44M 3 1/2-inch drives.

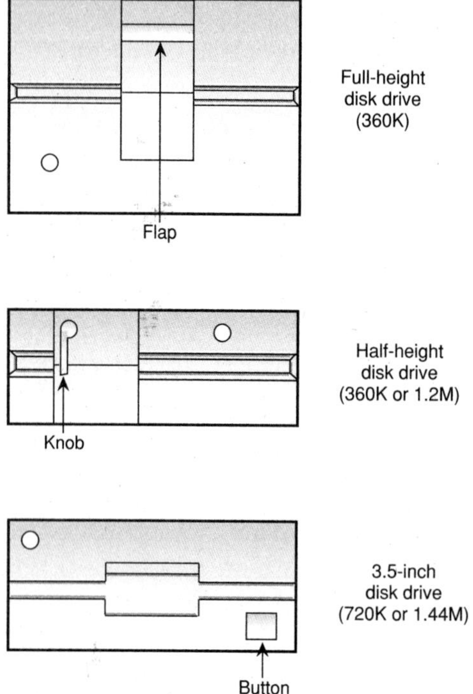

Fig. 2.1. Three kinds of disk drives.

Low-density drives spin at 300 rpm, which equates to 5 revolutions per second or 200 milliseconds per revolution. All standard floppy controllers (a *controller* is an electronic circuit that controls how the disk drive operates) support a 1 to 1 interleave, which means that each sector on a given track is numbered (and read) consecutively with no breaks or "wait sectors." To read and write to a disk, a controller sends data at a rate of 250,000 bits per second. Because all low-density controllers can support this data rate, virtually any controller supports low-density drives.

Because all standard IBM-compatible systems include ROM BIOS support for low-density drives, no special software or driver programs normally are required for you to use them. (This group may exclude some aftermarket [non-IBM] 360K drives for PS/2 systems, which may require some type of driver.) The built-in ROM support enables IBM units to work. The ROM BIOS is the basic input/output system, which is a factory-installed ROM-based program that controls the information flow to and from the computer. Usually, you need only to run the setup program for the system to recognize these drives properly.

1.2M 5 1/4-Inch Drive

The 1.2M high-density floppy drive first appeared in the IBM AT system introduced in 1984. This drive required the use of a new type of disk to achieve the 1.2M format capacity, but the drive still could read and write (although not always reliably) the 360K low-density disks.

The 1.2M high-density floppy drive records and numbers 80 cylinders with two tracks each, starting with cylinder 0 at the outer edge of the disk. A high-density drive can record twice as many cylinders as a low-density drive in approximately the same disk space. This capability suggests that the disk's recording capacity would double, but each track is recorded with fifteen 512-byte sectors, which increases the disk's storage capacity even further. In fact, high-density disks store nearly four times the amount of data that can be stored on 360K disks. The increased density for each track requires the use of special disks made of a modified media designed to handle this type of recording.

These disks initially were expensive and difficult to obtain, which prompted many users to attempt to format low-density disks as high-density disks in the high-density drives (see the section "Recording Problems with 1.2M and 360K Drives" later in this chapter). This practice resulted in data loss and (avoidable) data recovery operations.

The 1.2M drive's incompatibility with the 360K drive stems from the fact that the 1.2M drive can write twice as many cylinders as the 360K drive in the same space. Today a 1.2M drive easily can position its heads over the same 40 cylinder positions used by the 360K drive by *double-stepping*; the heads simply are moved every two cylinders to arrive at the correct positions for reading and writing the 360K disk's 40 cylinders. The real problem is that because the 1.2M drive normally has to write 80 cylinders in the same space in which the 360K drive would write 40, the heads of the 1.2M units have to be narrower than the heads in a 360K drive. These narrow heads can have problems overwriting tracks produced by a wider-headed 360K drive, because the narrow heads cannot cover the entire track area. Possible solutions to this problem are discussed later in the section titled "Recording Problems with 1.2M and 360K Drives."

The 1.2M high-density drive spins at 360 rpm, which equates to 6 revolutions per second or 166.67 milliseconds per revolution. High-density drives spin at this rate regardless of whether the disk is high or low density. To send or receive 15 sectors 6 times per second, a controller uses a data transmission rate of 500,000 bits per second (500 KHz). All standard high- and low-density controllers support this data rate and therefore support these drives.

A standard 360K disk running in a high-density drive spins at 360 rpm, which requires a data rate of 300,000 bits per second (300 KHz). All standard low- and high-density controllers support the 250 KHz, 300 KHz, and 500 KHz data rates. The 300 KHz rate is used only to enable high-density drives to read or write to low-density disks. Almost all standard AT-style systems have a ROM BIOS that supports the controller's operation of the 1.2M drive, including the 300 KHz data rate.

720K 3 1/2-Inch Drive

The 720K 3 1/2-inch low-density drives first appeared on a DOS computer when IBM introduced the convertible laptop system in 1986. All IBM systems introduced since 1986 have come standard with 3 1/2-inch drives. IBM also offers the 3 1/2-inch drive as an internal or external drive for AT and XT systems. Interestingly, vendors outside the IBM-compatible world (Apple, Hewlett-Packard, and so on) used 3 1/2-inch drives long before IBM did.

The 3 1/2-inch low-density drive records 80 cylinders of two tracks each, with 9 sectors per track. This process results in a formatted capacity of 720K. The actual capacity of these disks is 1M. The difference between the actual 1M capacity and the 720K usable after formatting exists because space on each track is occupied by the header and trailer of each sector, the intersector gaps, and the index gap at the start of each track before the first sector. These spaces are not usable for data storage and account for the differences between the unformatted and formatted capacities.

Most manufacturers report a disk's unformatted capacity, because they do not know the type of system on which you will be formatting the disk. Apple Macintosh systems, for example, can store 800K of data on the same disk because of a different formatting technique. Note also that the 720K of usable space does not include the areas that DOS reserves for managing the disk—boot sectors, file allocation tables (FATs), directories, and so on. With these nondata areas accounted for, only 713K remains for file data storage.

IBM-compatible systems have used 3 1/2-inch low-density drives mainly in XT systems because these drives can operate with any low-density controller. These drives spin at 300 rpm and therefore require only a 250 KHz data rate to operate properly. This same data rate is used for the 360K disk drives, which means that any controller that can support a 360K drive also can support a 720K drive. Therefore, virtually every PC has a controller that can support a 720K drive.

To use a 3 1/2-inch low-density drive, the computer's ROM BIOS must support the drive. Any IBM system with a ROM BIOS date of 06/10/85 or later has built-in support for 720K drives and requires no driver. If your system has a ROM BIOS date earlier than 06/10/85, the DRIVER.SYS program from DOS Version 3.2 or later versions is required to support the controller to operate these drives. When adding a 3 1/2-inch low-density drive to your system, the preferred method is to upgrade to a ROM BIOS with a date later than 06/10/85. To do so, you must physically replace one or more chips on the system board with new ROM chips. This process negates the need for any "funny" driver software.

Tip: You can use several methods to determine what version of ROM BIOS your computer is using. During the boot process, some computers display the name and date of the ROM BIOS in the upper left corner. If you have Norton Utilities Version 5.0, the SYSINFO command displays the name and date of your ROM BIOS on the System Summary screen. If you are familiar with the BASIC programming language, you can use the following program to determine the ROM BIOS date:

```
10 DEF SEG=&HF000
20 FOR X=&HFFF5 to &HFFFF
30 PRINT CHR$(PEEK(X));
40 NEXT
```

After you run the preceding program, the date of your ROM BIOS appears, such as 4/11/88.

1.44M 3 1/2-Inch Drive

The 3 1/2-inch 1.44M high-density drives first appeared when IBM introduced the PS/2 product line in 1987. Although IBM has not officially offered this type of drive for any of its older systems, most compatible vendors started offering these drives as system options right after the appearance of IBM's PS/2 system.

The 3 1/2-inch high-density drive records 80 cylinders of two tracks each, with 18 sectors per track. This process results in a formatted capacity of 1.44M. These disks actually hold 2M of data. The difference between the unformatted capacity (2M) and the formatted capacity exists because space on each track is occupied by the header and trailer of each sector, the intersector gaps, and the index gap at the start of each track before the first sector. Note that the 1,440K of total formatted capacity does not include the areas that DOS reserves for file management, leaving only 1423.5K of actual file storage area.

Like 720K drives, the 3 1/2-inch high-density drives spin at 300 rpm, a speed that they must maintain to operate properly with existing high- and low-density controllers. To utilize the 500 KHz data rate (the maximum data rate from most standard high- and low-density floppy controllers), these drives could spin at 300 rpm only. If these drives were to spin at the 360 rpm rate of the 5 1/4-inch drives, they would have to reduce the total number of sectors per track to 15 or the controller could not keep up. In a nutshell, 1.44M drives store 1.2 times the data stored by 1.2M 5 1/4-inch drives, and the 1.2M drives spin exactly 1.2 times faster than the 1.44M drives. The data rates used by both high-density drives are identical and compatible with the same controllers. In fact, because the 3 1/2-inch high-density drives can run at the 500 KHz data rate, any controller that can support a 1.2M 5 1/4-inch drive also can support the 1.44M drives. If you are using a low-density disk in the 3 1/2-inch high-density drive, the data rate is reduced to 250 KHz and the disk capacity is 720K.

The real issue in a particular system using a 3 1/2-inch high-density drive is ROM BIOS support. Any IBM system with a ROM BIOS date of 11/15/85 or later has built-in support for these drives, and no external driver support program is needed. Simply install the drive properly. One other problem, relating to the way the controller signals the high-density drive to write on a low-density disk, is discussed in detail in the next section.

Recording Problems with 1.44M 3 1/2-Inch Drives

Although you may have some success with saving data on 720K disks in 1.44M drives, incompatibilities exist and eventually may result in data loss. To prevent this unnecessary data loss, save data with 720K disks for 720K drives and 1.44M disks for 1.44M drives. You can read 720K disks in 1.44M drives with no problems.

Note that a serious problem awaits many users who use 1.44M 3 1/2-inch drives. If the drive is installed improperly, the possibility exists that any write or format operations on 720K disks will be performed incorrectly and will end up trashing the data. This situation arises because the controller cannot signal the high-density drive that a low-density recording is to take place.

When recording, high-density disks require a higher write current or signal strength than do low-density disks. A low-density drive can record only at the lower write current (correct for the low-density disks), but the high-density drive needs to record at both high and low write currents, depending on which type of disk is inserted into the drive. If a signal to reduce the write current level is not sent to the high-density drive, the drive stays in its high write current default mode, even when recording on a low-density disk. This signal normally is sent to the drive by the controller, but in many systems, an incorrect write current sent to the disk is the root of the problem.

Designed by Western Digital, the AT floppy controller used by IBM activated the reduced write current (RWC) signal only if the controller was transmitting at the 300 KHz data rate. (The 300 KHz rate indicates the special case of a low-density disk in a high-density drive.) The RWC signal is required to tell the high-density drive to lower the head writing signal to the strength proper for low-density disks. If the RWC signal is not sent, the drive defaults to the higher write current, which should be used only for high-density disks. If the RWC controller was transmitting at the 250 KHz data rate, the controller recognized that the drive was low density and that no RWC signal was necessary. (Low-density drives can write only with reduced current.)

Because 1.44M drives spin disks at 300 rpm, a serious problem arose when 720K disks were used in 1.44M drives. When writing to a low-density disk, the 1.44M drive uses the 250 KHz data rate, not the 300 KHz rate. This data rate "fools" the controller into thinking that it actually is sending data to a low-density drive; therefore, the controller does not send the required RWC signal. Without the RWC signal, the drive records improperly on these disks, possibly trashing data being written or data already present. Because almost all compatibles use controllers based on the design of the IBM AT floppy disk controller, most compatibles share the same problem as the IBM AT.

The drive and disk manufacturers came up with a solution to this problem short of redesigning the controller. Manufacturers built into the 1.44M drives a *media sensor* that can override the controller's RWC signal (or lack of RWC signal) and properly change the head current levels within the drive. When the media sensor is operational, the drive essentially chooses the write current level independent of the controller. The sensor itself is a small physical or optical sensor designed to feel or see the small hole opposite the write enable hole on high-density 3 1/2-inch disks. This extra hole (found only on high-density disks) is the media sensor's cue that the disk is high density and that full write current should be used when recording. When the sensor cannot see or feel the hole, the sensor prompts the drive to record in the reduced write current mode.

Some individuals foolishly attempt to override the function of this sensor by punching an extra hole into a low-density disk. Several con artist types of companies make a fast buck selling these hole punchers to unwary individuals. Some people may think that low- and high-density disks are identical except for the hole and that punching an extra hole can turn a low-density disk into a high-density disk. Those people are wrong! High-density disks are not the same as low-density disks, and the exact differences are explained in this section titled "Reviewing Disk Types and Specifications."

Punching an extra hole in a low-density disk is unnecessary. If you want to record a high-density format on a low-density disk, all you have to do is remove the jumper from the drive that enables the media sensor. Check your disk drive's specifications to find the jumper that enables the sensor. This technique also has problems, so it is not recommended. Removing the jumper enables the drive to continue working properly for high-density disks (writing at the full write current level) and enables the drive to write to low-density disks (at the full write current) as well. With the jumper removed, the drive has no way of determining whether an inserted disk is high or low density. The bottom line is that if you really want to risk your data to low-density disks formatted at high density, you can save yourself the cost of a $40 hole puncher; you need only remove the media sensor jumper from the drive. Note that if you attempt to format or record on a 720K disk after removing the jumper, your drive will be using the higher write current and the disk could be trashed. If you discover this problem on a drive, look for a removed jumper to see whether the media sensor is disabled. You can restore the drive by reenabling the sensor.

Many newer systems, including the IBM PS/2 series, Toshiba laptops, and most other computers with floppy controllers built into the motherboard, do not need media sensors with their 1.44M drives, because they can detect the density by reading data from the disk. Their controllers have been fixed to enable the RWC signal to be sent to the drive even when the controller is sending the 250 KHz data rate. As long as the disk is formatted properly, the system will operate correctly no matter what type of disk or drive is used. Because these systems do not have a media sensor, they easily can format low-density disks as if they were high-density disks, regardless of how many holes are on the disk. If you use a PS/2, for example, you can use low-density disks as if they were high-density disks. To avoid trashing your data, however, never use low-density disks as if they were high-density disks!

Recording Problems with 1.2M and 360K Drives

Although you may have some success with using 360K and 1.2M disks interchangeably in 360K and 1.2M drives, incompatibilities exist and eventually may result in data loss. To prevent this unnecessary data loss, save data with 360K disks for 360K drives and 1.2M disks for 1.2M drives. You can read 360K disks in 1.2M drives with no problems.

The 5 1/4-inch drives have their own special problems. One major problem is that tracks sometimes are recorded at different widths in different drives. Differences in recorded track width can result in unnecessary data destruction and problems with data exchange between 5 1/4-inch drives.

Table 2.2 lists the track widths (in millimeters) of the four types of floppy drives supported in PC systems.

Table 2.2
Track Widths of Four Floppy Drive Types

Drive Type	*Tracks*	*Track Width*
5 1/4-inch 360K	40 per side	0.330 mm
5 1/4-inch 1.2M	80 per side	0.160 mm
3 1/2-inch 720K	80 per side	0.115 mm
3 1/2-inch 1.44M	80 per side	0.115 mm

As you can see from table 2.2, differences in track width occur only in the 5 1/4-inch drives. The 5 1/4-inch low-density drives record a track width more than twice that of the 5 1/4-inch high-density drives. This difference presents a real problem if a high-density drive is used for updating a low-density disk that contains previously recorded data. The high-density drive (even in 360K mode) cannot completely overwrite the track left by the 40 track drive, which presents a problem when the disk is returned to the person with the 360K drive. The 360K drive sees the new data as "embedded" within the remains of the previously written track. The drive cannot distinguish either signal, and an `Abort, Retry, Ignore` error message appears.

Note that this problem will not happen if a brand new disk (that has never been recorded on) is formatted first in a 1.2M drive using the /4 option, which formats the disk as a 360K disk. Then you can use the 1.2M drive to fill the disk to its 360K capacity, and every file will be readable on a 40-track 360K drive. This trick is useful when you need to exchange data disks between AT systems that have a 1.2M drive and XT or PC systems that have only 360K drives (The section "Formatting Disks," later in this chapter, describes the FORMAT options you need to use 360K disks in 1.2M drives). The key to this trick is to start with a brand new disk or a disk that has been wiped clean magnetically by a bulk eraser. A *bulk eraser* is a device that can erase many disks in a short period of time by emitting a strong magnetic field. When a disk is exposed to this field, the magnetic information on the disk is erased. Simply reformatting the disk will not work, because during formatting, data written to the disk by a 1.2M drive is embedded in the bad 360K tracks, and the problem of distinguishing signals still exists.

> ***Warning***: Never use a bulk eraser close to your computer or valuable floppy disks.

Because 3 1/2-inch drives all write tracks of the same width, track-related disk-interchange problems do not occur with 3 1/2-inch drives. The other mixed-format problems mentioned in the previous section, however, still exist.

Examining Floppy Disk Construction

The 5 1/4-inch and 3 1/2-inch disks have unique constructions and physical properties. In both disk sizes, the flexible (or floppy) disk is contained within a plastic jacket. The jacket used for the 3 1/2-inch disks is more rigid than the jacket used for the 5 1/4-inch disks; however, the disks contained within the jackets appear similar except for the size. This section discusses the differences and similarities between the physical properties and construction of 3 1/2-inch and 5 1/4-inch disks.

When you look at a typical 5 1/4-inch floppy disk, you see several features (see fig. 2.2). Most prominent is the large round hole in the center of the disk, which is called the *hub access hole*. When you close the disk drive's door, a cone-shaped clamp grabs and centers the disk through this hole. Many disks come with hub ring reinforcements—thin plastic rings like those used to reinforce three-ring notebook paper—intended to help the disk withstand the mechanical force of the clamping mechanism. High-density disks usually lack these reinforcements.

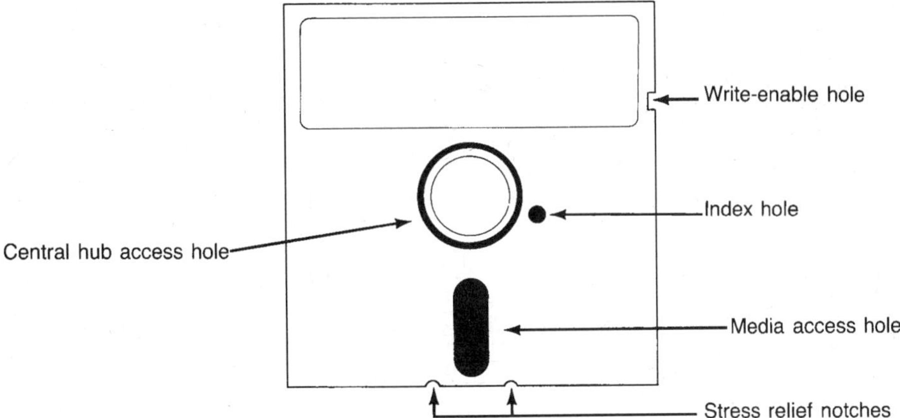

Fig. 2.2. *A 5 1/4-inch disk.*

To the right and just below the center of the hub hole is a smaller round hole called the *index hole*. If you carefully turn the disk within its protective jacket, you see at one point a small hole in the disk itself. The disk drive uses this index hole as the starting point for all sectors on the disk. The index hole serves as a "Prime Meridian" for the disk sectors. A disk with a single index hole is called a *soft-sectored disk*, indicating that the operating system software determines the number of disk sectors. Some older equipment (such as Wang word processors) uses *hard-sectored disks*, which have an index hole to demarcate each individual sector. Hard-sectored disks should not be used in a PC.

Below the hub hole is a slot shaped much like a long racetrack; through this slot, you can see the disk surface itself. This slot is the *media access hole* through which the disk drive heads read and write information to the disk surface.

At the right side of the disk, about 1 inch from the top, is a rectangular punch from the side of the disk cover. This punch is the *write-enable notch*. If this notch is present, writing to the disk has been enabled. Disks without this notch (or with the notch taped over) are known as *write-protected* disks, indicating that no information can be written to the disk. The write-enable notch may not be present on all disks, particularly on those you have purchased with programs on them.

On the rear of the disk jacket are two very small oval notches at the bottom of the disk, flanking the head slot. These notches relieve stress on the disk and help prevent the disk from warping. The drive also may use these notches to assist in keeping the disk in the proper position in the drive.

The 3 1/2-inch disks use a much more rigid plastic case that helps stabilize the disk, which is how these disks can record at track and data densities that are greater than the 5 1/4-inch disks. A metal shutter protects the media access hole (see fig. 2.3). This shutter is manipulated by the drive and remains closed whenever the disk is out of a drive, which helps insulate the media itself from the environment and your fingers. This shutter also eliminates the need for a disk jacket.

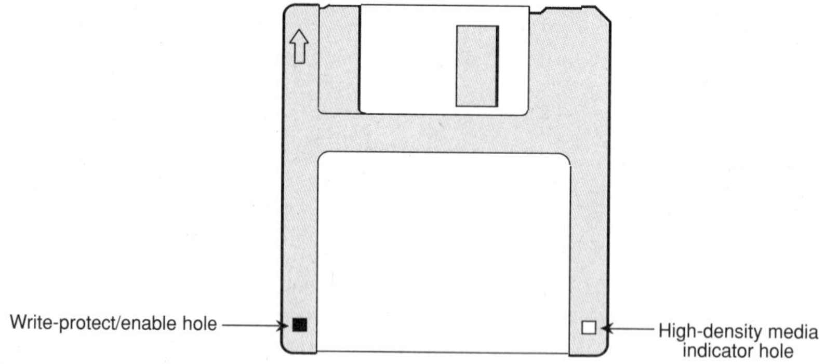

Fig. 2.3. *A 3 1/2-inch disk.*

Instead of using an index hole, the 3 1/2-inch disks use a metal center hub with an alignment hole. This metal hub is grasped by the drive, and the hole in the hub enables the drive to position the disk properly.

On the lower left part of the disk is a hole with a plastic slider—the *write-protect/enable hole*. When the slider is positioned so that the hole is visible, the drive is prevented from recording on the disk. When the slider is positioned to cover the hole, writing is enabled and you can record on the disk. More permanent write protection is available; some commercial software programs come on disks with the slider removed, which means that you cannot easily enable recording on that disk.

On the lower right part of the disk, you may find another hole in the disk jacket. This hole is the *media density selector hole*. If this hole is present, the disk is constructed of a special media and is therefore a high-density disk. The absence of this hole means that the disk is a low-density disk. Many modern 3 1/2-inch drives have a media sensor that controls recording capability based on the existence or absence of this hole.

The 3 1/2-inch and 5 1/4-inch disks actually are constructed of the same basic materials. Both types of disks use a plastic base (usually mylar) coated with a magnetic compound. The compound usually is a ferric-oxide (iron-oxide) based compound for the standard density versions (single- or double-density disks); a cobalt ferric compound usually is used in the high-coercivity (high-density) disks. The newly announced extended-density disk type uses a barium-ferric compound. Although the rigid jacket material of the 3 1/2-inch disks often causes people to believe (incorrectly) that these disks are some sort of "hard disk," the 3 1/2-inch disks themselves are just as floppy as the 5 1/4-inch variety. The following section contains information about different disk types and their appropriate use.

Reviewing Disk Types and Specifications

In this section, you examine all the types of disks you can purchase for your system. Of special interest are the technical specifications that can separate one type of disk from another. This section defines all the specifications used to describe a typical disk.

Single- and Double-Sided Disks

Whether a disk is single- or double-sided is really an issue only for low-density disks. No single-sided high-density drives have ever been made, so no need has ever developed for disks to match those drives. The original IBM PC did have single-sided drives, but they were discontinued in 1982.

A single-sided disk is constructed of the same material as a double-sided disk. The only difference is that the single-sided disks are certified (tested) only on one side, and the double-sided disks are certified on both sides.

Because single-sided disks are less expensive than the double-sided versions, many PC users decided that they could save a great deal of money if they used single-sided disks even in double-sided drives. This procedure can work. Making some disks with recording surfaces on one side and other disks with recording surfaces on both sides is economically impractical for manufacturers, so today's single-sided disks look and usually behave the same as double-sided disks. Therefore, depending on the brand of disks you buy, you generally can format and use successfully single-sided disks in double-sided drives at substantial disk cost savings.

The only danger in this practice is that some manufacturers do not burnish or polish the unused (top) side to the same smoothness level as the used (bottom) side. This situation may cause accelerated wear on the top head. (In single-sided drives, the top head was replaced with a soft felt pad.)

Fortunately, the formatting process enables you to "certify" your own disks. You must format each disk you use. When you format a disk, DOS determines whether the disk contains any bad sectors (sectors that cannot reliably hold information). If DOS finds any bad sectors, DOS tells you how many bytes are in bad sectors and seals off these places from any future attempts to put data there. So formatting really is your own "certification" of the disk. When you are formatting, if a floppy disk comes back with any bad sectors, seriously consider throwing away the disk. Given the cost, using a problem disk often is not worth the trouble. In fact, the highly recommended route is to spend the extra money for double-sided disks of the correct density.

Saving money by using single-sided disks is possible only with low-density disks. High-density single-sided disks do not exist, and mixing densities and formats is absolutely not recommended. IBM never used the single-sided versions of the 3 1/2-inch drives, but Apple and other manufacturers did. (Single-sided 3 1/2-inch disks are available.) Using the single-sided 3 1/2-inch disks in place of double-sided disks also is possible but not recommended.

Density

Density, in simple terms, is a measure of the amount of information that can be packed into a given area of a recording surface. Generally, the higher the density, the more information can be stored reliably on a disk. The key word here is *reliably*.

With disks, two types of densities exist: longitudinal density and linear density. *Longitudinal density* is indicated by how many tracks can be recorded on the disk. Longitudinal density often is expressed as a number of tracks per inch (tpi). *Linear density* is the capability of an individual track to store data. Linear density often is indicated as a number of bits per inch (bpi). Unfortunately, the two types of densities often are interchanged incorrectly when users discuss various disks and drives. Table 2.3 lists each of the disk types available.

Table 2.3
Floppy Disk Density Parameters

Media Density	*Tracks Per Inch (TPI)*	*Bits Per Inch (BPI)*	*Media Doping Material*	*Orsteds of Media Coercivity*	*Micro-inches of Coating Thickness*
5 1/4-inch					
Low-density	48	5,876	Ferrite	300	100
Quad-density	96	5,876	Ferrite	300	100
High-density	96	9,646	Cobalt	675	55
3 1/2-inch					
Low-density	135	8,717	Cobalt	665	78
High-density	135	17,434	Cobalt	720	35
Ext.-density	135	34,868	Barium	?	?

Note that IBM completely skipped over the quad-density disk type. No IBM personal computer of any type ever has used a quad-density drive or required quad-density disks. A quad-density disk is simply a better low-density disk. Quad- and low-density disks store the same linear data on each track. Both types of disks use the same formula for the magnetic coating on the disk, but the quad-density versions represent a more rigorously tested, higher quality disk.

High-density disks are different. To store the increased linear density, a different magnetic disk coating is required. High-coercivity coatings are used for this purpose. In the 5 1/4-inch and 3 1/2-inch high-density disks, this high-coercivity coating is used for achieving the tremendous bit density for each track.

> ***Tip:*** A high-density disk never can be substituted for a low- or quad-density disk because the *write current*—the magnetic signal that places information on the disk—must be different for these different media formulations and thicknesses.

The extended-density 3 1/2-inch disk listed in the table now is available in some systems. This type of drive was invented by Toshiba and currently is available from several other vendors as well. Extended-density disks are coated with a barium-doped compound that enables extremely high-density recordings. These types of drives also can read (and write to) any other type of 3 1/2-inch disk because of the similar track dimensions on all these formats.

Media Coercivity and Thickness

The *coercivity specification* of a disk refers to the magnetic field strength required to make a proper recording on the disk. Coercivity is measured in oersteds and is a value indicating magnetic strength. A disk with a higher coercivity rating requires a stronger magnetic field to make a recording on that disk. Lower ratings mean that the disk can be recorded with a weaker magnetic field. In other words, the lower the coercivity rating, the more sensitive the disk.

Thickness is another factor that determines a disk's sensitivity. The thinner the disk, the less a given region of the disk will influence an adjacent region. This relationship enables thinner disks to accept many more bits per inch without degrading the recording over time.

High-density disks are approximately half as sensitive as low-density disks. A high-density drive can record with a much higher volume level at the heads than the standard low-density drive can. For these high-density drives to record properly on a low-density disk, the drive must be capable of using a reduced write current mode and must enable RWC whenever the lower density disks are installed. Write current mode brings up a real problem with users and floppy disks.

Most AT system users cringe when they see the price of the high-density disks that their systems require. The same is true for PS/2 system users and the high-density 3 1/2-inch disks. The temptation is to use the low-density disks as a substitute in an attempt to save money. Formatting a "regular" disk at high-density capacity is foolish. This procedure is facilitated by DOS, which always attempts to format a disk to the maximum capacity of the drive unless you specifically order otherwise by using the proper parameters in the FORMAT command.

> ***Tip***: If you use no parameters and type *format a:*, the disk is formatted as if it is a high-density disk. Many users think that using low-density disks as high-density disks is somehow equivalent to using single-sided disks in place of double-sided disks, but they are wrong. Do not use low-density disks in place of high-density disks. If you do, you will experience severe problems and data loss.

The reasons for using the thin high-coercivity disks are simple. When designing the high-density drives, engineers found that the density of magnetic flux reversals became such that the adjacent flux reversals began to affect each other. They started to cancel each other out or, through attraction and repulsion, caused each other to migrate on the disk. Any data written at these high densities simply began to erase itself over time.

An analogy can be constructed by imagining a wooden track on which you place magnetic marbles evenly spaced 4 inches apart. At this distance, the magnetic forces from each marble are too weak to affect the adjacent marbles. Now suppose that the marbles are placed only 2 inches apart. The magnetic forces now may start to work on the adjacent marbles so that the marbles begin to move by themselves, possibly clumping together. Figure 2.4 illustrates this process.

You can eliminate this migration and clumping if you simply make the magnetic marbles weaker. If the marbles are made half as strong as before, you can put the marbles twice as close together without any interaction between them. This concept is the idea behind the thin high-coercivity disks. They are weaker magnetically, which is the reason that they need a higher recording strength for an image to be stored properly.

Try the following simple experiment to verify this principle. Attempt to format a high-density disk with a low-density format. You will find that DOS displays a `Track 0 bad - disk unusable` message. This disk apparently will not take a recording in low-density mode because the low-density recording also is low volume. The disk drive cannot make a recording on the disk, so the `Track 0 bad` message is displayed.

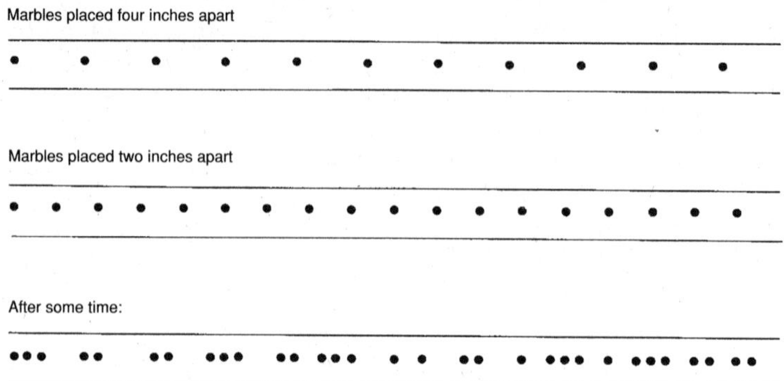

Fig. 2.4. The effect that adjacent magnetic domains can have on each other if magnets are too strong and too easily moved.

Unfortunately for users, the opposite attempt appears to work; you can format a standard low-density disk in a high-density drive, and DOS does not seem to protest. You may notice a high number of bad sectors, but DOS completes the format.

This situation is unfortunate for two reasons:

- You are recording strong magnetic signals to a media designed to hold weak magnetic signals. These strong magnetic signals begin to interact with adjacent signals over time. As a result, you will experience mysterious data losses over the next few days, weeks, or months.

- You have placed a recording on this disk at twice the signal strength it normally should be. This "industrial strength" recording may not be removable by any disk drive. You may never be able to reformat the disk correctly as a low-density disk because any low-density reformat is accomplished with reduced write current. The reduced write current may not be capable of overwriting the high write current signal that was recorded incorrectly. The best way to remove this "burned in" recording is to use a bulk eraser, which renews the disk by removing all magnetic information. In most cases, however, a fresh format is capable of overcoming the magnetic image of the previous format, even if the write current was incorrect.

Tip: Do not use the wrong media for the format you are attempting to perform. You must use the correct type of disk. You cannot get away with mixing densities like you can interchange single- and double-sided disks.

Note that the 3 1/2-inch disks have a perfect mechanism for foiling the naive user: the media sensor. A drive with the media sensor sets the write current and operating mode according to the actual disk that is inserted. You are prevented, for example, from placing 1.44M on a 720K disk. Remember that IBM does not use this sensor (because IBM fixed the controller problem that necessitated the sensor); therefore, incorrectly formatting a disk is easy on PS/2 systems. And, if you use an IBM PS/2 to format incorrectly a low-density 3 1/2-inch disk with a high-density format, you will not need a disk converter (hole puncher).

As mentioned previously, some companies sell disk converters, or hole punchers, that supposedly enable you to convert a low-density 3 1/2-inch disk into a high-density disk. You convert the disk simply by punching a hole in the disk to fool the disk drive media sensor. As you now know, many differences exist between a low-density and a high-density disk besides the hole in the case. Don't be fooled. Disk converters are designed and built by people who do not understand disk construction and use.

Soft- and Hard-Sectored Disks

Disks are soft sectored or hard sectored. For the PC, soft-sectored disks have only one index hole on the disk surface. Once per revolution, this hole is visible through the hole in the protective jacket, and the drive, controller, and DOS use this hole to establish the location of the first sector on any track. Hard-sectored disks have a hole for each sector, and thus each hole marks the beginning of a new sector. If you try to use a hard-sectored disk in a PC, the system will become confused. Sometimes hard-sectored disks are not specifically labeled as such, but they do specify 10 sectors or 16 sectors. Don't buy hard-sectored disks for use on a PC.

Formatting Disks

This section examines how the different density capabilities of high- and low-density drives sometimes cause problems with disk formatting. You always must ensure that a disk is formatted initially to the density in which the disk will run. In some cases, you may want to use a high-density drive to format a low-density disk. This procedure is possible if you use the correct FORMAT commands. This section describes how to use DOS correctly so that your disks are formatted properly.

Reading and Writing 360K Disks in 1.2M Drives

You can use a 1.2M drive to read or write to any 360K disk. Simply place into the 1.2M drive any 360K disk previously formatted at low density and then use the disk. You will find that the disk functions normally.

The problem arises when you attempt to read that same disk in a 360K drive. Remember that the recorded track width of the 1.2M drive is half that of the 360K drive, so any tracks recorded by a 360K drive are twice as wide as tracks recorded by a 1.2M drive. This difference implies that if you write to the 360K disk with the 1.2M drive, you do not overwrite the entire track width—only the center portion. When this disk is returned to a 360K drive, the wider head system in the 360K drive sees two signals on any overwritten tracks—the new data nestled within the image of old data that could not be overwritten completely by the 1.2M drive. This situation usually results in an immediate `Abort, Retry, Ignore` error message from DOS for any updated portions of the disk.

If you need to record data in a 1.2M drive and later read the data in a 360K drive, make sure that you format with a new 360K disk. A brand-new disk contains no magnetic information, which means that the smaller recorded track width can be written by the 1.2M drive and read properly in the 360K drive. The narrower track is written in "clean space," and the 360K drive is not confused by any "ghost images" of previously recorded, wider tracks.

The only other way to enable your 360K drive to read data recorded on a 1.2M drive is to use a disk that has been erased by a bulk eraser. You cannot just reformat a used disk. Formatting involves recording on the disk and therefore causes the track width problem. The new or bulk-erased disk must be formatted by the 1.2M drive for this procedure to work. Remember this simple rule: Any track recorded by a 360K drive cannot be overwritten by a 1.2M drive, even a 1.2M drive operating in the 360K format.

How do you correctly format a 360K disk in a 1.2M drive? If you simply execute the FORMAT command without any parameters, DOS attempts to format the disk to its maximum capacity. And because the 1.2M drives do not have any media sensing capability, DOS assumes that the disk capability is equal to the maximum capability of the drive itself. DOS attempts to create a 1.2M format on the disk. The write current also is increased during any recording in this format, which is incompatible with the 360K media. To format a 360K disk properly in a 1.2M drive, choose one of the following commands:

For DOS 4.0, 3.3, 3.2, 3.1, and 3.0, type

FORMAT A: /4

For DOS 4.0, 3.3, and 3.2, type

FORMAT A: /N:9 /T:40

For DOS 4.0 only, type

FORMAT A: /F:360

Each command places on a 360K disk a 40-track, 9-sector format using reduced write current mode.

Reading and Writing 720K Disks in 1.44M Drives

The 3 1/2-inch drives do not have the same data interchange problems as the 5 1/4-inch drive. Because the 3 1/2-inch high- and low-density drives write the same number of tracks and because the tracks are the same width, one type of drive has no trouble overwriting data written by another type of drive. For these reasons, IBM does not need to offer a low-density version of the 3 1/2-inch drives for the PS/2 50, 60, 70, and 80. These systems include only the high-density drive, which is completely capable of imitating the 720K drives found in Models 25 and 30. High-density drives, however, can be trouble in the hands of an inexperienced user.

Remember to format the 1.44M high-density disks using only the 1.44M format and format the 720K disks using only the 720K format. You will have serious problems if you simply place a 720K disk into a PS/2 Model 50, 60, 70, or 80 drive and enter the command *format a:*. You will need the services of a bulk eraser to extract you from your predicament. If you instead decide to use the incorrectly formatted disk, you will experience massive data loss over a period of time.

If IBM had decided to use media sensors in the PS/2 systems' drives, improper disk formatting might have been avoided. A media sensor informs the drive of which type of disk has been inserted. The drive then can control the write current and prevent improper formatting of disks.

IBM introduced the PS/2 systems before the media sensor had been agreed on by disk and drive manufacturers. In addition, IBM fixed the controller problem that required the use of a media sensor. Interestingly, many PS/2 systems shipped since mid-1988 have had drives with media sensors on board but not enabled. Because the media sensors in these systems are "permanently" disabled, the sensors can be enabled only if you cut a trace and solder a jumper.

If a standard FORMAT command is entered with no parameters, DOS always attempts to format the disk to the drive's maximum capacity. If you insert a 720K disk in a 1.44M drive and enter the FORMAT command with no parameters, DOS attempts to create a 1.44M format on the disk. If the drive has no media sensor (as with all PS/2 systems), the drive shifts into high write current mode and creates an 18-sector 80-track format on the disk. At that point, a 720K disk is ruined and should be thrown out or treated by a bulk eraser. If the drive has a media sensor, the FORMAT command formats the 720K disk properly.

Note that the media sensor does not communicate to DOS the correct information to format the disk; the media sensor simply prevents improper formatting. To format correctly a 720K disk in a 1.44M drive, choose one of the following commands:

For DOS 4.0 or 3.3, type

```
FORMAT A: /N:9 /T:80
```

For DOS 4.0 only, type

```
FORMAT A: /F:720
```

Note that DOS versions earlier than 3.3 do not support the 1.44M drive.

Handling Floppy Disks and Drives

Most computer users are aware of the basics of disk care. Disks easily can be damaged or destroyed by any of the following actions:

- Touching the disk's recording surface with your fingers or anything else
- Writing on a disk label with a ballpoint pen or pencil
- Bending the disk
- Spilling coffee or other liquids on the disk
- Overheating a disk (leaving the disk in the hot sun or near a radiator)
- Exposing your disk to stray magnetic fields

Disks are rather hardy storage devices. For example, writing on a disk label with a pen does not necessarily destroy the disk. (But be careful not to press too hard and crease the disk.) Touching a disk does not necessarily ruin it, but the oil and dust from your fingers can contaminate the disk and drive head. The real danger to your disks comes from magnetic fields, which are invisible and found in unusual places.

Stray Magnetic Fields

You can find several sources of magnetism around your home and office. Examples include

- Color TV sets and monitors
- Telephones
- Speakers
- Electric motors

All color monitors and color TV sets have a degaussing coil around the face of the tube. This coil is designed to remove any stray magnetism from the shadow mask at the front area of the tube when the unit is turned on. (Any residual magnetism in the shadow mask can bend the electron beams so that the picture appears to be out of focus or to have strange colors.) The degaussing coil is connected directly to the AC line and is controlled by a thermistor that passes a gigantic surge of power that tapers off to nothing as the tube warms up.

If you keep your disks anywhere near (within one foot of) the front of a color monitor, the disks are exposed to a very strong magnetic field every time you turn on the monitor. This is a bad situation, because the field is designed to demagnetize objects and is good at demagnetizing disks. Unfortunately, the demagnetizing effect is cumulative and irreversible; the more often a disk is exposed to a magnetic field, the more the magnetic signals on the disk are altered. When the magnetic signals on the disk are altered, the process cannot be reversed by removing the disk from the magnetic field. The damage is done!

Another major disk destroyer is the telephone. The mechanical ringer in a typical phone uses a powerful electromagnet to move the striker into the bell. The ringer circuit uses approximately 90 volts, and the electromagnetic fields generate enough power to degauss any disks next to or partially underneath the phone. Keep disks away from the telephone! A phone with an electronic ringer may not cause this kind of disk damage, but be careful anyway.

Stereo speakers contain magnets. Never put a disk near the rear of a speaker, particularly large speakers.

Electric motors are another source of powerful magnetic fields. Electric motors can be found in vacuum cleaners, heaters, air conditioners, fans, electric pencil sharpeners, and so on. You should not store your disks near these devices.

X-Ray Machines and Metal Detectors

Myths often are associated with things people cannot see. You certainly cannot see data stored on a disk or magnetic fields that can alter that data.

One myth is that airport X-ray machines somehow damage disks. I have a great deal of experience in this area, having traveled around the country for the last 10 years with disks and portable computers in hand. I currently fly about 150,000 miles per year, and my equipment and disks have been through X-ray machines more than 100 times each year.

Most people carrying disks or portable computers commit a fatal mistake when approaching the airport's X-ray machines: Most people do not pass the disks and the computer through the X-ray machine. X rays are a form of light; your disks and computers are not affected by X rays. A metal detector, on the other hand, makes an excellent degaussing coil and can damage your magnetic materials. The X-ray machine is the safest place to pass your disk or computer.

The X-ray machine is safe for your disks because it merely exposes a disk to electromagnetic radiation (discussed shortly) at a low frequency. Blue light is an example of electromagnetic radiation of a specific frequency. The only difference between X rays and blue light is the frequency of the emission.

A metal detector, on the other hand, emits a magnetic field and monitors for changes in that field. Any metal object inserted into the field causes the field's magnetic shape to change. This change is observed by the detector.

Most people without a background in physics don't know that electromagnetic radiation is not the same as a magnetic field. *Electromagnetic radiation* is a form of energy characterized by oscillating electric and magnetic fields that are perpendicular to one another. When electromagnetic energy is intercepted by matter, the energy is converted into thermal, electrical, mechanical, or chemical energy—but not into a magnetic field. Simply stated, an electromagnetic wave can generate heat or an electrical alternating current in any object that the wave passes through. Your microwave oven induces thermal (kinetic) or even electrical energy in objects by the same principle. Normally, microwaves cause kinetic energy in the molecules of the radiated substance, but most people know that if you place conductive (metal) objects in a microwave oven, an alternating electrical current is generated, and you may see sparks. The sparks, however, represent the generation of electrical or mechanical energy—not a magnetic field or magnetic force.

Because a disk is not a good conductor, the only noticeable effect of a high-powered electromagnetic field on your disk is the generation of kinetic (or thermal) energy. In other words, the only way that X rays, visible light, or any other radiation in this region of the electromagnetic spectrum can damage a disk is by heating it. The heat generated by X rays is insufficient to cause damage.

Consider, too, that if electromagnetic radiation could magnetize a disk as a magnetic field can, all magnetic disks and tapes in the world would be in extreme danger. At this moment, a large amount of electromagnetic radiation is passing through you and all your disks and tapes. Again, no magnetic danger exists because this radiation affects an object by imparting electrical, thermal, mechanical, or chemical energy but not by magnetizing the object.

Do not think, however, that you cannot harm a disk with electromagnetic radiation. You can. You know what the extremely powerful electromagnetic radiation emanating from the sun can do to a disk. (If you leave a disk in direct sunlight for a while, you can see the thermal effects of the sun's radiation.) But, at the normal levels of radiation that you and your disks are exposed to (in the airport X-ray machine, for example), you need not worry about the effects of electromagnetic radiation. Under normal conditions, the field strength is far too low to cook the disk.

Some users worry about the effect of X-ray radiation on their systems' erasable programmable read-only memory (EPROM). This concern may be more valid because EPROMs are erased by certain forms of electromagnetic radiation. Actually, you need not worry about this situation, either. EPROMs are erased by direct exposure to intense ultraviolet light. Specifically, an EPROM requires exposure to a 12,000 $\mu w/cm^2$ ultraviolet light source at a wavelength of 2537 Angstroms for 15 to 20 minutes at a distance of 1 inch. Increasing the power of the light source or decreasing the distance from the light source can shorten the erase times. The airport X-ray machine uses a different wavelength, and the exposure is nowhere near the strength, duration, or distance required for erasure. You should be aware that during quality control inspection, many manufacturers of circuit boards x-ray those boards with components (including EPROMs) installed.

I have conducted tests on my own. I have passed one disk through X-ray machines in various airports for two years, averaging two or three passes per week. All the original files and data have remained intact, and the disk never has been reformatted. I have several portable computers with hard disks installed, and one of those portables has been through X-ray machines every week for more than four years. In fact, I prefer to pass the computers and disks through X-ray machines because they offer the best protection from the magnetic fields produced by the adjacent metal detectors.

Solving Floppy Disk Problems

Several problems related to disks and disk drives can result in unreadable data. Some problems are caused by improperly installed or defective disk drives. Other problems involve using the wrong kind of disk in a drive—such as using a low-density disk in a high-density drive. A final problem is physical damage to the disk. Suggestions for dealing with these problems are presented in this section.

Improper Installation and Configuration

The majority of floppy drive problems are caused by improper installation, configuration, or operation of the drive. Unfortunately, floppy drive installation and configuration are much more complicated than the average technician understands. Even if your drive is installed by a "professional," the drive still may be installed incorrectly.

Unfortunately, a drive problem may not manifest itself immediately. Until you attempt to verify that the installation requirements have been performed properly, a drive problem often is difficult to detect.

For a floppy drive to be installed properly, you must do the following configuration procedures:

- Set the drive select jumper setting
- Enable/disable the terminating resistor
- Turn on the Disk Changeline (DC) signal setting on pin 34
- Enable the media sensor

The *drive select jumper* setting on the disk drive tells whether the drive is the first or second drive. The drive select jumper must be set to the first or second position, depending on what type of cable connection to the controller your system uses. IBM types of drives should be set to be the second drive in the system. The cable connecting the drive contains several twisted wires that make each drive operate in its proper identity. If your system's cable lacks these twisted wires, set drive A as the first drive select position and drive B as the second drive select position.

The *terminating resistor*, as the name implies, indicates to the computer the last drive connected to the controller. The resistor must be installed or enabled only in the drive at the connector farthest from the controller end of the cable—usually in drive A. The terminating resistor must be removed or disabled for drive B, which will be plugged into the connector at the center of the floppy cable between the controller and drive A. Note that most 3 1/2-inch drives have a form of automatic termination, and you don't have to configure the terminating resistor in these systems. Some 5 1/4-inch drives, such as those from Toshiba, have a permanently installed terminating resistor that is enabled or disabled by a jumper labeled TM.

On certain drives, the Disk Changeline (DC) signal setting on pin 34 should be turned on. This setting sends a signal to the computer that a disk change (a disk removal or insertion) has occurred in that disk drive.

The 360K low-density 5 1/4-inch drives should not send a signal of any kind along pin 34 of the disk interface cable. This position is farthest from pin 1. Pin 1 usually is identified by an odd-colored stripe on one side of the cable. Technically, these low-density drives must be set up this way for proper operation with a high-/low-density controller. If you are using a low-density controller only, such as with a PC or XT, pin 34 is ignored no matter what is sent on it.

All other drive types (1.2M, 720K, and 1.44M) must send the Disk Changeline signal on pin 34. The controller and DOS use this signal to flush all disk I/O buffers (close disk reads and writes) when a disk is removed or inserted. You usually invoke this signal by enabling a jumper on the drive labeled DS.

On a 3 1/2-inch high-density drive, the Enable Media Sensor setting enables the drive to tell the computer whether a high-density disk has been inserted. All 3 1/2-inch 1.44M high-density drives that you install in a standard IBM-compatible system must have a media sensor, and the media sensor must be enabled. The media sensor enables the proper write current for whatever type of disk you run in the drive. (The media sensor is required because of a defect in the controller design on most systems.) Many newer systems (such as the IBM PS/2) with floppy controllers built into the motherboard do not require that this sensor be enabled, but an enabled media sensor prevents improper density formats.

If you need more information on the proper installation of floppy disk drives, you can use several resources. *Upgrading and Repairing PCs*, published by Que Corporation, contains detailed information on proper floppy disk drive configuration and installation. In addition, you should obtain and use the original equipment manufacturer's (OEM's) documentation for your disk drives and controllers. These manuals indicate where the configuration items are located on your particular drive, what they look like, and how to set them. Often, you do not receive this detailed documentation with the drive or controller, and you have to contact the OEM directly to obtain the information.

The Phantom Directory

A common disk drive installation mistake involves the setting for signals sent to the controller by the drive on pin 34 of the cable. Every drive (except the 360K drive) must be configured so that a Disk Changeline (DC) signal is sent along pin 34 to the controller.

If you do not enable the DC signal, serious problems can result. For example, a PC user may come to you with a disk in hand and say, "Moments ago, this disk contained my document files, and now my entire word processing program has transferred mysteriously to this disk." The user then may say, "And, when I attempt to run the programs that now seem to be on this disk, the programs instantly crash or lock up the system." In this example, the damage has been done to the disk, and all you can do is perform data recovery techniques to get the information back for this user. One good thing about this problem is that recovery of most (if not all) of the information on this disk is entirely possible.

Another manifestation of a disabled DC signal is the "phantom directory" problem. Suppose, for example, that you have an AT-compatible system and you insert into drive A a disk containing files. You type *dir a:* and notice that the drive starts spinning, the drive's access light comes on, and the disk directory scrolls up the screen after a few seconds. Everything seems perfect. You then remove that disk, insert a different disk into drive A, and type *dir a:* again. This time, the drive barely spins (if at all) before the disk directory scrolls up the screen. Looking at the directory listing that has appeared, you find that it is the same listing displayed for the first disk that was removed from the drive.

You must understand that the contents of the disk currently in the drive are in danger. If you write on the disk in any way, the first disk's file allocation tables (FATs) and root directory sectors will be copied over those on the second disk, thereby trashing your FATs and root directory.

Underlying this problem is the fact that most AT-compatible systems with high-/low-density controllers use a floppy disk caching system. The caching system buffers in the system RAM the FATs and directories off the last-read floppy disk so that these areas do not have to be reread frequently. This process greatly speeds access to the disk. The door lever or eject button on the drive normally causes the Disk Changeline signal to be sent to the controller, which in turn causes DOS to flush out the floppy cache. The drive then rereads the FAT and directory areas when the next disk is inserted.

If the Disk Changeline signal is not sent properly, the cache is not flushed when you change a disk, and the system always thinks that the first disk is still in the drive. Any updates to subsequently inserted disks will have the new data written to the disk as well as a full or partial copy of the first disk's FAT and directory areas. In addition, new data will be written to what was free space on the first disk—space that may not be free on subsequently inserted disks.

Two solutions to this problem exist: a temporary solution and a permanent solution. A temporary solution is to press Ctrl-Break or Ctrl-C immediately after changing a disk, which forces DOS to flush the floppy I/O buffers manually. After you press these keys, the next time data on the disk is accessed, DOS rereads the FAT and directory areas of the disk, placing fresh copies in memory. Be sure that the buffer is flushed every time a disk is changed. These commands work only from the DOS prompt, so you cannot change a disk while you are inside any application.

A more permanent solution is simple: correct the drive installation. A common cause of the phantom directory problem is the installation. A simple rule is that if a jumper block labeled DC is on the disk drive, a jumper should be installed there. If you are absolutely certain that the installation was correct (for example, if the drive has worked perfectly but suddenly develops the phantom directory problem), check the following list of items that can prevent the Disk Changeline signal from being sent:

- User error. Check that the DC jumper is enabled.
- Bad cable. Check for continuity on pin 34, to make sure that the connection is good. The easiest way to test it is simply to replace the cable.
- Bad door switch. Replace the drive and retest.
- Bad drive logic board. Replace the drive and retest.
- Bad controller. Replace the controller and retest.
- Wrong DOS OEM version. User error.

The last item can stump you because the hardware seems to be functioning correctly. As a rule, you should use only the DOS supplied by the computer system's OEM. Use IBM DOS on IBM systems, for example, COMPAQ DOS on COMPAQ systems, Toshiba DOS on Toshiba systems, and so on. DOS compatibility problems are most noticeable with laptop systems or systems that are not completely hardware compatible with IBM, such as Toshiba. On such systems, be sure to use the correct version of DOS.

Inoperative Media Sensors

Inoperative media sensors are relevant only to 1.44M 3 1/2-inch high-density drives, because only these drives have media sensors. Media sensor problems often are attributable to an installer who does not enable the sensor when it should be enabled. You may think that the sensor is set correctly when you purchase the drive, but that is not usually the case. Never assume that the drives are preconfigured properly for your system. Remember that manufacturers also sell these drives for systems that are not IBM compatible.

If a media sensor is not enabled, locate the media sensor (ms) jumper on the drive (you may need to refer to the disk drive installation instructions to locate the jumper) and set it to enable.

If the media sensor is not operational, the controller is likely to leave the drive in high write current mode. This situation is fine for high-density disks, but when low-density disks are used, random and sporadic read and write failures occur. These failures usually are followed by an `Abort, Retry, Ignore, Fail` message.

Another inoperative media sensor symptom is low-density disks that seem to lose data over a period of time—a few weeks, several months, or longer. This data loss often can be traced back to an improperly installed drive. In some systems, the problem will be more obvious, as exhibited by the drive's incapacity to format or write on 720K disks or the drive's capacity to format a 720K disk to 1.44M even though you haven't punched any holes in the disk. These problems indicate that the media sensor is not operating. You can refer to *Upgrading and Repairing PCs*, published by Que Corporation, for specific information on how to ensure that your 3 1/2-inch drive is installed properly with an operational media sensor.

Low-Density Disks Formatted at High Density

If you attempt to format a 5 1/4-inch low-density disk at high density, DOS usually reports hundreds of kilobytes of bad sectors. When encountering a large number of bad sectors, most users refrain from using the disk. Because the types of 5 1/4-inch disks are radically different in coercivity and media formulation, the low-density disks do not work well when carrying a high-density format. The 3 1/2-inch low-density disks are not quite as different from their high-density counterparts; however, you should understand that 3 1/2-inch low-density and 3 1/2-inch high-density disks differ significantly.

A low-density 3 1/2-inch disk usually accepts a high-density format without reporting any bad sectors. This situation is unfortunate, because most users then think that they are safe in storing data on a 3 1/2-inch low-density disk formatted at high density.

A 3 1/2-inch low-density disk with a high-density format initially appears to work without any problems. If, however, you fill a low-density disk with 1.44M of data and store the disk on a shelf, over a period of time, you notice that the recording degrades and the data becomes unreadable. This degradation probably takes several months to become noticeable, and by then the data is lost. In fact, through talking to hundreds of my clients, I have found that the "half life" of such a recording is approximately 6 months; in other words, approximately 6 months from the time the data is written, one or more files suddenly have unreadable sectors. In 6 months to 1 year, much of the rest of the disk degrades rapidly and causes extensive damage to all data and files.

If the data periodically is reread and rewritten before any degradation is noticed, file damage will not be a problem. The problem occurs when data is written and stored on improperly formatted disks for six months or longer. Damage occurs because low-density disks are constructed of a media that is more magnetically sensitive than high-density disk media. A high-density disk recording is written with a higher write current level and with magnetic flux reversals spaced closely together. If this type of recording is written on a disk whose media is too sensitive, over time the individual magnetic domains magnetically affect one another, canceling each other out. In a sense, the disk performs a self-erasure operation over time.

Given the self-erasure problem, never use as backup disks any 3 1/2-inch low-density disks formatted at high density. Many users format low-density disks as high-density disks to save money. Today, however, 3 1/2-inch high-density disks are not prohibitively expensive. Data recovery, on the other hand, can be expensive. I charge $250 just to look at the problem (with no guarantees) and $200 per hour for any data recovery.

If you have an improperly formatted disk that is developing read problems, use the DOS DISKCOPY command to copy the disk to another (properly formatted) disk immediately. You then can survey the damage and repair the new copy. In the following chapters, you learn how to repair FAT, directory, and other management areas of the disk as well as how to recover data from files with unreadable sectors.

Differing Track Widths

As discussed previously, 5 1/4-inch high-density drives usually write a narrower track than 5 1/4-inch low-density drives. When a high-density drive is used for updating a low-density disk that was formatted or written to originally in a low-density drive, the wider tracks are not overwritten completely by the high-density drive. If the low-density disk first was formatted and subsequently written to only in a high-density drive (at the proper 360K format), no problem with overwriting occurs.

The overwrite problem occurs when that disk is updated with a low-density (wide-track) drive and then updated again with a high-density (narrow-track) drive. In that case, you have a narrow-track update embedded within (but not completely covering) a wider track. If you have a 5 1/4-inch disk that has been written by a low-density drive, remember never to update that disk with a high-density drive. That procedure renders the disk unreadable by the low-density drive (although the high-density drive still can read the disk). In fact, the best way to recover information from a disk that has been overwritten incorrectly in this manner is to use various high-density drives and perform a DOS DISKCOPY operation to a new, blank, never-before-formatted, low-density disk.

Off-Center Drives

The most frequently encountered problem with floppy drives is off-center clamping of the disk. In the PC troubleshooting seminars that I conduct around the world, the PC systems are run with the lid off for most of the course's duration. When someone has a floppy disk read or boot problem, I take a quick look at the exposed disk drive. I can see instantly whether the disk has been clamped by the drive hub in an off-center position. More often than not, off-center clamping is the problem. When not clamped properly, the disk appears to wobble as it rotates. This situation usually causes the disk's information to be unreadable. I simply eject the disk and reinsert it properly, and the read or boot problem disappears.

When inserting a disk into a floppy drive, always wiggle the drive lever down, up, and then down again to clamp the disk (instead of moving the lever down once to clamp the disk). The first partial closing of the lever serves to center the disk in its jacket so that the drive hub properly clamps the disk in a centered position.

The solution to an off-center disk is to eject the disk and reinsert it properly. This procedure is not helpful, however, if you have written to a disk in an off-center position. In that case, use the DOS DISKCOPY command to copy the data to another disk and attempt to recover the data on the files with unreadable sectors.

The 3 1/2-inch drives are almost totally immune from this type of problem; 3 1/2-inch drives use different types of clamping and centering mechanisms. The virtually foolproof clamping mechanism is one reason that the 3 1/2-inch drives are more reliable and easier to use than the 5 1/4-inch drives.

Misaligned Drives

If your disk drives are misaligned, you will notice that other drives cannot read disks created in your drive, and your drive may not read disks created in other drives. Misaligned drives can be dangerous if allowed to progress unchecked. If the misalignment is severe, your drive will not be capable of reading original applications program disks, although the drive still will be capable of reading disks created on your system.

One solution to this problem is to have the drive realigned. This solution may not be optimal because replacing the drive may be more cost-effective than realigning the drive. You also will find that your newly aligned drive may not be capable of reading all the backup or data disks created while the drive was out of alignment. If you replace the misaligned drive with a new drive but keep the misaligned drive, you can use the misaligned drive to copy the data to newly formatted disks in the new drive.

Dirty Drives

Sometimes disk read and write problems are caused by dirty drive heads. Many companies sell drive cleaning kits that work well in removing this dirt, which enables the drive to work properly. I recommend using the "wet" types of cleaning kits. These cleaning kits include a disk that contains a liquid cleaning solution (alcohol, Freon, or trichloroethelyne). When you insert the cleaning disk and the drive is accessed, the cleaning disk spins and washes the oxide particles and dirt off the drive heads. I do not recommend the "dry" types of cleaning kits, which rely purely on abrasive action to remove deposits from the heads; the abrasive action causes head wear as well.

Liquid Spills

Spilling liquid on a disk seems like a disaster. Actually, you can recover a disk quite easily from most liquid spills. Dry the disk and try normal recovery procedures. If those steps don't work, follow these steps:

1. Using a pocket knife, carefully slit the disk jacket along the seam and remove the disk itself. If you are working with a 3 1/2-inch disk, use the knife carefully to pry the two rigid jacket halves apart and free the disk inside.

2. Carefully wash off the disk with distilled water. You may have to let the disk soak for a minute or so if the liquid on the disk was allowed to dry.

3. Dry off the disk, being careful not to bend or crease the disk in any way.

4. Select a brand new disk of the same type, carefully slit the jacket with the knife, and remove the new disk. Be sure to do a careful, neat job because you want the jacket, not the disk inside. For a 3 1/2-inch disk, carefully split the new disk jacket apart.

5. Insert the cleaned disk in the jacket with the proper orientation—that is, right side up. If you are unsure which side originally was up, you have to guess.

6. Insert the newly jacketed disk into the drive and attempt to read the disk. If the read is successful, Use the DISKCOPY command to copy the disk's contents to another new (but uncut) disk. If the read is not successful, the disk probably is upside down in the jacket, and you should reverse the disk. (Remember to keep the jacket you used to recover the disk, because you can use that jacket again in this type of situation.)

This kind of repair illustrates that sometimes you need to be creative in finding your way out of a data recovery situation. Such creativity certainly can pay off.

Bent or Creased Disks

You may have had the experience of receiving a bent, unreadable disk in the mail. The solution to this problem is similar to the solution to the liquid spill problem, but the success rate is not quite as high.

You first need to get the disk out of the jacket and determine whether the disk itself has been harmed. If only the jacket has been damaged, simply inserting the disk into a new jacket (as described in the preceding section) should solve the problem. If the disk itself is creased or bent, you need to straighten out the disk. To flatten the disk, place it under a stack of books or encyclopedias. Do not attempt to heat the disk to remove creases; heating disks makes matters worse.

After pressing the disk for some time (a day or more of compression may be necessary to make the disk readable), insert the disk into a new jacket and use the DISKCOPY command to copy the disk's contents to a new disk. You then can work on recovering data from any unreadable files.

Chapter Summary

In this chapter, you examined the floppy disk drive and the floppy disk in great detail. You now are intimately familiar with floppy disk technology and operation. This knowledge will enable you to use the technology in an efficient and constructive manner.

The tips and information in this chapter should serve as a form of preventive maintenance for floppy drives and disks. Experience indicates that most floppy disk problems are caused by the user, not by the hardware. Now that you understand how your system works, you can prevent this type of problem.

3

Hard Disk Basics

When a hard disk drive fails, the results are almost never inconsequential. Loss of data rarely comes at a convenient time—such as immediately after you perform a backup. More likely, your hard disk loses data just after you enter all the information for your budget or finish writing your dissertation. If you consider the amount of time needed to retype or re-create important information, you will want to learn how to recover lost data and how to prevent future data loss from occurring.

To better recover information from a hard disk that has crashed or has damage to the file system or data contained on the drive, you must understand these units completely. Knowing how a hard disk functions also gives you an edge in reliability and performance because you can install, configure, and maintain a drive properly to ensure a long, trouble-free life.

In this chapter, you take a thorough look at the hard disk as it relates to data recovery. This chapter examines the physical construction and operation of a hard disk drive, as well as some of the types of drive units available. This chapter also addresses hard disk failures related to mechanical and electronic problems and discusses ways to recover.

Defining a Hard Disk Drive

A hard disk is similar to a floppy disk in many ways. Like a floppy disk, a hard disk is used for storing and retrieving information from your computer. Unlike a floppy disk, however, a hard disk usually is not removable, and a hard disk is capable of storing much more information than a floppy disk. The term *hard disk* refers to the way the disk is constructed—from a rigid disk platter in the drive. Unlike a floppy disk, this platter cannot bend or flex at all. Because the platter usually cannot be removed from the hard disk drive, IBM calls the platter a *fixed disk drive*. Removable platter hard disk drives exist, but their nonstandard nature, higher cost, and unreliability make these drives unpopular.

Hard disk drives often are called *Winchester* drives, a term dating back to the 1960s. During that time, IBM developed a high-speed hard disk drive that had 30 megabytes of fixed platter storage and 30 megabytes of removable platter storage. The drive had platters that spun at high speed and heads that floated over the platters while they were spinning in a sealed environment. This drive became known as the 30-30 drive and soon gained the nickname Winchester after the famous Winchester 30-30 rifle. After that time, all drives using a high-speed spinning platter with a floating head also became known as Winchester drives. The term has no technical or scientific meaning and now is used simply as slang for *hard disk*.

Defining Drive Components

A wide variety of hard disks is available. Nearly all drives share the same basic physical components. Some differences exist in the way hard disk components are built into the drive, as well as the quality of materials used, but the operational characteristics of most drives are similar. The components found in a typical hard disk drive include

- Disk platters
- Read/write heads
- Head actuator mechanism
- Cables and connectors, including interface signal connectors

The platters, heads, and head actuator mechanism usually are contained together in a sealed chamber called the head disk assembly (HDA). This assembly usually is treated as a single component because it rarely is opened. Parts that are external to the drive HDA—the logic boards, bezel, and any other configuration or mounting hardware—can be disassembled from the drive itself.

This section discusses several of the main components typical to most hard disks, including the platters, read/write heads, and head actuator mechanism. If you know a little about how hard disks are constructed, you will understand how certain operations can be helpful in a data recovery situation. For example, the type of actuator used in a hard disk can give you clues to the kinds of problems you can expect.

Platters

The disks or platters in a hard drive are the components that actually store information. This information is placed on the disk magnetically by the head, as described in Chapter 1. A typical hard drive has one or more platters or disks. The most common types of hard drives have 5 1/4-inch or 3 1/2-inch diameter platters. Larger drives with 8-inch or even 14-inch platters are available, but these expensive, high-capacity drives typically are not associated with PC systems. Drives with 2-inch platters also have been introduced and may become standard soon.

Most hard drives have several platters, although some of the smaller half-height drives have only one. The number of platters the drive has is limited by the drive's physical size. Currently, the maximum number of platters for full-height 5 1/4-inch drives is 11, and the maximum number of platters for half-height 5 1/4-inch and 3 1/2-inch drives is 8. The more platters you have in a drive, the more information you can store. Multiple platters lock and spin together, like a stack of records with space between each record, so the tone arms (the heads) can move in and out.

Most platters are made of an aluminum metal alloy for strength and light weight, but some platters are constructed of glass. Both the 5 1/4-inch and 3 1/2-inch platters are usually 1/8-inch thick. The platters are covered with a thin layer of a magnetically retentive substance, or *media*, which is actually responsible for the storing of information. As the following sections explain, the type and quality of the media used on a disk affect the reliability of the disk as a storage device. Two popular types of media are used on hard disk platters:

- Oxide media
- Thin film media

Oxide Media

Most older drives use oxide media on the drive platters. This media is popular because of its lower cost and ease of application.

Oxide media is made of various compounds containing iron oxide as the active ingredient. A magnetic layer is created by a process where the aluminum platter is coated with a syrup containing iron oxide particles. Spinning the platters at a high speed evenly spreads the media across the disk. The material flows from the center of the platter to the outside because of centrifugal force, which allows an even coating of material to be placed on the drive, with few imperfections. Then the surface is cured and polished, and a protective lubricating layer of material is added and burnished smooth. Normally, this media is about 30 millionths of an inch thick. If you could peer into a drive with oxide media coated platters, you would see that they are brown or amber.

This older method of coating does not give the kind of performance and reliability available in thin film media. Oxide media is also very soft, making the disk more prone to head crash damage if the drive is jolted during operation.

> ***Caution:*** A head crash occurs when the read/write head bangs against the platters, resulting in a scratch to the media surface. Jolting the computer or dropping it a short distance can instigate a head crash—even when the computer is turned off.

Thin Film Media

As drive densities increase, the media needs to be thinner and more perfectly formed. Thin film media is aptly named because it is much thinner than oxide media. When the media is thinner, the magnetic signals needed on the disks can be placed in smaller areas on the disk, enabling the disk to store more information in the same space as the old technology. Most higher capacity or higher quality drive systems use thin film media instead of the oxide coatings of the past.

Thin film media also is known as *plated* or *sputtered* media. These names describe the various processes used to get this thin film of media on the platters.

Plated media is manufactured by a process of placing the media material on the disk with an electroplating mechanism, much like chrome plating on the bumper of your car. The aluminum platter is immersed in a series of chemical baths that coat the platter with layers of metallic film. The final layer is about 3 millionths of an inch of a cobalt alloy that is the actual media itself.

Sputtering is a special procedure in which magnetic media is deposited on the platters in a near vacuum. Thin film sputtered disks are created by a process of first coating the aluminum platters with a layer of nickel phosphorus and then applying the cobalt alloy magnetic material by a continuous vacuum deposition process called sputtering. During this process, magnetic layers as thin as 2 millionths of an inch are deposited on the disk similar to the way silicon chip wafers are coated with metallic films in the semiconductor industry. The sputtering technique also is used for laying down an extremely hard protective carbon coating. The platters usually are electrically charged to attract the media particles as they are vaporized. This is the most expensive process because the requirements of a near perfect vacuum are difficult to meet.

The surface of a sputtered platter contains magnetic layers as thin as 2 millionths of an inch. The surface also is very smooth, enabling the head to float close to the disk surface. Therefore, a magnetic signal can be placed in a smaller area on the disk. With the head closer and writing areas smaller, the density of the magnetic field can be increased to provide greater storage capacity. The head can float over the surface as closely as 6 to 8 millionths of an inch. Additionally, the increased intensity of the magnetic field on the disk provides the higher signal amplitudes needed for good signal-to-noise performance when reading back a disk. That is, the magnetic signal must be stronger than any background magnetic signal (like static/noise on a radio) in order for the correct signal to be interpreted properly. Disks covered with the thin media are more reliable than disks using the older oxide coated disks.

Both the sputtering and plating processes result in a thin, hard film of media on the platters. The hardness of thin film media increases the likelihood of the disk surviving contact with the heads at high speed. The older oxide coatings are scratched more easily. Because the thin film media can handle much greater densities with accuracy, it is used on most larger-capacity drives, as well as on many of the newer 3 1/2-inch platter drives. If you could open a drive to peek at the platters, the thin film platters would look like the silver surface of a mirror: chrome-plated and highly polished.

Sputtering results in the most perfect, thinnest, and hardest disk surface that can be obtained commercially today and now is used in the majority of thin film media-equipped drives. This procedure translates into increased storage capacity in a smaller area, fewer head crashes, and a drive that gives you many years of trouble-free use. New techniques of creating even better disk surfaces probably will require a coating of the disk in a weightless environment. For this reason, disk drive media technology will benefit greatly when commercial manufacturing begins to exploit outer space.

Read/Write Heads

A component called a read/write head obtains information from the drive and stores information on the drive. As described in Chapter 1, the head produces a magnetic signal to write information to the disk. To read information from the disk, the head detects magnetic signals on the disk as it spins by. A hard disk drive usually has one read/write head for each platter side, which means a hard drive has between 2 and 22 read/write heads. The multiple heads are connected together on a single movement mechanism, causing the heads to move in unison across the platters.

The mechanical aspects of the heads are simple. Each head is on an arm that is spring loaded to force the heads into the platters. Each platter is squeezed by the two heads above and below it. If you could open a drive and lift up the top head with your finger, the head would snap back into the platter when released. Also, if you pulled down on one of the heads underneath a platter, the head would snap back up into the platter under spring tension when released.

When the drive is powered off, spring tension forces the heads into the platters, but when the drive spins at full speed, air pressure develops underneath the heads and lifts them up off the surface of the platter. The gap between the heads and the platter on a fully spinning drive is usually between 5 and 20 millionths of an inch. The small size of this gap is exactly the reason that you must never open up the disk drive's HDA. Any particle of dust or dirt that gets into this mechanism can cause the heads to read improperly or, worse, cause the heads to oscillate and strike the platters while at full speed, resulting in a head crash.

For the ensured cleanliness of the interior of the drive, the HDA is assembled in a class 100 or better clean room. In such a room, a cubic foot of air cannot contain more than 100 0.5 micron particles. One person while standing motionless breathes out 500 such particles in a single minute. Class 100 or better rooms contain special air filtration systems that continuously evacuate and refresh the air. A drive's HDA must not be opened unless it is inside such a room. Because these environments are excessively expensive to produce, few companies (except those that manufacture the drives) are prepared to service hard disk drives.

Two types of heads are used in modern hard disk drives:

- Composite ferrite heads
- Thin film heads

Composite ferrite heads often are used in low-cost disk drives. High-quality, high-capacity disk drives use the thin film heads. From a maintenance standpoint, disks with thin film heads are preferable.

Composite Ferrite Heads

The composite ferrite head is the traditional type of magnetic head design and is less expensive to produce. This type of head uses an iron oxide core with electromagnetic coils wrapping it. A magnetic field is generated when the coils are energized, and an electric field is induced in a head when a magnetic field is passed near the coils. This process gives the heads full read and write capability. These heads are larger and heavier than the thin film heads and must use a larger flying height to record on the disk. Because the flying height affects the size of the magnetic flux, the higher flying height makes the composite ferrite head capable of writing and reading less on an equivalent size disk than the thin film head. The heavier weight of the composite ferrite head makes it more likely to cause a head crash than the lighter thin film head.

Thin Film Heads

Thin film heads are a specially produced semiconductor chip. These heads themselves are a complex circuit. Thin film heads are produced by the same process as any semiconductor chip, but special care is given to their shape. The heads must have a U-shaped groove in the bottom to allow air pressure buildup. These heads are lightweight and can fly closer to the platter than the composite types of heads. The air pressure generated by the spinning disk controls the height at which the heads fly above the disk.

Flying height has been reduced to as little as 5 millionths of an inch in some designs. This reduced height enables the head and platters to pick up and transmit a stronger signal. As a result, the signal-to-noise ratio increases, which improves accuracy. In other words, the data signal on the disk is greater than any background noise signal (static) that may be on the disk. At the high track and linear densities in some drives, a standard composite head cannot pick out the data signal from the background noise. Most high-capacity drives today use thin film heads to achieve their tremendous densities.

Head Actuators

More important than the heads themselves is the mechanical system that moves the heads: the *head actuator*. This mechanism moves the heads across the disk and positions them accurately over the desired cylinder. Many variations of head actuator mechanisms are available, but they all are categorized as either *stepper motor actuators* or *voice coil actuators*.

Drives equipped with stepper motor actuators are much less reliable—often 5 to 10 times less reliable—than drives equipped with voice coil actuators. The use of one or the other type of positioner has profound effects on the drive's performance and reliability. These mechanisms affect the drive's speed; accuracy; sensitivity to temperature, position, and vibration; and overall reliability.

The head actuator is the most important specification in the drive. Knowing which head actuator mechanism is in a drive tells you a great deal about the drive's performance and reliability characteristics. A hard disk's documentation or installation guide often lists the type used.

Also, disk drives with the voice coil actuators tend to be more expensive, but price is not a definitive measure. Most large hard disks (60M or greater) used in name-brand computers, such as IBM and COMPAQ, use voice coil actuators.

Table 3.1 lists how the two types of head actuators affect certain parameters.

Table 3.1
Comparing the Effects Of
Stepper Motor and Voice Coil Actuators

Parameter	*Stepper Motor*	*Voice Coil*
Relative access speed	Average	Fast
Temperature sensitive	Yes	No
Positionally sensitive	Yes	No
Automatic head parking	Sometimes	Yes
Preventive maintenance	Periodic	Seldom
Relative reliability	Fair to Good	Excellent

A stepper motor-equipped drive has a slower average access rating. This type of drive is temperature sensitive during read and write operations; it also is sensitive to the physical orientation during read and write operations.

Most stepper motor-equipped drives do not automatically park the heads over a save zone during power down. And this actuator usually requires reformats once or twice per year to realign the sector data with the sector header information due to mistracking. Voice coil-equipped drives do not have these problems.

Note: A few stepper motor drives do feature automatic head parking at power down. If you have a newer stepper motor drive and want to know whether it features automatic head parking, check your technical reference manual. Sometimes you can hear a noise after power down, which can be deceptive. Some drives employ a solenoid activated spindle brake that makes a definite noise as the drive is powered off; this noise does not involve head parking.

All floppy disk drives position their heads with a stepper motor actuator. The accuracy of the stepper mechanism is suited to floppy drives because they have lower track densities than hard drives. As mentioned earlier, however, many less-expensive, low-capacity hard drives do use a stepper motor actuator.

Most hard disks with more than 40 megabytes use voice coil actuators, and *all* hard drives with more than 80 megabytes use voice coil actuators. IBM, for example, uses voice coil actuators in all drives with at least 40M.

The price difference between equal-capacity voice coil drives and stepper motor drives is approximately 30 to 50 percent. If you purchase a 40M stepper motor hard disk for $300, a 40M voice coil unit will cost between $390 and $450. This price increase usually proves true, but costs vary depending on where you shop. New 80M voice coil drives can be found for the same price as new 40M stepper motor drives. The price differential makes you factor the cost of a less expensive drive against the reliability and reduced maintenance of a more expensive drive.

Stepper Motor Actuator

A stepper motor is an electrical motor that "steps" or moves from position to position with mechanical detents (stopping mechanisms). These motors have a clicking or buzzing feel if you grip the spindle of one and spin it by hand. The feel is much like that of many volume controls on stereo systems. A stepper motor cannot position itself between step positions; instead, it must stop at one of the predetermined detent positions. These motors are physically small—1 to 3 inches in size—and they can be square, round cylindrical, or even round and flat like a pancake. These motors are outside the sealed HDA, but the spindle of the motor penetrates the HDA through a sealed hole. Stepper motors are located in one of the four corners of the hard disk drive, and usually they are visible from the exterior of the drive (see fig. 3.1).

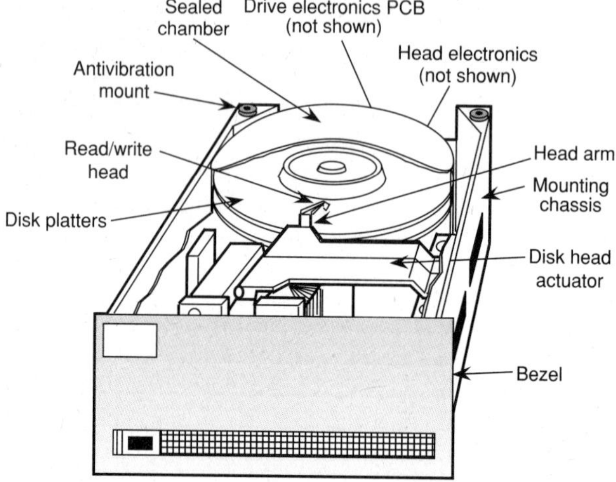

Fig. 3.1. *A stepper motor head actuator and other drive components.*

The stepper motor is linked mechanically to the head rack by either a split steel band coiled around the motor spindle or a rack and pinion gear mechanism. As the motor steps, each detent or click stop position translates to the movement of one track through the mechanical linkage. Some systems use several motor steps for each track. For example, in positioning the heads, if the drive is commanded to move to track 400, the motor begins the stepping motion, proceeds to the 400th detent position, and stops. The heads are now over the desired cylinder.

Temperature is the biggest problem affecting stepper motors. As the drive platters heat and cool, they expand and contract. This phenomenon causes the tracks to move in relation to some predetermined track position. The stepper mechanism cannot move in increments of less than a single track to correct for these temperature-induced errors. Therefore, the drive blindly positions the heads to a particular cylinder according to a predetermined number of steps from the stepper motor.

When the drive is low-level formatted, the initial track and sector marks are placed on the platters at the same positions the stepper motor commands the heads to be at. If all subsequent reading and writing occurs at the same temperature as the initial format, the heads always record precisely within the track and sector boundaries.

At different temperatures, however, the actual head position does not match the track position. When the platters are cold, for example, the heads miss the track location because the platters have shrunk and the tracks have moved inward toward the center of the disk. When the platters are warmer than the formatted temperature, the platters grow larger and the actual track positions are located outward from where the heads are located. Gradually, data is written inside, on top of, and outside the actual track and sector marks. As the mistracking builds up, the drive eventually fails to read one of these locations, and you receive a DOS `Abort, Retry, Ignore` error message.

If your hard disk begins showing these problems and you suspect a temperature problem, back up all files possible at a variety of temperatures. Then perform a low-level format and restore your data to the disk.

> ***Note:*** Because reformatting a hard drive usually requires a complete backup and restore operation, reformatting is an inconvenient and time-consuming operation to perform. To help with these periodic reformats, most commercially available low-level format programs offer a special reformat option. This option copies the data for a given track to a spare location, reformats the track, and then copies the data back to the original track. When this type of format operation is finished, you don't need to restore your data because the system has restored it for you.

> ***Caution:*** All these special reformat options wipe out the data as they operate. *Never* use these types of programs without first backing up your data completely. If, while you're using such a program, the power fails or a bug stops the program from finishing, you may lose some data. In such a case, you will need your backup to restore the data.

Voice Coil Actuator

Most hard disks with more than 40 megabytes use voice coil actuators, and *all* hard drives with more than 80 megabytes use voice coil actuators. Voice coil actuators provide greater performance and are more reliable than stepper motor actuators.

A voice coil actuator works by electromagnetic force. The construction of this mechanism is similar to that of a typical audio speaker, which uses a stationary magnet surrounded by a voice coil connected to the speaker's paper cone. Energizing the coil causes the coil to move, which produces sound from the speaker cone. In a typical hard disk voice coil system, an electromagnetic coil moves on a track through a stationary magnet. No contact occurs between the coil and the magnet other than magnetic interaction. The coil mechanism is connected directly to the head rack (see fig. 3.2). As the electromagnetic coils are energized, they attract or repulse the magnet and cause movement of the head rack. These systems are extremely quick and efficient, and most are much quieter than a system that is driven by a stepper motor.

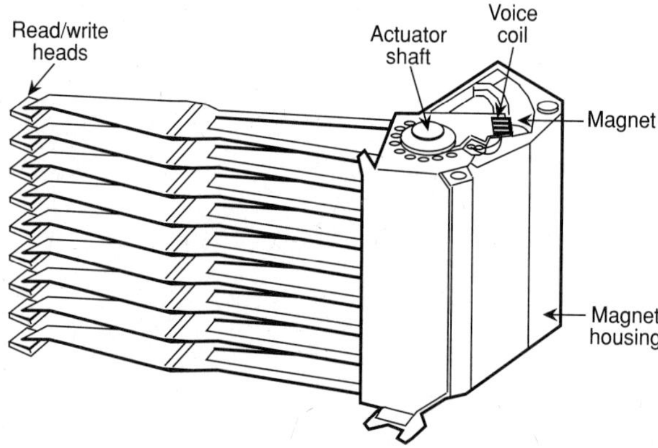

Fig. 3.2. *A voice coil head actuator, connected to the head rack.*

Unlike a stepper motor system, a voice coil system has no click stops or detent positions; therefore, some unique design parameters must be undertaken. In order for you to understand these parameters, you first must consider how the system works.

The system can slide the heads in and out smoothly, like a trombone mechanism, so a way needs to be available to stop the head rack over a particular cylinder. When the drive is manufactured, one side of one platter is deducted from normal read/write usage, and a special set of index marks indicating proper track positions is recorded. The head that sits above this surface has no recording capability, so these marks never can be erased.

As the drive is commanded to move the heads to a particular track—track 400, for example—the internal drive electronics use the signals received by this special head to indicate the position of the heads. As the heads move, the track counters are read from the index surface. When the correct track is under the head rack, the heads are commanded to stop moving. Then, before writing is allowed, the electronics fine-tune the position of the heads over the track where the strongest signals are received by the index head.

This parameter is called a *dedicated surface, closed loop, servo controlled* mechanism. *Dedicated surface* refers to the platter surface that is host for the storage of the special index tracks. For this reason, most voice coil drives have an odd number of heads (a giveaway clue indicating a voice coil actuator). *Closed loop* indicates that the index (or servo) head is wired to the positioning electronics in a closed loop, or feedback loop, system. The feedback from this index head is used for positioning the other heads accurately. The index head acts as a guide head to the rest of the rack. *Servo controlled* refers to the index or servo head itself, which is used for dictating or controlling head positioning accuracy.

Not all voice coil drives have an odd number of heads, however. Embedded servo drives bury the servo or guidance information in the sector gaps on each track. This method eliminates the need for an entire surface to be dedicated for this information. Also, some drives simply have an odd number of heads. After deducting the one used for servo purposes, only an even number remains.

A voice coil actuator with servo control is not affected by temperature changes in the same way as a stepper motor actuator. When the temperature is cold and the platters shrink, the voice coil system compensates. Voice coil systems never position to predetermined track positions; instead, these systems hunt down the particular track and, through the use of the servo head, position precisely over that track's current position, regardless of the formatted temperature. Likewise, when the temperature is hot, voice coil systems automatically compensate, and track positioning is precise.

A fringe benefit of using a voice coil positioner is *automatic head parking*. When a hard disk drive is powered off, the heads pull back into the platters to land by the spring tension in each head arm. Although the drive is designed to handle thousands of takeoffs and landings, the automatic head parking tries to ensure that this landing occurs where no data exists. Some amount of abrasion always occurs during the landing and takeoff process, which removes a "micropuff" of the media.

If the drive is jarred during the landing or takeoff process, the results can be worse. In a voice coil drive, the heads are positioned and held by magnetic force. When power is removed from the drive, the magnetic field holding the heads stationary over a particular cylinder dissipates. This dissipation enables the head rack to skitter loose back and forth over the drive surface, causing potential damage. Consequently, as part of the voice coil design, a weak spring must be attached to the head rack at one end and a head stop at the other end. This spring is normally overcome by the magnetic force of the positioner, but when the drive is powered off, the spring gently drags the head rack into a park and lock position before the drive slows down and the heads land. This process is automatic head parking and is a standard function of any voice coil positioner.

You activate the parking mechanism by turning off the system. You don't need to run any sort of park program, and the heads even park themselves automatically during a power outage. The drives automatically unpark when you turn on the system.

Cables and Connectors

Cables and connectors are overlooked often in discussions of recovery and reliability. However, improper installation or use of cables and connectors can cause problems with your hard disk operations. This section briefly examines the following cables and connectors: the interface connectors associated with the standard Seagate Technologies ST-506/412 interface and ESDI (Enhanced Small Device Interface), and the connectors associated with the SCSI (Small Computer System Interface) and IDE (Internal Drive Electronics) interface. The section "Examining Interface Specifications" later in this chapter provides a more in-depth discussion of these interfaces.

Several terms related to interface use appear in this section. You should understand the following terms before proceeding:

- A *cable*, also called a *flat ribbon cable*, is several wires attached in parallel fashion. A cable carries electronic signals from a hard drive controller. A cable can carry the signals of any kind of interface.
- The *connectors* are located at the ends of cables. One connector is plugged into the hard drive, and the other connector is plugged into the hard drive controller card.
- An *interface* is the electronic method by which information is transferred back and forth to a hard drive. Interfaces discussed in this section include the following: ESDI, SCSI, IDE, and ST-506.
- The *encoding method* is the way data is laid down on the disk platters (magnetically).

Note: Soon all hard drives will be mounted on main motherboards, eliminating the cable and connectors. As hard drives get smaller, they will change from being mounted on the chassis or frame of a computer to being mounted on the main motherboard. To some extent, this setup is being done now on laptops.

ST-506/412 and ESDI

The standard drives that interface via the ST-506/412 or ESDI nearly always have the following four connectors:

- Interface control connector
- Interface data connector
- Power connector
- Ground connector (tab)

The interface connectors are the most important because they carry the drive's instructions and also carry data to and from the drive. The control connector is a larger 34-pin connector that can be daisy-chained between two drives and a single controller. This cable and connector system is used for passing instructions from the controller to the drive to cause head movements and other operations (see fig. 3.3). The drive can acknowledge these actions to the controller through this cable. The daisy-chain arrangement is much like that used for floppy drives. The drive responds to two usable channels (out of a maximum of four), labeled drive selects 1, 2, 3, and 4. Only the first two channels are usable on PC controllers due to the design of the system as well as the controllers.

The data cable, which carries data to and from the drive, is a smaller 20-pin cable that runs from the controller to each drive separately (see fig. 3.4). This cable is not daisy-chained. A two-drive system has one control cable from the controller to each of two drives and two separate data cables, one for each drive. The controllers have three connectors to support the two-drive maximum limit.

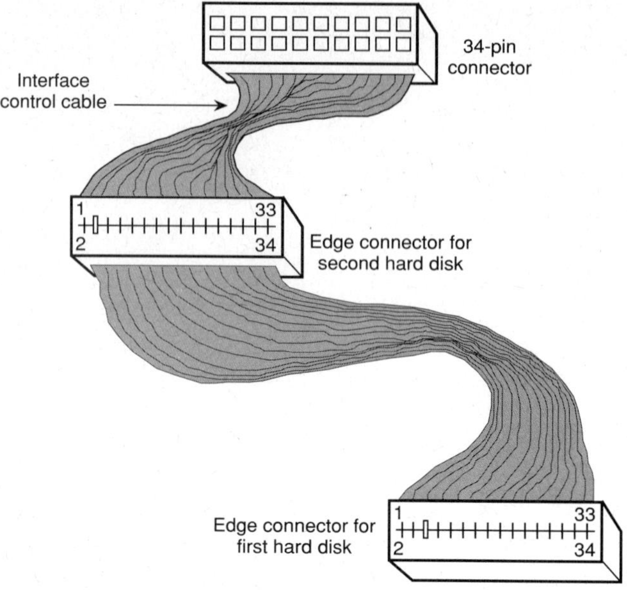

Fig. 3.3. *The interface control connector.*

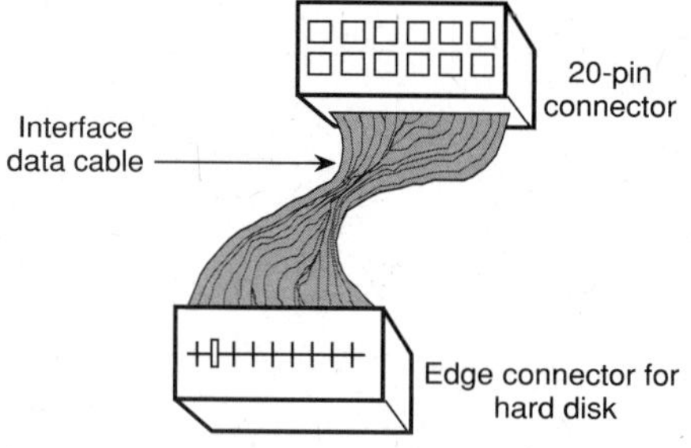

Fig. 3.4. *The interface data connector.*

The power connector that is used to connect to your hard disk is the same as the one used for a floppy disk drive. The drives use both 5- and 12-volt power; the 12-volt power is used for running the drive's motors and head actuator. Make sure that your power supply can adequately supply power for the hard disk drives you install; many hard drives draw a great deal more power than floppy drives do. You can determine your power supply's capability by checking the number of amps supplied. Older PCs' power supplies may not have adequate amperage to support additional floppy or hard disk drives not originally designed for the computers. Also, you must verify that the connectors on your power supply provide enough amps for all devices connected.

IBM AT systems, for example, have a power supply with three disk drive power connectors, labeled P10, P11, and P12. Both P10 and P11 have 2.8 amps of 12-volt current available; connector P12 has 1.0 amp of 12-volt current available. Most full-height hard drives draw much more power than 1.0 amp, especially at start-up. Therefore, the P12 connector is usable by floppy drives or smaller 3 1/2-inch hard drives only. You can compensate for this situation by plugging the hard drive into the right power connectors, which are P10 or P11. Most compatibles have a power supply with four or more disk drive power connectors, and each connector usually provides the same outlet power. However, a few compatibles may still use power supplies designed like IBM's.

Most drives contain a grounding tab, which provides a positive ground connection between the drive and the chassis of the system. In a PC or XT system, the hard disk is mounted with screws that hold the drive directly to the chassis of the PC, so the ground wire is unnecessary. On AT systems, however, the drives are on plastic or fiberglass rails, which do not provide a proper ground path. These systems must provide a grounding wire, which is plugged into the drive through this grounding tab. Failure to ground the drive may result in improper operation, intermittent failure, or general read and write errors.

> ***Note:*** A cable can be installed backward sometimes (if a key is missing). The computer then cannot "talk" to the hard drive. After the cable is installed correctly, the problem no longer exists.

SCSI and IDE

The SCSI host adapter and the IDE drives do not use the same standard control and data connections as the ST-506/412 and ESDI.

The SCSI (pronounced *scuzzy*) host adapter uses a SCSI interface, which has a single, large, 50-pin cable. In this adapter, power and grounding are normally separate from this 50-pin cable. Because the SCSI system is a daisy-chain arrangement, more than one drive can be strung out along the same cable. Usually, the system is limited to seven SCSI devices in addition to the SCSI host adapter, the eighth device.

IDE drives are ESDI or ST-506/412 drives that combine the entire disk controller with the drive. The drive and controller are contained in a single physical unit that plugs directly into the computer's bus slots instead of using a cable. For example, PS/2 Model 70 systems use MicroChannel IDE drives that plug directly into a MicroChannel bus slot (usually through an angle adapter or interposer card). Systems from other companies, such as COMPAQ, use AT-bus (16-bit) IDE drives or XT-bus (8-bit) IDE drives. The first XT-bus IDE drives were called *hardcards*.

Examining Interface Specifications

A hard disk interface is the connection scheme—the logic—used to link your hard disk to its controller. To properly connect these two vital pieces of equipment, you must use the right interface and connect it properly. Several popular hard disk drive interfaces are available for use in PC systems, including the following:

- ST-506/412
- ESDI
- SCSI
- IDE

Of these interfaces, only the ST-506/412 and ESDI are true disk interfaces. The SCSI and IDE interfaces are system-level interfaces that incorporate one of the other two disk interfaces internally. Most SCSI or IDE drives incorporate an ESDI interface into the disk drive electronics; the higher level SCSI or IDE interfaces are used for talking to the drive controller. Although these interfaces are hardware-specific, you should know the disk interface with which you are working (as described in the following sections) because many data recovery problems are related to the drive setup and installation.

Because data recovery operations are tied directly to the disk drives in your system, you need a high level of knowledge of several of the disk drives and interfaces to become an expert at data recovery. Each of these interfaces involves a slightly different method of installation and drive configuration; if these procedures are done incorrectly or altered by the system user accidentally, you may be prevented from accessing any data on the drive. Expertise in data recovery requires proficiency in installing and configuring the various types of hard disks and controllers available. If you are primarily concerned with your own system, however, you only need to understand your type of controller and drive.

ST-506/412

The ST-506/412 interface was developed by Seagate Technologies in 1980. The interface was designed specifically for the ST-506 drive, a 6M unformatted/5M formatted drive in a full-height 5 1/4-inch form factor. By today's standards, this drive is huge. In 1981 Seagate introduced the ST-412 drive, which added to the interface a feature called *buffered seek*. The buffered seek read more information from the disk than necessary, so the next piece of information requested by the computer was likely to be in memory already. This feature improved the effective read performance of the disk. The ST-412 is one of the drives IBM originally selected for the XT. The ST-412 is a 10M formatted/12M unformatted drive—also huge by today's standards.

Other drive manufacturers wanting to introduce a PC hard disk decided to adopt the Seagate-developed standard rather than reinvent the wheel, which has made this interface extremely popular today. The interface's design has remained constant, which means it is compatible with virtually any drive. You don't need custom cables or special modifications.

The only item requiring customization is the drive table support in the system. The drive table gives the computer information about your hard disk, such as how many disks and heads are included in the drive.

This interface's only problem is its aging design, which doesn't meet the needs of current high-performance drives. This interface was designed originally for a 5M drive. The maximum drive capacity also is limited; currently, no manufacturers of drives larger than 152M or 233M use this interface.

The ST-506/412 interface specifies that the data separator, or *encoder/decoder*, is located on the controller (see "Examining Data Encoding Schemes" later in this chapter). This *en*coder/*dec*oder (endec) converts the digital signal into a series of magnetic flux transitions for storage on the drive. The idea is similar to a modem that converts digital information into tones for transmission over phone lines. The particular method used for the conversion of digital information into the analog flux change signals is called the *encoding scheme*. The original specification for ST-506/412 indicates that the encoding scheme to be used is modified frequency modulation.

ESDI

The Enhanced Small Device Interface (ESDI) is a specialized hard disk and tape drive interface established as a standard in 1983 by Maxtor Corporation. Maxtor led a consortium of drive manufacturers to adopt its proposed interface as a new high-performance standard. The company also made provisions for increased reliability, such as building the encoder/decoder (endec) into the drive. The ESDI is a high-speed interface capable of transferring 24 megabits per second as a specified top-end limit. Most drives running the ESDI are limited to a maximum of 10 or 15 megabits per second at this time.

One of the ESDI's most important features is that it has been adopted throughout the industry without changes from individual manufacturers. The ESDI has enhanced commands so that the controller can read the drive's capacity parameters directly off of the drive and control defect mapping in the same way. This feature enables the controller or motherboard ROM BIOS to read the drive parameters directly off of the hard disk, which means users no longer need a setup program to tell the system what type of hard disk has been installed.

With this method, IBM completely avoids the drive table problem in high-end ESDI systems. COMPAQ also adopted the ESDI in high-end Deskpro 386 systems. Also, because a standard way exists for reading a defect map from a drive, you can write the manufacturer's defect list to the drive in the form of a file. The controller and low-level format software can read this file, eliminating the need for you to type these entries manually. This feature enables the format program to update the defect list if any new defects are discovered during the low-level format or the surface analysis. See Chapter 4 for detailed information about low-level formatting.

Currently, few ESDI interface controllers are available for the PC or XT systems because these systems cannot handle the greater throughput (sending data though the interface). Western Digital has a WD1007V-WA2 controller, which is an ESDI controller supporting two hard drives and two floppy drives. Adaptec and DTC also have popular ESDI hard disk/floppy disk controllers that can be used in AT systems.

Most ESDI implementations have drives formatted to 32 sectors per track or higher. Sixty or more sectors per track are possible. This number is much higher than the standard ST-506/412 MFM or RLL implementation of 17 or 26 sectors per track and results in two or more times the data transfer rate with an interleave of 1 to 1. Any ESDI controller can support a 1 to 1 interleave, which allows a 1,020K-per-second or greater transfer rate.

The *interleave* denotes how information is read from the disk. If the head reads each sector on the disk one after another, the interleave is 1 to 1. If the head reads a sector, skips a sector, and reads a sector, the interleave is 1 to 2, and so on. The transfer rate measures the speed at which the information can be read from the disk.

In the PC world, controlled by IBM, the ESDI has become the new standard interface, replacing the older ST-506/412 interface. IBM now uses the ESDI on all PS/2 systems incorporating 70M or greater drives. For example, the PS/2 Model 80-041 comes with a 44M ST-506/412 drive that runs a 1 to 1 interleave at 17 sectors per track using MFM encoding, and the PS/2 Model 80-071 comes with a 70M ESDI drive that runs a 1 to 1 interleave at 36 sectors per track using RLL encoding.

At 1 to 1 interleaving, the 44M drive can transfer all 17 sectors of data to the system in a single revolution of the disk. With 60 revolutions per second, the result is a maximum transfer rate of 510K per second. The ESDI drive running 1 to 1 interleaving can transfer all 36 sectors in a single revolution. With 60 revolutions per second, the result is a maximum transfer rate of 1,080K per second. The 70M drive has more than twice the data transfer rate of the 44M drive—entirely due to the ESDI. COMPAQ and other high-end compatible systems manufacturers also supply 1 to 1 interleave ESDI systems on their systems.

Because the ESDI is much like the older ST-506/412 interface, the ESDI can replace the ST-506/412 compatibly. Most ESDI controllers are register-compatible with the ST-506/412 controllers, which means the ESDI can understand the signals sent by the ST-506/412 interface. OS/2 and other non-DOS operating systems also run with little or no problems. The ROM BIOS interface to the ESDI is similar to the ST-506/412 standard, and many of the same low-level disk utilities that run on one interface run on the other. To take advantage of the ESDI defect-mapping and other special features, you need to use a low-level format and surface analysis utility designed for the ESDI, such as the ones built into the controller ROM BIOS and called by DEBUG.

IDE

The Internal Drive Electronics (IDE) interface was originally used as the interface for hardcards that plug directly into a system board or expansion slot. The disk controller is built into the drive, and the drive/controller assembly plugs into a slot on the motherboard. This type of drive/controller combination greatly simplifies installation because no separate power or signal cables go from the system or controller to the drive. Also, assembling the controller and the drive as a unit reduces the total number of components. Signal paths are shorter, and the electrical connections are more noise resistant, resulting in a more reliable design.

Instead of being mounted directly into a slot like hardcard types of drives, an IDE drive is mounted in the more secure positions that standard hard disks occupy. A cable connects the drive/controller unit to a slot on the motherboard.

Many people using IDE drives think that they have a hard disk controller built into their motherboards. These users get this impression because the hard disk seems to plug directly into the motherboard. However, the controller is really in the drive. PC systems with hard disk controllers built into the motherboards do not currently exist but will be introduced in the near future.

Three main types of IDE interfaces are available. The differences are based on three different bus standards. Expansion cards are attached to the computer's bus. If you plug the expansion card into an expansion slot connector on the system board, the bus carries signals to a component in the computer. The three most commonly used bus types follow:

- XT IDE (8-bit)
- AT IDE (16-bit)
- MCA IDE (MicroChannel 16-bit)

The XT and AT versions have standardized on a 40-pin single connector at the drive and motherboard, and the MCA versions have standardized on a 72-pin connector. If the motherboard does not have a dedicated IDE connector for an IDE drive, an adapter card can be plugged into a slot that adapts the standard bus slot physical configuration to the standard IDE 40-pin or 72-pin connectors.

Sometimes these card adapters have some buffer circuitry to improve the bus connection to the drive, but this buffer circuitry is nothing more than a signal adapter, not a controller. *Buffering* means that when information is requested from the disk, more information is read than is really needed. For example, the sector requested is read as well as the few sectors on the disk (perhaps the entire track on which the original sector was located). Then, when the next sector is requested to be read, it's already in memory, which often improves the effective speed of reading information from the disk.

Seagate and Western Digital offer these adapter cards for XT and AT IDE drives to plug into systems that do not have dedicated 40-pin IDE connectors. In PS/2 systems, IBM sometimes uses an *interposer card*, which is an adapter that changes the physical MicroChannel slot to the 72-pin MCA IDE edge connector.

XT IDE drives work in XT-class, 8-bit ISA slot systems only; AT IDE drives work in AT-class, 16-bit ISA bus systems only; and MCA IDE drives work in MicroChannel systems only, such as the IBM PS/2 Model 50.

Because of the simplified physical installation and connection, IDE drives are becoming popular for newer systems. Fewer physical components, fewer cables (or none at all), and a shorter signal path from the controller to the drive greatly improve reliability and performance, especially when higher drive densities are used. To take advantage of the IDE interface drive in an older system that lacks the special IDE connector, all you need is the correct adapter, which plugs into a slot and gives your system a place in which to plug the IDE drive.

SCSI

SCSI (pronounced *scuzzy*) stands for *small computer systems interface*. It is a systems-level interface as opposed to a disk interface, which means SCSI is not a type of controller. Instead, you plug controllers (up to eight) into a SCSI system, and SCSI enables the controllers to talk to one another. One of the controllers acts as a host adapter and functions as the gateway between the SCSI bus and the system.

SCSI does not work directly with a hard disk; the disk drive still needs a controller to talk to SCSI. For example, you can use both ST-506/412 and ESDI drives and their respective controllers, which plug into the SCSI interface. A SCSI host adapter in your system enables the SCSI interface to talk to all the attached devices much like a small local area network.

One SCSI bus can support up to eight *logical units*, or ports. One of these logical units is the adapter card in your PC; the other seven can be other peripherals such as the following:

- Graphics scanner
- Tape backup unit
- Optical CD ROM drive
- ST-506/412 hard disk controller with two drives
- ESDI controller with two drives

Instead of having a standard controller with two drives attached and plugged into a SCSI adapter, most disk drive/controller/SCSI port combinations are in one unit. When you purchase a SCSI interface hard disk, you get the drive, controller, and SCSI attachment all in one circuit. This type of drive is called an embedded SCSI drive because the SCSI interface is built into the drive. This feature prevents you from attaching another drive into the controller portion of the unit because the controller inside the embedded SCSI drive is not directly accessible. These embedded SCSI drives are used today.

The design interface of SCSI limits you to seven total hard disk drives attached to one SCSI host adapter because each of the seven available SCSI bus addresses supports only one drive rather than two. However, you can add a second, third, and fourth SCSI adapter to your system and support a total of 28 hard disks! Unfortunately, DOS recognizes only the first 24 of those drives.

You don't need to know what type of controller (ESDI, ST-506/412, etc.) is inside the SCSI drive because your system does not communicate directly with the controller. Instead, all communication goes through the SCSI host adapter installed in your system bus. You only talk to the drive by using SCSI protocols. Because of devices with embedded controllers and SCSI ports, you probably will see a great number of SCSI-based peripherals in the future.

One SCSI host adapter in your system can expand your system a great deal because of the number of other items that you can connect. Apple Computer, Inc., offers a good example. Apple originally rallied around the SCSI interface as an inexpensive way out of a problem with the Macintosh. Apple designed the Macintosh as a closed system (no slots). The easiest way to gain expandability was to build in a SCSI port, which enabled users to add external peripherals to the slotless Macs. Unlike Apple's Macintoshes, PC systems always have been expandable. With eight bus slots supporting different devices and controllers, these systems had little need for SCSI.

SCSI is gaining popularity in the PC arena because it can expand your system and because many devices are being developed with built-in SCSI interfaces. Acceptance of SCSI in the PC marketplace is slow, however, because it lacks a true standard. The loose SCSI standard that exists has been designed primarily by a committee, and no single manufacturer has led the way—at least in the IBM arena. A little too much flexibility is available, and each manufacturer has his or her own idea of how SCSI should be implemented.

The current SCSI standard defines only the hardware connections and not the driver specifications required for communicating with the devices. Software ties the SCSI subsystem into your PC, which complicates usage of

SCSI because most driver programs supporting SCSI devices work only for a specific device and host adapter.

Suppose, for example, that you buy a graphics scanner to connect to your PC. The scanner comes with its own SCSI host adapter to connect to the system. Suppose that you also want to add a CD ROM drive to the system. The drive comes with a different SCSI host adapter. You can tell the vendor that you already have a SCSI adapter, but the vendor's driver software works only with the adapter the vendor supplies. You must get a third SCSI host adapter to run your SCSI hard disk drives because the host adapters supplied by the scanner and CD ROM companies don't include a built-in BIOS that supports hard disk drives and self-booting.

The "promise" that you can connect all your SCSI devices to the same single SCSI host adapter has not been fulfilled. Many PC-related SCSI problems exist because the SCSI lacks a host adapter standard, as well as a software interface and ROM BIOS support for hard disk drives attached to the SCSI bus.

Running hard disks off the SCSI bus presents some difficulties that do not exist in the older interfaces. The standard IBM XT and AT ROM BIOS software was designed to talk to ST-506/412 hard disk controllers. These systems easily were modified to work with ESDI because ESDI controllers are similar to ST-506/412 controllers at the register level. This modification enabled companies to come out easily with self-booting ROM BIOS-supported ESDI drives. IBM adopted this interface into the PS/2 systems and incorporated an ESDI BIOS into either the disk controller or the motherboard on the PS/2 systems—not the case for SCSI.

The SCSI interface is so different from standard disk interfaces that an entirely new set of ROM BIOS routines is necessary for the system to be supported properly and self-boot. Companies such as Future Domain have produced SCSI cards with built-in ROM BIOS support for the SCSI interface, but these BIOS routines are limited; they run the drives with DOS only. The BIOS doesn't run in the AT protected mode, and other operating systems such as OS/2 include drivers for the standard ST-506/412 and ESDI controllers only. Thus, running the SCSI interface is impossible with many non-DOS operating systems.

In the Apple arena, the development of systems software support (operating systems and ROM) for SCSI enables Apple users to connect peripherals in fairly standard ways. Until recently, IBM users couldn't do so because IBM didn't supply SCSI adapters and devices with their own support. On March 20, 1990, however, IBM introduced several standard SCSI adapters and peripherals for the PS/2 systems, with complete ROM BIOS as well as full operating systems support.

Soon, many third-party companies will ship SCSI products with drivers that support these IBM adapters. Hard disks are already no problem because the support is built into the card. All companies currently making SCSI host adapters will have to update their adapters so they emulate the IBM adapters. With IBM's support, the SCSI bus probably will become the standard peripheral interface for IBM compatibles, just as it has for the Apple Macintosh.

Examining Data Encoding Schemes

Data encoding and decoding schemes are used to speed up the transmission of information to and from the hard disk. Because the *en*coder/*dec*oder (endec) is on the controller and the drive is a passive element in these encoding schemes, some controller manufacturers changed the type of endec that they were using to enable the drive to store data in different ways. Although many different encoding schemes are used for disk drives, two schemes are most popular in PC applications:

- Modified frequency modulation (MFM)
- Run length limited (for example, RLL 2,7 or 1,7)

The difference between the two encoding schemes is the density that they achieve. In the standard ST-506/412 MFM format, the drive contains 17 sectors per track, with each sector containing 512 bytes of data. With an RLL encoding scheme, the number of sectors per track is raised to 25 or 26, which results in approximately 50 percent more data on each track and, at the same interleave value, a 50 percent greater transfer rate. Thus, the method of encoding can make a difference in the efficiency (increased transfer rate) of how data is stored on disk. Because the encoding schemes also contain some error correction algorithms, this section also considers how the encoding scheme affects data integrity.

Using MFM

MFM converts digital information into magnetic flux changes that are stored on a disk drive. As previously mentioned, encoding schemes are used in telecommunications for converting digital data bits into various tones for transmission over a telephone line. For disk drives, the digital bits are converted or encoded into a pattern of magnetic impulses or flux reversals that are stored on disk. In telephone system encoding, a *mo*dulator/*dem*odulator (modem) performs the conversion to and from the encoded data. For the disk interface, an *en*coder/*dec*oder (endec) performs the conversion to flux reversals and the reconversion back to digital data.

MFM is a fixed-length scheme, which means a set pattern of bits always consumes the same number of linear spaces on the disk. The encoding scheme determines the efficiency of the recording on the disk. The MFM encoding scheme originally was devised as a way to build in clocking information with data pulses. With this particular method, flux reversals on the disk always are evenly spaced in time so that the beginnings of one bit can be separated from another. This type of scheme enables the controller electronics to detect and correct even single bit errors easily.

With the ST-506/412 interface, 17 sectors per track exist if the data is encoded with MFM. Floppy disk drives, including all the 5 1/4-inch and 3 1/2-inch formats, also use MFM encoding for data storage.

Using RLL

The acronym RLL usually is followed by two numbers, such as RLL 2,7. The first number represents the minimum run of 0 bits between two 1s, and the second number indicates the maximum number of 0s between two 1s, or the limit. RLL encoding has fewer regular intervals between flux changes and is more prone to errors than MFM encoding. Essentially, each MFM bit cell is broken down into three RLL bit cells, each of which may have a flux reversal. Much greater demands are placed on the timing of the controller and drive electronics because these flux reversals now may arrive at highly irregular intervals. No clocking information exists, so accurately reading the timing of the flux changes is now paramount. Also, because this code is not a fixed-length code, a single bit error cannot be detected and may corrupt as many as five total bits. Consequently, the controller must have a more sophisticated error detection and correction routine.

The great benefit of RLL is the increased density and increased transfer rate. The nominal increase in density and transfer rate over MFM encoding is 50 percent. A drive that stores 20M with MFM encoding can store 30M with RLL encoding. The density of the flux reversals per inch of track does not change. The feature that changes is the timing between the flux reversals and the bit or byte meanings of various groups of these flux reversals. Consequently, change occurs in data density rather than magnetic density.

An analogy to this encoding scheme can be made with the secret codes children often use. Many children devise secret codes so they can send each other messages that only they can read. Suppose, for example, that two children devise a code in which each letter of the alphabet is converted to the letter at the opposite end of the alphabet. The letter A is converted to Z, B is converted to Y, and so on. This encoding scheme creates a message that is no more dense than the same message written in standard form. If the original message is 500 letters long, the encoded message also is 500 letters long.

Now suppose that a new code is developed in which a unique letter or symbol represents each word. A message 500 letters long may be coded as a 50-symbol message because each symbol represents an entire word. This new encoding scheme is 10 times more efficient than the previous one. Some drawbacks do exist, however. This scheme may be more difficult to interpret quickly. Also, any error in the new scheme results in the loss of an entire word rather than a single letter (which could be corrected easily in context). Finally, users must memorize many symbols if every possible word is to be encoded.

This denser encoding scheme is exactly how RLL works. With approximately the same flux density, the drive can store 50 percent more information. Reliability and data integrity are RLL's two main problems.

Changing the Encoding Method

In some situations, you may be able to change from the slower MFM encoding to the faster, more efficient RLL encoding on a hard drive. This section examines some of the possibilities and ramifications of changing encoding methods.

Because of the ST-506/412 interface's design, the MFM endec or RLL endec resides on the controller card. This card is located in a slot in the PC, and this card is where encoding and decoding take place. Unfortunately, this location places the endec far from the data transmitting and receiving source.

Accurate RLL encoding and decoding place more demands on the drive and controller. In particular, the sensitivity to timing means the drive must be a high-quality unit with a voice coil positioner. A stepper motor drive has too many tracking and temperature-induced errors to enable accurate RLL encoding and decoding.

Another issue is the media. Thin film media has a much greater signal-to-noise ratio and bandwidth (which determines the maximum frequency on which the signal can be sent) than conventional oxide media, resulting in a drive that is less likely to have errors using RLL encoding. Most drive manufacturers only RLL-certify ST-506/412 drives that use a voice coil head actuator and have thin film media.

This chapter repeatedly mentions ST-506/412 when discussing RLL encoding. In the ESDI and SCSI interface schemes, the data separator or endec is part of the drive and cannot be changed. This situation holds true for IDE versions of ST-506/412 as well. In these cases, only pure digital information is sent to the drive (or drive/controller combination), which does all the encoding and decoding internally. For this reason, any ESDI, SCSI, or IDE versions of ST-506/412 interfaces are more reliable than the older non-IDE ST-506/412 interfaces. These versions share none of the problems associated in the past with RLL encoding over the non-IDE ST-506/412 interface. Nearly all ESDI, SCSI, and IDE ST-506/412 drives use RLL encoding.

The encoding scheme under these interfaces is much less of an issue for discussion because you have little choice in the matter. The endec is built into the drive and has nothing to do with the type of interface card in your system.

Purchasing a Quality Drive

Part of the data recovery process is *preventing* data loss in the first place. You can minimize data loss problems related to poor hard disk quality by selecting a hard drive that exhibits the qualities of high performance and reliability. A high-quality drive has two basic properties:

- Voice coil actuator mechanism
- Thin film media

Only select a stepper motor drive when cost far outweighs all other considerations. Do not use a stepper motor drive in a portable system or in a system that must operate under extremes of temperature, noise, or vibration. Do not use stepper motor drives when you cannot provide preventive maintenance, because these drives require periodic reformats to maintain data integrity. Finally, do not use these drives under any demanding situations such as with a network file server.

Stepper motor drives are acceptable in low-volume usage, where preventive maintenance can be provided at least annually or semiannually. As long as you can control the environment and reasonably "baby" the drive, it will perform adequately.

Use voice coil drives in all other situations, especially if you need to place extreme demands on the drive. These types of drives are ideal for portable systems; for systems that must operate under extremes of temperature, noise, or vibration; or for systems with which a fast drive must be used, such as a network file server. A voice coil drive requires no preventive maintenance; the first low-level format is usually the only one done. You can use voice coil drives in high-volume situations, such as when one person must support many systems. These drives are more expensive, but they provide payoffs in reliability, performance, and maintenance that eventually offset the initial cost.

When possible, choose a drive that uses thin film media rather than oxide media. Although oxide media drives are less expensive, they run a higher risk of head crashes than thin film media drives. Also, thin film media drives provide better performance and more years of service than oxide-coated drives.

Purchasing a voice coil drive with oxide media disks is acceptable but only if cost is the major concern.

Understanding Hard Disk Operation

In most ways, a hard drive operates in the same way as a floppy drive. A hard drive uses spinning disks with heads that move over the disks and store data in tracks and sectors. Although hard drives function like floppy drives at a basic level, hard disk drives have many unique features.

Hard disks usually have multiple platters, each with two sides on which to store data. Most drives have at least two or three platters, meaning four or six sides. Together the identically positioned tracks on each side of each platter are called a cylinder (see fig. 3.5). One head is available for each platter side, and all the heads are mounted on a common carrier device or rack. The heads are moved in and out across the disk in unison and cannot move independently.

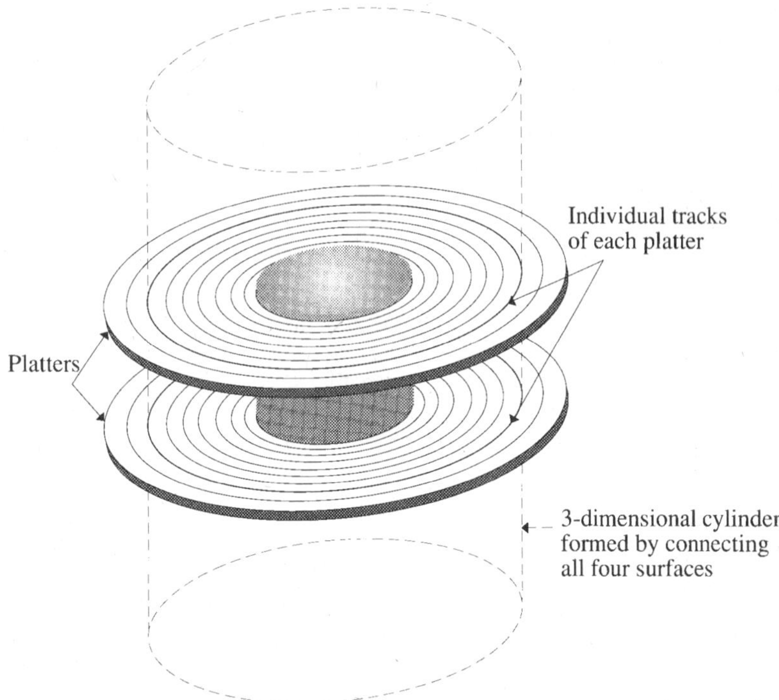

Fig. 3.5. *Tracks, sectors, and cylinder.*

Hard drives operate much faster than floppy drives. Most hard drives spin approximately 10 times faster than floppy drives—at 3,600 rpm. Until recently, this rotational speed was constant among drive manufacturers; now, however, a few hard drives spin even faster—at up to 5,600 rpm. High rotational speed combined with a fast head positioning mechanism and more sectors on a given track make some hard disks faster than others. Those same factors make hard drives in general much faster at storing and retrieving data than floppy drives.

The heads in a hard disk do not touch the platters during normal operation. When the drive is powered off, the heads land on the platters as the platters stop spinning. When the drive is turned on, a cushion of air keeps each head suspended a short distance above the platter. If this cushion is disturbed by a particle of dust or shock of some kind, the head may come in contact with the platter spinning at full speed. If the contact with the spinning platter is hard enough to do damage, the contact is called a *head crash*. Damage can range from a few lost bytes of data to a totally trashed disk. Most drives today have special lubricants on the platters and hardened surfaces that can withstand the daily takeoffs and landings as well as more severe abuse.

Because the platter assemblies (HDAs) are sealed from the environment and are not removable, the disks are protected from damage caused by dust particles and other foreign materials floating in the air. Dust and other materials can limit the precision with which heads read information from the disk. With less pollutants in the air, the hard disk can ride closer to the platter, and the head can place the magnetic signals more precisely on the disk and yield high track densities. Many platters have 1,000 or more tracks per inch of media.

Because platter assemblies are assembled in clean rooms under absolutely sanitary conditions, few companies are capable of actually repairing a hard disk's HDA. Consequently, repair or replacement of any item inside the sealed HDA can be expensive. If the data on the disk is important and cannot be recovered by other means, however, you may find that repairing the disk and recovering the data is worthwhile.

Recovering from Major Hard Disk Disasters

This section examines connections and mechanical and electronic problems that can cause hard disk failure. Many times, finding the solution to a problem is much easier than locating the problem itself. The information presented here helps you identify problems as well as find solutions.

Hardware Error Codes

When a failure occurs in the hard disk subsystem at power-on time, the POST sees the problem and reports it with an error message. If you receive 17*xx*, 104*xx*, or 210*xxxx* errors during the POST or while running the advanced diagnostics, you have a problem with your hard disk, controllers, or cables. The 17*xx* errors apply to the ST-506/412 interface drives and controllers, 104*xx* errors to the ESDI drives and controllers, and 210*xxxx* errors to the SCSI drives and host adapters.

Table 3.2 lists the17*xx* and 104*xx* error messages and their meanings.

Table 3.2
17*xx* and 104*xx* Error Messages

17xx	*ST-506/412 Fixed Disk Errors*
1701	Fixed disk general POST error
1780	Fixed disk 0; seek failure
1781	Fixed disk 1; seek failure
1782	Fixed disk controller test failure
1790	Fixed disk 0; diagnostic cylinder read error
1791	Fixed disk 1; diagnostic cylinder read error
104xx	*ESDI Fixed Disk Errors*
10480	Fixed disk 0; seek failure
10481	Fixed disk 1; seek failure
10482	Fixed disk controller test failure
10483	Fixed disk controller reset failure
10490	Fixed disk 0; diagnostic cylinder read error
10491	Fixed disk 1; diagnostic cylinder read error

The 210*xxxx* error codes represent a SCSI host adapter or drive failure. The first *x* is the SCSI ID number, the second *x* is the logical unit number, the third *x* is the host adapter slot number, and the fourth *x* is the drive capacity.

Most of the time, a seek failure indicates that the drive is not responding to the controller. This lack of response usually is caused by one of the following situations:

- The drive select jumper setting is incorrect.
- The control cable is loose, damaged, or backward.
- The power cable is loose or bad.
- Stiction occurs between drive heads and platters.
- The power supply is bad.

If a diagnostics cylinder read error has occurred, you usually encounter these problems:

- An incorrect drive type setting
- A loose, damaged, or backward data cable
- A temperature-induced mistracking

The ways to correct most of these problems are obvious: If the drive select jumper setting is incorrect, correct it. If a cable is loose, tighten it. If the power supply is bad, replace it. The following procedures will help you diagnose the possible problem:

1. Determine whether the computer is operating under conditions that are different from usual—particularly a condition that is causing the computer to be hotter than usual. If so, temperature-induced tracking may be the problem. You often can solve temperature-related problems by allowing the drive to operate at the same temperature at which the data was written. Either allow the drive to warm up or cool and reread the disk.

2. Open the computer and check all connections. (Make sure that the unit is unplugged.) A thorough check includes removing the connection, cleaning the leads on the connection of dirt or other foreign materials, and reseating the connection. If the hard disk uses a controller that is connected to the computer bus, be sure to take the controller out of the bus slot, check it, and reseat the controller back into the slot. After verifying that connections are tight and correct, reboot the computer to see whether you have solved the problem.

3. When a power supply begins to go bad, it often makes noise or the exhaust fan on the supply quits working. If you have voltage-checking equipment, you can check whether the power coming from the power supply cables is correct. If the power supply is bad, replace it with an equivalent or better power supply and check whether the problem is corrected.

Causes and solutions for past errors are found in the section "Tracing the Boot Process" in Chapter 5. If you get controller test or reset errors, perhaps your controller is going bad. If you have a similar computer that uses the same controller, swap controllers to check. If you cannot check the controller this way, have a technician take a look.

The stiction problem and problems related to logic boards may not have obvious solutions. Therefore, the next two sections discuss these problems in detail.

Failure of Drive To Spin

Besides a faulty power supply or power supply connection cable, stiction is the primary cause of a no-spin situation with a hard disk drive. If the disk is not spinning, you should be able to detect that the normal slight vibration and hum is missing from the hard disk. *Stiction* occurs when the drive heads stick to the platters, preventing the platter motor from spinning the drive up for operation. This problem occurs frequently in hard drives.

The heads become mired in the lubricant coating found on the platters. This situation is especially noticeable if the drive has been turned off for a long period of time, such as a week or more. This situation also is noticeable if the drive is operated under very hot conditions and then shut down. In this case, the lubricant has been softened by the excessive heat buildup in the drive, and after the drive is powered off, the lubricant cools rapidly and contracts around the heads, which have settled in on the lubricant coating. Drives with many platters and heads are more prone to this problem than drives with fewer ones.

To solve this problem, you must spin the platters with enough force to "rip" the heads loose from the platters. Usually you accomplish this feat by twisting the drive violently in the same plane as the platters, using the platter's inertia to overcome the sticking force. The heavy platters tend to remain stationary while you twist the drive and, in essence, make the heads move around the platters. Another technique you can use is to spin the spindle motor, which rotates the platters inside the drive. To do this procedure, remove the circuit board from the bottom of the drive to get to the spindle motor. You also can try inserting a stick into the gap between the bottom of the drive and the circuit board and then pushing on the spindle motor with the stick. You will feel heavy resistance to rotation, and then suddenly the platters will feel free as the heads are unstuck.

Some drives use a spindle motor brake that is released by an electric solenoid. This setup may make turning the platters more difficult. Also, the brake may have failed, preventing the platters from spinning. If the brake has failed, you need to remove the brake from the spindle motor to allow it to spin. Because each drive is designed differently, you need to consult the drive manual to see whether your drive has such a spindle braking system.

After you free the platters, reapply the power; the drive should spin up normally. Solving stiction problems with these methods rarely—if ever—results in data loss. If you are nervous about handling your drive in this manner, consult a professional drive-repair facility.

Logic Board Failures

All disk drives have one or more logic boards mounted on the drive. These boards contain the electronics that control the drive's spindle and head actuator systems, as well as present data to the controller in some agreed-on form. Some drives even have built-in controllers directly on the drive. If you are satisfied that the possible problems listed in the preceding sections are not present, then you may have a logic board problem.

Logic boards on hard disk drives fail more often than the mechanical components. Most professional data recovery specialists stock a number of functional logic boards for popular drives that they expect to see. When a customer brings in a dead drive, the data recovery specialist first checks the drive for installation or configuration problems, temperature mistracking, or stiction; if problems don't exist in these areas, the specialist replaces the logic board on the drive. Often, this solution solves the problem, and data can be read off the drive.

On most hard disks, you can remove and replace the logic boards because they simply plug into the drive. Usually, you can mount logic boards with standard screw hardware. If a drive is failing and you have a spare, you may be able to verify a logic board failure by taking the board off of the good drive and mounting the board on the bad one. If your suspicions are confirmed, you can order a new logic board from the manufacturer of the drive.

Be prepared for sticker shock. Buying a new logic board may cost more than replacing the entire drive with a new or refurbished unit. The drive manufacturer can give you details on these costs, the availability of a refurbished unit, and the possibility of taking your old drive as a trade-in. Although purchasing a new logic board may not always be cost-effective, borrowing one from another drive that works costs nothing and enables you to recover the data from the dead drive.

Chapter Summary

This chapter examined the hard disk from the inside out, including its material and electrical components. The components used in manufacturing the hard disk are related to the drive's long-term reliability.

When using data recovery techniques, you should know what kind of hard disk you have and what problems are associated with the components comprising your particular hard disk.

The chapter discussed quality issues related to the disk media, the read/write heads, the actuators, and the components related to the hard disk interface. This chapter also explained ways to recover from hard disk disasters. With this information, you will be more able to understand some of the other concepts covered in the remainder of this book.

4

Hard Disk Formatting

Operating your system is easier when you understand how it works. How can you understand what is "correct" or "incorrect" without knowledge of the system? Preceding chapters and this chapter provide information about hard disk drives to clarify your understanding of the recovery process.

Even with a properly installed disk, an improper setup can cause problems. This chapter examines the proper setup and configuration of a hard drive to ensure that data is stored properly and that all defective areas are mapped out. These formatting or initialization operations are critical for proper drive performance and long-term data integrity. Proper setup and configuration are preventive maintenance. This chapter also examines problems that can arise from an improperly configured and installed drive and offers solutions to these problems.

This chapter concludes with some tips and tricks I have developed over the years for recovering from major hard disk disasters. Sometimes you can perform simple operations to recover data from what may seem like an impossible situation—even recovering data from what may appear to be a "dead" drive. In essence, you can combine proven hardware troubleshooting and repair techniques with software data recovery procedures to bring back data from the most difficult situations.

Formatting a Hard Disk

Properly setting up and formatting a drive is critical to the drive's performance and reliability. This section discusses the procedures for correctly formatting a hard disk drive, thereby giving that drive the best chance to run trouble-free. Use these procedures when you first install a drive in a system or immediately after you recover data from a hard disk that has been exhibiting problems.

You follow three major steps to complete the formatting process for any hard disk drive subsystem:

1. *Low-level format*. Scan for existing defect mapping, select an interleave, format and (re)mark manufacturer defects, and run a surface analysis.
2. *Partition.* Define the area for operating systems to use.
3. *High-level format*. Create the FAT and system directory.

> ***Warning:*** These three operations can cause loss of current information on a hard disk. These operations primarily are for use on a new hard drive or on a hard drive that must be reinitialized to correct problems.

Of these procedures, the low-level format is most important in ensuring trouble-free operation of the drive, so it must be done correctly. The low-level format is like a building's foundation, which supports the structure of the disk's data storage. If the low-level format of a disk is not sound, then the information on this disk has a greater chance of being damaged and lost.

Besides the low-level format itself, you should perform several other procedures as part of the low-level format process. These procedures include finding and dealing with disk defects. On some systems, such as the IBM PS/2, these procedures are performed automatically without operator intervention. IBM simplified the initialization of a hard disk because many users do not perform these procedures properly.

Performing a Low-Level Format

The low-level format includes drive defect mapping, the selection of an interleave, and a surface analysis of the drive. To perform these operations, you probably need information about your drive, controller, and system—each of which usually has its own manual and documents. Be sure to get complete documentation for your drive and controller products when you purchase them.

A *low-level format* (LLF) is a *real format*, which means that it thoroughly tests the disk drive's media and, in the process, erases data on the drive. Usually, when you hear someone speaking of formatting a hard drive, the person is referring to a *high-level format* (HLF). You can recover data—unformat—from a high-level format. Before you perform either type of format, you should back up the data on your hard drive.

During the low-level format, the disk's tracks are divided into a specific number of sectors. Within each sector, header and trailer information is recorded, as are *intersector* and *intertrack gaps*—gaps between sectors and tracks. Each sector's data area also is filled with a dummy value, usually consisting of 512 bytes with a value of hexadecimal F6. For floppy disks, the actual number of sectors recorded on each track depends on the type of disk and drive. For hard disks, the number of sectors per track depends on the drive interface and controller used.

Although the data portion of each sector is always 512 bytes, the header and trailer information for each sector occupies additional space on the track. The actual numbers may vary, but for most hard drives, 571 bytes of information actually are recorded for each sector. Note that only during an LLF operation is this header and trailer information ever written or updated. During normal read and write activity, only the 512 bytes plus a checksum value in the trailer actually receive data. The discrepancy between the number of bytes required for a format and the number actually written causes the instability of many drives during read and write operations.

For a proper low-level format, be sure that your drive is at normal operating temperature and in normal operating position. If the drive is not shock-mounted or isolated from the drive frame by rubber bushings, it should be mounted in the host system. Most new drives are shock-mounted.

If a 5 1/4-inch disk drive is formatted only 5 minutes after it has been turned on, the platter temperature is a relatively cold 70 degrees Fahrenheit. After the drive runs for several hours, the platter temperature rises to 140 degrees Fahrenheit. With the drive platters now as much as 70 degrees warmer than before, each disk has expanded in size by .0025 inch. Each track may have moved a distance of approximately .0013 inch outward.

Most 5 1/4-inch hard disks have track densities of between 500 to 1,000 tracks per inch, with 1 to 2 thousandths of an inch between adjacent tracks. The thermal expansion of a typical hard disk platter can cause the tracks to migrate anywhere from one-half to more than one full track of distance underneath the heads. If the drive head movement mechanism cannot compensate for these changes in the platters, severe mistracking results. The data areas within each sector that have been updated at the higher temperature would not line up with the sector header and trailer information. If it cannot read sector header and trailer information, DOS usually issues an error message such as

```
Sector not found reading drive A
Abort, Retry, Ignore, Fail?
```

In effect the data is misaligned with the sector boundaries on those tracks. Note that this situation also can work in reverse. If the drive is formatted and written to while extremely hot, the drive may not read properly while cold. If you let the drive warm up for some time, it may boot and run normally. Then back up the drive completely and initiate a new low-level format at the proper operating temperature.

For you to format a hard disk properly, the platters should be at normal operating temperature for dimensional stability. Allow at least one half hour of operating time before low-level formatting. Also allow any hard disk to warm up for several minutes to a half hour before storing any data on the drive. You even can leave the drive running constantly, which actually does wonders for a trouble-free life span because the temperature and dimensions of the platters stay relatively constant.

Now you can understand the differences between the open loop stepper motor type of actuator mechanism, which offers no thermal compensation, and the closed loop voice coil system. The voice coil system follows temperature-induced track migration and compensates completely, resulting in no tracking errors even with large changes in platter dimensions. Because a voice coil system tracks dimensional changes in the platters, it prevents mistracking errors (see Chapter 3).

Temperature changes are not the only thing to interfere with proper formatting. Gravity can place different loads on the head actuator and cause a mistracking error between a vertical or horizontal position. To account for gravity, be sure that the drive is formatted in the proper operating position.

For drives that are not properly shock-mounted (like the Seagate ST 2xx series), you should format the drive only with it installed in the host system. If you use screws that are either too long or the wrong type when mounting this drive, you can cause undue force on the sides of this drive. This force can cause mistracking. If you format the drive with the mounting screws installed tightly, it may not read from the drive with the screws out and vice versa. Also, to prevent stress on the HDA in any drive, be careful not to overtighten the mounting screws. Newer drives with the HDA isolated from the frame by rubber bushings rarely have this problem.

Because controllers differ from one another in how they write data to a drive, you usually should use the same make and model of controller that will be used in the host system. Some different brands of controllers do work exactly alike, so this suggestion is flexible. If the controller uses its own onboard ROM for establishing the drive type instead of the system setup program, the controller will be incompatible with any other controllers.

Mapping Defects

Before formatting a hard drive, you should map out any defects on the drive. Most manufacturers supply a list of defects that were discovered during the quality control testing of the drive. These defects should be marked off on the drive so that you will not use them to hold programs or data. To understand the defect mapping procedures, you first must understand what exactly happens when a defect is mapped on a drive.

Defect mapping always is done properly during the low-level format. Most drives have several defects, which are printed on a sticker on the top of the drive, as well as included on a printed sheet in the box from the manufacturer. The defects usually are indicated by cylinder and track. Entering this information causes the low-level format program to mark these tracks with invalid checksum figures in the header of each sector. Then data cannot be read from or written to these locations.

Later, when you use DOS to high-level format the disk, the DOS FORMAT program will be (guaranteed) incapable of reading these locations and also will mark the file allocation table (FAT) with information indicating which clusters were involved so that they never are utilized. Failing to enter these locations properly at low-level format time may allow these defective tracks to be used by data and program files. Any files that "land" in these locations become candidates for corruption.

The list of defects the manufacturer provides is probably more extensive than any program can ever determine on your system. Because the manufacturer's test equipment is far more sensitive than your controllers, do not expect any format program to find the defects automatically. You probably will have to enter defects manually—unless you have a new PS/2 system. With these systems, the defect list is encoded in a special area of the drive that is not accessible by normal software. This map is read by the IBM PS/2 low-level format program included on the Reference disk that comes with the PS/2 systems.

Always perform your own low-level format on drives after you receive them. Most of the time, new drives are not low-level formatted by the manufacturer. If formatting was done, the temperature and operating position may be problems. If the drive is supplied in a system as already installed by the manufacturer or dealer, the low-level format was probably performed. For your protection, though, do your own low-level format.

Usually, a hard disk is supplied with a piece of paper that contains a list of sectors that should be marked as bad. When you run your own low-level format, it probably finds and marks a number of bad sectors. Make sure that the sectors on the list are marked as bad by your LLF program. (Your program may find additional bad sectors besides those on the list.) If a sector on the list is not marked as bad by your LLF program, mark it as bad when prompted by your software to manually enter sectors to mark as defective.

You can perform several tasks to learn more about your hard disk and to prepare it to receive the low-level format. These tasks are explained in the next three sections. The disks should be scanned for marked defects to determine what sectors already have been marked as bad (usually at the factory). This feature is important if you do not have the manufacturer's list of defects. The sections also discuss how to interpret "defect free" hard disks.

Scanning for Currently Marked Defects

Several reasons exist for scanning a disk for (marked) defects before running a fresh low-level format on it. You can ensure that the previous low-level format was correctly used to mark all the manufacturer's defects on the drive. You should compare the report of the defect scan to the manufacturer's list on the drive and note any discrepancies. Any defects on the manufacturer's list but not on the defect-scan report were not marked properly.

> ***Note:*** A scan for marked defects does not locate new defects—just those that are already marked. A surface analysis, on the other hand, locates new defects.

Another thing to look for are tracks that show up as marked defective but that are not on the manufacturer's list. They may have been added by a previously run surface analysis program, or they may have resulted from typographical errors. If the additional tracks are found via another surface analysis, they should be retained. If the tracks are simply a typographical error, you can unmark the tracks and use them. I had a drive whose manufacturer's list showed cylinder 514 head 14 as defective, but a defect scan marked that one as good and marked cylinder 814 head 14 as bad. Because the 814 location was not on the manufacturer's list, and transcribing 5 and 8 can happen easily, a typographical error was the likely cause. I reformatted the disk accordingly.

To perform a (marked) defect scan using most low-level format programs, locate the menu item or command labeled Defect Scan. IBM calls this procedure Read Verify in the Advanced Diagnostics. This operation is nondestructive and merely reports that track locations (by cylinder and head position) are currently marked as bad from the previous low-level format. You should not mistake this operation with a *surface analysis,* a destructive scan for defective tracks on a disk (see the section "Performing a Surface Analysis" later in this chapter for more information).

Mapping the Manufacturer's Defect List

When a hard disk is new, the manufacturer extensively analyzes the drive platters, using sophisticated test instruments. After test results are interpreted, the manufacturer prints a list of bad areas and usually places it on a sticker on the drive. These tests are done with special test instruments—not a PC with a standard controller. This testing indicates the functionality of any area of the disk in great detail; information such as the signal-to-noise ratio, as well as recording accuracy, can be measured precisely. A PC disk controller cannot ascertain such information. All any surface analysis running on your system can do is to write 512 bytes of data, read it back, and compare what has been read to what has been written. Digital testing gives only a pass/fail analysis, a far cry from the information factory testing provides.

Suppose that a spot in the sector is only performing at 51 percent of its capacity. On a normal day, that would be good enough for a passing grade by a PC-based surface analysis. The next day, variances in the drive and electronics result in 49 percent capacity at that same spot, prompting a failing grade by a surface analysis. You may find that on some test runs, an area passes, but on other runs, the area fails. For this reason, most of the PC-based surface analysis programs have the option of running multiple passes, so you can identify a marginal location.

> ***Note:*** If a spot on the disk is marginally acceptable, multiple passes of the surface analysis program may eventually detect it as bad.

The manufacturer testing is far more accurate and can note precisely how any area of the disk is performing. Any area below the manufacturer's standards (whatever those standards may be) is added to the defect list printed on the drive.

Some manufacturers are fussier than others about what is "passing." Good manufacturers rigorously check the disk media, yielding disks that have more defects listed than other companies. Many individuals are bothered when a new drive comes with a list of defective locations. These individuals sometimes even demand that a defect-free drive be installed before they accept the system. To satisfy that buyer, the seller merely can substitute a less-expensive drive made by a company whose quality control is lacking.

Because defects often are small flaws left over from when the magnetic media was placed on the platter, almost every platter has some defects. You should not be concerned if a disk reports 10 to 20 defects; this rate is normal.

I tested an inexpensive stepper motor 40M drive that had only three defects on the list. Most of the surface analysis programs found those three plus another one. In cases such as this one, if the warranty is applicable, return a drive that shows more defects than are on the manufacturer's list. After the warranty period, reformat the drive with the additional defects marked.

To mark the manufacturer's defects listed on the drive, consult the documentation for your low-level format program. At some point in the low-level format, you can enter these defects manually so that these tracks are wiped out. If you have a defect scan option, you can determine whether manufacturer's defects were entered properly by the previous formatter, but make sure that all the manufacturer's defects are entered before proceeding with the low-level format.

Most drives record the defects by cylinder and head. Some lists also provide you with a number like Bit from Index. This number locates the defective bit, starting with the index location, which defines the beginning of the track.

Some systems mark the manufacturer's defects automatically, using a special file recorded on the drive by the manufacturer containing a list of the known defect locations. You would require a special low-level format program that knows how to find and read this file. These programs can update this file if any additional defects are found during a surface analysis of the drive. Automatic defect map entry is standard for all IBM PS/2 systems and also common on most ESDI and SCSI systems. Consult the drive or controller vendor for the proper low-level format program and defect handling procedures for your drive.

Evaluating Defect-Free Drives

Some manufacturers claim that all the drives they sell or install are "defect free." This claim is not really true. Defects on a drive can be hidden so that normal software cannot find them. Therefore, DOS does not have to work around the defects in the FAT. Creating a defect-free drive usually is accomplished by the use of spare sectors and tracks.

Normally, after the low-level format and surface analysis of a hard disk, you have marked several areas defective. These marks are actually implemented by the corruption of the checksum values in the appropriate sector headers on the indicated tracks. Anytime these sectors (or tracks) are read later, the read operation is guaranteed to fail. When the high-level format scans the disk, it locates the defective sectors by failing to read them during its defect scan. The clusters or allocation units that contain these unreadable sectors then are marked as bad in the FAT. When you execute the CHKDSK command, you receive a report, such as the following, of how many bad clusters exist:

```
Volume DRIVE_C created 06-02-1990 9:14p
Volume Serial Number is 3311-1CD3

117116928 bytes total disk space
    73728 bytes in 3 hidden files
   593920 bytes in 268 directories
106430464 bytes in 4068 user files
   143360 bytes in bad sectors
  9875456 bytes available on disk

     2048 bytes in each allocation unit
    57186 total allocation units on disk
     4822 available allocation units on disk

   655360 total bytes memory
   561216 bytes free
```

The 143,360 bytes in bad sectors are really only 70 clusters or allocation units because 2,048 bytes are in each allocation unit. When I low-level formatted that disk, I entered 14 defects, which corrupted 14 tracks. This disk drive has 17 sectors per track, so 17 sectors times 14 tracks, or 238 total sectors, have been corrupted by the low-level format program. Multiplying 238 sectors times 512 bytes per sector yields 121,856 total bytes marked as bad. This total does not agree with the total reported by CHKDSK because DOS must mark entire allocation units as bad, not individual sectors.

Each track on the disk has 17 sectors, but 4 sectors (2,048 bytes) are taken for each allocation unit; 17 sectors equals 4 allocation units plus 1 sector of a fifth unit. Because DOS must mark a whole unit as bad even if only one sector is bad inside the unit, DOS actually marks 5 allocation units as bad for each marked track; 5 allocation units equals 20 sectors, which equals 10,240 bytes marked as bad in the FAT for each track marked in the low-level format. And 10,240 bytes per track marked as bad times 14 total marked tracks equals 143,360 total bytes marked as bad, matching the total listed by the program.

These calculations show that all the correct defect mapping is in place. Those bytes in bad sectors never will be used by any files. This number should not change over the life of the drive except to increase if any new defects are entered in a subsequent low-level format or surface analysis program.

I also have an IBM PS/2 Model 70-121 with a 120M IBM drive with an embedded ESDI controller. The controller is built into the drive unit rather than as a separate card. Normally this is called IDE (Internal Drive Electronics) by the industry. I formatted this drive using the IBM Advanced Diagnostics for the PS/2 (included free with the system). After finishing the high-level format and running CHKDSK, I was skeptical when no bad sectors were indicated. Later I found that this particular drive has more than 140 defects, and all of them are marked correctly. How can that be? If the defects were marked, then the high-level format should not have been capable of reading those locations, and CHKDSK should have reported the `*xxxxxx* bytes in bad sectors` message.

The answer lies in how the drive and controller operate together. IBM advertises this drive as having 32 sectors per track and 920 cylinders with 8 heads, but this drive actually has 33 sectors per track or a spare sector on every track. When a defect location is given to the low-level format program, it removes the defective sector from use and gives the spare sector the number of the defective one. The defective sector then becomes the spare. A defect can occur in every track on the drive (7,360 total) without causing any loss in capacity or without you knowing that the defects exist. If more than one sector on a given track is defective, entire spare tracks are available on several spare cylinders past 920. Spare sectors and tracks exist to accommodate all the possible defects on the drive.

This defect mapping, called *sector sparing*, is standard on many newer drives. All PS/2 systems now come with drives that automatically handle defects in this manner.

Although some companies advertise that their drives are "defect free," defects (perhaps many of them) exist, but they are mapped out and replaced by spare sectors and tracks. Sector sparing insulates the operating system from handling the defects, so CHKDSK will not report any bytes in bad sectors on such drives.

Selecting Interleave

Suppose that you pick up your luggage at an airport on one of those circular conveyor belts. If your three suitcases are next to one another, and the belt is going fast, you may be unable to pick up more than one suitcase each time the belt goes around. In other words, the belt must go around three times before you can retrieve all your luggage. If the belt moves slower or your luggage is spaced farther apart, however, you can pick it up on one pass. This method exemplifies how the head on your disk drive retrieves data as the disk spins. The way the data is read—called the *interleave ratio*—is determined by the spacing of the data and the speed of the hard disk.

A low-level format numbers sectors in a way that enables the head to read the data efficiently. The interleave ratio determines how consecutive sectors are put on the disk. For example, a 1 to 1 ratio means that after one sector is read, the adjacent sector is read, and so on. A 4 to 1 ratio means that after one sector is read, the head skips the next three sectors, reads the fourth sector, skips three more sectors, and so on. (The head reads the skipped sectors later.) An incorrect interleave ratio can cause your hard disk to read data inefficiently, resulting in slow access.

The information stored on a floppy or hard disk is arranged in concentric rings called *tracks*. A popular specification for disk drives, especially hard drives, is the drive's reported *average access time*—the average time required for the heads to be positioned from one track to another. The average access time often is calculated from hundreds or thousands of individual random seeks across the disk, the observation of the total time taken, and the division of that time by the number of actual random seeks completed. Unfortunately, the importance of this specification often is overstated, especially in relation to a specification known as the *data transfer rate*.

The actual transfer rate of data between the drive and the motherboard is more important than access time because most drives spend more time reading and writing information than simply moving the heads around on the disk. Sorting large files, which requires a great deal of "random access" to individual records of the file and many seek operations, is helped by a faster-seeking disk drive. But common load and save operations are affected most by the rate of data transfer, which depends on the disk controller—not on the drive itself.

The disk controller controls the data transfer of information to and from the drive. Each track on a disk is divided into sectors, which are shaped much like slices of a pie. The actual number of sectors on a disk can vary, depending on the density of the disk and the encoding scheme used. Disks are available currently with 17, 25, 26, 32, 34, 35, 36, and even more sectors per track. Among different drives, two features remain consistent: the rotational speed of the drive (usually 3,600 rpm) and the number of bytes in each sector (512). Some drives today spin faster than 3,600 rpm. The number of sectors per track therefore dictates a disk's maximum transfer rate.

Although drives with the same number of sectors per track have the same transfer rate, not all controllers can accept and transfer data at the rate possible for the drive. Also, even if the controller can match the transfer rate of the drive, not all motherboards can accept data at the full rate.

For example, consider a disk with 17 sectors on each track, with the sectors on each track numbered consecutively:

1, 2, 3, 4, 5, 6, 7, 8, 9, 10, 11, 12, 13, 14, 15, 16, 17

If you command the controller to position the heads at a particular track and to read all 17 of its sectors, the heads move and arrive at the desired track. After an average of 1/2 disk revolutions, the sector numbered 1 arrives under the heads. As the disk is spinning at 3,600 rpm (60 revolutions per second), the data is read from sector 1, and as it is being transferred to the system board, the disk continues to spin. Finally, the data is moved into the motherboard, and the controller is ready for sector 2.

Because the disk continues to spin at such a high rate of speed, several sectors pass under the head as the controller does its work; now the heads are coming up on sector 5. The controller has to wait as the disk spins until sector 2 comes under the heads and is read. While the controller is transferring the data to the motherboard, sectors 3, 4, and 5 move under the heads. When the controller is finally ready to read sector 3, the heads are on sector 6. The controller again has to wait until sector 3 comes underneath the heads before it can be read. At this pace, 17 revolutions are taken, each at 1/60 of 1 second, to read all these sectors. Nearly 1/3 of 1 second is a long time by computer standards.

You can improve this performance by numbering the tracks out of order. After reading a particular sector from the disk, this controller takes time to transfer the 512 bytes to the motherboard. The controller skips three sectors, and the next one it catches is four from the first one. The controller catches every fourth sector, which in the original sector numbering scheme looks like figure 4.1.

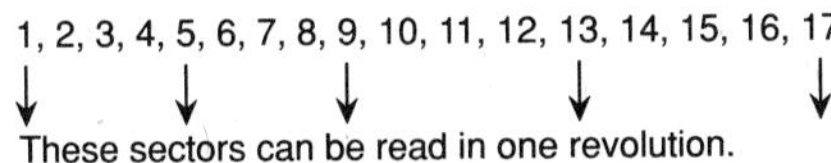

Fig. 4.1. The controller catching every fourth sector.

Reading or writing the sectors out of order would confuse the controller, not to mention DOS, but numbering the sectors out of order works. Our new numbering scheme can take into account the speed of the controller and number the sectors so that the sector coming under the heads is always the "next" sector the controller encounters. The sector numbering scheme now looks like figure 4.2.

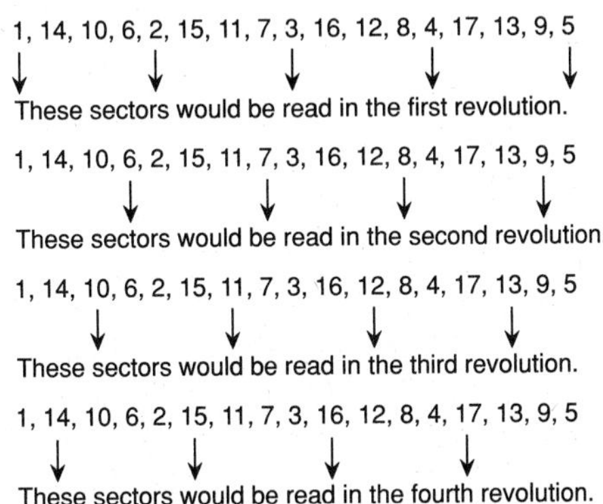

Fig. 4.2. Numbering sectors on the disk.

Now only 4 rather than 17 revolutions are needed to read all 17 sectors on the disk. This renumbering of sectors on the disk is called *interleaving*. The interleave ratio here is 4 to 1. This ratio means that the next numbered sector is 4 sectors away from the previous one on the disk.

Theoretically, changing the interleave ratio to 3 to 1 would be even faster, requiring only 3 revolutions to read a single track. The problem is with the controller. Interleaving is set too short. Therefore, data cannot be transferred as fast as the defined interleaving setting. This discrepancy causes more problems than it corrects.

The correct interleave for any system depends primarily on the controller and secondarily on the speed of the system the controller is plugged into. A controller and system that can handle a consecutive sector or 1 to 1 interleave must be capable of transferring data as fast as the disk drive can present it. Table 4.1 lists transfer rates for various sectored disks at a 1 to 1 interleave to a 6 to 1 interleave.

Table 4.1
Transfer Rates in Kilobytes per Second

Interface	*Speed (rpm)*	*Sectors*	*Interleave Ratio* 1:1	2:1	3:1	4:1	5:1	6:1
ST-506/412 MFM	3,600	17	510	255	170	128	102	85
ST-506/412 RLL	3,600	25	750	375	250	188	150	125
ST-506/412 RLL	3,600	26	780	390	260	195	156	130
ESDI or SCSI	3,600	32	960	480	320	240	192	160
ESDI or SCSI	3,600	34	1,020	510	340	255	204	170
ESDI or SCSI	3,600	35	1,050	525	350	263	210	175
ESDI or SCSI	3,600	36	1,080	540	360	270	216	180
ESDI or SCSI	4,300	48	1,720	860	573	430	344	287

The disk controller in the example can handle 128K per second from the drive. The 1 to 1 interleave may seem unattainable, but advances in controllers have made it possible and affordable. All AT and PS/2 systems are capable of this transfer rate. The only system units that cannot use a 1 to 1 interleave, regardless of the controller, are the original 4.77 MHz PC and XT systems. These systems have a maximum throughput to the slots of just under 400K per second, which is not quite fast enough for a 1 to 1 interleave.

All IBM PS/2 systems, including Model 50 and later models, have default 1 to 1 interleaves. A 1 to 1 interleave with a 17 sector disk is one thing, but with the ESDI interface on the Models 60, 70, and 80, IBM is using disks with 32, 34, 35, 36, and 48 sectors per track, which results in more than 1 1/2 megabytes of data transfer each second.

The standard interleave ratio listed for an IBM XT system is 6 to 1 and for an AT is 3 to 1 (both with hard disks), but I suggest using lower ratios in each case. The best interleave for the Xebec 1210 controller in a 4.77 MHz PC or XT is 5 to 1, and the best interleave for the Western Digital 1002 and 1003 controllers in a 6 MHz or 8 MHz AT system is 2 to 1. If you reformat these systems to the lower interleave number, you gain about 20 to 30 percent in data transfer performance—at no cost.

The interleave factor can be either too "loose" or too "tight" (a number that is high is too loose, and a number that is low is too tight). Operating with an interleave factor that is too loose reduces performance—the speed of reading and writing. Operating with an interleave factor that is too tight is more serious because it causes the controller to miss the next sector every time and slows the disk to pathetic rates of speed.

No matter what the interleave is, whether too loose, right on, or too tight, the disk functions with no errors. Many systems are interleaved incorrectly because you have no indication of incorrect interleaving other than some performance tests. Such tests can show your system's performance at different interleaves, so you can compare these results with performance figures from your disk as it is now. Your system should be set for the interleave value that yields the best transfer rate.

The Norton Utilities 5.0 Calibrate test is one program that performs an interleave performance comparison to determine the optimal interleave factor for your hard disk (refer to *Using Norton Utilities*, published by Que Corporation).

The only way to change an interleave is through a low-level format, but setting the interleave factor can be done with software that works one track at a time, saving and restoring tracks as it operates. Be sure to back up a disk completely before attempting such an operation.

Running the Low-Level Format Program

You can choose from several types of low-level format programs. Unfortunately, because of the wide variety of different drive interfaces and system designs, no single low-level format program works for all drives or on all systems. Because low-level format programs must operate closely with the controller, they are often specific to a certain controller or controller type. You should ask the controller manufacturer for the software recommended to perform a format.

If the controller manufacturer has his or her own low-level format program, use it because it best understands your system and controller. If any special defect mapping features exist, for example, the manufacturer-supplied programs can use these capabilities. A foreign format program may fail to use a manufacturer-written defect map or may even overwrite and destroy it.

Many aftermarket disk controllers in non-IBM systems have built-in format programs that usually are activated by the DOS DEBUG program. If the controller contains such a program, use it because the controller manufacturer developed it.

For a general-purpose ST-506/412 or ESDI low-level format program, I usually recommend the Htest/Hformat program by Kolod Research. For the ST-506/412 interface only, I recommend the IBM Advanced Diagnostics or the HDtest program by Jim Bracking. The latter is available as a user-supported product on many bulletin boards across the country and on CompuServe. These programs work on a variety of different controllers and systems. You can use the Htest/Hformat on more systems, and this program offers the most power. The HDtest program sports a nicer user interface and is easier to use for most standard format jobs. For SCSI systems or systems on which the other recommended programs do not work, I recommend that you contact the controller or interface manufacturer and find out what he or she can supply or recommend to you. Each of these programs is discussed in the following sections.

Controller ROM-Based Format Software

If the controller on your hard disk contains a ROM-based, low-level format program, you probably are limited to using this program to perform an LLF on the disk. You should use this formatter because it is the only way to write special information to disk for the controller. Special information includes the number of cylinders and heads in the disk. The technical documentation for a controller usually specifies whether a ROM-based format controller is built into the controller.

IBM Advanced Diagnostics

The standard low-level format program for IBM systems is the Advanced Diagnostics, which comes with the hardware maintenance service manuals. For the PS/2 Model 50 and later models, this formatting software is provided on the Reference disk included with the system. Other PS/2 systems earlier than Model 50 do not include this software, so you must purchase the service manuals.

To access the Advanced Diagnostics portion of the Reference disk, press Ctrl-A (for Advanced) at the Reference disk main menu and the “secret” advanced diagnostics appear. IBM does not document this feature in the regular system documentation because the company does not want the average user wandering around in this software. This Ctrl-A procedure is documented in the service manuals that cost several hundred dollars.

> ***Warning:*** A low-level format overwrites existing information on your disk. If the disk contains valuable data, back up the disk before performing the format.

The PS/2 low-level format programs are excellent. In fact, they are just about the only format programs you ever should use on these systems. Most foreign format programs cannot read the IBM-written defect map placed on the drive. Only the IBM format tools can get to this map, use it, and update it.

For standard AT or XT systems, the Advanced Diagnostics low-level format program is fine for formatting and testing hard disks. This program has all the expected standard features, but the AT version does not allow an interleave selection of 1 to 1. This hindrance may not be a problem for most users but makes this program useless if you upgrade to a controller that can handle a 1 to 1 interleave.

The XT version allows only one interleave selection (6 to 1), which renders this routine useless on PC or XT systems because most controllers can handle between 2 to 1 and 5 to 1 interleaves. Using the IBM XT format program results in a slow system. The PC or XT version does not allow the entry of the manufacturer's defect list. This oversight makes the XT low-level format program an unwise choice. Fortunately, the problem is minimal because IBM no longer manufacturers the PC, XT, or these controllers. Thus, most PC or XT users use an aftermarket autoconfigure controller with a proper, built-in ROM-based formatter.

Htest/Hformat

For AT systems or other systems with controllers that do not have an autoconfigure routine, I recommend the Htest/Hformat program from Kolod Research. This program is probably the most sophisticated hard disk technician's tool available. With the sophistication of this program comes some degree of difficulty of use. The number of options and capabilities is bewildering to those who are not well versed in hard disk technology.

This program has many capabilities that make it a desirable addition to your toolbox. Htest/Hformat includes an interleave testing program called Hoptimum, which tests your disk at different interleave values and determines which value offers the best performance. After this determination, the program actually can redo the entire disk at the new interleave by performing a low-level format of one cylinder at a time, backing up and restoring each cylinder as it goes. The program can calculate the best interleave, reset the disk to that interleave, and retain all the data on the drive, all while you are eating lunch. Be sure to back up the disk before you start this process because any power interruptions or problems can corrupt the disk. Never trust any program like this one with data that is not backed up.

This program also can perform perhaps the best surface analysis or surface scan of any program available. The low-level format and surface analysis tools are in full control of the disk controller and can detect errors that the controller normally will mask with error detection and correction capabilities. Also, the analysis can be made to run for a number of passes on each track, thus improving the capacity to detect a marginal track that may seem OK after a single pass. This program is for you if you suspect that your drive has defects in addition to those the manufacturer indicated on his or her defect list. If you lost the original defect list and need to mark any improper areas of the disk, this program will be invaluable.

Htest/Hformat also works independently of any operating systems, so it is compatible with DOS, OS/2, XENIX, Novell NetWare, or any other software. Other minor functions, such as controller and drive test programs and a program that prints out the currently marked defects on the drive, make this program worth your investment. This program costs around $100 and is an essential part of my tool kit.

HDtest

HDtest by Jim Bracking is an excellent user-supported software program, distributed through electronic bulletin boards and public domain software libraries. The program costs $35, but you can try it for free.

This program has an easy-to-use interface and pull-down menu system. The program offers all functions normally associated with a standard low-level format program and then some. Besides the normal formatting and defect mapping, this program has a surface analysis routine, interleave test routine, and nondestructive low-level reformat routine. This program also includes a duplicate of the IBM Advanced Diagnostics hard disk tests, which includes tests for drive seek, head selection, and error detection and correction, as well as a read/write/verify of the diagnostics cylinder. This program also includes the capacity to detect hard disk errors that are minor enough to be corrected by the disk controller's own correcting code.

All in all, this program includes most of what you ever will want in a low-level format program and hard disk diagnostics utility. The only limitation is that the system must be compatible with the IBM XT or AT and use ST-506/412 drives supported by a correct installation (that is, the drive type has been defined properly). This program does not work on ESDI or SCSI drives and does not support the PS/2 defect map written on the drive. With this in mind, you can use the program effectively on any standard XT or AT compatible with standard ST-506/412 drives.

Performing a Surface Analysis

After the low-level format has been completed for a hard disk, you can perform a *surface analysis* in an attempt to locate any defects besides what you already have entered.

A surface analysis is different from a defect scan. A defect scan scans only for marked defects, but a surface analysis scans for true or actual defects. A surface analysis ignores tracks that have been marked defective already by a low-level format program and instead focuses only on unmarked tracks. The surface analysis program writes 512 bytes to each sector on the good tracks, reads the sectors back, and compares the written and read versions. If the data does not match, that track is marked as bad exactly as in the low-level format by the corruption of the checksum values for each of the sectors on that track.

Surface analysis programs are destructive because they write over every sector on the disk except those already marked as bad. Some surface analysis programs work by performing a track backup and restore operation before and after corrupting that track, but as always, back up the disk before using any of this software. The correct time to run a surface analysis program is immediately after a low-level format, to determine whether any defects have cropped up beyond the manufacturer's defects entered during the low-level format. A defect scan after the LLF and surface analysis shows the cumulative tracks marked as bad by both programs as unreadable tracks.

If you lost the manufacturer defect list for a drive, you can get by with the surface analysis program to indicate which tracks are bad, but remember that this software never can duplicate the accuracy or sensitivity of the manufacturer testing. Manufacturers do not keep defect records for each drive they sell, so a surface analysis probably will be your only alternative.

Some surface analysis programs offer the option of increasing the redundancy, or the number of times each track is tested. If you have trouble locating a bad track, use this option to run the program during an evening or weekend.

With high-quality disks, I usually omit a surface analysis after a low-level format because it is thorough and much faster than a surface analysis. With low-quality (stepper motor) or second-hand drives, or those with long-since-expired warranties, I may run the surface analysis after the low-level format. Although some users think that finding a few defects beyond those indicated by the manufacturer is normal, I disagree. Finding more defects indicates that the drive is starting to have problems or that the manufacturer has taken extreme shortcuts in quality control.

Because of variations in read and write accuracy, you only should perform the surface analysis immediately after a fresh low-level format. Then the surface analysis accurately will interpret misread data as a real defect on the drive and not as a mistracking problem caused by temperature variations in the platters.

Maintaining a Defect List

A defect list usually is printed on a sticker found on the cover of most hard disks. You have to update this list manually if any additional defects are found during the life of the drive. Also, if the defect list is printed on the drive, you usually have to enter these defects manually during the low-level format.

Before running a low-level format on a drive that has been formatted previously, you always can run a nondestructive scan for tracks currently marked as bad. This scan does not look for a drive bound table but scans each sector of the disk, looking for the corrupt sector header checksum bytes. This type of defect scan is nondestructive; that is, no writing is done to the disk. The scan only shows which current track or sector locations are marked.

You can compare the scan report to the written list on the drive sticker to see whether the previous formatter marked all the defects. Sometimes, you may discover typographical errors in the previous transcription of defect locations from the sticker to the low-level format program.

Whatever type of defect management your drive and controller combination performs, you should make sure that all defects have been entered correctly and marked. If you trust the marking of additional areas to subsequent surface analysis scans, you may be surprised to see that some marginal areas will read as OK one time and defective another. Make sure that whenever any area is reported as bad, that area is marked as bad by all subsequent low-level format operations.

Using Surface Analysis Software

Surface analysis routines are provided in any good low-level format program. The original IBM XT and AT Advanced Diagnostics low-level format programs include surface analysis as an option to perform after the format. On the PS/2 Advanced Diagnostics, the surface analysis is performed automatically during the low-level format procedures, slowing the process with multiple passes through the disk. The first pass is the actual format, the second pass is a destructive write test, and the last pass is a read and verify of all the disk's sectors. The time required to finish a format depends on the disk size and speed, but 30 minutes usually is sufficient.

All the commercial aftermarket low-level format programs also include surface analysis routines. The Htest/Hformat and HDtest programs include comprehensive surface analysis capability. A controller-based format program may include a surface analysis routine. If the program does, use it. If the program does not, you may use one of the aftermarket software products mentioned in the section "Running the Low-Level Format Program" to perform the surface analysis.

Partitioning the Drive

After you perform a low-level format on a disk, you must partition the drive before performing a high-level format.

Partitioning a hard disk is simply defining areas of the disk for an operating system to use as a volume. To DOS, a *volume* is an area of a disk denoted as a drive letter. Drive C, for example, is really volume C, and drive D is volume D. Some users mistakenly think that they have to partition a disk only if they're going to divide it into more than one volume. However, a disk must be partitioned even if it will be the single volume C.

Partitioning the disk writes a master partition boot sector on the drive at cylinder 0, head 0, sector 1—the first sector on the entire hard disk. This boot sector contains the partition table describing the partitions by their starting and ending cylinder and head and sector locations. The partition table also indicates to the ROM BIOS which partition is bootable and where to look for an operating system to load.

A single hard disk can have between 1 and 24 partitions. You can split the drive into many more partitions, but DOS only recognizes the first 24 partitions it sees. The 24-partition limit includes all the hard drives currently installed in the system, which means that I can have up to 24 separate hard disks with one partition each, a single hard disk with 24 partitions on it, or any combination of disks and partitions totalling or less than 24. DOS does not recognize more than 24 partitions although other operating systems may. DOS is limited because it letters volumes, and Z is the 24th volume including C.

Before you use a hard disk, you *must* partition it to make your hard disk work properly. You can create a partition with the DOS-supplied FDISK program or with an aftermarket program. I recommend using FDISK for reasons explained in the following sections.

Using the DOS FDISK Program

The DOS FDISK program is the standard for partitioning hard disks. Partitioning is merely preparation of the boot sector of the disk so that the DOS FORMAT program can operate correctly. Partitioning was first needed so different operating systems could coexist on a single hard disk.

If a disk is set up with two or more partitions, FDISK shows only two DOS partitions, called the *primary* and *extended* partitions. The extended partition then is divided into logical DOS volumes, which are actually partitions. Although FDISK says it sets up a disk divided into C, D, E, and F as two partitions (a primary or first partition C and an extended partition with logical DOS volumes D, E, and F), in the structure of the disk each logical DOS volume is a separate partition complete with an extended partition boot sector describing it.

Partitioning capabilities differ among DOS versions. DOS 2.x and later versions support hard disks and partitioning. The minimum partition size for any DOS version is one cylinder. The DOS 4.0 or 5.0 FDISK program allocates primary or extended partitions in multiples of 1M, so the minimum partition size that DOS 4.0 FDISK can create is 1M. DOS 4.0 or 5.0 allows a partition as large as 4 gigabytes, but I never have tested a partition this large. DOS versions before Version 4.0 or 5.0 have a maximum partition size of 32M. Because many disks now use more than 32M, you need DOS 4.0 or 5.0 to use these disks as one huge partition.

DOS 3.3 allows a partition of up to 32M. Although FDISK shows that a single extended partition can fill the rest of the disk not used by the primary partition, this picture of the disk structure is inaccurate. This so-called single extended partition is not really a partition but points to the remainder of the disk where the DOS extended partition resides. This extended partition must be split into logical DOS volumes, which are partitions themselves, with no more than 32M. The primary partition is assigned drive letter C, and the extended partitions are assigned drive letters sequentially from D through Z. Each drive letter designates a volume or partition that can be assigned no more than 32M of disk space with DOS 3.3.

DOS 2.x supports only 16M maximum partitions because of limitations of the 12-bit FAT system. A 12-bit FAT can manage up to 4,096 total clusters on a disk. The 16M limit came from the high-level DOS FORMAT command and not from the FAT. This command aborted with a `Track 0 bad - disk unusable` error message if the partition was larger than 16M. If no marked-as-bad tracks existed beyond the first 16M of the disk, you could have ignored the error and continued the setup of the disk with the SYS command. If defects existed beyond 16M, those defects would not have been marked properly in the FAT and you would have had problems when attempting to store data to these areas of the disk. These problems were corrected by modified high-level format programs supplied with hard disks sold by most disk vendors at the time. These programs allowed a partition of up to 32M to be formatted properly. The only problem then was that the 12-bit FAT defined each cluster or minimum allocation unit on the disk at 8,192 bytes (8K). Because each file would use the disk in increments of 8K, a great deal of disk space was wasted, especially with smaller files.

Using Aftermarket Partitioning Utilities

If you have DOS 3.3, 4.0, or 5.0, you probably do not need aftermarket partitioning utilities except for special cases. Instead of purchasing a partitioning utility, I recommend that you upgrade to a newer version of DOS. Using a nonstandard partitioning program jeopardizes the data in these partitions and makes data recovery difficult if not impossible.

Prior to DOS 4.0, the partition size limit is 32M for DOS 3.x and 16M for DOS 2.x. These limits are bothersome for people with hard disks much larger than these limits; users have to split their hard disk into many partitions so they can use all of the disk.

If you have a 120M hard disk, for example, using DOS 3.2 or an earlier version, you can access only 32M of that disk as a C partition. Several software companies came up with enhanced partitioning programs to create multiple partitions recognizable by DOS and to make many of them larger than 32M. Some examples of these enhanced partitioning programs are Disk Manager by Ontrack, Speedstor by Storage Dimensions, and Vfeature Deluxe by Golden Bow. The Ontrack Disk Manager is probably the most popular because Seagate shipped it with all drives having more than 32M.

These partitioning programs also include a high-level format program because the DOS FORMAT program in Version 3.3 and earlier versions can format only a 32M partition. Low-level format capabilities were included so the program can be used as a single tool for setting up a hard disk. The partitioning programs even included the capability to override the physical type selections available in a ROM BIOS. In this way, a system can use all of a disk, even though the type table in its ROM BIOS does not have an entry that matches the hard disk exactly.

If you are interested in data recovery, you must not use any of these programs or any others like them to partition or high-level format your hard disks. Also, never use the capability of these programs to override your ROM

BIOS drive type settings. DOS defines specific ways to write information to disk. If a program writes information to disk without following the DOS guidelines, the data may be written to the disk in a nonstandard way. Most data recovery methods assume that the DOS methods were followed. If a program circumvents these methods, the normal recovery procedures may not work. Overriding your ROM BIOS disk table settings is especially dangerous. As an example, a disaster scenario follows.

Suppose that you have a Seagate ST-4096 hard disk with 1,024 cylinders and 9 heads. This disk requires that your controller never perform a data write modification called "write precompensation" to any cylinders of the disk. Some drives require this precompensation on the inner cylinders to compensate for "bit crowding" resulting from the higher density of data on the (smaller size) inner cylinders. The ST-4096 internally compensates for this effect, so no precompensation is needed from your controller.

You install this drive in an IBM AT, which does not have a ROM BIOS drive table that matches this drive exactly. The built-in information in the ROM BIOS drive table, which includes specifications about a number of hard disks, does not include the proper specifications (drive type) for this hard disk. The best matching type you can select for this drive is Type 18, which enables you to use only 977 cylinders and 7 heads, or 56.77M of what should be a 76.5M hard disk. If your AT has a ROM BIOS dated 01/10/84 or earlier, the situation is even worse because that table ends with Type 14 as the highest usable type. In this case, you have to pick Type 12 as the best match within the first 14 table entries, which gives you access to 855 cylinders and 7 heads, or only 49.68M of the 76.5M drive.

Most compatibles have a more complete table than IBM's, and most likely have an exact table match for this drive, allowing the full 80M to be used with no problems. For example, for most compatibles with a Phoenix ROM BIOS, Type 35 supports the drive entirely.

Suppose that you don't feel content with using only 50M or 57M of an 80M drive, so you invoke the Disk Manager program that came with the drive and low-level format the drive. Then you use Disk Manager to override the Type 18 or Type 12 settings in the drive table. (This table instructs you to set up a small C partition of only 1M and then partition the remainder of the disk's 75.5M as partition D.) Because you are using DOS 3.3 on this system, this program also overrides the 32M partition limitation. If you had a compatible system that did not require the drive type override, you still would need to use the Disk Manager partitioner to create any partitions larger than the DOS 3.3 standard 32M. Next, you use Disk Manager to high-level format the C and D partitions, because the DOS high-level format in DOS 3.3 works only on 32M or smaller volumes.

The Disk Manager program creates a special driver file called DMDRVR.BIN, which it installs in the CONFIG.SYS file through the DEVICE command. After you boot from this C partition and load the DMDRVR.BIN device driver, the 75.5M D partition is completely accessible.

Now suppose that along comes an innocent user of the system who always boots from his or her own DOS floppy disk. After booting from the floppy, the user attempts to log into the D partition because that is where almost all the programs and data must reside in this system. Remember that C is only 1M in size and cannot hold many programs or files. No matter what DOS version this user has booted from on the floppy disk, including Version 4.0, the D partition seems to have vanished. Any attempt to log into that partition results in an `Invalid drive specification` error message. No standard version of DOS recognizes the D partition without the DMDRVR.BIN device driver loaded.

Any attempt by this user to recover data on this drive with the Norton, Mace, or PC Tools utility programs results in failure. These programs can see the drive as having only 977 cylinders and 7 heads (Type 18) or 855 cylinders and 7 heads (Type 12). In fact, any attempt at correcting what seems to be partition table damage by these programs will corrupt any of the data in the "vanished" D partition.

Assuming that a physical problem exists with the disk, the user boots and runs the Advanced Diagnostics software to test the hard disk. Because the Advanced Diagnostics software incorporates its own special boot code rather than standard DOS, the software is not concerned with partitioning but looks to the ROM BIOS drive type table to determine the capacity of the hard disk installed. The Advanced Diagnostics program sees the unit as having the 977 or 855 cylinders indicated by the Type 18 or 12 settings, as well as only 7 heads, also indicated by both of these types. The user then runs the series of hard disk tests found on the Advanced Diagnostics disk, which uses the last cylinder of the disk as a test cylinder for diagnostics read and write tests. This cylinder is subsequently overwritten by the diagnostics tests, which all pass, because the drive has no physical problem.

This user has just wiped out all the data in the D drive that happened to be on either cylinder number 976 or 854 (depending on whether Type 18 or Type 12 originally was selected in the CMOS setup program). Had the drive been partitioned with the standard FDISK software, the last cylinder indicated by the ROM BIOS drive tables would have been left out of any partitions and reserved for diagnostics tests on the drive without damaging any data.

If the user boots from drive C, the data in drive D is accessible. After the partition information is wiped out by diagnostics, the user must resort to special disk recovery programs, such as Norton's DiskEdit, to recover the information from the drive.

Using any other software to access the disk based on the hardware type setting also may cause you to innocently wipe out data on a disk set up with these "enhanced" partitioning programs. For example, OS/2, UNIX, XENIX, Novell Advanced NetWare, or any other non-DOS operating system cannot recognize the disk or the nonstandard partitions you have set up. In fact, running Windows 3.0 messes up everything because that program also looks to the ROM BIOS for the disk parameters. Writing to the drive with any of these operating systems destroys data.

Nonstandard partitions also can botch things up when you attempt to upgrade from one DOS version to another or install another operating system, such as OS/2, on your hard disk. Another way to wipe things out is by using any low-level format utilities to run an interleave test of your hard disk. These tests normally use the Diagnostics Cylinder as the test area, which with Disk Manager contains data (or I should say, "used to contain data"). Accidentally deleting or overwriting the DMDRVR.BIN driver file causes the D partition to "disappear" after the next reboot.

Because these nonstandard partitions do not follow the rules and guidelines of Microsoft and IBM, you cannot document their structure. Data recovery on these partitions is difficult if they are damaged in any way. The sizes and locations of the FATs and root directory are not standard, and the detailed reference charts in this book (which are valid for any standard FDISK-created partitions) are inaccurate when applied to these nonstandard partitions.

> ***Note:*** This discussion applies to Disk Manager, Speedstor, Vfeature Deluxe, or any other programs that provide the same features. If you use these programs for low-level formatting only, however, you should have no problems. Problems arise from the drive type override, partitioning, and high-level format operations.

Following Partitioning Guidelines

To ensure data integrity and your best chance of data recovery, follow these disk support and partitioning rules:

1. Your hard disk should be supported properly by your ROM BIOS, with no "software overrides." If your system does not currently

have a table that supports the full capacity of your drive, you either live with what is in the table or modify the table through hardware. You may patch your existing ROM BIOS, upgrade to a new ROM BIOS, or use a disk controller with an onboard ROM BIOS for drive support. Drive type changes done with these methods cannot be misunderstood by software that reads the absolute disk parameters from your BIOS and enables the drives to work under any operating system.

2. Use only FDISK to partition your disk. If you want partitions larger than 32M, you must use DOS 4.0 or a later version. With DOS 4.0 and later versions, you have no excuse for using any program like Disk Manager, Speedstor, or Vfeature Deluxe for partitioning.

To save data to a floppy disk or tape, use FDISK to repartition the disk and reload the data. If you decide to repartition a disk, follow these steps:

1. Back up all information from the current hard disk to tape or floppy disks. For added safety, create two backups in case one has problems.

   If your hard disk is several years old, you may want to perform a low-level format to identify defects that have developed since the last low-level format.

2. Repartition your hard disk by using the DOS FDISK program.

3. Perform a high-level format on the hard disk.

4. Reload information from the backup to the hard disk.

Completing the DOS High-Level Format

The third and final step in the software preparation of a hard disk is to complete the DOS high-level format. The primary function of the high-level format is to create a FAT and directory system on the disk so DOS can manage files. You usually perform a high-level format with the standard DOS FORMAT program, using the following syntax:

```
FORMAT C: /S /V
```

This command high-level formats drive C (or volume C if the drive is a multivolume drive) and places the hidden operating system files on the first part of this partition. This command also prompts for the entry of a volume label to be stored on the disk.

Functions and procedures performed by the FORMAT program in this operation include the following:

1. Scan the disk (read only) for tracks and sectors that have been marked as bad during the low-level format. The high-level format notes these tracks as unreadable.

2. Return the drive heads to the first cylinder of the partition and at that cylinder, head 1, sector 1, write a DOS volume boot sector. This sector contains information such as the version of DOS used to format the disk, the number of bytes per sector, and the number of heads.

3. Immediately following the DOS volume boot sector (at head 1, sector 2), write a FAT. Immediately after this FAT, write a second copy of the FAT. These FATs are essentially blank except for bad cluster marks made after the marked defect scan. After files are stored on the disk, the FAT tells DOS which clusters on the disk are in use by files and which are available for use.

4. Write a blank root directory. The root directory is used for storing information about files located in the root directory.

5. If the /S parameter was specified, copy the files IBMBIO.COM, IBMDOS.COM, and COMMAND.COM to the disk in that order. These files contain the necessary information for DOS to boot the computer when it is turned on. If you are formatting the hard disk from which the computer is to be booted (usually drive C), use the /S parameter. If you do not include the /S option, your computer cannot boot from the C drive. If the disk is only for data storage and not for booting, do not use the /S parameter.

6. If the /V parameter was specified, prompt the user for a volume label, which should be written as the fourth file entry in the root directory. The volume enables you to name your disk. You may use information like your name, company name, size of disk, or date as the name for future reference. Then, when you enter a DIR command, the name of the disk appears in the directory listing. If you do not include the /V option during the format, you can add a volume label later by using the DOS LABEL command.

Now the disk is prepared for DOS to store and retrieve files; the disk also now is bootable in this example.

When you perform a marked defect scan as the first part of a high-level format, defects marked by the low-level format show up as totally unreadable tracks or sectors. When the high-level format encounters one of these areas, the high-level format automatically performs up to five retries to read these tracks or sectors. If the unreadable area was marked by the low-level format, the read fails on all retries. After five retries, the DOS FORMAT program gives up on this track or sector and moves on to the next. The FAT notes any unreadable areas as bad clusters.

DOS 3.3 and earlier versions only can mark an entire track as bad in the FAT, even if only one sector was marked in the low-level format. DOS 4.0 or 5.0 individually checks each cluster on the track and recovers those that do not involve the low-level marked-as-bad sectors. Because most low-level format programs mark all the sectors on a track instead of the individual defective sector, the results with DOS 3.3, 4.0, or 5.0 are the same.

Some newer low-level format programs, however, mark only the individual sector that is bad instead of an entire track. This capability occurs on the IBM PS/2 low-level formatters, which are on the PS/2 Advanced Diagnostics or Reference disk. In this case, high-level formatting with DOS 4.0 or 5.0 results in fewer lost bytes in bad sectors because only the clusters containing the marked-as-bad sectors are marked as bad in the FAT. DOS 4.0 or 5.0 gives the message `Attempting to recover allocation unit x`, where *x* is the number of the cluster, in an attempt to determine whether only a single cluster or all the clusters on the track should be marked as bad in the FAT.

If your controller and low-level format program together support sector and track sparing, the high-level format sees the entire disk as being defect-free because all defective sectors have been exchanged for spare good ones. If you have low-level formatted your disk correctly, the high-level format always should show the same number of bytes in bad sectors each time the high-level format is performed. Some people claim that after redoing the high-level format on their hard disks, the number of bytes in bad sectors reported changes—fewer bytes in bad sectors are reported or none at all. Whoever did the high-level format probably did it incorrectly and perhaps did not mark the manufacturer's defects. Any defect marks made in the low-level format show as bad bytes in the high-level format, no matter how many times you run it.

People who use data recovery utilities such as Norton, Mace, or PC Tools to mark defective clusters on the disk sometimes find that these programs cannot mark the sectors or tracks at the low level. The bad-cluster marks the utilities make are stored only in the FAT, and they are erased during the next high-level format operation. Remember that only a low-level format or a surface analysis tool can mark defects correctly on a disk. Anything else you use makes only temporary bad-cluster marks in the FAT. Temporary markings are sometimes OK, but you should redo the low-level format of the disk and mark the area manually or run a surface analysis and make the mark permanent.

The speed of the high-level format command for DOS 4.0 has improved tremendously as of the DOS update known as SYSLEVEL UR29015. In particular, the handling of marked defects has improved. This SYSLEVEL also corrected a bug in the FORMAT command that caused the program to abort with an `Invalid media or Track 0 bad - disk unusable` error message. This message appeared if you were high-level formatting a partition larger than 32M and a marked defect was located in the area of the disk from 32M to 32M plus *x*, where *x* equals the size of the DOS volume boot sector, FATs, and root directory on that partition.

Prior to receiving the patched FORMAT command in SYSLEVEL UR29015 or later, I had to boot OS/2, high-level format the partition with the OS/2 1.1 high-level format program, and then reboot DOS 4.0 and use the SYS command to make the disk bootable. The DOS 4.0 corrective service disks eliminate this problem (see Chapter 6 for more information on the corrective service disks and how to get them).

Recovering from Improper Formatting Problems

This section summarizes a few simple rules for proper formatting of a hard disk. These rules are mostly common sense now that you have a better understanding of how the drive works. At this point in the chapter, you are equipped with enough knowledge of hard disk drives to understand the following situations.

Properly Marking Defects

You must enter the manufacturer's defect list properly during the low-level format. Because the manufacturer uses highly sensitive analog test equipment to locate defects, no ordinary software can locate all the defects the manufacturer finds. Do not fall for the inaccurate claims of some disk utilities that they can locate media defects more accurately than the drive manufacturers.

When the actual tracks are properly marked as bad, any high-level format attempting to read that track cannot. This reading failure causes the high-level format to create a FAT that contains marks causing the particular sectors in that track to be marked as unavailable. These defective locations show up as bad sectors with the DOS CHKDSK command, which indicates that the protection from using these areas is in place and operating properly.

Many newer systems have controllers and low-level format programs that support track and sector sparing, as well as a specially recorded machine-readable media flaw table. These systems automatically mark the manufacturer's defects as bad. They also may utilize spare sectors and tracks in place of the marked-as-bad ones so that the DOS high-level format command never detects unreadable locations on the disk. This approach gives the impression (to anything except the low-level format program) that the disk is free of defects.

Checking the Temperature

Always format your hard disk at a normal operating temperature. Never begin a low-level format immediately after you turn the power on. Until the drive has warmed up, changes occur in the size and dimensions of the platters and in the head positioning system. To ensure that the format information is written exactly where data will be when it is read later, allow the drive to warm up for at least 30 minutes before beginning a low-level format. Also be sure that the environmental temperature is close to what is normal for the drive's use. For example, don't set up and low-level format a hard disk in a cold warehouse and then ship the system to a warmer office for use.

Most of the time, thermal problems show up as a failure to boot in the morning when the drive platters are at an ambient temperature. By letting the system run and the platters warm up and expand, the system usually boots normally. Failures to read or write data after the system has warmed up fully—especially when running hotter than normal—also are caused by thermally induced variations in head and platter positions. Normally, redoing the low-level format at normal operating temperature (not too cold or too hot) restores the drive to normal operation. Leaving the system on continuously or reducing the number of power on/off cycles also minimizes the number of thermal expansion and contraction cycles, extends the life of the drive, and prevents many read and write problems.

Checking Position

Always format your hard disk in the position in which you will operate it. If the drive is to be positioned on its side, format the drive in exactly the same position. Don't low-level format the drive horizontally and then turn the drive sideways. Gravity places loads on the head actuating mechanism, and these loads differ with the position of the drive. To ensure that all data actually is written within the precise sector boundaries determined during the format time, you must format the drive in the running position.

Hard disks with a stepper motor head actuator are extremely sensitive to this problem, but voice coil actuated drives are more immune.

Avoiding Drives That Are Not Shock-Mounted

Most hard disks manufactured today have a shock-mounted head disk assembly (HDA). Some sort of rubber cushion is between the disk drive body and the mounting chassis. The only way to tell whether your computer has shock-mounting (unless it is mentioned in the product literature) is to examine the hard disk mountings. Most HDAs have shock isolation mounts, but low-cost drives (like the Seagate ST-2xx series) are exceptions. Never use drives that are not shock-mounted in a portable system or where the environment subjects the drive to any vibration or mechanical stress.

Many manufacturers of portable systems, such as IBM and COMPAQ, install a drive that is already shock-mounted in a cradle that is further shock-mounted to the system chassis. This double shock-mounting system increases the reliability of the hard disk systems used in the portables.

Parking the Heads

When any hard disk is powered off, the heads normally rest on the disk's surface. This contact between the heads and platter surface happens as the platters spin down so that when the head finally lands, the drive is not turning very fast. Usually the heads land on whatever cylinder they were positioned over last, which means the heads usually land over areas that actually contain data.

Any drive that uses a voice coil head actuator offers a feature known as automatic head parking. These systems have a spring attached to the head. While the drive is operational, the electric voice coil mechanism overcomes the spring tension and can move the heads across the surface of the disk. In this setup, when power to the drive is lost, the spring automatically pulls the head rack away from data areas of the disk to a special landing zone, before the velocity of the platters slows to the point where the heads actually land. All voice coil drives automatically park the drive heads, but almost no stepper motor drives do.

A few stepper motor drives incorporate a parking mechanism. Out of the hundreds of brands, makes, and models on the market today, only a few exceptions exist, such as the Seagate ST-251/252 and Seagate ST-277. These drives are stepper drives that autopark using an ingenious system whereby the spindle motor is driven as a generator by the flywheel effect of the spinning platters. This free energy then is used to power the head stepper motor and park the heads in a nondata area of the disk. Some of Seagate's 3 1/2-inch stepper motor drives also use this feature to autopark. To learn how your drive works, check the drive manufacturer's technical reference manual.

All the stepper motor actuated drives without an auto parking feature can be parked with software. Before you shut down the system, run a park program to secure the heads. If the power goes off unexpectedly, you cannot park the heads. The head parking program is on your system Setup, Diagnostics, or Reference disk supplied by the manufacturer. Usually, the same parking program is supplied also on the Advanced Diagnostics disks found with the service documentation for your system. With many of these disks, you just need to boot the disk and select the Prepare System for Moving option; then the heads of any attached disks are parked. After the disks are parked, shut down the system. This action invokes a program called SHIPDISK.COM. SHIPDISK.COM files differ for XT and AT systems.

In 1984, IBM issued a warning to its dealers recommending against running SHIPDISK.COM from the DOS prompt. The memo warned about a slight chance of data loss if the program wiped out track 0 of the disk. Therefore, run SHIPDISK.COM only from the menu.

For AT systems, IBM supplies a separate program, SHUTDOWN.EXE, that you can run from the DOS prompt. This program is on the AT Diagnostics and Advanced Diagnostics disks. Copy this program to the hard disk and enter the command *shutdown* at the DOS prompt. You see a graphic picture of the system's red power switch, which turns itself off as the heads are parked. The program then halts the system, requiring a complete power down. This program works only on AT systems.

Both the SHIPDISK.COM and SHUTDOWN.EXE programs work by placing the heads at the cylinder indicated as the landing zone for the drive type selected and entered in CMOS RAM from the ROM BIOS drive table found in the system. Exactly where the heads are placed depends on what "type" you have selected for your hard disk, as well as what landing zone is indicated for that particular type. Consult your technical reference manual for a listing of drive types found in your system ROM BIOS.

Do not run a hard disk parking program on your system unless it is designed for that system. A parking program cannot physically hurt a drive although you may hear some strange noises. Many drives make different sounds when resetting the heads to track 0 or when forced into a parking mode by a seek to a high enough cylinder.

If you use an inappropriate parking program for your system, an attempt is made to force the heads past either the inner or outer cylinder of the disk. In these cases, the drive automatically truncates the seek operation and recalibrates the heads to cylinder 0. You may think that you are parking your disk heads in a data-free zone, but you really are placing the heads over cylinder 0, which contains some of the most important information on your drive.

Some people think that you should park the heads every time you shut down the drive. IBM states that you do not have to park the heads on a drive unless you plan to move it. My own experiences follow IBM's recommendation, but nothing is wrong with a fail-safe approach. If you are using voice coil drives, this point is moot because these drives automatically park the heads every time. For stepper motor drives, I recommend that you park the heads before every shutdown; doing so is easy and cannot hurt.

Chapter Summary

This chapter examined the process of formatting a hard disk (including low-level and high-level formatting) and recovering from improper formatting problems. You have read some tips and tricks that I have developed over the years for recovering from a number of hard disk problems. These are simple operations that you often can perform to get your data back from what may appear to be a "dead" drive. In essence, you now can combine simple, proven hardware troubleshooting techniques with what you will learn about software data recovery procedures for the ability to bring back data from the most difficult situations.

5

DOS Background

You can think of DOS as the computer's manager. DOS is a necessary component in managing information on disk and in the computer's memory. DOS regulates virtually all data storage on your computer. Therefore, your knowledge of how data recovery processes operate will be enhanced if you understand the inner workings of DOS. In this chapter, you examine the structure of DOS in relation to your system and disks.

This chapter explains the components of DOS and focuses on the system files and command processor components. These components form the kernel of DOS and are loaded during the boot process. This chapter also examines the boot process. If you have a boot failure, understanding the boot process helps you determine whether the problem is hardware-related or a software data recovery problem.

Some data loss problems are caused by DOS itself—an imperfect operating system. Knowing the problems associated with different versions of DOS enhances your data recovery abilities. You may be tempted to replace hardware that is working perfectly, or you may blame other applications software for problems—to no avail. Knowing DOS quirks often saves you from hours of unproductive problem solving.

Understanding System Memory Allocation

The system's *memory map* shows the memory that is possible for the system to address and how the memory is used in a particular type of system. This section examines the three types of available memory: *conventional*, *extended*, and *expanded*. Understanding the memory map helps you deal with programs that use these memory locations and memory-chip problems.

This section describes how the three kinds of memory work with DOS and how they relate to the different kinds of processors (8088, 80286, and so on). Different processors have varying capabilities when using memory. To address problems that can arise from these processors, you must understand how the processors use memory.

Conventional Memory

All IBM-compatible systems have at least a 1M processor addressable memory workspace. AT-compatible systems have at least a 16M map. The first megabyte of memory in an IBM-compatible system is called *conventional memory*, a form of random-access memory (RAM). The 1M of RAM is divided into several sections. The portion of RAM space where conventional programs and data can reside is called *user memory*. Under normal conditions, only the first 640K of the 1M can be allocated as user memory.

The remaining 384K of memory is reserved for special-purpose system use. The first 128K of this special-purpose area is reserved for *video RAM*, where text and graphics reside when displayed. The next 128K is reserved for read-only memory (ROM) control programs and other special-memory uses for adapter boards. The last 128K of RAM is reserved for motherboard ROM, where the Basic Input/Output System (BIOS), the power-on self test (POST), and the bootstrap loader reside. These programs are the master test and control programs for the system, enabling the system to load the operating system.

ROM is a subset of RAM that stores programs that cannot be changed. The programs are stored on special chips by a fusion of circuits on the chip so that the PC cannot alter them. ROM stores permanent programs that must be present while the system is running. Graphics boards, hard disk controllers, communications boards, and expanded memory boards are examples of adapter boards that may use some of this memory.

Figure 5.1 represents conventional memory and shows how it may be allocated. Each symbol on a line is equal to 1K of memory. Each line or *segment* is 64K, and the entire map is 1,024K (1,024K equals 1M). Figure 5.1 uses the following symbols:

- . = Program accessible memory
- v = Video RAM
- a = Adapter board ROM and RAM
- r = Motherboard ROM BIOS
- b = IBM cassette BASIC

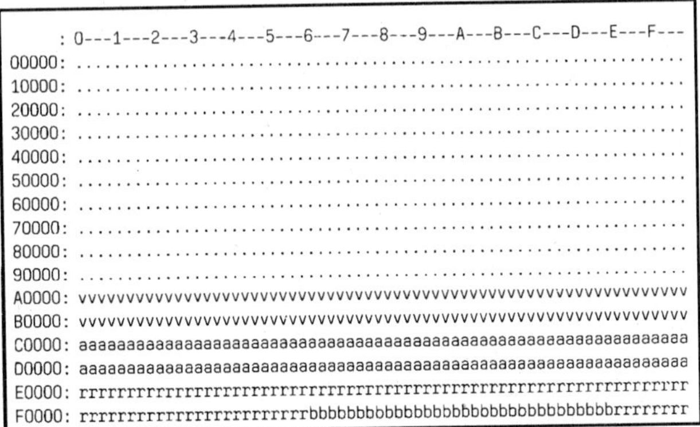

```
      : 0---1---2---3---4---5---6---7---8---9---A---B---C---D---E---F---
00000: ................................................................
10000: ................................................................
20000: ................................................................
30000: ................................................................
40000: ................................................................
50000: ................................................................
60000: ................................................................
70000: ................................................................
80000: ................................................................
90000: ................................................................
A0000: vvvvvvvvvvvvvvvvvvvvvvvvvvvvvvvvvvvvvvvvvvvvvvvvvvvvvvvvvvvvvvvv
B0000: vvvvvvvvvvvvvvvvvvvvvvvvvvvvvvvvvvvvvvvvvvvvvvvvvvvvvvvvvvvvvvvv
C0000: aaaaaaaaaaaaaaaaaaaaaaaaaaaaaaaaaaaaaaaaaaaaaaaaaaaaaaaaaaaaaaaa
D0000: aaaaaaaaaaaaaaaaaaaaaaaaaaaaaaaaaaaaaaaaaaaaaaaaaaaaaaaaaaaaaaaa
E0000: rrrrrrrrrrrrrrrrrrrrrrrrrrrrrrrrrrrrrrrrrrrrrrrrrrrrrrrrrrrrrrrr
F0000: rrrrrrrrrrrrrrrrrrrrrrrrbbbbbbbbbbbbbbbbbbbbbbbbbbbbbbbbrrrrrrrr
```

Fig. 5.1. IBM 1M memory map.

Note that memory segments from A0000 to F0000 (addresses of memory in hexadecimal notation)—consisting of 384K—are reserved for special purposes. This reserved space may be used completely in some systems, but other systems may use only a bit of the space. For example, the monochrome display adapter (MDA) and color graphics adapter (CGA) do not use all 128K of the space allocated to them. The unallocated space can be used as a path into *expanded memory*, a type of memory discussed later in this chapter.

Extended Memory

In an AT system, the memory map can be extended up to 16M. For this reason, the industry calls memory beyond 1M *extended memory*. A small portion of the last megabyte is reserved for a duplicate of the AT ROM BIOS, so not all of extended memory can be used for programs and data. This memory is where the BIOS resides as well as the POST and bootstrap loader. These programs are the master test and control programs for the system and also enable the system to load an operating system from floppy or hard disk. This 128K reserve causes the total reserved space in an AT to be 512K, which is up from the 384K reserved in an XT system.

To recognize memory beyond the standard 1M address space, the 80286 and later processors must be operating in *protected mode*. Protected mode, the native mode of these advanced processors, possesses greater access to memory, a modified instruction set, and other operational differences. Unfortunately, these operational differences prevent the system from being compatible with the original IBM PC systems. So Intel designed an 8086/8088 mode within the 80286 and later processors, called *real mode*, which permits full compatibility. Real mode inhibits the speed and capabilities of these later processors.

Figures 5.2 and 5.3 show the 16M map for an AT system in protected mode. Figure 5.2 shows where the real-mode addressable memory ends. Figure 5.3 shows where extended memory picks up. An 80286 or later system running in protected mode is required to address memory beyond the 1M boundary.

In the figures, the following symbols are used:

- . = Program accessible memory
- v = Video RAM
- a = Adapter board ROM
- r = Motherboard ROM BIOS
- b = IBM cassette BASIC

```
       : 0---1---2---3---4---5---6---7---8---9---A---B---C---D---E---F---
000000: ................................................................
010000: ................................................................
020000: ................................................................
030000: ................................................................
040000: ................................................................
050000: ................................................................
060000: ................................................................
070000: ................................................................
080000: ................................................................
090000: ................................................................
0A0000: vvvvvvvvvvvvvvvvvvvvvvvvvvvvvvvvvvvvvvvvvvvvvvvvvvvvvvvvvvvvvvvv
0B0000: vvvvvvvvvvvvvvvvvvvvvvvvvvvvvvvvvvvvvvvvvvvvvvvvvvvvvvvvvvvvvvvv
0C0000: aaaaaaaaaaaaaaaaaaaaaaaaaaaaaaaaaaaaaaaaaaaaaaaaaaaaaaaaaaaaaaaa
0D0000: aaaaaaaaaaaaaaaaaaaaaaaaaaaaaaaaaaaaaaaaaaaaaaaaaaaaaaaaaaaaaaaa
0E0000: rrrrrrrrrrrrrrrrrrrrrrrrrrrrrrrrrrrrrrrrrrrrrrrrrrrrrrrrrrrrrrrr
0F0000: rrrrrrrrrrrrrrrrrrrrrrrrbbbbbbbbbbbbbbbbbbbbbbbbbbbbbbbbrrrrrrrr
```

Fig. 5.2. *IBM 16M memory map to the point where real-mode addressable memory ends.*

```
       : 0---1---2---3---4---5---6---7---8---9---A---B---C---D---E---F---
100000: ................................................................
110000: ................................................................
120000: ................................................................
130000: ................................................................
140000: ................................................................
     \
     /
     \
A large break occurs
     \
     /
     \
E80000: ................................................................
E90000: ................................................................
EA0000: ................................................................
EB0000: ................................................................
EC0000: ................................................................
ED0000: ................................................................
EE0000: ................................................................
EF0000: ................................................................
       : 0---1---2---3---4---5---6---7---8---9---A---B---C---D---E---F---
F00000: ................................................................
F10000: ................................................................
F20000: ................................................................
F30000: ................................................................
F40000: ................................................................
F50000: ................................................................
F60000: ................................................................
F70000: ................................................................
F80000: ................................................................
F90000: ................................................................
FA0000: ................................................................
FB0000: ................................................................
FC0000: ................................................................
FD0000: ................................................................
FE0000: rrrrrrrrrrrrrrrrrrrrrrrrrrrrrrrrrrrrrrrrrrrrrrrrrrrrrrrrrrrrrrrr
FF0000: rrrrrrrrrrrrrrrrrrrrrrrrbbbbbbbbbbbbbbbbbbbbbbbbbbbbbbbbrrrrrrrr
```

Fig. 5.3. *IBM 16M memory map where extended memory picks up.*

Note the duplicate of the ROM BIOS at the end of the 16th megabyte. The memory in these last two segments is a mirror image of what is in the last two segments of the first megabyte. This duplicate ROM BIOS is required by the 80286 and later processors to provide for switching between real and protected mode.

Expanded Memory

Some systems incorporate a type of memory called *expanded* memory, which is addressable by the processor through a small 64K window. Expanded memory operates through a segment-switching scheme in which a memory adapter has many 64K segments on board. The system uses one available segment to map into the board. When this 64K fills, the board simply rotates that segment out, replacing it with a new segment.

Three prominent companies—Lotus, Intel, and Microsoft—decided to standardize expanded memory by starting it at segment E000 in the first megabyte. (The standard, LIM EMS, stands for Lotus-Intel-Microsoft Expanded Memory Specification.) The LIM standard has the following drawbacks:

- Programs must be specially written to take advantage of this segment-swapping scheme.
- Because DOS cannot address this segment, programs can put only data there.
- A program cannot run while it is "swapped out" (placed in the expanded memory).

Because of expanded memory's limitations, it should not be used in systems that can use extended memory.

Figure 5.4 shows the logical locations and relationships among conventional, extended, and expanded memory. Notice that only the conventional and extended memory locations are directly addressable by the processor. The expanded memory can be accessed through a small window in the conventional memory space.

Examining the System Architecture

The way DOS provides access to memory is just one aspect of a computer's architecture. A PC system contains a hierarchy of software that controls the system. Even when you are operating within an applications program, such as a spreadsheet or word processor, several other layers of programs always are executing underneath.

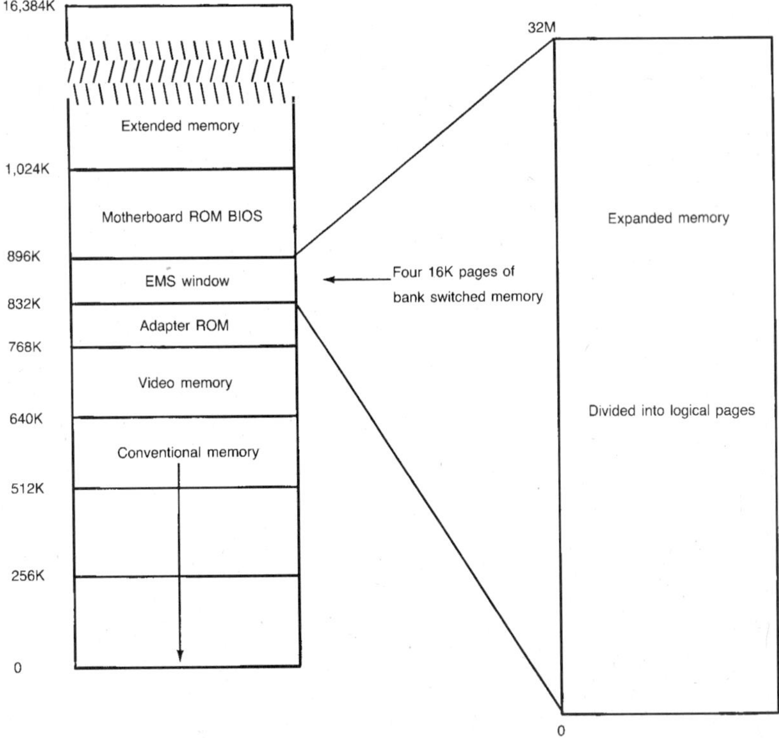

Fig. 5.4. Memory location.

Think of the layers like this: the applications program talks to DOS, DOS talks to the ROM BIOS, and the ROM BIOS talks to the computer's microprocessor. For example, when your word processor saves your letter to disk, the word processor actually tells DOS to save the letter. DOS passes the information to the BIOS, and the file is saved to disk. Some renegade programs skip a layer or two to talk directly to the BIOS or to the hardware. Although skipping layers can improve the speed of programs, it can damage the way data is stored and manipulated on your computer—resulting in the need for data recovery.

At the lowest level of the system architecture exists the computer system itself. If you examine the system at this level, you find that by placing various bytes of information at certain ports or locations within the memory structure of the system, you can control virtually anything that is connected to the CPU. Control at this level is difficult for you to maintain; this type of control requires complete knowledge of the system architecture. Commands to the system here are in *machine language*, binary groups of information applied directly to the microprocessor itself. These instructions are quite limited in their function, and many instructions are required to perform even the smallest amount of useful work. These instructions are executed rapidly, with little wasted overhead.

When personal computers are started, a series of machine code programs—the ROM BIOS—assumes control. This action is the beginning of the boot process. The ROM BIOS programs always are present in the system, and they do the talking (in machine code) to the hardware. The BIOS accepts commands supplied by programs and translates these commands to machine code for the microprocessor. Commands at this level are called *interrupts* or *services*. A programmer can use almost any language to supply these instructions to the BIOS. A complete list of these services is supplied by IBM in the *BIOS Interface Technical Reference Manual*.

DOS is the second layer of architecture, located just above the ROM BIOS. DOS has the following functions:

- DOS attaches to the BIOS, and a portion of DOS actually becomes an extension to the BIOS—providing more interrupts and services for other programs to use.
- DOS provides for communications with the ROM BIOS in PCs and also for communications with higher level software such as the applications (third-level architecture) you run daily.
- DOS gives the programmer additional interrupts and services to use in programs in addition to what is already provided by the ROM BIOS. This feature prevents a great deal of "reinventing the wheel" as far as programming routines are concerned. For example, DOS provides an extremely rich set of file-handling functions that can open, close, find, delete, create, and rename files on a drive. A programmer can rely on DOS to do most of the work.

This standard set of DOS functions to read and write data makes data recovery possible. Imagine how tough programming the process of reading and writing information to the disk would be if every applications program had to implement its own custom disk interface, with a proprietary directory and file retrieval system!

Examining DOS Components

DOS is a series of components that makes up the DOS system. These major components of DOS follow:

- The *system ROM BIOS* sends messages to the computer hardware.
- The *DOS file allocation* determines how and where information is stored to disk.
- The *I/O (input/output) system* sends messages to the ROM BIOS to control the movement of data within the system.
- The *command processor (COMMAND.COM)* interprets the commands typed at the DOS prompt and sends that information to the I/O system.

This section describes in detail the workings of these four important components of DOS.

The System ROM BIOS

Think of the system ROM BIOS as glue that attaches hardware to the operating system. The same copy of DOS runs on the original IBM PC as well as the latest 80486 computers. If DOS was written to talk directly to the hardware on all systems, then it would be a very hardware-specific program. Instead, IBM developed a set of standard services and functions that each system should be able to perform, and IBM coded these services and functions as programs in the ROM BIOS. Each system gets a completely customized ROM BIOS that talks directly to the hardware in the system and knows exactly how to perform each specific function on that hardware only.

The operating systems can be written to a standard interface. Applications written to the operating system standard interface can run on that system. Two different hardware platforms each can have a custom ROM BIOS that talks directly to the hardware on one hand but provides a standard interface to the same operating system on the other.

The actual ROM BIOS code for each computer can differ. Therefore, you usually cannot run a ROM BIOS from one system in a different system. ROM upgrades must be customized for that particular hardware.

You can find the system files on any bootable DOS disk; these files usually are named IBMBIO.COM and IBMDOS.COM. These files should be the first and second files listed in the directory on any bootable DOS disk. Although applications programs should be isolated from the hardware by the ROM BIOS and DOS, many programmers write programs that circumvent DOS and the ROM BIOS to talk directly to the hardware. Some programs do not work on certain hardware, even if the proper DOS and ROM interfaces are present.

Programs that go directly to hardware perform quickly. For example, many programs directly access the video hardware to improve screen update performance. These applications often have installation programs that require you to specify your hardware so the program can load the correct routines into the applications.

Some utility programs, such as a low-level format program, must talk directly to hardware. These programs are specific to a certain controller or controller type. Another system-specific utility is a driver program that enables extended memory to function as expanded memory on an 80386-based system.

DOS itself communicates directly with the hardware. In fact, much of the IBMBIO.COM file consists of low-level drivers that are designed to supplant and supersede ROM BIOS code in the system. People who own both IBM systems and compatibles may wonder why IBM never seems to have ROM upgrades as quickly as compatible vendors. In a way, IBM distributes its ROM patches and upgrades in DOS. When PC DOS loads, it determines the system type and ID information from the ROM and loads different routines depending on the version of ROM. For example, DOS contains at least four hard disk code sections, but only one section is loaded for a specific system.

The user interface program, or *shell*, is stored in the file COMMAND.COM, which is loaded during a normal DOS boot-up. The shell provides the DOS prompt and communicates to the user.

DOS File Allocation

Allocation of disk space for a file is performed on demand. The space is allocated one *cluster*, or allocation unit, at a time. A cluster is always one or more sectors. Chapter 4 contains more information about sectors and clusters.

The clusters are arranged on a disk to minimize head movement for multisided media. The space on a disk cylinder is allocated before the head moves on to the next cylinder. This scheme uses the sectors under the first head, the sectors under the next head, and so on, for all sectors of all heads of the first cylinder. Then the head moves on to sector 1 of head 0 on the next cylinder.

DOS 2.x uses a simple algorithm—the First Available Cluster algorithm—for allocating file space on a disk. Each time a program requests disk space, DOS scans from the beginning of the file allocation table (FAT) until it finds a free cluster in which to deposit a portion of the file. DOS continues searching and filling until the file is written. The First Available Cluster algorithm causes erased files near the beginning of the disk to be overwritten during the next write operation, because those clusters are the first available to the next write operation.

This algorithm also promotes file fragmentation, because the first available cluster found is used regardless of whether the entire file can be written there. DOS simply continues searching for free clusters in which to deposit the remainder of the file.

DOS 3.x and later versions use a different algorithm, the Next Available Cluster algorithm. The search for available clusters in which to write a file starts where the last write occurred, not at the beginning of the disk. Disk space freed by the erasure of a file is not necessarily reused immediately, unlike with earlier versions of DOS. The pointer that tracks the last written cluster is maintained in system RAM. This pointer is lost when the system is reset or when a disk is changed in a floppy drive.

Because the pointer is lost on system resets and disk changes, files still become fragmented using the Next Available Cluster algorithm. But the new algorithm has one great benefit: Recovering files is more likely to succeed even if the disk has been written to since the erasure. The file just erased is not likely to be the target of the next write operation.

Even when you replace a file under the Next Available Cluster algorithm, the clusters occupied by the file are not overwritten (unless the file is huge or disk space is limited). Suppose that you accidentally save a file using the same name as an existing file; in other words, you replace the file. The existing file's clusters are marked as available, but the pointer ensures that the new file is written to the disk in the next available clusters. You probably can retrieve the original copy of the file.

Of course, replaced files no longer appear in a directory listing, even if the data still is recoverable on the disk. Most quick unerase utilities cannot find any record of a replaced file on the disk. Because quick unerase utilities do not look at the FAT or the data clusters, the utilities see no record of the file's existence. By scanning the free clusters on the disk individually with a disk editor tool, you can locate the actual data from replaced files and rebuild the FAT and directory entries manually. Then you can recover the files. This operation is discussed in Chapters 9 and 10, the problem-solving chapters of this book.

The I/O System

To know how to read and write data, DOS must have some way of sending requests for storage and retrieval to BIOS. The programs that send requests are called the I/O (input/output) system. These I/O programs are contained primarily in the DOS system files IBMBIO.COM and IBMDOS.COM. The CHKDSK command reports these hidden files. The following sections describe these important DOS system files and some of the problems that can result from having these programs placed incorrectly on a disk.

IBMBIO.COM

The IBMBIO.COM file contains the low-level programs that interact directly with devices on the system and the ROM BIOS. This program usually is customized by the original equipment manufacturer (OEM) of the system to match perfectly with the OEM's particular ROM BIOS. IBMBIO.COM contains low-level drivers that are loaded in accord with a particular ROM BIOS based on the ROM ID information, as well as a system initialization routine. During boot-up, this file is loaded by the DOS volume boot sector and given control of the system. IBMBIO.COM loads into low memory, and it remains in memory during normal system operation—except for the system initializer part of the file.

The actual file name may vary with different OEM versions of DOS. Many non-IBM OEM versions of DOS use IO.SYS as the name of this file, including the Microsoft MS-DOS Packaged Product version. Some other manufacturers call this file MIO.SYS, and Toshiba calls it TBIOS.SYS. Although different names for this file may not seem to be a problem, different file names can be a problem when you are upgrading from one OEM version of DOS to a different OEM version. If the different OEMs have used different names for this file, the SYS command may fail, giving the error message `No room for system on destination`. Today, most OEMs use the standard IBMBIO.COM name for this file to eliminate problems in upgrading.

For a bootable disk, this file must be listed as the first file in the directory and occupy at least the first cluster on the disk (cluster number 2). The remainder of this file may be placed in clusters anywhere across the rest of the disk. This file is marked with hidden, system, and read-only attributes and is placed on a disk by the DOS FORMAT or the SYS command.

IBMDOS.COM

The file IBMDOS.COM contains the DOS disk-handling programs and represents the main core or kernel of DOS. IBMDOS.COM is loaded into low memory at system boot-up by the DOS volume boot sector and remains resident in memory during normal system operation.

IBMDOS.COM is not likely to be customized by an OEM, but you may find it under different names. The most common alternative name is MSDOS.SYS, which is used by some OEM versions and the Microsoft MS-DOS Packaged Product version. Toshiba uses the name TDOS.SYS. Most OEMs stick to the IBM convention to eliminate problems in upgrading.

IBMDOS.COM must be listed as the second entry in the disk's root directory for a bootable system disk. This file is marked with hidden, system, and read-only attributes. The DOS FORMAT command or the SYS command usually puts the file on a disk. No special requirements exist for the physical positioning of this file on a disk.

System File Problems

Special requirements exist for the positioning of the system files on a hard disk. These requirements can cause problems when you upgrade from one DOS version to another.

To upgrade your DOS version on a hard disk, you normally use the SYS command to replace the old system files with the new ones. The SYS command can copy the system files in the correct position with the correct names and attributes. The COPY command, on the other hand, cannot copy hidden or system files, nor can COPY put the files in the right position.

The SYS command transfers the two hidden, system files from one disk to another. SYS also updates the DOS volume boot sector on the destination disk, to correct the sector for the new version of DOS. The format for the command follows:

SYS [*d:*][*path*] *d:*

For DOS 4.x and later, the [*d:*][*path*] part of the command specifies an optional source drive and path for the system files. If you omit this information, the boot drive is used. DOS versions earlier than 4.0 automatically look for system files on the default drive.

The *d:* part of the command specifies the destination drive for the transfer.

The SYS command may fail if the destination disk already contains data. The error message `No room for system on destination disk` often brings up a popular misconception. Some people think that the larger system files in new versions of DOS cannot fit into the same space allocated by the older versions. Moreover, many think that they must move data away from the beginning of the destination disk to make room. These beliefs are incorrect.

Stated simply, the system files can be placed virtually anywhere on the destination disk, but the first clusters of the disk must contain the file IBMBIO.COM. For DOS 3.3 or later, even the IBMBIO.COM file can be fragmented and spread out all over the disk, as long as the first cluster of the file occupies the first cluster of the destination disk (cluster 2). The names IBMBIO.COM and IBMDOS.COM must use the first and second directory entries.

The following paragraphs list the conditions—depending on DOS version—that must be met for the SYS command to execute successfully.

DOS 5.x and earlier versions

The disk must have enough free clusters to contain the system files or enough additional free clusters to contain the extra length of any new system file versions if overwriting older system files.

The disk must have at least two unused directory entries in the root directory.

The first byte in the FAT must be a proper media identification byte.

DOS 3.3 and earlier versions

The first and second directory entries in the root directory must contain deleted files, unused file names, or file names that match the new system file names.

The first cluster (cluster 2) on the disk must be available or in use by the system files currently on the disk.

DOS 3.2 and earlier versions

Starting with the first cluster (cluster 2), the destination disk must contain enough consecutive free clusters or consecutive clusters occupied by the current system files to hold the new IBMBIO.COM file.

DOS 2.1 and earlier versions

Starting with the first cluster (cluster 2), the destination disk must contain enough consecutive free clusters or consecutive clusters occupied by the current system files to hold the new IBMBIO.COM and IBMDOS.COM files.

With DOS 4.x or later, the SYS command is more powerful. Because the system files use the first two entries in the root directory and the first cluster (cluster 2) of the disk, the DOS 4.x SYS command moves nonsystem files that occupy the first two entries to other available entries in the root directory. Also, the DOS 4.x SYS command moves the portion of a foreign file that occupies the first cluster to other clusters on the disk. In other words, the DOS 4.x SYS command makes adjustments automatically, whereas earlier DOS SYS commands fail.

The DOS 3.3 SYS command cannot update a DOS OEM version to another OEM version with different system file names. The new system files do not overwrite the old system files because the names differ. To fix this problem, use a directory editing tool to change the names of the old system files to match the new names.

DOS 3.2 requires the IBMBIO.COM file to be contiguous, starting with cluster 2 (the first cluster) on the disk. The other system file, IBMDOS.COM, can be fragmented or placed anywhere on the disk. The second system file does not have to follow the first one physically on the disk.

DOS 2.x requires that both system files, IBMBIO.COM and IBMDOS.COM, occupy contiguous clusters on the disk, starting with cluster 2 (the first cluster). This requirement does not cause problems with updating from Version 2.0 to 2.1, however, because the 2.1 system files are not larger than the 2.0 system files in terms of cluster allocation. Although the Version 2.1 files are larger in bytes, the size change is not enough to require additional clusters on the disk.

Updating DOS to a later DOS version from the same OEM is easy with just the SYS command. You can update DOS for a bootable hard or floppy disk without reformatting the disk. Most problems occur when you change OEM versions with different names for the system files. For other problems, examine the list of requirements stated at the beginning of this section to see whether you are overlooking something.

The SYS command can update the DOS volume boot sector of the destination disk. Later versions of SYS perform this update more completely. Therefore, downgrading DOS versions with SYS is difficult. You cannot use SYS, for example, to install DOS 2.1 on a disk that currently boots Version 3.0 or later. The DOS 3.x and later boot sectors are compatible, but 3.x boot sectors do not support 4.x partitions larger than 32M.

Note that the system file names are stored in the DOS volume boot sector, and these names must occupy the first and second entries in the root directory as system files. Therefore, a DOS volume boot sector from Phoenix DOS 4.01 is incompatible with a DOS volume boot sector from IBM DOS 4.01 due to differences in the system file names.

Chapters 9 and 10 examine how to use the volume boot sector creation/update feature of the SYS command to restore a volume boot sector that has been corrupted.

The Command Processor (COMMAND.COM)

The DOS command processor, COMMAND.COM, is the interactive part of DOS. The user interface program (the shell) is stored in COMMAND.COM. This part of DOS gives you the DOS prompt and communicates with you.

Although commands can be categorized by function, IBM categorizes the commands by how they are made available: either *resident* or *transient*. (These commands also are referred to as *internal* or *external*.) When you look up the definition of a command in the DOS manual, the manual identifies whether the command is resident (internal) or transient (external). These two types of commands are examined in this section. This section also discusses the DOS command file search procedure, which determines how to act on commands that are typed at the DOS prompt. Finally, this section shows where DOS resides in the computer's memory.

Resident Commands

Resident commands, built into COMMAND.COM, are available any time at the DOS prompt. Resident commands include simple, frequently used commands such as CLS and DIR. These commands execute rapidly, because the instructions for them already are loaded into memory (these commands are called resident because they are memory resident).

Transient Commands

Transient commands often are called utilities. These commands are not resident in memory, so the instructions to execute the command must be located on disk. The instructions are loaded into memory for execution only and are overwritten after their use—hence the name transient commands. The majority of DOS commands are transient; otherwise, the memory requirements for DOS would be astronomical. Transient commands are less frequently used than the resident commands and take longer to execute because these commands must be found and loaded before they can be run.

DOS looks in specific places for a transient command's instructions. The instructions that represent the command or program are contained in files on one or more disk drives. The files that contain the instructions have specific extensions to indicate to DOS that these instructions are programs and not normal files. The extensions must be COM (command files), EXE (executable files), or BAT (batch files). The COM and EXE files are machine code programs; BAT files are a series of commands and instructions using the DOS batch facilities. The places where DOS looks for these files can be controlled by the current directory and the PATH command.

File Search Procedure

DOS performs a two- or three-level search for program instructions (the file) on the disks. DOS checks whether the command is resident, and if so, DOS runs the command from the program code already loaded in COMMAND.COM. DOS then looks in the current directory for COM, EXE, and BAT files—in that order. The first file DOS finds is loaded and executed. Next, DOS looks for files—in the same order—in the directories specified in the path setting, which you control. If DOS fails to locate the file of command instructions, you see the error message `Bad command or filename`. This message may be misleading, because the file is probably missing from the search areas—not "bad" in any way.

Suppose that you enter the command *xyz* at the DOS prompt and press Enter. You now have sent DOS on a search for the XYZ program's instructions. If the search succeeds, the program begins running in seconds. If DOS cannot find the instructions, DOS returns an error message. In this example, DOS performs the following steps:

1. DOS checks to see whether the XYZ command is one of the resident commands. This command is not resident, so DOS finds nothing.

2. DOS looks in the current directory on the current drive for files named XYZ.COM, XYZ.EXE, or XYZ.BAT—in that order. Again, DOS fails to find the file.

3. DOS checks whether a path has been specified. If not, the search ends. Because, in this example, you do have a path specified when your system starts, DOS checks every directory listed in the path for the files XYZ.COM, XYZ.EXE, or XYZ.BAT—in that order within each directory. Your PATH statement lists several directories, but DOS cannot find the files in any of them. At this point, the search ends, and DOS displays the message `Bad command or filename`.

For a successful search, you must ensure that the desired program or command file is in the current directory on the current drive or set your path to point to the program's drive and directory. The common practice is to put all of your simple command files or utility programs in a directory and point the PATH statement to it. The resulting effect is that these programs (commands) are available, just like resident commands. Thus, if you attempt to run a program (such as a transient DOS command) and get the message `Bad command or filename`, you should check your path specification to see whether it includes a path to the directory that contains the command.

This practice works well for most single-load programs, such as commands and other utilities. Major applications software, which can consist of many individual files, may have problems with this practice. When the applications look for the overlay and accessory files, the DOS PATH setting has no effect.

On a hard disk system, install your transient commands and utilities in subdirectories and ensure that the path points to those directories. Major applications can be called through batch files. Sometimes, programs can "force feed" a path type of setting to the programs, making the applications believe that files are present even when they are in some other directory. The best utility for this purpose is the APPEND command, found in DOS 3.3 and later versions. For example, to enable an application to open files in a directory named D:\DATA as if it is the current directory, use the command

APPEND D:\DATA

Then, when the application is prompted to access a file, the application searches the current directory and the D:\DATA directory for the file.

You can short-circuit the DOS command search procedure by entering the complete path to the file at the command prompt. Instead of entering *chkdsk* at the DOS prompt, for example, you can enter the complete path:

C:\DOS\CHKDSK

This command immediately locates and loads the CHKDSK program, without searching through the current directory or path setting. Typing paths is a good way to speed up the loading and execution of a program—especially batch file execution.

Locations of COMMAND.COM

When COMMAND.COM is loaded into memory by IBMBIO.COM, COMMAND.COM is loaded in two places. The core resident portion of COMMAND.COM is loaded into low memory right after IBMBIO.COM, IBMDOS.COM, and device drivers—usually within the first 128K of memory. This core portion of COMMAND.COM is fairly small—usually less than 7K—depending on the DOS version. The remainder of COMMAND.COM, 30K or more, is loaded in the high end of regular memory, up against the 640K barrier.

Figure 5.5 shows the memory locations occupied by the resident and transient portions of COMMAND.COM in my PS/2 Model 70, which runs DOS 4.01. Figure 5.5 uses the following symbols:

- d = IBMBIO.COM, IBMDOS.COM, and device drivers
- R = Resident portion of COMMAND.COM
- . = Empty memory
- T = Transient portion of COMMAND.COM
- X = PS/2 extended BIOS data area (for mouse)
- v = Video RAM

- a = Adapter board ROM
- r = Motherboard ROM BIOS
- b = IBM cassette BASIC

```
     :0--1---2---3---4---5---6---7---8---9---A---B---C---D---E---F---
00000:dddddddddddddddddddddddddddddddddddddddddddddddddddddddddddddddd
10000:dddddddddddddddRRRRRR...........................................
20000:................................................................
30000:................................................................
40000:................................................................
50000:................................................................
60000:................................................................
70000:................................................................
80000:................................................................
90000:....................................TTTTTTTTTTTTTTTTTTTTTTTTTTTX
A0000:vvvvvvvvvvvvvvvvvvvvvvvvvvvvvvvvvvvvvvvvvvvvvvvvvvvvvvvvvvvvvvvv
B0000:vvvvvvvvvvvvvvvvvvvvvvvvvvvvvvvvvvvvvvvvvvvvvvvvvvvvvvvvvvvvvvvv
C0000:aaaaaaaaaaaaaaaaaaaaaaaaaaaaaaaaaaaaaaaaaaaaaaaaaaaaaaaaaaaaaaaa
D0000:aaaaaaaaaaaaaaaaaaaaaaaaaaaaaaaaaaaaaaaaaaaaaaaaaaaaaaaaaaaaaaaa
E0000:rrrrrrrrrrrrrrrrrrrrrrrrrrrrrrrrrrrrrrrrrrrrrrrrrrrrrrrrrrrrrrrr
F0000:rrrrrrrrrrrrrrrrrrrrrrrrbbbbbbbbbbbbbbbbbbbbbbbbbbbbbbbbrrrrrrrr
```

Fig. 5.5. *DOS memory map showing location of resident and transient portions of COMMAND.COM.*

Note that the resident part of COMMAND.COM occupies about 6K and resides about 80K from the beginning of memory. The transient part occupies about 27K and resides about 612K from the beginning of memory. Because I am using a PS/2 system, a 1K extended BIOS data area is located at 640K, which leaves 639K for DOS (the PS/2 BIOS needs this 1K for mouse control).

When certain applications load, they overwrite the transient portion of COMMAND.COM, freeing this memory to be used by the applications for whatever it wants. When the applications are terminated, the resident part of COMMAND.COM checks whether the transient part has been overwritten. If so, the resident part reloads COMMAND.COM from disk using the file name indicated by the environment variable COMSPEC. If the required file cannot be found or loaded, the following error message is displayed:

```
Insert Disk with \COMMAND.COM in drive A
Press any key to continue . . .
```

This error probably occurs because the user booted from drive A, changed to drive C, and ran applications that overwrote the transient portion of COMMAND.COM. To solve this problem, set the COMSPEC variable to something like C:\COMMAND.COM so the file is reloaded from the hard disk rather than the floppy.

> ***Warning:*** If you set COMSPEC to point to a nonremovable drive that doesn't contain the file, the system hangs (it asks you to insert a disk with the proper file—which is impossible).

Tracing the Boot Process

The term *boot* describes the method by which the PC becomes operational. Just as you pull on a large boot by the small strap attached to the back, you can load a large operating system program by first loading a small program—a *bootstrap program*—which pulls in the operating system. A chain of events begins with the applications of power and ends with a running operating system and software. Each event initiates the next event.

Tracing the system boot process can tell you the location of a problem. If you see an error message that is displayed only by a certain program, you know that program was loaded. Combine this information with the knowledge of the boot sequence, and you can tell how far your system has progressed. Look at files or disk areas that were being accessed during the failure in the boot process.

The error messages are tough to decipher at times, but the first step to decoding the error message is to know which program actually sent the message. The following programs can display error messages during the boot process:

- Motherboard ROM BIOS
- Adapter card ROM BIOS extensions
- Master partition boot sector
- DOS volume boot sector
- System files (IBMBIO.COM and IBMDOS.COM)
- Device drivers (loaded through CONFIG.SYS)
- Shell program (COMMAND.COM)
- Programs run by AUTOEXEC.BAT

This section examines the system start sequence and many error messages that occur during this process.

The following steps take you through a typical system start-up. If you have a problem with your system during start-up and you can determine where in this sequence of events your system has stalled, you may be able to eliminate some areas as a cause of the problem.

> ***Note:*** The following steps mention where in memory certain information needed during start-up is located, such as the memory address FFFF:0000 for the ROM BIOS code. You may need to know what data is at a specific location to diagnose problems.

1. You apply power by turning on the switch.
2. The power supply performs a self-test. When all voltages and current levels are acceptable, the supply sends the power-good signal to the motherboard, indicating stable power. The duration between switch on and power good is normally from 0.1 to 0.5 second.
3. The microprocessor timer chip receives the power-good signal, which causes it to stop resetting the microprocessor.
4. The microprocessor begins executing the ROM BIOS code, starting at memory address FFFF:0000.
5. The ROM BIOS tests the central hardware to verify basic system functionality. Any errors that occur at this time are indicated through audio codes, because the video system has not been initialized yet. Audio codes that may occur during the boot process follow:

Audio Code	*Probable Fault Domain*
No beep	Power supply
Continuous beep	Power supply
Repeating short beeps	Power supply
1 long and 1 short beep	Motherboard
1 long and 2 short beeps	Video adapter card
1 short beep and bad or no display	Video cable and/or display
1 short beep and no boot	Disk cable, adapter, or drive

6. The BIOS scans for video adapter ROM programs contained on a video adapter card in a slot. Memory locations from C000:0000 through C780:0000 are scanned for a video adapter ROM BIOS.

   If a video ROM is found, it is tested by a checksum procedure. If the video ROM passes the checksum test, then the ROM is executed. The video ROM code initializes the video adapter, and a cursor appears on-screen.

   If the video ROM is found, but the checksum test fails, this message appears:

   ```
   C000 ROM Error
   ```

   This message usually indicates a bad video adapter, and you must replace the adapter to correct the problem.

   If no video adapter ROM is located, the motherboard ROM video drivers are used. The video display hardware is initialized, and a cursor appears on-screen.

7. The motherboard ROM BIOS scans locations C800:0000 through DF80:0000 in 2K increments for any other ROMs located on any other adapter cards. If any ROMs are found, they are checksum tested and executed. These adapter ROMs can alter existing BIOS routines and establish new ones.

   A failure of the checksum test for any of these ROM modules causes this message to appear:

   ```
   XXXX ROM Error
   ```

   The address *XXXX* indicates the segment address of the failed ROM module. In this case, you should have a technician replace the bad ROM or replace the motherboard.

8. The ROM BIOS checks the value at memory location 0000:0472 to see whether this start should be a cold or warm start. A value of 1234h in this location indicates a warm start, which skips the memory test portion of the power-on self test (POST). Any other value in this location indicates a cold start and full POST.

9. The ROM BIOS performs the POST. Any errors found during the POST procedures are reported by audio codes and on-screen messages. A single beep indicates a successful POST.

10. The ROM BIOS searches for a DOS volume boot sector at cylinder 0, head 0, sector 1 (the very first sector) on drive A. This sector is loaded into memory at 0000:7C00 and tested.

If the sector cannot be read or no disk is present, the BIOS continues with the next step.

If the first byte of the DOS volume boot sector loaded from the disk in drive A is less than 06h or if the first nine values contain the same data pattern, the following error message appears and the system stops:

```
602-Diskette Boot Record Error
```

If the disk was formatted or SYSed by DOS 3.3 or an earlier version and the specified system files are not the first two files in the directory, the following message appears:

```
Non-System disk or disk error

Replace and strike any key when ready
```

If the disk was formatted or SYSed by DOS 3.3 or an earlier version and the boot sector is corrupted, you may see the following message:

```
Disk Boot failure
```

If the disk was formatted or SYSed by DOS 4.0 or a later version and the specified system files are not the first two files in the directory or the boot sector is corrupted, the following message appears:

```
Non-System disk or disk error

Replace and press any key when ready
```

In all of these cases, you must replace the boot disk with one containing DOS or correct the current disk and retry the boot.

11. If no DOS volume boot sector can be read from drive A, the BIOS looks for a master partition boot sector at cylinder 0, head 0, sector 1 (the first sector) of the first fixed disk.

    If found, this sector is loaded into memory address 0000:7C00 and tested for a signature. A *signature* is an identifier in the boot record that tells DOS the kind of disk being read. If the last two (signature) bytes of the master partition boot sector are not equal to 55AAh (which is the code placed on a disk to signify that it is bootable), software interrupt 18 tells the computer that this disk is not bootable.

    On an IBM system, this error invokes the cassette BASIC interpreter in ROM BIOS. But, on a non-IBM-compatible system, a message indicates some type of boot error. For example, systems with the Phoenix AT ROM BIOS display the following message:

```
No boot device available -
Strike F1 to retry boot, F2 for setup utility
```

12. The master partition boot sector program searches its partition table for an entry with a system-indicator byte indicating an extended partition. If one is found, the extended partition boot sector at the location indicated by the entry is loaded. The disk's boot sector also has a table that is searched for another extended partition. If another extended partition entry is found, then that extended partition boot sector is loaded from the location indicated, and the search continues until no more extended partitions are indicated or the maximum number of 24 total partitions has been reached.

13. The master partition boot sector searches its partition table for a boot-indicator byte marking an active (bootable) partition.

    If no partition is marked active, cassette BASIC is invoked on an IBM system (some type of disk error message is displayed on most IBM compatibles).

    If any of the boot indicators in the master partition boot record table are invalid or if more than one indicates an active partition, the following message is displayed and the system stops:

    ```
    Invalid partition table
    ```

14. If an active partition is found in the master partition boot sector, the volume boot sector from the active partition is loaded and tested.

    If the DOS volume boot sector cannot be read from the active partition within five retries (due to read errors), the following message appears and the system stops:

    ```
    Error loading operating system
    ```

    The hard disk DOS volume boot sector is tested for a signature. If the DOS volume boot sector does not contain 55AAh as the last two bytes in the sector, the following message appears and the system stops:

    ```
    Missing operating system
    ```

If either of these errors occurs, boot from a floppy disk and back up as much as possible from the hard disk. Then perform a low-level format on the hard disk, run the FDISK program, and reformat the disk with a high-level format. If this procedure does not solve the problem, the disk needs to be scrapped or sent to a qualified technician for repair.

15. The volume boot sector executes as a program. This program checks the root directory to ensure that the first two files are IBMBIO.COM and IBMDOS.COM. If present, these two files are loaded.

    If the disk was formatted or SYSed by DOS 3.3 or an earlier version and the specified system files are not the first two files in the directory, the following message appears:

    ```
    Non-System disk or disk error
    Replace and strike any key when ready
    ```

    If the disk was formatted or SYSed by DOS 3.3 or an earlier version and the boot sector is corrupted, you may see the following message:

    ```
    Disk Boot failure
    ```

    If the disk was formatted or SYSed by DOS 4.0 or a later version and the specified system files are not the first two files in the directory or the boot sector is corrupted, the following message appears:

    ```
    Non-System disk or disk error
    Replace and strike any key when ready
    ```

    To correct these problems, reboot the computer from a floppy. Then use the SYS command to reload the system to the hard disk. Also, copy a fresh copy of COMMAND.COM to the root directory. Then reattempt booting from the hard drive.

16. The DOS volume boot sector executes IBMBIO.COM. The initialization code in IBMBIO.COM copies itself into the highest region of contiguous DOS memory and transfers control to the copy. The initialization code copy relocates DOS over the portion of IBMBIO.COM in low memory (overwrites IBMBIO.COM), which contains the initialization code, because it is no longer necessary.

17. The initialization code executes IBMDOS, which initializes the base device drivers, determines equipment status, resets the disk system,

resets and initializes attached devices, and sets the system default parameters. The full DOS filing system now is active. Then the IBMBIO initialization code is given back control.

18. The initialization code reads CONFIG.SYS several times. During the first read, statements except for DEVICE, INSTALL, and SHELL are read and processed in a predetermined order. In other words, the order in which statements other than DEVICE, INSTALL, and SHELL appear in CONFIG.SYS is meaningless. During the second read, DEVICE statements are processed in order, and any device driver files named are loaded and executed. During the third read, INSTALL statements are processed in order, and the programs named are loaded and executed. During the fourth read, the SHELL statement is processed, loading the specified command processor with the specified parameters. If no SHELL statement is located, the default COMMAND.COM processor is loaded with default parameters. Loading the command processor overwrites the initialization code in memory.

19. If AUTOEXEC.BAT is present, COMMAND.COM loads and runs AUTOEXEC.BAT. Otherwise, COMMAND executes the internal DATE and TIME commands, displays a copyright message, and displays the DOS prompt.

20. The commands contained in AUTOEXEC.BAT are executed, and when these commands are completed, the DOS prompt finally appears.

Some minor deviations exist for this scenario. Other ROM programs in adapters may introduce such variations, for example, but the preceding steps list the chain of events that the computer follows. Depending on the ROM BIOS programs involved, some error messages and sequences may vary from this presentation.

By altering the CONFIG.SYS and AUTOEXEC.BAT files, you can change the configuration of DOS and permit special start-up programs to execute every time the system starts. For example, the CONFIG.SYS file often contains the FILES= and BUFFERS= commands. The default setting for FILES= is 8, which means that the system can open and access eight files at one time. Some programs (such as dBASE) require more files. Thus, if you place the command FILES=25 in CONFIG.SYS, you change the system settings so that 25 files can be opened at one time.

In the same way, the BUFFERS= command controls the number of buffers that DOS uses to hold data during read and write operations. The command BUFFERS=25 sets the number of buffers to 25. The default number of buffers for DOS depends on your system's RAM. For systems with 512K or more of RAM, the default is 15.

The AUTOEXEC.BAT file often is used for beginning programs that you want to run each time the computer is booted. AUTOEXEC.BAT also often contains DOS commands such as PATH and PROMPT. For example, the PATH command

```
PATH C:\;C:\DOS;C:\NORTON
```

sets up the system path to look in the root directory (C:\), the DOS directory (C:\DOS), and the NORTON directory (C:\NORTON) for commands that you enter at the DOS prompt if the command file (program) is not in the current directory.

You use the PROMPT command to customize the DOS prompt. The most commonly used version is

```
PROMPT $P$G
```

which causes the DOS prompt to display the current directory as a part of the prompt.

Chapter Summary

In this chapter, you examined the structure of DOS, especially as it relates to your system and disks. This information helps you understand the principles and procedures behind data recovery operations.

You now know the components of DOS, especially the system files and command processor components, which form the kernel of DOS. The boot process was explained to provide information that helps determine what went wrong when a boot failure occurs.

6

DOS Versions

The disk operating system (DOS) manages the functions of the computer. If DOS has a problem, your computer does not operate properly. This chapter examines the variety of DOS versions that exist and the problems and features of each version. This chapter also explains how to ensure that your copy of a particular DOS version contains all known bug fixes.

Examining How Versions of DOS Differ

Most people know nothing more than the number of the DOS version they use. However, each DOS version has the following identifying features or aspects:

- Original equipment manufacturer (OEM)
- Version number
- Revision level (corrective service level or SYSLEVEL)

The original equipment manufacturer (OEM) is the manufacturer who produced the DOS. Knowing this piece of information is important. The version number indicates the particular version of the OEM's DOS. The revision level indicates a subversion of a DOS version with patches or bug fixes.

If someone asks you which DOS you use, the correct answer should include the preceding information. For example, COMPAQ DOS 3.31 Revision B and Phoenix DOS 4.01 are accurate descriptions of specific DOS systems. Responding that you use MS-DOS 3.3 is technically correct but not very specific. IBM, COMPAQ, and Zenith all have versions of MS-DOS. Saying that you use MS-DOS is like saying that you drive a General Motors automobile; the statement is correct, but it's not specific. The reason you should be more specific is that the various OEM versions of MS-DOS differ, and these differences may have an impact on what the DOS can or cannot do.

OEM DOS Versions

DOS is produced under a joint development agreement between IBM and Microsoft. This agreement covers DOS 3.3 and later versions and OS/2. Under this agreement, IBM and Microsoft are coauthors of DOS and OS/2, and Microsoft retains ownership.

After IBM and Microsoft jointly complete the product, IBM releases its OEM version and Microsoft then begins to license the code to all the other OEMs. Microsoft provides a binary adaptation kit (BAK) to each OEM who enters a license agreement with Microsoft for DOS. The OEM uses this kit to modify the DOS code and produce a custom version and custom documentation. The DOS is changed to support any quirks or enhancements found in systems relative to one of IBM's systems. The licensee and producer of a custom MS-DOS version then writes the manuals, copies the disks, packages the product, and puts its name on the product—Zenith MS-DOS, for example.

The interaction between a computer and its operating system is complex; the DOS you use should be made by the same manufacturer that made your computer hardware. Using a different OEM version of DOS can cause myriad problems due to incompatibilities. For IBM equipment, use IBM DOS. For COMPAQ computers, use COMPAQ DOS. For AT&T systems, use AT&T DOS.

Each version has minor differences. Examples of differences among different OEM versions of MS-DOS include the following:

- *BASIC.* When you receive DOS from IBM, a BASIC interpreter is supplied and can be loaded by either the BASIC or BASICA commands. About half of the BASIC interpreter code in IBM systems is contained in the motherboard ROM. (No other company places BASIC in ROM.) This interpreter as it exists on the DOS disk is an incomplete program and needs to link with the remainder of BASIC in the IBM ROM to function as a whole. Therefore, IBM BASIC or BASICA runs only on an IBM computer. Consequently, to run BASIC on an IBM clone, you need to get a version of BASIC from the OEM DOS designed for that system. Most of the time, the OEM provides the standard Microsoft version, called GWBASIC.

- *Display*. Some compatibles use display hardware that is different from IBM's. For example, the COMPAQ CGA-compatible display adapter is better than IBM's CGA in most respects, including scrolling speed. Therefore, COMPAQ adjusted its DOS to enable faster scrolling of the screen. If you use IBM DOS on a COMPAQ, the screen operates perfectly but at the slower IBM scrolling speed. If you use COMPAQ DOS on an IBM with a CGA card, the screen scrolls faster than the card can handle and you see a *chromablizzard* of snow as the screen scrolls. Other OEMs include additional EGA or VGA drivers with their versions of DOS to support nonstandard EGA and VGA hardware in their systems.

- *Clock*. The PC AT has a battery-operated CMOS clock that DOS uses to set the system time when the computer is started up. Non-IBM computers may have clocks that are addressed by a different means in the system, and their clocks usually are not recognized correctly without the proper OEM version of DOS. Many AT&T computers have this problem and must use the AT&T version of DOS for proper clock operation.

- *Backup*. Many computers are available with a manufacturer-installed tape backup system as an option. The software to operate this system usually comes with the manufacturer's custom version of MS-DOS. Also, many OEMs have customized their floppy backup programs, which are incompatible with the RESTORE program from any other OEM version of DOS.

- *Mode*. Some computer systems offer additional features, such as speed switching control. With a COMPAQ system, for example, you can use the MODE command from COMPAQ DOS to change the operating speed of the system. Using the wrong OEM version of DOS disables this feature or causes unexpected results if you're invoking a feature supported by the DOS version but not by the hardware.

For 100 percent IBM-compatible computers (some "compatibles," such as many Zenith models, are only partially compatible), you can use the IBM version of DOS. You should note, however, that the BASIC or BASICA interpreters do not work. On COMPAQ computers, you can run IBM DOS and use the BASIC interpreter and ANSI screen drivers from a COMPAQ DOS disk. However, this procedure is not advisable. The best situation is to use the correct OEM DOS for a particular system.

IBM DOS is the best choice if you have a true IBM-compatible computer. IBM provides excellent documentation for its DOS, and IBM DOS enables you to configure all your systems in the same way, even if they are different brands. You should avoid purchasing a system that is not hardware compatible enough with IBM to run unmodified IBM DOS and IBM OS/2. COMPAQ and all other compatible manufacturers get the latest version of DOS or OS/2 much later than IBM, or they may not have all the latest corrections in their DOS to match the latest IBM corrective service disk (CSD) level. When you want the new features of the latest DOS, your only choice is IBM.

Generic DOS Versions

Although you usually can run the IBM version of DOS on a true compatible, a generic version of DOS is sold with many compatible systems. Microsoft produces a generic DOS, but Microsoft has placed restrictions on its distribution. Microsoft states that DOS is not—and never has been—a retail product and that DOS should not be sold over the counter. DOS needs to be tested on each system on which DOS is to run, and this testing is the responsibility of the system manufacturer. Because of the variety and complexity of differences among various manufacturers' systems, Microsoft cannot be responsible for a given MS-DOS implementation working on a particular brand of computer. Therefore, the only authorized channels for distribution of DOS are the computer manufacturers themselves. But what about this generic version?

Until DOS Version 3.2, Microsoft only licensed DOS to other companies to customize and sell with their hardware. These companies created their own packaging and manuals, and they sold DOS as they desired. Thus, no generic version of DOS existed prior to Version 3.2. Only custom OEM versions existed.

With DOS 3.2 and later versions, Microsoft adopted a new policy. Small-business manufacturers whose resources preclude licensing and creating a custom version can buy prepackaged, finished versions of MS-DOS (called the Microsoft MS-DOS Packaged Product) that they can sell with their hardware. This version is designed to run on IBM hardware. Computer manufacturers who are interested in licensing this version should ensure that their hardware is IBM compatible to the extent that this DOS runs correctly. One of the provisions of the contract to license this Packaged Product version is that this DOS only can be sold with one of the manufacturer's computers—never by itself. Most computers built by small-business manufacturers use this version of DOS.

You easily can identify the Microsoft Packaged Product (or generic) Version 3.3 or later by specific markings on the box. In the upper left corner of the gray box, a circle contains the words "Not for retail sale except with a computer system." In the middle of the box front, another notice states

> DISTRIBUTION LICENSEE (i.e., the OEM): You must place a label here indicating that this copy of MS-DOS is intended for use only on your computer systems. In addition, the label must provide your customer support telephone number and notice to purchaser that they should call this number for support. PURCHASER: Do not accept this product if this notice is visible.

Although Microsoft states that the Packaged Product version of DOS must not be sold without a computer, many clone makers violate their contracts with Microsoft. A large gray market for this generic version of DOS exists. This version of DOS is not a problem as long as it works correctly on your system. If this version does not work properly, however, you may have problems getting any support. Some people who want to upgrade their old DOS versions on clone computers purchase generic DOS, particularly if the clone manufacturer is out of business.

Recently, Microsoft changed its support policies for DOS. Microsoft now offers fee-based technical support to all MS-DOS users in the United States. This new support applies to all OEM versions of MS-DOS. Because Microsoft licenses MS-DOS only to OEMs rather than end users, product support previously has been the responsibility of the individual OEM. Under the new plan, OEMs continue to serve as the primary source of MS-DOS support for their customers, and Microsoft provides supplementary support. The kinds of support you may need from Microsoft include information about the quirks of a particular DOS version or information on fixes to bugs in DOS.

Microsoft offers its support service through a 900 number at a cost of $2 per minute. Customers are not charged until they reach a technician. The 900 service operates from 8 a.m. to 5 p.m. PST, Monday through Friday (excluding holidays). The service number is 1-900-896-9000.

As a side note, Microsoft does have a large problem with piracy and counterfeiting of DOS. This piracy extends to the entire DOS package—not just copies of disks. These copies are produced without any license from Microsoft, and they are illegal, although the copies come in packaging that makes them look official. You can identify the counterfeit copies of MS-DOS by looking for a nine-digit registration number stamped on the label. Bona-fide copies of MS-DOS have this number; fake copies usually do not.

If you suspect a fake, call Microsoft and the company will help you determine whether your copy is real. Fake versions of DOS may be more susceptible to carrying a virus because the bogus manufacturer is not as careful in the reproduction of the disks. Also, a fake version is probably not the latest release of a particular version. Finally, continuing to use a known illegal version may make you or your company legally vulnerable.

No generic version of OS/2 is available from Microsoft. Microsoft produces an OS/2 software development kit (SDK) that is available for $2,600. This kit contains a beta test copy of the newest OS/2 Version 2.x. This version is only for software developers who want to get a jump on program development with the new OS/2 version and does not constitute a normally available release. You only can purchase OS/2 by buying an OEM version from a hardware vendor. IBM, COMPAQ, Zenith, AST, and Tandy, along with other major hardware manufacturers, all have their own OS/2 versions. Like DOS, these versions are customized to the hardware on which they are sold to run.

Because on a standard AT system OS/2 bypasses the motherboard ROM BIOS, OS/2 can be very hardware specific. OS/2 loads a protected mode BIOS from disk. For the IBM version of OS/2 to work on a compatible, the system hardware must be extremely like the original AT. Although many compatibles and clones do run the IBM version of OS/2, few guarantees are made as to compatibility. Never purchase a compatible system unless the manufacturer provides a custom OEM version of OS/2 or guarantees in writing that the IBM release works with no problems.

Reviewing the History of DOS

Many different DOS versions exist, and many more versions will be created. DOS 5.0 is the current version. This section examines the differences among the available versions of DOS. This information will help you make a decision as to which DOS version to use, as well as whether to upgrade an existing version.

When buying DOS, your choice is limited to Version 4.01 or 5.0 because these two versions are the only ones currently being sold and supported by IBM. However, millions of computers still in existence use obsolete versions of DOS. Because different versions affect the way you handle data recovery problems, this section provides you with information about all the DOS versions—not just versions currently being sold.

DOS 1.0

Version 1.0 appeared in 1981 when the IBM PC was introduced. This DOS was named the IBM *Personal Computer Disk Operating System*, or *PC DOS*. PC DOS was the standard operating system for the PC and cost less than $60. This operating system only supported single-sided disk drives with a capacity of 160K. PC DOS had no hard disk support.

When PC DOS 1.0 was introduced, it contained several commands and limited batch processing facilities. Half the commands were internal parts of PC DOS, and the disk utilities were external assembly language programs. The commands in DOS at that time follow:

Command	*Function*
BASIC	Activates BASIC language mode
CHKDSK	Checks disk
COMP	Compares files
COPY	Copies files
DATE	Sets date
DEBUG	Activates DEBUG program
DIR	Runs directory of files
DISKCOMP	Compares disks
DISKCOPY	Copies disks
EDLIN	Activates line editor
ERASE	Erases files
FORMAT	Formats disk
LINK	Links program files
MODE	Sets device parameters
PAUSE	Pauses and waits for you to press Enter
REM	Enables remarks to be made
RENAME	Renames files
SYS	Transfers system
TIME	Sets time
TYPE	Displays contents of file to monitor

DOS 1.0 supported single-sided disks with 40 tracks of 8 sectors per track. Each sector held 512 bytes of information. The total capacity for these disks was 160K. PC DOS also came with interpretive BASIC, a text editor called EDLIN, a linker, a debugger, and a series of BASIC programs. All these programs were sold on one single-sided floppy disk.

DOS 1.1

In 1982, IBM introduced an updated version of PC DOS, called Version 1.1. The major difference between DOS 1.0 and 1.1 is that the latter can operate double-sided disk drives. All of the external and most of the internal commands were rewritten to accommodate double-sided drives. This version of DOS remained available for quite some time. Version 1.1 offered no support for hard disks explicitly, but several manufacturers supplied kits with software patches to DOS that enabled a hard disk to be used. Many different companies offering expansion products for the PC emerged at this time, and many of these products came with software that patched DOS directly. IBM and Microsoft finally introduced a new version that was so changed and improved that it brought all patching to an abrupt halt.

DOS 2.0

In 1983, IBM and Microsoft introduced the PC XT and, with it, PC DOS 2.0. Most applications will run with DOS 2.0 or a later version, so many people still use this version of DOS. DOS 1.1 was rewritten entirely with the hope of evolving into a significant competitor to Bell Laboratories' operating system, UNIX. (Microsoft had been licensed to sell its version of UNIX, called XENIX.) UNIX is an operating system that has a larger number of command options than DOS. Also, UNIX was the first operating system to offer the use of the powerful C programming language.

For DOS to compete against the up-and-coming UNIX rival, DOS needed to be designed so that it could support the C language. The methodology was simple: increase the number of assembly language functions available through PC DOS, via INT 21h, so the C language can be implemented easily on a microcomputer. That is, provide a way to pass information to DOS through an interrupt vector (INT 21h), which would allow the implementation of the C language on the PC—giving the PC access to the kinds of programming power previously available only in UNIX. This setup would make the PC a truly powerful software development system.

In achieving their objective, IBM and Microsoft tripled the size of IBMDOS.COM, IBMBIO.COM, and COMMAND.COM. The new commands available in DOS 2.0 follow:

Command	*Function*
BACKUP	Backs up files
BREAK	Controls Ctrl-Break
BUFFERS	Determines number of disk buffers
CHDIR	Changes directory
CLS	Clears screen
DEVICE	Installs device driver
FILES	Determines number of files that can be opened
GRAPHICS	Enables print screen of graphics
MKDIR	Makes directory
PATH	Sets DOS search path
PRINT	Prints text file to printer
RECOVER	Recovers defective sectors
RESTORE	Restores backed up files
RMDIR	Removes directory
SHELL	Starts secondary processor
TREE	Displays list of directories
VER	Displays DOS version number

The major feature of PC DOS 2.0 was support for the use of a hard disk and a hierarchical file structure in order to support the new PC XT. This file structure enabled the user to create, change, and remove subdirectories. This feature greatly increased the flexibility of the operating system, making it look almost like UNIX.

DOS 2.0 increased the storage capacity of both single- and double-sided drives significantly. 160K drives became 180K drives, and 320K double-sided drives became 360K under the new DOS. This increased capacity was achieved by the addition of another sector onto each track of the disk, from 8 sectors to 9. DOS 2.0 also could read and write any of the older formats, ensuring total downward compatibility.

Another major feature of this DOS version was support for *installable device drivers*. This feature enabled DOS 2.0 to offer support for various hardware and software that could be installed directly into DOS. If the manufacturer of a plotter wanted it to be usable on a PC, for example, the manufacturer wrote a device driver, which interpreted commands from DOS into the language the plotter needed to operate. A good word for describing this feature is *slots*. Physical slots enabled you to plug in expansion products, and software slots enabled you to add support for new devices and programs without patching DOS directly. This feature saved IBM DOS from a great deal of problems because IBM did not have to alter DOS each time a new device became available.

DOS 2.1

In 1983, IBM introduced the PCjr, and with this system came PC DOS 2.1. Version 2.1 corrected some problems found in 2.0 but offered few new features. Bugs found in 2.0's BACKUP and RESTORE commands were fixed, along with other minor bugs in different areas. The only new feature was a reconfiguration that enabled DOS 2.1 to work properly with the half-height disk drives on the new PCjr and the soon-to-be-announced portable PC.

DOS 3.0

In 1984, IBM introduced the PC AT and a new DOS, PC DOS 3.0. DOS 3.0 was rushed to the market primarily to support the new AT. Although Version 3.0 ran on all IBM computers, including the PCjr, Version 3.0 quickly was superseded by DOS 3.1.

DOS 3.0 contained the following major new features: system level support for sharing files, support for the AT's 1.2M, 5 1/4-inch floppy drive (80 cylinders, 15 sectors per track), support for RAM beyond 1M (as a RAM disk only), and several extensions to and bug fixes for DOS 2.1.

The resident size of DOS in RAM increased from about 24K in Version 2.1 to 36K in Version 3.0. The resident size increased further as the GRAPHICS screen dump, background PRINT spooler, and other DOS-resident programs were loaded. The larger size of DOS 3.0 made it less attractive to users with small amounts of RAM and users whose systems had no hard drive.

DOS 3.0 permitted the execution of external commands (files with extensions of EXE, COM, and BAT) without you having to set first a path or change the default directory. DOS 2.x (x stands for all versions of DOS 2) was inconsistent in this regard, enabling data files to be specified completely by path name but failing to permit the execution of the external commands preceded by path name.

Several new commands were added to DOS 3.0, including the following:

ATTRIB marks a file's attribute.

LABEL enables the addition, change, or deletion of a volume label on a disk.

KEYBxx permits selection of alternative keyboards.

VDISK is an installable device driver that enables the creation of one or more RAM drives.

DOS 3.1

At the same time that IBM introduced the PC AT and DOS 3.0, IBM also introduced Version 3.1. The fact that both Versions 3.0 and 3.1 were announced on the same day indicates that Version 3.0 was a release rushed to market simply to get the AT operational. DOS 3.0 had all the problems associated with a rushed release. Version 3.0's sole function was to make the AT operational until IBM could release 3.1.

DOS Version 3.1 provides all the functions contained in DOS 3.0 plus enhancements for support of the IBM PC network hardware and software. DOS 3.1 operates on all IBM personal computers.

Features added from DOS 3.0 include the following:

> Network support enables the addition of the File Server and Print Server package to DOS 3.1. This package is available separately from DOS and requires the IBM PC network hardware. This package enables users to access printers and other devices located on other computers on the IBM network.
>
> Error recovery provides additional error reporting facilities to enhance support in the network environment.
>
> JOIN enables the splicing of directories.
>
> SUBST enables you to substitute a virtual drive name for a path name.
>
> DOS Version 3.1 uses approximately 36K of RAM (the same as DOS 3.0). This amount is an increase over DOS 2.1 and DOS 1.1 (DOS 2.1 was 24K). On some systems, additional memory may be required to permit an applications program to be loaded and run. In general, 96K to 128K is a minimum memory requirement for DOS 3.1 systems.
>
> DOS 3.1 and later versions are required to support the PC network program with the broadband hardware. If the Token Ring hardware is used, Version 3.1 does not work, and Version 3.21 or later versions must be used instead.

DOS 3.2 and 3.21

In 1986, IBM announced DOS Version 3.2. DOS 3.2 provides all the functions contained in the prior version of DOS (3.1) and is a prerequisite for the IBM Token Ring network and the IBM PC Convertible. Version 3.2 contains two new commands—REPLACE and XCOPY—and some modified commands to improve usability.

DOS 3.2 features include the following:

BASIC 3.2 is enhanced to include EGA high-resolution graphics modes and support for the IBM PC network and the IBM Token Ring network via the OPEN statement. The BASIC interpreter program Version 3.2 was shipped with DOS 3.2. The *BASIC Language Reference Manual 3.2* also was created and available separately.

SHELL enables the DOS environment area to be reserved. A new option of the SHELL command enables this area to be expanded to 32K. This expansion enables you to specify more extensive PATH, PROMPT, and SET commands without running out of environment space.

FORMAT now requires you to specify the drive letter; FORMAT no longer uses the current drive as the default. When you're formatting a hard disk, the FORMAT command requires you to specify the volume ID of the disk. A warning message also is displayed, indicating that all data on the hard disk will be lost if you choose to proceed with the formatting.

REPLACE, a new command, replaces all occurrences of a file on a disk. This command is ideal for upgrading old software to new versions, including DOS.

XCOPY, a new command, enables you to copy files in more than one subdirectory. Options enable you to select which files to copy, verify after a write, copy lower level directories even when they're empty, copy files modified after a specified date, and copy archived files only (with or without modifying the archive bit). XCOPY can be performed where the source and target drives are of different densities.

DOS Version 3.2 uses approximately 44K of memory. DOS 3.2 requires a minimum of 96K to 128K of memory.

IBM issued a maintenance release update to DOS 3.2 called 3.21. This new version was available from your dealer free of charge if you had Version 3.2. This upgrade corrected problems with BASIC and the keyboard of the IBM Convertible PC, as well as some other problems. DOS 3.21 was considered a replacement for Version 3.2.

DOS 3.3

In 1987, IBM introduced the IBM PS/2 Models 30, 50, 60, and 80. At the same time, IBM announced DOS Version 3.3, which is required to support these PCs. Shortly thereafter, IBM quit marketing DOS 3.1 and DOS 3.20.

New features include the following:

FASTOPEN is a new terminate-and-stay-resident (TSR) command for installing file name cache support. This command enables files that have been accessed recently to be reopened rapidly and provides fast access to nested files that are opened and closed frequently, such as files shared by multiple users on a PC network.

CALL, a new command, allows for nested batch files. A batch file can call another batch file that can return control to the calling batch file. This com-mand enhances support for applications such as automated test programs.

APPEND, a new command, enables the use of application and data files not contained in the currently active directory. This command enables you to be in one subdirectory and find files in another subdirectory, to eliminate duplication of files or file profiles in each directory.

BACKUP and RESTORE are enhanced to provide greater performance and usability. A disk not previously formatted will be formatted if you use a new /F parameter. The backup mode more efficiently uses the backup media capacity and correctly handles file sharing and record locking. The BACKUP command produces a log file that records each file processed and identifies the disk on which the file resides. The RESTORE command is enhanced to prevent the creation of an unbootable system due to inadvertent restoration of system files.

DATE and TIME (for systems with a CMOS clock) are enhanced so you can set and update the system date and time. Previously, the CMOS clock date and time only could be changed through the SETUP routine on the system diagnostic disk.

ATTRIB is enhanced so you can modify most file attributes for a single file, for selected files in a directory, or for all files at or below a directory level. This command gives you greater control over file access and usage.

MODE is enhanced to provide support for up to four asynchronous communications ports to exploit new hardware capability. This command also enables you to set the asynchronous adapter to 19.2K transmission rates.

SYS is enhanced so you can upgrade previous system release disks with checking to prevent the creation of an unbootable disk.

Batch facility is enhanced to give access to environmental values. This enhancement results in increased flexibility of batch files by enabling appropriate actions to occur based on the content of the environmental area.

Hard disk operation uses the enhanced BIOS support for hard disk drives by enabling data to be accessed by a single operation independent of the number of tracks the data spans. When data, such as clusters, spans tracks on a disk, DOS 3.3 issues a single operation for all tracks, which speeds up input/output for large data file processing on hard disks.

Logical partitioning of hard disks provides access of media greater than 32M by enabling the user to divide large hard disks into logical drives up to 32M, depending on physical space available. This feature provides support for larger hard disks. Each disk volume created as an extended DOS partition can be any size from one cylinder up through 32M.

`Abort, Retry, or Ignore` is enhanced to display only the appropriate action subset of a new prompt, `Abort, Retry, Ignore, or Fail`. A `Fail` return code has been added to aid applications in handling of critical errors.

Support is provided for U.S. English, U.K. English, German, French, Italian, Spanish, Danish, Dutch, Norwegian, Portuguese, and Swedish.

COUNTRY is enhanced to provide more extensive country information to extend national language support. All extended country information is supplied by an external data file (COUNTRY.SYS). The COUNTRY command indicates the location of this file.

KEYB, a new command, provides a single keyboard driver routine for all keyboards supported in DOS (17) instead of individual drivers (KEYBXX) for each keyboard supported.

NLSFUNC, the new external TSR command, expands DOS 3.3 interrupt function capability to allow for extended country information and code page support.

CHCP, a new command, can initiate code page switching if hardware support is available for this feature. A *code page* is a set of characters and symbols appropriate to a given country. In addition, the MODE command is enhanced to support code pages.

A DOS 3.3 technical reference manual is packaged and sold separately and covers topics for the experienced DOS user, system programmer, and application developer. For DOS Version 3.3, the following programs and associated documentation have been transferred from DOS to the DOS 3.3 technical reference manual: LINKER, EXE2BIN, LIB, VDISK.ASM, and DEBUG.

The DEBUG utility is shipped with DOS 3.3 and with the technical reference manual. A detailed command description for DEBUG is only included in the technical reference manual. DEBUG can be used for displaying, changing, or tracing a program in memory. The DEBUG program also is included on the regular DOS distribution disks; however, the documentation is only included as part of the technical reference manual.

LINKER, the linker program, can be used for combining separately produced object modules into a relocatable load module.

EXE2BIN is used for converting the output of files created by the LINKER (EXE files) to command files (COM).

VDISK.ASM is a file containing the assembler language source code for virtual disk (RAM memory disk) device driver (VDISK.SYS). The assembled object code for VDISK.SYS and instructions for its use are included in the DOS 3.3 package. The VDISK.ASM file is provided on the DOS 3.3 technical reference utilities disk for programmers who want to use it as a model for creating device drivers.

LIB, an additional program, has been added to the DOS 3.3 technical reference utilities disk. This program provides the Library Manager function, which enables programmers to maintain a library of assembled subroutines. Subroutines from this library then can be linked into a program.

The DOS 3.3 product includes the BASIC Interpreter Program Version 3.3. A new BASIC Reference Manual Version 3.30 (6280189) describes BASIC 3.3 and is available separately.

DOS Version 3.3 uses approximately 54K of memory on an IBM AT if loaded with a default configuration. Most of this increase is due to the new default configuration selections in DOS. DOS 3.3 determines a default BUFFERS setting that is much higher than earlier versions of DOS.

If BUFFERS= is not specified in CONFIG.SYS, then the setting is determined as follows:

```
IF memory size > 512K, then                    BUFFERS=15
OR IF memory size > 256K, then                 BUFFERS=10
OR IF memory size > 128K, then                 BUFFERS=5
OR IF any diskette drive > 360K,then           BUFFERS=3
ELSE                                           BUFFERS=2
```

If you have a system with 640K of conventional memory, your default buffer setting is 15. If you have only 128K of memory and are using an XT with two 360K floppies, your default buffer setting is 2. And, if you have an AT with 512K of memory, your default buffer setting is 10. The earlier versions of DOS only set the default buffers to 2 or 3, using the capacity of the largest disk drive as a guide. Because each buffer consumes 528K of memory, a setting of 15 costs about 8K of memory, or 7K more than with any earlier version of DOS.

DOS 3.3 also interrogates the system ROM BIOS to determine what type it is and installs itself differently depending on the version of the ROM BIOS. For example, booting the same DOS 3.3 disk on an XT and AT system results in different amounts of memory being used. The AT system causes about 3K more DOS code to become memory resident. DOS 3.3 requires a minimum of 128K of memory.

Table 6.1 lists the part numbers for DOS 3.3.

Table 6.1
DOS 3.3 Part Numbers

Part Number	*Item*
6280060	DOS 3.3 (3 1/2- and 5 1/4-inch media)
6280059	DOS 3.3 technical reference manual
80X1011	Additional DOS licenses
6280224	Documentation only

DOS 4.0 and 4.01

In 1988, IBM announced DOS Version 4.0. IBM considers this version to be the primary operating system for 8086/8088 microprocessors and to serve as an interim entry-level operating system solution for 80286, 80386, and 80486 systems until they migrate to OS/2. A new user shell provides a front-end menu for interaction with the system. Large hard disk support and integrated expanded memory support also are included in DOS 4.0.

DOS 4.0 is compatible with DOS 3.3 and supports all IBM PS/2s and IBM PCs except the PCjr, AT/370, and XT/370. An upgrade to DOS 4.0 from all prior levels of DOS was initially offered at a reduced charge but has been discontinued.

DOS 4.0 features include the following:

> Large hard disk partition support is provided. The new sector addressing format of 32 bits versus 16 bits removes the limitation of 32M partitions. For compatibility, DOS 4.0 retains the capacity to install on and use currently formatted hard disks. After DOS 4.0 is installed with

larger than 32M partitions, the user cannot boot from DOS 3.3 and read the hard disk. Some applications may be incompatible with the SHARE command, which is automatically installed if any partition is greater than 32M.

A DOS shell is provided as an alternative to the DOS prompt to increase usability. The DOS shell is similar in appearance to the OS/2 Presentation Manager. You can start up and use applications when necessary, access information and data in the file systems, obtain hard copy output, and get help information relevant to the task. You can accomplish these actions by making straightforward selections from menus, using either a mouse or the keyboard. The shell runs in text or graphics mode. Installation of the DOS shell is optional.

DOS 4.0 provides support for the Lotus, Intel, and Microsoft (LIM) Expanded Memory Specification 4.0. Expanded memory is addressed through a combination of an EMS device driver and an IBM hardware adapter capable of expanded memory. The drivers provided function only on adapters compatible with the IBM XMA specification (which is not the same as any other EMS card) or on IBM-compatible 80386-based systems.

For 80286-based systems with an IBM XMA adapter, the driver XMA2EMS.SYS (which is included with DOS 4.0) converts this XMA type of memory into true LIM EMS 4.0 memory. For the 386 systems, an XMA type of adapter is not needed. The XMAEM.SYS driver included with DOS 4.0 can use the 386 memory paging functions to emulate an IBM XMA card. Standard non-IBM EMS types of adapters must continue to use the drivers supplied by the adapter manufacturer. The DOS commands that can take advantage of EMS 4.0 work with any EMS 4.0-compatible board and driver combination. The XMA2EMS.SYS driver converts IBM's own normally incompatible XMA memory into true standard LIM EMS 4.0 memory.

The EMS support in DOS 4.0 is fairly limited. The drivers included with DOS simply enable IBM 386 systems or systems with IBM XMA memory adapters to function as true LIM EMS 4.0. These drivers are not necessary for any non-IBM system or memory adapter, because the drivers for non-IBM systems and memory cards always have been supplied by the system or adapter manufacturers. After you have LIM EMS 4.0 memory regardless of the source, DOS 4.0 only can use expanded memory for the BUFFERS, FASTOPEN, and VDISK functions. Otherwise, EMS memory can be used only by applications programs that comply with the EMS specification, which always has been the case, even with earlier versions of DOS.

Additionally, the early versions of 4.0 were defective in the EMS handling routines of these commands, and many users who tried to use these commands experienced problems. These problems were corrected by the patched 4.01, which was patched again with additional update disks.

Installation is easier. One interesting new feature in DOS 4.0 is in the operation of the SYS command. If files other than the system files are the first two directory entries on a disk, instead of displaying the message `No room for system on destination`, SYS moves the first two entries in the root directory to place IBMBIO.COM and IBMDOS.COM as required. This feature makes upgrading from non-IBM OEM versions of DOS much less difficult.

In video and graphics, DOS 4.0 now supports more than 25 lines of text on Enhanced Graphics Adapter (EGA) and Video Graphics Array (VGA) displays with the appropriate capability. Also the GRAPHICS command has been extended to support the graphics display modes of the EGA, VGA, IBM PS/2 Display Adapter, and IBM PS/2 Display Adapter 8514/A. Graphic print screen support is provided for any IBM PC printer with compatible graphic print modes.

ANSI.SYS has a new /x parameter that enables extended keyboard reassignments and a new /l parameter that tries to enforce the number of lines set through the MODE command—even within an application.

APPEND is enhanced to enable more control of its searching operations.

BACKUP automatically formats the target disk if it is not already formatted.

BUFFERS has new parameters to improve DOS buffer cache support and to utilize buffers in EMS.

CHKDSK displays the volume serial number, if found, and the allocation units in the status report.

COUNTRY provides support for the countries Japan, Korea, the Peoples Republic of China, and Taiwan.

DEBUG provides EMS support. Detailed information is contained in the DOS 4.0 Technical Reference Application Programming product, available separately.

DISPLAY.SYS checks the hardware to select the type of active display, if the display adapter type is omitted.

ERASE or DEL has a new /p parameter that displays each file name and a message to verify that the file is to be deleted.

FASTOPEN has a new /x parameter that enables FASTOPEN to perform its function by using expanded memory, saving space in low memory for applications programs. FASTOPEN now stores file information in memory to enable faster retrieval of recently opened files.

FDISK now uses 80 display columns, accepts disk partition sizes in megabytes or percentages, and displays the volume label and file system for each partition.

FORMAT accepts a new /f:*size* parameter. This feature indicates the size of the disk to format, which makes easier the process of formatting media less than the maximum capacity of a drive.

MEM, a new program, displays the memory configuration of the system. The /debug or /program switches give a detailed description of the memory usage.

MODE is enhanced to enable selection of keyboard typematic rates and lines per screen.

REM is enhanced to enable comments or line spacing in a batch or CONFIG.SYS file.

REPLACE has a new /u parameter. This parameter restricts REPLACE to update only files with a date and time on the source disk more recent than the date and time on the target disk.

TREE displays block graphics and indent at each subdirectory level.

VDISK has a new /x:*size* parameter for using expanded memory using XMA2EMS.

The DOS 4.0 product includes the BASIC Interpreter Program 4.0. The existing *BASIC Reference Version 3.30* (6280189) manual describes BASIC 4.0 and is available separately.

The DOS 4.0 documentation library has been redesigned. *Getting Started with DOS 4.0* assists with the installation process and provides a tutorial on the new DOS 4.0 shell. *Using DOS 4.0* describes how to use DOS 4.0 to complete daily tasks and routines. These two manuals are included with the DOS 4.0 package but do not cover each and every DOS command. World Trade keyboard information is contained in *IBM Keyboard Layouts For Your PC and PS/2* and is available free of charge if you mail the postcard included in the DOS 4.0 package.

A new DOS 4.0 command reference provides detailed command descriptions and is available separately. A new DOS 4.0 *Technical Reference Application Programming* product is also available separately. The manual that comes with the DOS 4.0 package does not always have information about all the DOS commands. You may have to purchase the command reference manual if you want to have the same level of documentation that used to be provided with earlier versions of DOS. The command reference does contain the detailed ANSI.SYS information that was formerly in the technical reference manual only; however, you still may need the technical reference for detailed documentation on the DEBUG command.

A DOS 4.0 technical reference manual is also available separately. This manual provides reference and system architecture information for the experienced user, system programmer, and application developer. The manual assumes that the user is familiar with the 8088/8086, 80286, or 80386 microprocessor architecture. This new product has been updated with DOS 4.0-related topics. As with DOS 3.3, the DOS 4.0 technical reference contains the DEBUG, LINK, EXE2BIN, VDISK.ASM, and LIB programs, as well as documentation for these programs.

DOS now must be purchased separately in 3 1/2-inch and 5 1/4-inch versions. This packaging is a change from DOS 3.3, which included both sizes in a single package.

DOS 4.0 consumes 64K for a default configuration on an AT system, which is an increase of about 11K over DOS 3.3. If you create any disk partitions larger than 32M, DOS also needs to load the SHARE command, which increases memory consumption to 70K for a default configuration on an AT. DOS 4.0 consumes different amounts of memory on different types of systems by evaluating the type of system indicated by the ROM BIOS and installing appropriate routines and drivers. Also, the default configuration settings vary depending on your system's memory and disk sizes. IBM lists 256K as the minimum memory requirement for DOS 4.0 systems.

IBM has released several sets of corrective service disks (CSD) or patch disks for DOS 4.0 that correct various problems with DOS. Only the first of these CSDs was included in an updated release of DOS called 4.01. You can tell whether you have the 4.01 release only by looking at the original DOS disks. In the fine print on the label, you will see either 4.00 or 4.01 as the version. The DOS VER command always reports 4.00 for any version. Because several CSD levels beyond 4.01 exist, to have the latest version of DOS you need to get the current CSD. Also, each CSD release contains all the previous CSDs as well. No matter what version or CSD level you are at now, if you get the latest version, you will be completely up to date. These CSD disks are available free from your IBM dealer.

Table 6.2 lists the part numbers for DOS 4.0.

Table 6.2
DOS 4.0 Part Numbers

Part Number	*Item*
6280256	DOS 4.0 3 1/2-inch media
6280225	DOS 4.0 5 1/4-inch media
6280253	DOS 4.0 command reference
6280254	DOS 4.0 technical reference
6280273	Additional DOS licenses
6280258	User documentation only

DOS 5.0

Although DOS 5.0 contains many features, the amount of memory taken by this version is actually less than Version 4.0. Therefore, applications you are running may handle larger files. DOS 5.0 also incorporates a number of data recovery features. These features are similar to those found in DOS utility programs, such as PC Tools and Norton Utilities. These data recovery features include the capacity to unformat a disk and undelete a file.

For data recovery to be supported in DOS 5.0, an important change was made in the way a floppy disk is formatted. Previously, a DOS format of a floppy disk was a combination of a low-level and high-level format, which meant that information on the disk was overwritten and couldn't be recovered. In DOS 5.0, the format used (by default) on a floppy disk is only a high-level format, where the actual data in files is not overwritten (like the high-level format previously used for hard disks only).

Therefore, you can use the UNFORMAT command to restore the information on the floppy disk after a format. In order to get the most out of the UNFORMAT and UNDELETE commands, you should use the new MIRROR command each time you boot your computer. Doing so saves a duplicate copy of the disk's directory information. Then, when an unformat or undelete is needed, the information in the MIRROR file can assist in making the restoration successful. Normally, you will want to place the MIRROR command in the AUTOEXEC.BAT file so that the MIRROR file is updated each time the computer is booted. If the MIRROR command is not used, the unformat and undelete still may work to some extent, but they will not be as effective.

Changes in DOS 5.0 include the following:

The improved graphical shell can make use of higher resolution screens than the DOS 4.0 shell.

When you use DOS from the command line, you can request help information about DOS commands by typing a command at the DOS prompt followed by a /? switch.

The BASIC language has a new help procedure that you call up by pressing F1.

DOSKEY, a new command, enables you to recall commands that you previously entered. This TSR program causes the computer to remember a certain number of commands you previously entered. You can recall a command with the up-arrow key, the down-arrow key, PgUp, or PgDn, edit the command, and reenter it.

EDIT is a full-screen editor that is a substitute for the old EDLIN line editor. This command enables you to create, edit, save, and print ASCII files.

UNFORMAT enables you to unformat a disk that has been formatted accidentally. This procedure is similar to those used in Norton Utilities and PC Tools.

MIRROR enables you to store an image of important directory and system information, which enables the UNFORMAT command to work.

UNDELETE undeletes deleted files. This procedure is similar to those used in Norton Utilities and PC Tools.

You can sort directory listings by file name, type, time, and size.

You can search for files through multiple levels of directories by using the search option in the DOS shell.

Partitions of up to 2 gigabytes now are possible, as well as more than two hard disks.

DOS 5.0 supports the use of 2.88M 3 1/2-inch floppy disks.

DOS Bugs

Discovering that the software you depend on has some bugs and problems is extremely frustrating. Unfortunately, every version of DOS has had bugs and problems. Some of the problems are never resolved; you simply live with the problem. However, when the problems are severe enough, IBM and Microsoft issue a patch disk that corrects the problems. When you are involved in data recovery or the prevention of problems that can lead to the need for data recovery, you need to keep abreast of DOS problems, how they can cause data problems, and how you can update your DOS versions.

You must keep in touch with your dealer to find out about these patches. Neither IBM nor your dealer will call you. Check in periodically to see whether any patch disks are available. Part of an IBM dealer's job is to distribute these patch disks and fixes to customers at the customer's request. These patches are provided free, except for the media, and are provided on request. You do not have to go back to the dealer where you purchased your DOS. If a dealer does not know about these patches, or will not provide the patches for any reason, have the dealer contact his or her IBM representative. DOS is a warranted product, and these patches are part of the warranty service that a dealer must provide.

To correct minor problems, IBM has released patch disks for virtually all versions of DOS. These patch disks are called corrective service disks, or CSDs. The release of CSDs has been especially noticeable since Version 3.1.

Bugs in DOS 3.3

DOS 3.3 contains several problems. IBM issued several CSDs to correct these problems shortly after introducing DOS 3.3. The bugs that are fixed in the latest version of DOS 3.3 follow:

> The DOS BACKUP command does not work properly when backing up a large number of subdirectories in a given directory.
>
> DOS 3.3 may falsely display an out of paper error message if the printer is slow or has a small input buffer. A bug fix to this problem is the program I17.COM.
>
> DOS 3.3 gives intermittent read failures on 720K original applications software floppy disks on PS/2 Models 50, 60, and 80. You may see `Not Ready Error Reading Drive A` when attempting to install an application. Attempts to perform DIR or COPY commands from the disk also produce the error message.
>
> DOS 3.3 has highly intermittent problems with a floppy drive `Not Ready` or a hard disk `General Failure` message. This problem may be aggravated by certain programming practices that mask off interrupts for long periods of time. An update to DOS 3.3 ensures that interrupts are unmasked on each disk or disk request.

FORMAT fails on multiple 3 1/2-inch disks. The failure appears as a `Track 0 bad or invalid media` message, when you press Y in response to the prompt `Format another (Y/N)?` after you complete the first format. The failure message appears when you attempt to format the second disk. If you boot the system from disk, the format problem does not occur.

If the power to the computer is interrupted or switched on and off quickly on a PS/2, a keyboard error (301) or mouse error (8062) may be displayed. Also, you may see a CMOS checksum/configuration error (162) or a clock-not-updating (163) error. This problem can cause the computer to fail to update the date, causing the computer's system clock to be a day behind.

DOS 3.3 may prompt you to enter a password when you boot, even though no password security has been implemented. Also, you may be told incorrectly that a password already exists when you attempt to install the power-on password function.

Bugs in DOS 4.0 and 4.01

DOS 4.0 has several patches for various problems. As of this writing, IBM has released five patch disks. The disks are released as a CSD package. Each level of CSD always contains all the previous levels of CSD patches. The first CSD issued (UR22624) contained a series of problem fixes that later were incorporated into the standard released version of DOS 4.01. The other CSDs contain many further updates, but currently no commercial packaged release of IBM DOS has incorporated these newer fixes.

Therefore, if you go to an IBM dealer today and purchase DOS 4.01, you get the equivalent of DOS 4.0 plus CSD UR22624. You immediately have to ask the dealer for the current CSD disks to really have the latest release. A responsible dealer automatically includes the latest CSD disks with a DOS purchase. Unfortunately, many dealers do not include these disks; many do not even have the CSDs on hand.

The VER command in any level of DOS 4.x always lists 4.00. This version number has caused much confusion as to which level of CSD fixes is installed on a given system. To eliminate this confusion and allow for the correct identification of installed patches, CSD UR29015 and later levels have introduced a new SYSLEVEL command to DOS 4.x. This command is resident in COMMAND.COM and designed to identify conclusively to the user which level of corrections is installed. With CSD UR31300 installed, the SYSLEVEL command reports the following:

```
DOS Version:    4.00                U.S. Date: 06/17/88
CSD Version: UR31300                U.S. Date: 06/29/90
```

The following CSDs are available for DOS 4.x:

- CSD UR22624 as of 08/15/88 (this CSD equals 4.01)
- CSD UR24270 as of 03/27/89
- CSD UR25066 as of 05/10/89
- CSD UR29015 as of 03/20/90
- CSD UR31300 as of 06/29/90

The following problems are corrected by these CSDs. The latest CSD contains all the previous CSD fixes. The CSD indicated for each problem is the one in which the fix first appeared:

CSD	*Item*	*Problems Addressed or Solved by the CSD*
UR22624	XMA2EMS	PS/2 Model 50Z cannot use DOS 4.00 EMS.
UR22624	APPEND	APPEND /PATH:OFF not working properly.
UR22624	IBMBIO	INT 2Fh for INT 67h causes a hang.
UR22624	SHELLC	SHELL HELP index entries not alphabetic.
UR22624	MODE	MODE overwrites user's application.
UR22624	SELECT	Using Ctrl-Break with SHELL causes a hang.
UR22624	MODE	MODE now allows 19200 baud rate on PS/2 Models 25 and 30.
UR22624	SHELLC	Problem with Shift in SHELLC.
UR22624	SHELLC	Pull-down menu in files gives wrong help.
UR22624	IBMDOS	BUFFERS=XX /X problem (BUFFERS to XMA).
UR22624	SHELLC	Problem with Shift in SHELLC.
UR22624	IBMDOS	Problem in copying large files across a network.

CSD	*Item*	*Problems Addressed or Solved by the CSD*
UR22624	PRINT	First-time PRINT nonexisting file message appears.
UR22624	SHELLC	SHELL doesn't give an error for / or \.
UR22624	SELECT	Listing of printers should be reordered.
UR22624	XMA2EMS	Hang occurs with Token Ring network card in slot 0.
UR22624	SHELLC	SHELL doesn't run after you run compiled BASIC.
UR22624	MODE	MODE not handling translation correctly.
UR22624	SHELLC	SHELL not handling translation correctly.
UR22624	SELECT	Select correct defaults for keyboards.
UR22624	SELECT	SELECT/SHELL translated too big for 256K.
UR22624	SHELL	Corrects PS/2 Model 30 with 8512 error color change.
UR22624	XMA2EMS	You receive unpredictable results using DMA to EMS.
UR24270	CMOSCLK	Date doesn't change at midnight.
UR24270	README	CSD UR22624 documentation unclear.
UR24270	IBMDOS	CHKDSK shows allocation errors with 32M.
UR24270	COMMAND	APPEND /X:ON not working with DIR.
UR24270	BACKUP	BACKUP command cannot find FORMAT with LAN 1.3.
UR24270	IFSFUNC	'freopen()' doesn't work with LAN 1.3.
UR24270	MODE	Wrong number of lines on the display.
UR24270	RESTORE	Files backed up in Version 3.1 not restored.
UR24270	FASTOPEN	Internal stack overflow occurs with CHKDSK /F.
UR24270	FASTOPEN	FASTOPEN /X hangs the system.
UR24270	FASTOPEN	Error occurs in EMS-check.
UR24270	FDISK	32M partition yields only 31M.

CSD	*Item*	*Problems Addressed or Solved by the CSD*
UR24270	SELECT	Wrong partition message appears during SELECT.
UR24270	SHELLC	The SHELL file system is not consistent.
UR24270	COMMAND	Corrects DisplayWrite 4 reloading with LAN 1.3.
UR24270	COMMAND	Batch file causes corrupted work space.
UR24270	IFSFUNC	DOS 4.0 not working with LAN 1.3.
UR24270	IFSFUNC	Problems when printing to a network printer.
UR24270	IFSFUNC	Certain command sequence on network server.
UR24270	ANSI	ANSI doesn't allow use of Shift-PrintScreen.
UR24270	SHELLC	SHELL PSC doesn't accept null variables.
UR24270	XMAEM	IBMCACHE in extended memory hangs Model 70-A21.
UR24270	SHELLC	SHELL Add a Program doesn't accept directory slash.
UR25066	FASTOPEN	FASTOPEN 2nd parameter causes database to abort.
UR25066	IBMDOS	File gets two clusters allocated.
UR25066	IBMBIO	DOS checks for "IBM" for valid boot sector.
UR25066	XMA2EMS	Fixes sort map table problem.
UR25066	IBMBIO	Problem when using /X and page below 640K.
UR25066	XMA2EMS	EMS mapping returns hex 80 from a restore operation.
UR25066	IBMDOS	Implement dynamic EMS page selection.
UR25066	IBMDOS	Fixes look-ahead buffers for file greater than 32M.
UR29015	FASTOPEN	Fixes FASTOPEN and Business Adviser RENAME/RESTORE operations.
UR29015	SHELLC	Adding programs overlays end of disk.

CSD	*Item*	*Problems Addressed or Solved by the CSD*
UR29015	SHELL	File system hangs with maximum program name.
UR29015	SHELL	File system doesn't handle write-protect correctly.
UR29015	SHARE	Multiple FCBs refer to same file.
UR29015	BACKUP	Ctrl-Break doesn't terminate properly.
UR29015	FORMAT	Fixes problem when COMMAND.COM not in boot drive when /S used.
UR29015	MEM	Added MEM command and LIM EMS support.
UR29015	COMMAND	COMMAND.COM became invalid when APPEND changed.
UR29015	IFSFUNC	File locking errors with PCLAN and application.
UR29015	FORMAT	Explicit SHARE load and FORMAT /V error.
UR29015	CMOSCLK	Year end in 00 causes error on some PS/2s.
UR29015	XCOPY	Picks up wrong DBCS character for path.
UR29015	NLSFUNC	Set code/page not clearing DBCS vector.
UR29015	XMA2EMS	Return codes incorrect.
UR29015	MODE	Allows MODE to support 19200 baud.
UR29015	SYS	DOS 4.0 cannot be installed on systems over OS/2 Version 1.2.
UR29015	IBMBIO	DOS 4.0 hangs with more than two hard disks.
UR29015	KEYB	Multiple interrupts may cause abend.
UR29015	KEYB	Keyboard error causes an NL failure.
UR29015	KEYB	Loss of control of SDLC interrupt.
UR29015	FDISK	32M partition yields only 31M in FDISK.
UR29015	KEYB	Lock keys and PS/2 mouse conflict exists.
UR29015	IBMBIO	Device status check returns wrong status.
UR29015	IBMBIO	Buffer /XS doesn't load properly.

CSD	*Item*	*Problems Addressed or Solved by the CSD*
UR29015	SHELL	Copy to/from VDISK not working properly.
UR29015	XCOPY	Hang occurs when downloading S/36 files.
UR29015	XCOPY	Source file deleted when disk is full.
UR29015	IFSFUNC	INT 2F, AX=120A extended error incorrect.
UR29015	IFSFUNC	INT 2F, AX=120B treated as critical error.
UR29015	IBMBIO	DOS 4.01 doesn't accept an ECC error.
UR29015	COMMAND	No way to tell the level of service.
UR29015	FDISK	Doesn't display drives correctly with more than two hard disks.
UR29015	XMA2EMS	Version 4.01 XMA2EMS command fails intermittently.
UR29015	SHELLB	SHELL abends if a lowercase path is entered.
UR29015	SHARE	LOCK violation error occurs when using LOCKs.
UR29015	IBMDOS	IOCTL returns errors for off-line printer.
UR29015	XMAEM	Conflict with UR25066 XMA drivers.
UR29015	SHELLC	SHELL hangs if mouse isn't attached.
UR29015	IFSFUNC	SHARE parameters ignored when using PCLP.
UR29015	FORMAT	FORMAT quits on certain disk defects.
UR29015	XMAEM	Stack alignment error affects performance.
UR29015	FASTOPEN	FASTOPEN fails with WordPerfect 5.0.
UR29015	XMA2EMS	Memory adapters not found in all slots.
UR29015	BACKUP	Cannot BACKUP kanji (Japenese) subdirectory.
UR29015	IBMBIO	Hardware-related stack error occurs.
UR29015	IBMBIO	Disk drives not assigned properly.
UR29015	IBMBIO	Problem occurs when trying to access more than two hard disks.

CSD	*Item*	*Problems Addressed or Solved by the CSD*
UR29015	KEYB	Model 70 keyboard fails when reconnected.
UR31300	KEYB	Bad output occurs from a key press in German.
UR31300	SHARE	Character device driver causes abend.
UR31300	SHELLC	SHELL causes file system warning message.
UR31300	XMA2EMS	You see "overlap has occurred" message with expanded memory.
UR31300	IBMBIO	You cannot see non-HPFS drives when one is HPFS.
UR31300	FDISK	Large message size causes failure in FDISK.
UR31300	FDISK	HPFS not supported correctly in DOS FDISK.
UR31300	IBMDOS	Program loader overlays program data area.
UR31300	XMA2EMS	Hang occurs on installation on Family-1 computers.
UR31300	BACKUP	Abort BACKUP to hardfile deletes \BACKUP files.
UR31300	XMAEM	Hang occurs on device installation on 486 systems.
UR31300	MORE	First line missing with NLS MORE - Germany.
UR31300	XMAEM	INT 15h, FUNC 87h hangs with XMAEM installed.

These CSD disks are only valid for the IBM version of DOS 4.0. Other OEMs may provide patches or corrections in different ways; some OEMs may not even offer these corrections. Because most OEMs release their versions of DOS long after IBM, they have had a chance to incorporate many (but not all) of these fixes in their standard version without having to release any patch disks. Contact your DOS OEM to find out what you need and what you can get in terms of patches.

Integrating Systems Running Different DOS Versions

Integrating systems that run different versions of DOS can be difficult. Usually, a later version of DOS is downwardly compatible with an earlier one, but the later version offers features that the earlier one does not have. This difference in features can be found in many areas. Batch files provides one example. If you write batch files that use many of the new features added in Version 3.3, most of your batch files will not run properly on any earlier version of DOS. Writing different batch files that perform the same functions yet run with different versions of DOS is difficult or impossible if these batch files depend on features only found in the newer versions.

Troubleshooting problems greatly increases if you run different versions of DOS in-house. This increase is because different versions of DOS have different bugs and problems, especially in the areas of supporting peripherals or new types of hardware. Also, various applications can react to these different versions of DOS in different ways, complicating software troubleshooting as well as hardware troubleshooting.

If you are in a support position at an organization, keeping up with the bugs in all DOS versions has to be a nightmare. You may want to encourage your organization to allow the use of only the last two releases of DOS on the organization's computers.

Upgrading DOS

Deciding which DOS version to buy is a simple choice. Barring any special problems, you always should use the latest version of DOS available from your hardware OEM. However, making a decision to upgrade your DOS is not a decision you should make without careful consideration.

When a new major version of DOS is released—from Version 3.3 to 4.0, for example—you should take several precautions before blindly upgrading. Recognize that most new DOS versions have a few minor problems that usually will be corrected with a patch disk a few months after release. Run any new DOS on a test system to see whether the new version has any major problems that may affect you. If you don't see any problems, or a patch disk becomes available, then you can be more comfortable about upgrading your DOS.

You should test all your important applications with the new DOS before upgrading your hard disks to boot the new version. You can do this procedure by booting your own system from a floppy disk formatted with the new DOS. This way you can test the new DOS on your own system without having to copy the new files onto the hard disk. If you determine that everything will be OK, you can proceed with the transfer of the new DOS to your hard disk.

Sometimes a new DOS version causes problems with utility programs. In DOS 4.0, for example, the partitioning system was changed slightly from DOS 3.3 and many hard disk utility programs no longer worked with this new DOS. Of course the producers of these utility programs rapidly upgraded them so that they would support the new partitioning scheme, and then all was well.

If you have a certain utility that is important to you (such as those used in data recovery operations), make sure that the utility works on the newer version of DOS before you upgrade.

DOS is a personal piece of software, and many people resist upgrading because they have become attached to the version they currently use. Also, many people think that "if it isn't broke, don't fix it!" If you are satisfied with everything provided by your version of DOS (or any software for that matter), don't upgrade. However, be sure that you look into the new version to ensure that you're not missing out on features you want.

Contrary to what some people believe, you should never have to reformat a hard disk when upgrading from one version of DOS to another, although valid reasons for reformatting may exist.

You can perform a DOS upgrade in two ways. The first method is done without reformatting the hard disk. This "easy" method is the preferred way to upgrade because it takes fewer than five minutes. The second method, or "hard" method, involves a complete backup and restore operation of all data and program files on the disk. Depending on what media and systems you have in place for backup, this method can take a great deal of time.

You have to use the hard way if you want to take advantage of any special privileges of the newer DOS's disk formatting capabilities. For example, you easily can use a simple procedure to upgrade a hard disk running any version of DOS so that the hard disk boots IBM DOS 4.01. However, if you do not use DOS 4.01 to partition and format the disk, then you cannot take advantage of the more than 32M partition sizes that DOS 4.01 is capable of.

You also may want to reformat a disk when doing a DOS upgrade if doing so will result in a change in the cluster size on the disk. For example, disks greater than or equal to 16M that were formatted by DOS 2.x have an abnormally large cluster size. Also, non-IBM OEM versions of DOS sometimes use larger than necessary cluster sizes on a disk. One example is COMPAQ DOS, which jumps to larger cluster sizes much earlier than IBM DOS. In these cases, you need to repartition the disk by using the new DOS FDISK program and then high-level format the disk with the DOS FORMAT program. This process will enable the new version of DOS to implement the new cluster size properly on the disk.

In cases where you do not want or need to change the partition sizes (or cluster size), then the easy way is the one for you; otherwise, you must use the hard method. Both of these methods—especially the easy method—depend on the SYS and REPLACE commands. Besides the SYS command, which was discussed earlier in this chapter, the only other command required for upgrading from one DOS version to another is the REPLACE command. This command is a specialized form of a copy command designed primarily to examine a set of new files and copy these files over older files that need to be updated. This command also can add files to a disk like a regular copy. REPLACE was designed primarily to be used in upgrading software or files from older versions to newer versions. REPLACE is available in DOS Version 3.2 and later versions.

The syntax of the REPLACE command follows:

REPLACE [*d:*][*path*]*filename* [*d:*][*path*][/A][/P][/R][/S][/U][/W]

[*d:*][*path*]*filename* specifies the name of the file on the source disk that will replace the file on the destination disk.

[*d:*][*path*] specifies the destination drive and directory of the files that are to be replaced.

/A causes REPLACE to copy only the files that do not already exist on the destination disk.

/P causes REPLACE to ask whether you want to replace each file. You are prompted as each file is copied.

/R causes REPLACE to replace the read-only files.

/S causes REPLACE to search all subdirectories on the destination disk for matching files. Matching files found in any subdirectory are replaced. /S and /A cannot be used together.

/U replaces files on the target disk if they are older than those on the source disk. With /U, you can replace files from the source disk that have a newer date/time attribute than those on the target disk. You cannot use /A and /U together.

/W causes REPLACE to wait for you to insert a disk.

Upgrading the Easy Way

The following steps list the easy way to do a DOS version upgrade:

1. Boot the new DOS version from drive A.
2. Transfer the system files to drive C (which is the hard disk you normally boot from) by using the following command:

   SYS C:

3. Replace all transient files on drive C with new versions by using this command:

   REPLACE A:*.* C: /S /R

4. Change the disk in drive A to the second DOS disk and repeat the preceding steps; continue until all DOS floppies have been inserted and then place the boot disk back into drive A.
5. Add any new transient files to the C:\DOS directory with the following command:

   REPLACE A:*.* C:\DOS /A

6. Change the disk in drive A to the second DOS disk and repeat the preceding step; continue until all DOS floppies have been inserted.

When you reboot the system (normally from drive C), the new DOS version is in use. One potential problem for DOS new users is that the SYS and REPLACE commands are themselves transient commands, and they have to be "findable" by DOS in order to run. You must ensure that these commands are either in the current directory or somewhere in your PATH setting for them to be executed.

This easy method upgrades any OEM version of DOS to any later version of DOS from the same OEM. You can use this method on systems from IBM DOS 2.0 to 2.1, 3.0, 3.1, 3.2, 3.3, and 4.0 without ever reformatting or even repartitioning any disks. For DOS versions prior to Version 3.2, you have to substitute the COPY command for the REPLACE command because REPLACE did not exist in DOS Versions 3.1 and earlier. If for some reason you are working with a DOS version earlier than Version 3.2, be sure that you overwrite all the DOS files in all hard disk subdirectories, which REPLACE would do automatically for you.

One assumption is made with these steps—that you will store your DOS program files in a directory called C:\DOS. If you use any other directory for this purpose, change the C:\DOS specification in the procedure to whatever you use. This method ensures that all previous DOS files are overwritten with the new versions.

If you have any problems with the SYS command, you have an abnormality in your installation. You can cause this abnormality by mixing different OEM versions of DOS or by using "funky" driver files to address limitations in DOS's partitioning capabilities. Unfortunately, these problems are the result of a nonstandard setup, and you should proceed to correct the situation accordingly. As a last resort, you can upgrade DOS the hard way.

Upgrading the Hard Way

The hard way to do a DOS version upgrade involves completely backing up and restoring all the files on your disk. This backup is necessary because the disk partition will be removed and recreated with FDISK. The procedure follows:

1. Boot the system from the old DOS.
2. Execute a complete backup by using the method of your choice.
3. Use the old DOS FDISK to remove the DOS partition(s).
4. Boot the new DOS from a floppy disk.
5. Use the new DOS FDISK to create partitions to your liking.
6. Perform a high-level format and install the new DOS system files by using this command:

   ```
   FORMAT C: /S
   ```

7. Reboot the system with the old DOS and—using the same RESTORE.COM (on floppy)—restore all the old floppy files to the hard drive by typing

   ```
   A:RESTORE A:C:
   ```

8. Reboot as usual from the hard drive.

> ***Note:*** If you restore from a version earlier than DOS 3.3, that version will replace the DOS system files on your hard disk. You then must boot with your new DOS from a floppy disk and use the SYS command to replace IBMBIO.COM and IBMDOS.COM and copy COMMAND.COM to the hard disk.

9. Replace all transient files on drive C with new versions by using this command:

   ```
   REPLACE A:\*.* C: /S /R
   ```

10. Change the disk in drive A to the second DOS disk and repeat the preceding step; continue until all DOS floppies have been inserted and then place the boot disk back into drive A.

11. Add any new transient files to the C:\DOS directory by using this command:

    REPLACE A:*.* C:\DOS /A

12. Change the disk in drive A to the second DOS disk and repeat the preceding step; continue until all DOS floppies have been inserted.

Now the system will boot from the hard disk. An assumption in these steps is that you will store your DOS program files in a directory called C:\DOS. If you use any other directory for this purpose, replace C:\DOS with whatever you use. This method ensures that all previous DOS files are overwritten with the new versions.

If you have a proper tape or other specialized backup system, this method will not be too difficult. If you use a backup procedure other than that in DOS 3.3 or a later version, you will have to prevent your particular backup/restore system from restoring the system files. This decision is up to you because the method you choose depends on what you use for backup and restore. If you use the DOS 3.3 or later BACKUP and RESTORE commands, preventing the overwriting of the system files is greatly simplified because RESTORE never can restore the files IBMBIO.COM, IBMDOS.COM, and COMMAND.COM, which eliminates the chance of overwriting these files.

Also, you must use the new DOS's FDISK procedure on the disk in order for any of the newer partitioning capabilities to become available. You also should use the older FDISK to remove the partitions it has created. As an alternative to using the old DOS FDISK to remove the partitions, you can redo the low-level format of the disk, which wipes everything clean. A disadvantage is that the low-level format also wipes clean any other non-DOS partitions. Using the hard method examined earlier in this section, those other non-DOS partitions survive. However, the low-level format remarks the sectors and tracks, which you may want done if your hard disk is a stepper motor type.

Chapter Summary

This chapter covered the differences among the various versions of DOS. You learned that MS-DOS is a general term that can apply to a wide number of specific OEM products on the market. A list of known DOS bugs was presented, along with an explanation of the various patch disks or CSDs that are available for correcting these problems.

This chapter also explained two methods you can use to upgrade a system from one DOS version to another.

The DOS information presented here and in Chapter 5 is important for you to know in order to understand data recovery completely. The next chapter examines the components of a disk from the physical as well as the DOS point of view. Damage to some of the more important areas of a disk can cause many problems with accessing the data and files present on the remainder of the disk. The next chapter focuses on disk structure and format so that recovery of damaged areas will be understood easily.

7

Disk Format and Structure

Storing data is not a perfect process, which is why data recovery is necessary. Information is susceptible to loss of magnetic signals on disk or accidental overwriting of information by a program. Many times when data is "lost" on disk, the data itself is intact, but the address information that tells DOS where to find the data has been corrupted. In other words, DOS cannot find the data. If you correct the address information, then the data will be usable again.

Data recovery procedures often involve the correction of address information on disk. The data recovery technician must probe the disk for the location of the problem and correct it—often by transplanting good information where corrupted information exists. This "surgery" often takes place in the most critical areas of the disk, where the changing of one bit of information can heal the problem or cause more problems.

This chapter looks at the critical system and file information on floppy and hard disks, stored in areas called *structures* or *tables*. Most of these structures are important and depend on other structures. If a structure becomes damaged, you may see a domino effect that leads to bigger problems.

Problems can appear to be catastrophic, even to the point of total inaccessibility to the disk. However, an informed data recovery technician may be able to locate that small cause and correct the situation. This chapter helps you locate and fix critical disk areas that can cause information loss.

Disk Interfaces

The DOS interface is the communication path by which instructions from applications interact with the disk to store and retrieve files. To use some of the recovery techniques discussed in this chapter, you need to know what aspects of the DOS interface are used for communicating with the disk structures. By understanding how the DOS interface and the DOS disk structure areas work together to access disks, you can improve greatly your troubleshooting skills with data recovery operations.

To fix damage, you need to know what a correct and valid structure looks like. This chapter familiarizes you with the DOS interface and disk structures.

You carry out disk and file management by using a combination of DOS features and facilities. These components differ slightly between floppy and hard disks and also among disks of different sizes. These components determine how a disk appears to DOS and applications programs. Each component describes the disk system and forms a layer in the complete system. Each layer talks to the layer above and below it. When the components work together, an application can access the disk to store data.

Three primary layers of interface exist between an applications program and disks:

- DOS Interrupt 21h, 25h, and 26h routines
- ROM BIOS disk Interrupt 13h routines
- Disk controller I/O port commands

Each layer accepts various commands, performs various functions, and generates results. These interfaces are available for both floppy disk drives and hard disk drives; the floppy disk and hard disk Interrupt 13h routines and controllers differ, but the layers perform the same functions. The following sections examine these layers.

Interrupts 21h, 25h, and 26h

The DOS Interrupt (INT) 21h routines exist at the highest level and provide the most functionality with the least work. Interrupts are built-in routines of DOS that enable the program to use the DOS interface to the disk. An *interrupt* is essentially a path into the DOS system whereby the program can get DOS's attention and request a service. If an applications program needs to create a subdirectory on a disk, the program can call Interrupt 21h, Function 39h.

A program can request different services of INT 21h by calling a function. For example, Function 39h performs the necessary operations for creating the subdirectory on the disk, including updating the appropriate directory and file allocation table (FAT) sectors. The only information this function needs is the name of the subdirectory to create. More programming steps are required for creating a subdirectory on the disk with the use of one of the lower level access methods.

Most applications programs access the disk through this level of interface. Other interrupt routines are mentioned throughout the chapter as their services are needed.

The DOS INT 25h and 26h routines provide a much lower level of access than the INT 21h routines. INT 25h only reads specified sectors from a disk, and INT 26h only writes specified sectors to a disk. If you write a program that uses these functions to create a subdirectory on a disk, the amount of work is much greater than with the INT 21h method. For example, your program must calculate which directory and FAT sectors must be updated. Then the program uses INT 25h to read these sectors, modify them appropriately to contain the new subdirectory information, and then use INT 26h to write the sectors back out.

The number of steps increases with the difficulty in determining exactly which sectors need to be modified. According to INT 25/26h, the DOS-addressable area of the disk consists of sectors numbered sequentially from 0. A program that accesses the disk with these functions must know where anything is by this sector number. A given program may have to be modified to handle disks with different numbers of sectors or different directory and FAT sizes and locations. Because of all the overhead required to get the job done, accessing the disk in this manner isn't recommended. Instead, programs that want to access the disk services should use the higher level INT 21h, which does all the work for you.

Disk- and sector-editing programs typically access a disk drive at this level. These programs can edit only areas of a disk that have been defined as logical volumes (drive letters) to DOS. For example, DEBUG can read and write sectors to and from disks with this level of access.

Interrupt 13h

INT 21h provides extensive disk services. Like a waiter at a fine restaurant, DOS takes care of the details for your requests, such as updating the system files, directories, and so on. The problem with this approach is that a program can order only what is on the menu. Using INT 13h routines is like cooking a meal from scratch. A program has more control over the outcome, but it has to do more work than making a simple request.

INT 13h routines are in ROM chips on the motherboard or an adapter card in a slot. These routines enable a program to access the information on the disk more directly than with INT 21h.

If a program is reading or writing information to or from a disk using a 13h routine, the program must specify the cylinder, head, and sector coordinates and update all necessary system tables and directories itself. If the program forgets to update a piece of information when writing information to disk, the data may not be accessible properly because of incorrect information. Therefore, programs that access the INT 13h routines for disk access are more powerful than those using the INT 21h routines, but they also require more care in use.

DOS provides INT 13h functions that read the disk parameters, format tracks, read and write sectors, park heads, reset the drive, and perform other operations.

Programs that implement disk programs such as a low-level format must work at the INT 13h level or lower. If the disk drive controller is designed to use INT 13h routines, implementing the low-level format is more straightforward than if the controller does not use a standard INT 13h interface. For example, most ST-506/412 controllers format programs access at the INT 13h level.

Other types of controllers, such as ESDI or SCSI, use different defect mapping and other operations. Controllers that must perform special operations during low-level formatting—such as defining disk parameters to override the motherboard ROM BIOS drive tables—do not work with formatters that use only the standard INT 13h interface. Most controllers require a special custom formatter designed to bypass the INT 13h interface, communicating directly with the disk drive controller.

Most low-level reformat programs that initiate a nondestructive format—such as Norton Calibrate or SpinRite—access the controller through the INT 13h interface. Therefore, you cannot use these programs for an initial low-level format. The initial format must be done by a controller-specific utility.

Because the partition tables and non-DOS partitions exist outside of the disk area defined by DOS, only programs that work at the INT 13h level can access these areas of a disk. Other than some basic formatting software, a few disk utility programs can talk to the disk at the INT 13h level. The Norton DiskEdit and NU programs can communicate with a disk at this level in Absolute Sector mode. The Kolod Research Htest/Hformat utilities also can communicate at the INT 13h level. These programs can be used for the worst data recovery situations—when the partition tables have been corrupted.

Disk Controller I/O Port Commands

At the lowest level, a program talks directly to the disk controller—in the controller's specific, native language. The program sends commands through the I/O ports that the controller responds to. These commands are specific to the particular controller involved. The commands even can differ among different controllers of the same type, such as different ESDI controllers. The ROM BIOS in the system must be designed specifically for the controller; the ROM BIOS talks to the controller at this I/O port level.

Most manufacturers' low-level format programs must talk to the controller directly; the higher level INT 13h interface does not provide enough specific features for many of the custom ST-506/412, ESDI, and SCSI controllers.

The Relationship among Interface Levels

Figure 7.1 shows the relative relationships among the various interface levels.

From figure 7.1, you can see that most applications programs work through the DOS INT 21h interface, which passes commands to the ROM BIOS as INT 13h commands. The ROM BIOS converts the commands into direct controller commands, and the controller executes the commands and returns the results through the layers back to the application. Applications can be written without you worrying about low-level system details, which are left up to DOS and the ROM BIOS.

Although software can bypass a level of interface and communicate at a lower level, this procedure requires more work. The lowest level available is to talk directly to the controller via I/O port commands. As you can see from figure 7.1, each type of controller has different I/O port locations and differences among the commands presented at the various ports. When software communicates directly with the controller, you can lose data if the program alters data on the disk without having the proper updates in necessary tables and directories.

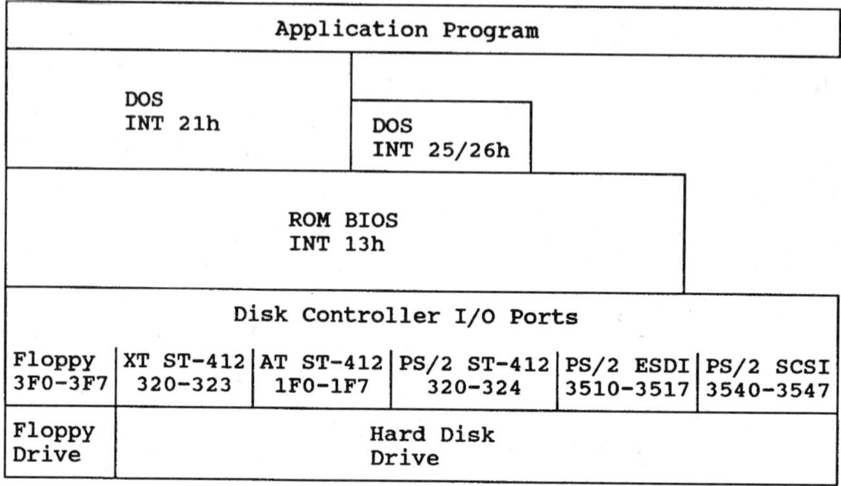

Fig. 7.1. *The relative relationships among interface levels.*

DOS Structures

To manage the files and data on a disk and allow all applications programs to see a consistent disk interface no matter what type of disk is used, DOS constructs and uses several structures. All the structures and areas defined and used by DOS to manage a disk follow:

- Partition boot sectors (master and extended partition boot sectors)
- DOS volume boot sector
- Directories
- File allocation tables (FATs)
- Data area
- Diagnostics read and write cylinder

A hard disk has all the preceding areas allocated; a floppy disk has all but the partition boot sectors and the diagnostic read and write cylinder allocated. Because floppy disks cannot be partitioned, these structures have no use.

Figure 7.2 shows the relative locations of these areas on a 32M hard disk in an IBM AT Model 339. Notice that track 0 contains important system and file information about the disk. When you're repairing a disk with a disk editor, you access this location to correct many problems. The middle area of the disk is the data section. The last part of the disk contains a diagnostic cylinder.

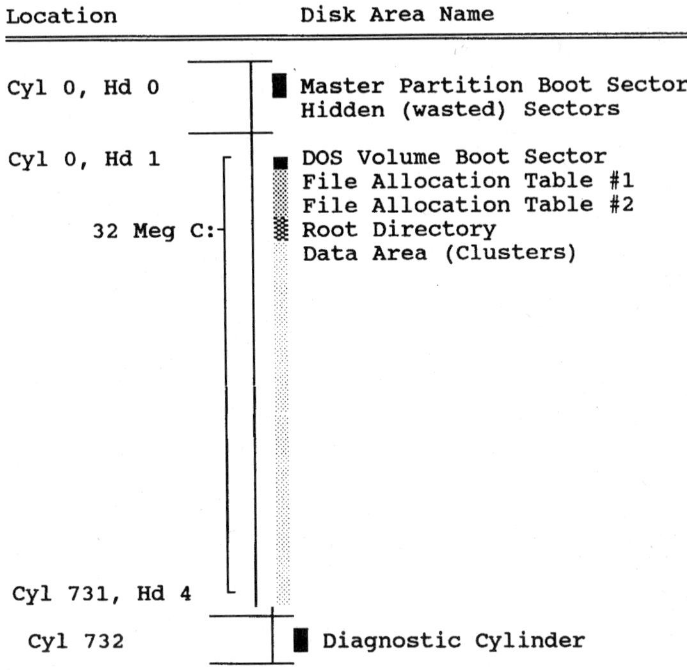

Fig. 7.2. Disk areas on a 32M hard disk.

If one of these special structures is damaged, such as the FAT, serious consequences can result, often causing a domino effect. Damage to one area can cut off access to other structures, limiting access to other areas of the disk or causing further problems in using the disk. For example, DOS cannot read and write files if the FATs are damaged.

You should know these data structures and their functions well enough to repair them when necessary. Rebuilding these special tables and areas of the disk is essential to the art of data recovery. Techniques for rebuilding these areas are covered in Chapter 9.

This section defines these structures and disk areas in more detail.

Partition Boot Sectors

A hard disk must be partitioned for it to be accessible by any operating system. A *partition* is an area set aside on the disk that holds the information about a particular operating system. You must partition a disk even if you want to create only a single partition. To share a hard disk among different operating systems, you can divide the disk logically into 1 through 4 partitions.

The DOS FDISK program enables you to select the size of each partition. For example, you may want your primary operating system to have a large partition of your disk and save only a small partition of your disk for a secondary operating system.

You can set up multiple partitions, all using DOS, which you must do if you're using a version of DOS up to Version 3.2 and have a hard disk with a capacity larger than 32M.

The partition information is kept in several partition boot sectors on the disk; the main table is embedded in the master partition boot sector. The master partition boot sector always is located in the first sector of the entire disk—cylinder 0, head 0, sector 1.

Through DOS 3.2, each operating system on the disk can be assigned to only one partition. DOS 3.3 and later versions have the extended DOS partition, which allows for multiple DOS partitions on the same hard disk. The extended partition boot sectors are located at the beginning of each extended partition volume.

Each DOS partition contains a DOS volume boot sector as the first sector within the partition. This volume boot sector holds the information needed to boot the computer into the operating system (see the section "The DOS Volume Boot Sector" later in this chapter).

With the DOS FDISK utility, you can designate a single partition as *active*, which means that it is bootable. The master partition boot sector causes the active partition's volume boot sector to receive control when the system is started or reset. Suppose that you have PC DOS and XENIX partitions on your disk. If you designate the PC DOS partition as the active partition, the computer boots into the PC DOS operating system. If the XENIX partition is made the active system, the computer boots into the XENIX operating system.

After you boot into an operating system, information from other operating systems is not available. If you have booted with XENIX, for example, then DOS files in the DOS partition are inaccessible. OS/2 and DOS partitions share FAT partitions; a corrupted FAT may affect both partitions.

Early DOS versions had another limitation—32M maximum per partition. Other operating systems could use the remaining space. Many old aftermarket utilities produced non-DOS partitions that were addressable to DOS with a device driver. Unfortunately, these drivers conflicted with many programs and were incompatible with the extended partitioning scheme of DOS 3.3 and later versions.

DOS 3.3 retains the 32M limit for a DOS partition, but DOS 3.3 enables you to create multiple partitions addressable as volumes (drive letters). A 115M drive with DOS 3.3, for example, can be split into several DOS partitions: C, D, E, and so on.

To remain compatible with old disk systems and versions of DOS, DOS 3.3 kept the structure of the master partition boot sector, including the four slots for partition tables. The second entry, however, was an extended partition—a pointer to another partition boot sector. Two of those slots are used—the first as an entry describing the defined partition and the second pointing to the start of the next partition boot sector.

With this scheme, no limits exist on the maximum number of partitions on a disk. Of course, creating more than 24 partitions on attached drives is futile, because DOS runs out of drive letters after Z.

On a system with DOS 3.3 and a 115M hard disk, you have a master partition boot sector with a partition table containing two entries. The first entry describes a 32M DOS primary partition, and the second entry describes an 83M extended partition—the rest of the disk. As DOS sees it, this 83M extended partition defines the area of the disk that will be searched for extended partition boot sectors. The first extended partition boot sector is found at the beginning of the extended partition area indicated by the second entry in the master partition table. DOS swings the heads over to that area and reads this extended partition boot sector. This sector also contains two entries; it looks much like the master partition boot sector.

The first entry is a 32M primary DOS partition called volume D; the second entry is an extended partition entry used by DOS as a pointer to find the next extended partition boot sector. DOS chains from one sector to the next, working its way through all partitions on the disk, until the chain ends or is broken somehow.

You end up with one partition boot sector for each DOS volume, or drive letter. The first one is the master partition boot sector; the rest (up to 23 more) are extended partition boot sectors. These sectors are examined next.

Master Partition Boot Sectors

A master partition boot sector has a 64-byte, embedded partition table. This structure is found on hard disks only, and it must reside on the first sector of the first cylinder and head (track) of the hard disk. The coordinates are cylinder 0, head 0, sector 1.

The master partition boot sector must contain the following items:

- A *program code* to examine the partition table within the sector. This program uses the data in the table to locate and load a volume boot sector for one of four possible operating systems.

- A *partition table* with four entries embedded within the boot sector. Each table entry is 16 bytes long and contains information concerning the locations and sizes of the partitions, as well as which one is to be the bootable partition. This design permits a single hard disk to be shared by several (up to four) operating systems.

Chapter 9 covers information about several disk editing programs. These programs enable you to change information on disk, correcting errors to important structures such as the master partition boot sector. For example, a partition on a hard disk becomes corrupted, making the information on the disk unavailable—lost! If you can edit the partition to correct the problem, you can regain access to the information on disk.

Before you begin changing this information, you must understand what is included in the partition. The listing that follows is a copy of the actual master partition boot sector from my current system, which is an IBM P70 portable with a 320M SCSI drive split into two partitions, sized at 300M for drive C and 5M for drive D.

In this type of listing, the offset of each byte in the sector is indicated by the far left column and top row numbers. For example, the offset 0A3 (hexadecimal) is 45 (hexadecimal), which you can determine by finding row 0A0 at the far left and column 3 at the top of the page. The intersection of the row and column contains the entry 45. The main columns in the center are the actual hexadecimal values of each byte in the sector, and the equivalent displayable ASCII text characters for bytes are shown in the right column.

As you can see from this listing, a machine code program starts the sector, with three error messages near the end of the program portion of the sector. The middle is mostly unused space.

```
Cylinder 0, Head 0, Sector 1:

Hexadecimal Byte Values                                      ASCII Text

    0  1  2  3  4  5  6  7  8  9  A  B  C  D  E  F  0123456789ABCDEF

000 FA 33 C0 8E D0 BC 00 7C-8B F4 50 07 50 1F FB FC .3.....¦..P.P...
010 BF 00 06 B9 00 01 F2 A5-EA 1D 06 00 00 BE 07    ................
020 B3 04 80 3C 80 74 0E 80-3C 00 75 1C 83 C6 10 FE ...<.t..<.u.....
030 CB 75 EF CD 18 8B 14 8B-4C 02 8B EE 83 C6 10 FE .u......L.......
040 CB 74 1A 80 3C 00 74 F4-BE 8B 06 AC 3C 00 74 0B .t..<.t.....<.t.
050 56 BB 07 00 B4 0E CD 10-5E EB F0 EB FE BF 05 00 V.......^.......
060 BB 00 7C B8 01 02 57 CD-13 5F 73 0C 33 C0 CD 13 ..¦...W.._s.3...
070 4F 75 ED BE A3 06 EB D3-BE C2 06 BF FE 7D 81 3D Ou...........}.=
080 55 AA 75 C7 8B F5 EA 00-7C 00 00 49 6E 76 61 6C U.u.....¦..Inval
090 69 64 20 70 61 72 74 69-74 69 6F 6E 20 74 61 62 id partition tab
0A0 6C 65 00 45 72 72 6F 72-20 6C 6F 61 64 69 6E 67 le.Error loading
0B0 20 6F 70 65 72 61 74 69-6E 67 20 73 79 73 74 65  operating system
0C0 6D 00 4D 69 73 73 69 6E-67 20 6F 70 65 72 61 74 ..Missing operat
0D0 69 6E 67 20 73 79 73 74-65 6D 00 00 00 00 00 00 ing system......
0E0 00 00 00 00 00 00 00 00-00 00 00 00 00 00 00 00 ................
0F0 00 00 00 00 00 00 00 00-00 00 00 00 00 00 00 00 ................
100 00 00 00 00 00 00 00 00-00 00 00 00 00 00 00 00 ................
110 00 00 00 00 00 00 00 00-00 00 00 00 00 00 00 00 ................
120 00 00 00 00 00 00 00 00-00 00 00 00 00 00 00 00 ................
130 00 00 00 00 00 00 00 00-00 00 00 00 00 00 00 00 ................
140 00 00 00 00 00 00 00 00-00 00 00 00 00 00 00 00 ................
150 00 00 00 00 00 00 00 00-00 00 00 00 00 00 00 00 ................
160 00 00 00 00 00 00 00 00-00 00 00 00 00 00 00 00 ................
170 00 00 00 00 00 00 00 00-00 00 00 00 00 00 00 00 ................
180 00 00 00 00 00 00 00 00-00 00 00 00 00 00 00 00 ................
190 00 00 00 00 00 00 00 00-00 00 00 00 00 00 00 00 ................
1A0 00 00 00 00 00 00 00 00-00 00 00 00 00 00 00 00 ................
1B0 00 00 00 00 00 00 00 00-00 00 00 00 00 00 80 01 ................
1C0 01 00 06 3F 60 2B 20 00-00 00 E0 5F 09 00 00 00 ...?‘+...._.....
1D0 41 2C 05 3F 60 30 00 60-09 00 00 28 00 00 00 00 A,.?‘0.‘...(....
1E0 00 00 00 00 00 00 00 00-00 00 00 00 00 00 00 00 ................
1F0 00 00 00 00 00 00 00 00-00 00 00 00 00 00 55 AA ..............U.
```

Near the end of the sector, starting with the byte at offset 1BEh, is what seems to be a random collection of bytes, but these bytes are actually the partition table. The table in this example has two (out of four) 16-byte entries occupied. At the end of the sector at offset 1FEh is the special 2-byte signature 55AA. This signature helps the system identify a valid boot sector. All master, extended, and DOS volume boot sectors must contain this signature as the last 2 bytes (offset 1FEh).

Checking the Master Partition Boot Sector

The master partition boot sector is loaded by the system ROM BIOS. After loading the sector into memory at address 0000:7C00, the ROM BIOS checks to see that the 55AAh signature bytes are present at offset 1FEh in the sector. If these bytes are not correct, the ROM BIOS refuses to execute the sector program code and halts the system.

On an IBM PC XT or AT (non-PS/2) system, the cassette BASIC is invoked by an INT 18h instruction. The screen shows the following information:

```
The IBM Personal Computer Basic
Version C1.10 Copyright IBM Corp 1981
62940 Bytes free
Ok
```

The function key settings are displayed at the bottom of the screen. You cannot proceed from this point except by rebooting the system from a floppy. Then you can correct the master partition boot sector (see Chapter 9 for information on editing disk information). When the system boots into cassette BASIC, you know that the signature bytes on the hard disk are invalid.

When an IBM-compatible system invokes the INT 18h instruction, however, a boot error message is displayed (non-IBM systems do not have cassette BASIC built into ROM). The message displayed on a system with a Phoenix ROM BIOS follows:

```
No boot device available -
strike F1 to retry boot, F2 for setup utility
```

You can run the setup program or boot from a floppy disk to correct the master partition boot sector on the hard disk. Other IBM-compatible systems display similar messages. An IBM PS/2 system, for example, displays a screen instructing you to insert a floppy disk into drive A and press the F1 key.

Executing the Master Partition Boot Sector Program

After the sector loads and the ROM BIOS determines that the signature bytes are correct, the ROM executes the sector as if it is a COM program. Under control of this small boot sector program, several tests determine the integrity of the system before proceeding. After these tests are executed, one of the following situations occurs:

- *Blank screen, cursor displayed, system locked*. This situation indicates that the master partition boot sector program has been corrupted. The sector must be partially OK for the ROM to evaluate the signature bytes as correct, but if bytes have been altered accidentally, the program can lock the computer. You can tell whether the system is locked up totally by pressing the Caps Lock key. If the lights on the keyboard don't turn on, the system is hard-locked, which means that the system cannot even respond to the Ctrl-Alt-Del warm-boot sequence. You must reset the computer by turning it off and then on.

  To correct the problem, you must boot from a floppy disk to start the system. Use a disk edit program such as Norton DiskEdit to correct the master partition boot sector program (see Chapter 9 for more information on disk editing).

- *Blank Screen, cursor displayed, enabled loop*. The screen here appears like the previous example—blank with a flashing cursor in the upper left corner. In this case, though, the system is in an *enabled loop*, executing a set of instructions over and over. The lights on the Caps Lock key turn on when you press it, indicating that the system is still alive and processing. You can use the Ctrl-Alt-Del sequence to warm-boot the system.

  This enabled loop is invoked by the program code in the boot sector when none of the master partition table entries has a valid (nonzero) system indicator byte. This situation occurs, for example, if you use FDISK to remove all partitions on the disk and then attempt to boot from it. Correcting this problem involves booting from a floppy and repairing the master partition table entries to contain proper system indicator bytes. Use a disk edit program such as Norton DiskEdit to correct the problem (see Chapter 9 for more information on disk editing).

- *Cassette BASIC*. Cassette BASIC is invoked through an INT 18h instruction if valid system indicator bytes exist in at least one of the four partition table entries but none is marked active. In this case, even an IBM PS/2 displays the cassette BASIC screen. IBM compatibles without cassette BASIC in ROM display a `No boot device available` message or something similar.

  Suppose that you use an IBM AT and cassette BASIC appears on-screen during an attempted hard disk boot. You do not know whether the ROM BIOS invoked the BASIC because of a signature byte test failure or because the system already executed the boot sector program code and failed the test for an active partition.

The correction in this case is to boot from a floppy disk, run FDISK, and simply make the primary partition active. Users commonly fail to mark one of the partitions as active when using FDISK in creating multiple partitions. When FDISK is not allowed to create the primary partition through its default method, FDISK does not automatically make the partition active.

- *Invalid partition table*. This message is displayed if any boot indicator bytes in the master partition boot record table are invalid. Valid indicator bytes are 00h or 80h. If the boot record contains any other value, the table is invalid. Also, the 80h value indicates that the partition is active. Because only one partition can be active, an invalid partition table message also appears if more than one 80h code exists.

  To fix this problem, boot from a floppy disk and run FDISK to correct the problem with too many active partitions. In some cases, you may need to use a utility program that directly patches the sector. Use a disk edit program such as Norton DiskEdit to correct the problem (see Chapter 9 for more information on disk editing).

- *Error loading operating system*. This message indicates that the master partition boot sector located a single active partition and attempted to load the DOS volume boot sector from that partition but failed. If the DOS volume boot sector cannot be read successfully from the active partition within five retries due to read errors, the error message appears.

  To correct this problem, you must boot from a floppy disk and use a utility program to examine or correct the volume boot sector in the active partition. In some cases, you can use the SYS command to correct a damaged volume boot sector. If the SYS command does not correct the problem, use a disk edit program such as Norton DiskEdit to correct the problem (rebuild the DOS volume boot sector). Chapter 9 provides more information on disk editing.

- *Missing operating system*. This message appears if the DOS volume boot sector from the active partition doesn't have a valid signature. Just as the master partition boot sector partition is tested by the ROM BIOS, the volume boot sector is tested by the master partition boot sector—for a valid signature of 55AAh as the last two bytes in the sector.

To correct this situation, you must boot from a floppy disk. Then replace the signature bytes in the volume boot sector or restore the entire sector. You often can use the SYS command to perform this operation with the least effort. If SYS does not work, use a disk edit program such as Norton DiskEdit to correct the signature bytes in the volume boot sector (see Chapter 9 for more information on disk editing).

If you pass these tests, the DOS volume boot sector executes and the master partition boot sector program code finishes its job.

Reviewing the Partition Table

Besides the short piece of program code in the master partition boot sector, the four-entry partition table is important. If the information in the table is corrupted, you cannot access information on disk. The format for this table and the offsets for the values contained within are listed in table 7.1. You may be able to use this information to edit a corrupted table and restore it to working order.

Table 7.1
Master Boot Sector Partition Table Format

Partition Table Entry #1

Offset	*Length*	*Item*
1BEh 446	1 byte	Boot indicator byte (80h = active, else 00h)
1BFh 447	1 byte	Starting head (or side) of partition
1C0h 448	16 bits	Starting cylinder (10) and sector (6)
1C2h 450	1 byte	System indicator byte
1C3h 451	1 byte	Ending head (or side) of partition
1C4h 452	16 bits	Ending cylinder (10) and sector (6)
1C6h 454	1 dword	Relative sector offset of partition
1CAh 458	1 dword	Total number of sectors in partition

continues

Partition Table Entry #2 (continued)

Offset	*Length*	*Item*
1CEh 462	1 byte	Boot indicator byte (80h = active, else 00h)
1CFh 463	1 byte	Starting head (or side) of partition
1D0h 464	16 bits	Starting cylinder (10) and sector (6)
1D2h 466	1 byte	System indicator byte
1D3h 467	1 byte	Ending head (or side) of partition
1D4h 468	16 bits	Ending cylinder (10) and sector (6)
1D6h 470	1 dword	Relative sector offset of partition
1DAh 474	1 dword	Total number of sectors in partition

Partition Table Entry #3

Offset	*Length*	*Item*
1DEh 478	1 byte	Boot indicator byte (80h = active, else 00h)
1DFh 479	1 byte	Starting head (or side) of partition
1E0h 480	16 bits	Starting cylinder (10) and sector (6)
1E2h 482	1 byte	System indicator byte
1E3h 483	1 byte	Ending head (or side) of partition
1E4h 484	16 bits	Ending cylinder (10) and sector (6)
1E6h 486	1 dword	Relative sector offset of partition
1EAh 490	1 dword	Total number of sectors in partition

Partition Table Entry #4

Offset	*Length*	*Item*
1EEh 494	1 byte	Boot indicator byte (80h = active, else 00h)
1EFh 495	1 byte	Starting head (or side) of partition

Offset	*Length*	*Item*
1F0h 496	16 bits	Starting cylinder (10) and sector (6)
1F2h 498	1 byte	System indicator byte
1F3h 499	1 byte	Ending head (or side) of partition
1F4h 500	16 bits	Ending cylinder (10) and sector (6)
1F6h 502	1 dword	Relative sector offset of partition
1FAh 506	1 dword	Total number of sectors in partition

In this table, the left two columns contain the offset into the sector where the described field is located. The first column lists the offset in hexadecimal; the second column lists the offset in decimal format. The third column lists the length of the field. Some fields are to be interpreted as bits, some as bytes, and some as double words (*dwords*).

A *dword* consists of two words read in reverse order; a *word* consists of two bytes read in reverse order. The uninitiated may find this reverse order confusing, but this procedure reflects the fact that the least important part is stored first. This procedure is a result of the register design of the Intel 16- and 32-bit processors.

The partition table stores the starting and ending cylinder, sector, and head for each of four possible partitions, as well as the number of sectors preceding the partition and the number of sectors occupied by the partition.

Examining the First Partition Table

The following listing shows the end of the master partition boot sector, which contains the partition table:

```
Hexadecimal Byte Values                                     ASCII Text

     0  1  2  3  4  5  6  7  8  9  A  B  C  D  E  F  0123456789ABCDEF

1B0 00 00 00 00 00 00 00 00-00 00 00 00 00 00 80 01  ................
1C0 01 00 06 3F 60 2B 20 00-00 00 E0 5F 09 00 00 00  ...?‘+...._.....
1D0 41 2C 05 3F 60 30 00 60-09 00 00 28 00 00 00 00  A,.?‘0.‘...(....
1E0 00 00 00 00 00 00 00 00-00 00 00 00 00 00 00 00  ................
1F0 00 00 00 00 00 00 00 00-00 00 00 00 00 00 55 AA  ..............U.
```

The 16 bytes that are underlined comprise Table Entry #1. To see just how a partition table entry is constructed, you need to examine the entry byte by byte:

Boot Indicator Byte

Starting with the beginning of the first table entry at offset 1BEh, you can see that the value is 80h; this field is called the *boot indicator byte*. The master partition boot sector uses the boot indicator byte to determine whether one of the partitions contains a loadable operating system. A value of 00h indicates a nonbootable partition; a value of 80h indicates a bootable partition. FDISK marks a partition as bootable by placing a value of 80h in the corresponding boot indicator and setting all other boot indicators to 00h. Only one partition at a time can be marked as bootable. The partition shown in the preceding partition table has a value of 80h, indicating that the partition is bootable.

Head Start Byte

The next byte at offset 1BFh is a field indicating at which head this partition starts with. Our example is 01h, which indicates that the first partition actually starts at head 1.

Cylinder and Sector Start Byte

The next field is 16 bits (2 bytes) located at offset 1C0h, which indicates the cylinder and sector where the first partition starts. The cylinder and sector 16-bit field contains both values intermingled. The low-order 8 bits (the first 8 bits) of the 16-bit field are the low-order 8 bits of the cylinder number.

The high-order 8 bits of the 16-bit field are split; the low-order 6 bits of this byte represent the sector, and the high-order 2 bits of this byte are actually the high-order 2 bits of the complete 10-bit cylinder number. Sound confusing? Perhaps table 7.2, showing the organization of these 16 bits, can help.

Table 7.2
Partition Table Cylinder and Sector Fields

	Cyl #	*Sector #*	*Cylinder #*
Bit #	F E	D C B A 9 8	7 6 5 4 3 2 1 0
Bit Value	C C	S S S S S S	C C C C C C C C

In this chart, a bit value of *C* stands for cylinder and *S* for sector. The table simplifies sending proper information to the ROM BIOS that loads the appropriate boot sector. Only two MOV instructions—instructions that move information—are required to place the appropriate values in the DX and CX registers (memory locations) that supply the information for the ROM BIOS call that will cause the boot to take place.

Hard disk booting is only possible from the first hard disk in the system, where a BIOS drive number of 80h corresponds to the boot indicator byte, which corresponds with the ROM BIOS INT 13h (disk I/O) requirements, permitting a 10-bit cylinder number. Because the cylinder value can be represented by a maximum of 10 bits, the highest possible value would be 1111111111b, or 1,024 in decimal notation.

Today, ESDI, SCSI, and most ST-506/412 RLL controllers allow for a translation of the drive's actual number of cylinders and heads to something that fits this limitation. For example, the drive I currently am using in my system is a 320M SCSI with the following physical makeup:

- 949 cylinders
- 14 heads
- 48 sectors per track

However, my SCSI software translates these parameters to the following makeup:

- 305 cylinders
- 64 heads
- 32 sectors per track

Although translation is not strictly necessary in this case because the drive had less than 1,024 cylinders, IBM PS/2 systems with ESDI or SCSI controllers translate their drives to 64 heads and 32 sectors per track. This procedure results in a convenient 1M of disk space for each cylinder.

To decode the actual values in my example, you convert the hexadecimal value of these two bytes (0100h) to binary (00000001 00000000b). Then the least significant (rightmost) 8 bits (numbered 0 through 7), combined with the most significant (leftmost) 2 bits (numbered 14 and 15), make up the number corresponding to the cylinder value. The remaining 6 bits (numbered 8 through 13) make up the number corresponding to the sector value. The cylinder value is figured as 0000000000b = 0, and the sector value is figured as 000001b = 1 (see fig. 7.3).

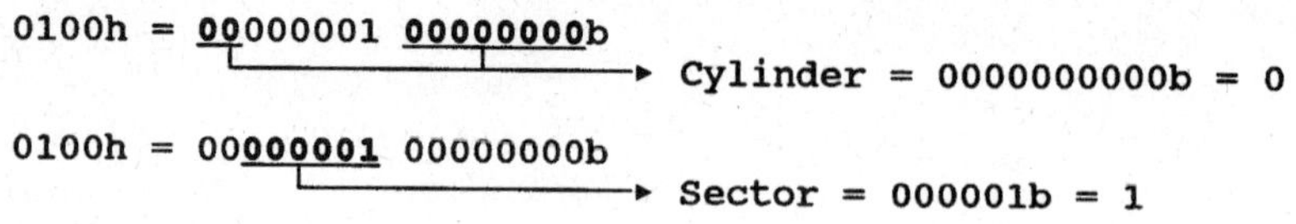

```
0100h = 00000001 00000000b
                              ──► Cylinder = 0000000000b = 0

0100h = 00000001 00000000b
                              ──► Sector = 000001b = 1
```

Fig. 7.3. Cylinder and sector start bytes.

The values so far indicate that the first partition is active, and it starts at cylinder 0, head 1, sector 1. All partitions are allocated in cylinder multiples and begin on sector 1, head 0, except the partition that is allocated in the first entry of a table. The partition in the first table entry must indicate a start at head 1 on the starting cylinder to account for the track that contains the master or extended partition boot sector.

System Indicator Byte

The next field is called the system indicator byte and is located at offset 1C2h for the first table entry. The system indicator byte dictates the operating system that "owns" the partition and describes the partition type. Table 7.3 lists many of the system indicator bytes used by different operating systems and partitioning schemes.

Table 7.3
System Indicator Bytes

Value	*Indication*
00h	No partition allocated in this entry
01h	Primary DOS, 12-bit FAT (partition < 16M)
02h	MS-XENIX partition
04h	Primary DOS, 16-bit FAT (16M <= partition <= 32M)
05h	Extended DOS partition
06h	Primary DOS, 16-bit FAT (partition > 32M)
07h	OS/2 HPFS partition
50h	Ontrack Disk Manager partition
56h	Golden Bow Vfeature partition
61h	Storage Dimensions Speedstor partition
63h	386/ix UNIX partition
64h	Novell NetWare partition
75h	IBM PCIX partition
DBh	Digital Research CPM-86 partition
FFh	UNIX bad block table partition

DOS and OS/2 systems normally use system indicator bytes from 00h to 07h. The others are used by foreign operating systems and disk partitioning schemes that are incompatible with DOS.

Head End Byte

The next field stores the head on which the partition ends—a byte at offset 1C3h. In the partition table, this byte has a value of 3Fh—63 in decimal. This first partition ends at head 63.

Partition End Byte

Now you come across another 16-bit field at offset 1C4h that contains a cylinder and sector number. They indicate the ending locations for this partition. In my example, these two bytes have values of 602Bh, which equals 0110000000101011b. To decode this value, combine the least significant (rightmost) 8 bits (00101011) with the most significant (leftmost) 2 bits (01) to arrive at the number 0100101011 (in binary), which equals 29; the remaining 6 bits (1100000) equal 32 (see fig. 7.4). Therefore, in this example, the first partition ends at cylinder 299 (head 63), sector 32.

```
602Bh = 01100000 00101011b
                           ──► Cylinder = 0100101011b = 299

602Bh = 01100000 00101011b
                           ──► Sector = 100000b = 32
```

Fig. 7.4. Partition end byte.

Relative Sector Offset Byte

The next field, located at byte offset 1C6h for the first table entry, indicates the relative sector offset of the partition. The *relative sector specification* is the number of sectors preceding the partition on the disk. You obtain this value by counting the sectors beginning with cylinder 0, head 0, sector 1, of the disk, up to the beginning sector of the partition.

For the first partition on any hard disk, the relative sector offset is the number of sectors on the first track; only one track precedes the first partition on the disk. For a hard disk with 17 sectors per track, the relative sector offset for the first partition is 17. If the disk has 17 sectors per track, 4 heads, and a second partition that begins at cylinder 150, head 0, sector 1, the second partition's starting relative sector offset is 10,200 (17 x 4 x 150).

This relative sector offset field is a dword, which is 4 bytes long. In the partition table example, the 4 bytes at offset 1C6h represent the relative sector offset, and their hexadecimal values are 20 00 00 00. To convert this dword to a standard 32-bit hexadecimal number, you must reverse the words and the bytes within the words. After you reverse the words, you get the result shown in figure 7.5.

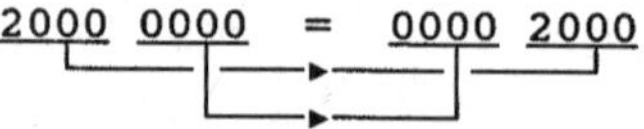

Fig. 7.5. Relative sector offset field: reversing the words.

Now reverse the individual bytes in each word for the result shown in figure 7.6.

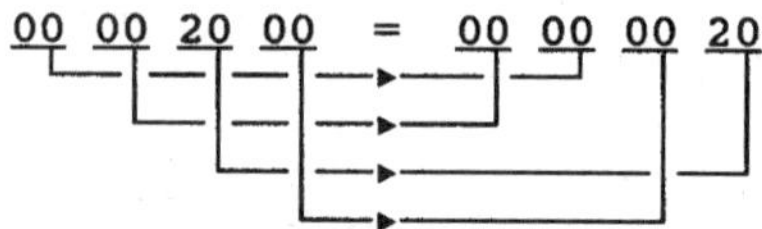

Fig. 7.6. Relative sector offset field: reversing the bytes.

You can translate the 32-bit hexadecimal number into a decimal value that indicates the relative sector offset:

00000020h = 32

Therefore, the first partition has a relative sector offset of 20h, which is equal to 32 sectors. This result is appropriate, because my hard disk has 32 sectors per track and only 1 track precedes the first partition on most disks.

Total Sector Number Byte

The last field in a partition table is the total number of sectors. This field is also a dword (4 bytes long) stored at offset 1CAh in the first partition table entry. Because this field is stored in dword format, you must reverse the byte and word values before the number can be read properly. This field stores the total number of sectors on the disk within the partition. In the sample partition entry, the 4 bytes starting at 1CAh follow:

E0 5F 09 00

To translate this entry from a dword into a standard 32-bit number, you must reverse the read order of the bytes:

E0 5F 09 00 (dword) = 00 09 5F E0 = 00095FE0h

Now you can translate the hexadecimal 32-bit number to a decimal value:

00095FE0h = 614,368

In the example, the first partition is 614,368 sectors long, which equals the following:

614,368 sectors x 512 bytes/sector = 314,556,416 bytes

314,556,416 bytes ÷ 1,024 bytes/kilobyte = 307,184 kilobytes

307,184 kilobytes ÷ 1,024 kilobytes/megabyte = 299.98 megabytes

Incidentally, the reason that this partition is 0.02M short of an even 300 is because of the sector occupied by the master partition boot sector and the 31 other wasted sectors on the first track.

Decoding the Second Table Entry

Now decode the values for the second table entry in the sample master partition boot sector. Here again is the end portion of the master partition boot sector, which contains the partition table:

```
Hexadecimal Byte Values                                        ASCII Text

    0  1  2  3  4  5  6  7  8  9  A  B  C  D  E  F   0123456789ABCDEF

1B0 00 00 00 00 00 00 00 00-00 00 00 00 00 00 80 01  ................
1C0 01 00 06 3F 60 2B 20 00-00 00 E0 5F 09 00 00 00  ...?'+...._.....
1D0 41 2C 05 3F 60 30 00 60-09 00 00 28 00 00 00 00  A,.?'0.'...(....
1E0 00 00 00 00 00 00 00 00-00 00 00 00 00 00 00 00  ................
1F0 00 00 00 00 00 00 00 00-00 00 00 00 00 00 55 AA  ..............U.
```

The underlined 16 bytes comprise the second partition table entry, which begins at offset 1CEh. To decode the values in this table entry, follow the procedures used for the first entry.

To derive the cylinder and head numbers from the byte values stored at offsets 1D0h and 1D4h, you must translate the 2 bytes to a 16-bit binary number and then combine the correct bits to determine the cylinder and head values. To derive the starting cylinder and sector located at 1D0h, follow the procedure shown in figure 7.7.

```
412Ch = 01000001 00101100b
                              ──► Cylinder = 0100101100b = 300

412Ch = 01000001 00101100b
                              ──► Sector = 000001b = 1
```

Fig. 7.7. Decoding the starting cylinder and sector location.

To derive the ending cylinder and sector located at 1D4h, follow the procedure shown in figure 7.8.

```
6030h = 01100000 00110000b
                          ──► Cylinder = 0100110000b = 304

6030h = 01100000 00110000b
                          ──► Sector = 100000b = 32
```

Fig. 7.8. Decoding the ending cylinder and sector location.

Determining the relative sector offset requires reversing the 4 bytes at offset 1D6h to get the 32-bit number for translation to decimal as follows:

00 60 09 00 (dword) = 00096000h = 614,400 sectors

Deriving the total number of sectors also requires reversing the 4 bytes at offset 1DAh to get the 32-bit number for translation to decimal as follows:

00 28 00 00 (dword) = 00002800h = 10,240 sectors

The rest of the values translate in a more straightforward manner. The full decoding is listed in table 7.4.

Table 7.4
Decoding Partition Table Entry #2

Offset	*Item*	*Value*	*Translation*
1CEh	Boot indicator	00h	Nonactive
1CFh	Starting head	00h	Head 0
1D0h	Starting cylinder and sector	412Ch	Cylinder 300, sector 1
1D2h	System indicator	05h	Extended DOS partition
1D3h	Ending head	3Fh	Head 63
1D4h	Ending sector and cylinder	6030h	Cylinder 304, sector 32
1D6h	Relative sector offset	00600900h	614,400 sectors
1DAh	Total number of sectors	00280000h	10,240 sectors (5M)

DOS interprets this table entry in a special way because the system indicator says that this is an extended DOS partition. Actually, DOS doesn't even treat this table entry as a partition; instead, DOS sees this partition as a pointer to another partition boot sector that does define another partition. When DOS sees the extended DOS partition indicator in the master boot sector, DOS looks at the beginning and ending locations for the partition. These locations define the area of the disk that is allocated by all additional DOS partitions.

In this example, DOS sees that the disk area from cylinder 300, head 0, sector 1, to cylinder 304, head 63, sector 32, may be allocated by one or more additional DOS partitions.

DOS uses the starting location information as a pointer to the next partition boot sector. This sector contains tables that define another DOS partition. In this example, the numbers say that the extended partition boot sector is located at cylinder 300, head 0, sector 1. DOS reads that sector and examines the tables contained in it.

Usually a partition is defined by it as a primary DOS partition, which then is assigned the volume designator D. If an extended partition table entry also exists, that information is used as a pointer for locating the next extended partition boot sector. This sector has a table with a primary DOS partition defined, assigned a volume of E. The chain goes on until DOS reaches one of the following: an extended partition boot sector that does not define additional primary or extended partitions, the maximum of 24 volumes (drive Z), or the end of the extended partition area defined by the extended DOS partition table entry in the master partition boot sector.

In the next section, you examine the structure of the extended partition boot sectors to see how they fit into the scheme of things.

Extended Partition Boot Sectors

Although they serve the same purpose as the master partition boot sector, extended partition boot sectors contain no program code and reside on the first track of the cylinder that begins the partition they represent. One extended partition boot sector is required for every DOS volume or logical drive from D through Z.

These sectors contain the four partition table entries in the same positions as the master boot sector. The format and structure of the table entries contained in these partitions is exactly the same as the master partition boot sector.

The decoding of partition tables sometimes can seem complicated unless you understand where they are and what the values mean. This section explains the meaning of each part of the partition table entries so that if you ever find that you need to correct an entry that has been modified or destroyed accidentally, you can perform the repair.

Also, you will see how the master and extended partition boot sectors chain together to enable DOS to allocate multiple volumes on a single drive. Because of the difficulty of deciphering the partitioning scheme used by DOS, few people can repair damage to these areas of a disk. Considering that situation and the fact that only programs using the INT 13h ROM BIOS interface to the disk can even get to these areas, you can have a difficult data recovery situation on your hands. You can use this book as a reference to the partition table structure. You can use some useful software tools to perform most of the partition table value translations and math operations automatically.

An extended partition boot sector is positioned at the beginning of each logical DOS drive area within the extended DOS partition. The entry for an extended partition in the master partition boot sector does not define a single extended partition. Instead, the entry defines the range over the whole disk that is further divided into extended partitions. The extended partition boot sectors are linked together; the starting cylinder, head, and sector entries in the partition table are pointers to the location of the next extended partition boot sector.

Decoding the Extended DOS Partition Table

Now continue with the example presented earlier. The following listing shows additional information about my 320M drive. Understanding this information is important in case you are required to edit the contents of the partition to restore it to operating form. The second table entry in the master partition boot sector on my 320M drive defined a start location for the extended DOS partition of cylinder 300, head 0, sector 1. This location is not really the start of a partition but, instead, is the exact location of the next partition boot sector. Here is a copy of the extended partition boot sector located at cylinder 300, head 0, sector 1, on the example disk:

```
Hexadecimal Byte Values                                   ASCII Text

     0  1  2  3  4  5  6  7  8  9  A  B  C  D  E  F     0123456789ABCDEF

000 00 00 00 00 00 00 00 00-00 00 00 00 00 00 00 00     ................
010 00 00 00 00 00 00 00 00-00 00 00 00 00 00 00 00     ................
020 00 00 00 00 00 00 00 00-00 00 00 00 00 00 00 00     ................
030 00 00 00 00 00 00 00 00-00 00 00 00 00 00 00 00     ................
040 00 00 00 00 00 00 00 00-00 00 00 00 00 00 00 00     ................
050 00 00 00 00 00 00 00 00-00 00 00 00 00 00 00 00     ................
060 00 00 00 00 00 00 00 00-00 00 00 00 00 00 00 00     ................
070 00 00 00 00 00 00 00 00-00 00 00 00 00 00 00 00     ................
080 00 00 00 00 00 00 00 00-00 00 00 00 00 00 00 00     ................
090 00 00 00 00 00 00 00 00-00 00 00 00 00 00 00 00     ................
0A0 00 00 00 00 00 00 00 00-00 00 00 00 00 00 00 00     ................
0B0 00 00 00 00 00 00 00 00-00 00 00 00 00 00 00 00     ................
0C0 00 00 00 00 00 00 00 00-00 00 00 00 00 00 00 00     ................
0D0 00 00 00 00 00 00 00 00-00 00 00 00 00 00 00 00     ................
0E0 00 00 00 00 00 00 00 00-00 00 00 00 00 00 00 00     ................
0F0 00 00 00 00 00 00 00 00-00 00 00 00 00 00 00 00     ................
100 00 00 00 00 00 00 00 00-00 00 00 00 00 00 00 00     ................
110 00 00 00 00 00 00 00 00-00 00 00 00 00 00 00 00     ................
120 00 00 00 00 00 00 00 00-00 00 00 00 00 00 00 00     ................
130 00 00 00 00 00 00 00 00-00 00 00 00 00 00 00 00     ................
140 00 00 00 00 00 00 00 00-00 00 00 00 00 00 00 00     ................
150 00 00 00 00 00 00 00 00-00 00 00 00 00 00 00 00     ................
160 00 00 00 00 00 00 00 00-00 00 00 00 00 00 00 00     ................
170 00 00 00 00 00 00 00 00-00 00 00 00 00 00 00 00     ................
180 00 00 00 00 00 00 00 00-00 00 00 00 00 00 00 00     ................
190 00 00 00 00 00 00 00 00-00 00 00 00 00 00 00 00     ................
1A0 00 00 00 00 00 00 00 00-00 00 00 00 00 00 00 00     ................
1B0 00 00 00 00 00 00 00 00-00 00 00 00 00 00 00 01     ................
1C0 41 2C 01 3F 60 30 20 00-00 00 E0 27 00 00 00 00     A,.?‘0....’.....
1D0 00 00 00 00 00 00 00 00-00 00 00 00 00 00 00 00     ................
1E0 00 00 00 00 00 00 00 00-00 00 00 00 00 00 00 00     ................
1F0 00 00 00 00 00 00 00 00-00 00 00 00 00 00 55 AA     ..............U.
```

Notice that this sector is devoid of program code. You see 16-byte partition tables starting at offset 1BEh in the sector. Only table entry #1 is used in this example. The decoded values are listed in table 7.5.

Table 7.5
Decoding Partition Table Entry #1

Offset	*Item*	*Value*	*Translation*
1BEh	Boot indicator	00h	Nonactive
1BFh	Starting head	01h	Head 1
1C0h	Starting cylinder and sector	412Ch	Cylinder 300, sector 1
1C2h	System indicator	01h	Primary DOS, 12-bit FAT
1C3h	Ending head	3Fh	Head 63
1C4h	Ending sector and cylinder	6030h	Cylinder 304, sector 32
1C6h	Relative sector offset	20000000h	32 sectors
1CAh	Total number of sectors	E0270000h	10,208 sectors (5M)

This entry describes the first extended DOS partition on the disk, known by DOS as volume D. As you can see from the system indicator byte, this entry is for a primary DOS partition with a 12-bit FAT system, because the partition is less than 16M in total size. Although the system indicator says that this partition is a primary DOS partition, it is still inside the extended DOS partition area allocated in the master partition boot sector.

If this disk had additional space and more extended partitions, the second entry in this table would be filled and the system indicator would denote an extended DOS partition, which again would be simply a pointer to the next extended partition boot sector. This sector would have an entry for a primary DOS partition and possibly another extended DOS partition entry pointing to yet another extended partition boot sector.

Figure 7.9 shows the physical relationship between the master and extended partition boot sectors. This figure shows the location of the master partition boot sector and an extended volume boot sector. Associated with each boot sector are areas allocated by the entries in the partition tables inside these sectors. These areas included the FATs, the root directory, and the data area. Figure 7.9 shows the areas on a disk allocated to these items—in particular, the structure of the 320M disk divided up into two volumes of 300M (the first volume boot sector area, associated with the master partition boot sector) and 5M (the second volume boot sector area, associated with the extended partition boot sector).

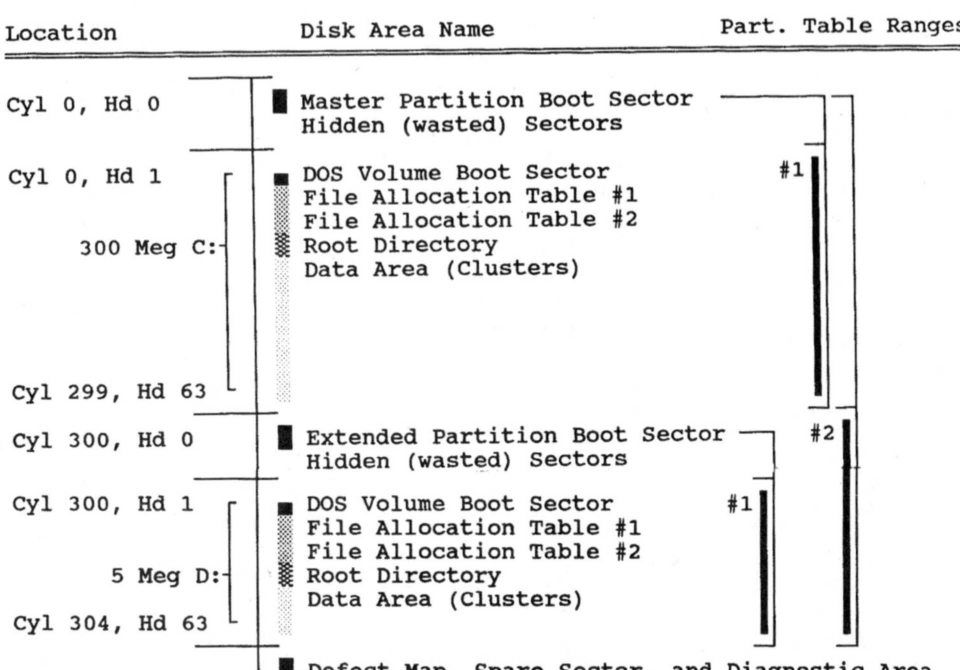

Fig. 7.9. The physical relationship between the master and extended partition boot sectors.

In this figure, you can see that the master partition boot sector has two table entries. The first entry (beginning at cylinder 0, head 1, and ending at cylinder 299, head 63) describes an area that defines the boundaries for volume C, and the second table entry (beginning at cylinder 300, head 0, and ending at cylinder 304, head 63) describes the boundaries for volume D, the rest of the disk. At the beginning of the area denoted by master partition table entry #2, DOS finds the first (and only, in this example) extended partition boot sector. This sector's partition table has only one entry, which describes the area known as volume D. Because this table has no entry #2 describing an extended DOS partition, the DOS drive addressing stops. Each volume ends up having its own personal partition boot sector, and these sectors require the use of a whole track that ends up outside the actual volume or partition area.

Decoding Another Example

For this example, you will explore an IBM PS/2 Model 70 that has a 120M hard disk. To the system, this disk has the following characteristics:

- 115 cylinders
- 64 heads
- 32 sectors per track
- 512 bytes per sector
- 115M total capacity

In this example, the drive is partitioned with DOS 3.3 or 4.0 and has one primary DOS partition of 32M as volume C. One extended partition of 83M exists (the rest of the 115M disk). This extended partition is split into three volumes: D (32M), E (32M), and F (19M).

The master partition boot sector is on cylinder 0, head 0, sector 1 (the first sector on the disk) and contains two partition entries. The first table entry allocates a partition from cylinder 0, head 1, sector 1, to cylinder 31, head 63, sector 32. This partition has a system indicator byte of 04h because it is less than or equal to 32M of space. The partition cannot actually begin until head 1, because the first sector under head 0 is used by the master partition boot sector and a partition must begin on a cylinder or head boundary. In other words, the next 31 sectors are wasted. Because these sectors cannot be used for anything, they sometimes are called *hidden sectors*.

The second partition table entry in the master partition boot sector contains an extended DOS partition that starts at cylinder 32, head 0, sector 1, and ends at cylinder 114, head 63, sector 32. This partition table entry has a system indicator byte of 05h, indicating an extended partition.

At this point, DOS has defined an extended partition, but that partition has no disk drive volumes assigned to it. DOS calls these *logical* DOS drives. To locate and assign the logical DOS drives, DOS looks to the first sector in the extended partition to see whether an extended partition boot sector resides there (at cylinder 32, head 0, sector 1). That sector has an extended partition boot sector with two table entries.

The first entry indicates a normal DOS partition—the system indicator equals 04h—that starts at cylinder 32, head 1, sector 1, or on the track following the track containing the extended partition boot sector. This partition ends at cylinder 63, head 63, sector 32. This first entry is an entry for the logical DOS drive D within the extended partition indicated by the original master partition boot sector.

The second table entry has an extended DOS partition that starts at cylinder 64, head 0, sector 1, and ends at cylinder 95, head 63, sector 32. This partition has a system indicator of 05h, which indicates an extended partition. This table entry is another pointer to the next extended partition boot sector, which can be found on the first sector of this extended partition.

At this point, DOS has defined drive C, the primary partition, and drive D, the first logical DOS drive in the extended partition. To find the next extended partition boot sector, DOS looks to cylinder 64, head 0, sector 1, which is the first sector in the extended DOS partition area defined by the table entry. This sector contains another extended partition boot sector, which also has two entries in its embedded table.

The first entry is a normal DOS partition (the system indicator equals 04h) that starts at cylinder 64, head 1, sector 1, and ends at cylinder 95, head 63, sector 32. This scheme defines the logical DOS drive E. Notice that each of these logical DOS partition entries starts the logical DOS drive on the second head or track. This method leaves room for the extended partition boot sector and 31 other wasted sectors.

The second entry in this extended partition boot sector is an extended partition. The system indicator starts at cylinder 96, head 0, sector 1, and ends at cylinder 114, head 63, sector 32. This entry is the pointer to the next extended partition boot sector.

At this point, DOS has defined drives C, D, and E. DOS now looks to cylinder 96, head 0, sector 1, for the next extended partition boot sector. This location has only one entry, which is for a normal DOS partition (the system indicator equals 04h) that starts at cylinder 96, head 1, sector 1, and ends at cylinder 114, head 63, sector 32. No other entry with a system indicator of 05h exists, so you have come to the end of the line.

To sum up, this 115M disk contains one master partition boot sector and three extended partition boot sectors. But still more boot sectors exist. When FDISK partitions the disk, in addition to creating the master and extended partition boot sectors, FDISK also creates a volume boot sector inside each logical DOS drive area. That fact translates to another four boot sectors on the example disk.

Boot sector types and positions on the example 120M drive are listed in table 7.6.

Table 7.6
Boot Sector Types and Positions

Boot Sectors	*Cylinder*	*Head*	*Sector*
Master partition boot sector	0	0	1
Volume boot sector for 32M C:	0	1	1
Extended partition boot sector	32	0	1
Volume boot sector for 32M D:	32	1	1
Extended partition boot sector	64	0	1
Volume boot sector for 32M E:	64	1	1
Extended partition boot sector	96	0	1
Volume boot sector for 19M F:	96	1	1

The partition boot sectors are in the first sector of any primary partition or extended partition logical DOS drive area. The volume boot sectors are in the first sector of the second track in the primary partition and extended partition logical DOS drive areas.

Figure 7.10 shows the 120M disk used in these examples.

In this figure, you can see how the partition tables chain from one to the next, using the extended DOS partition table entry #2 as the forward link. The partition tables in each of the partition boot sectors have two table entries except for the last one. The second entry is the forward pointer that informs DOS to look further for more volumes. You can see that another type of boot sector, called the DOS volume boot sector, leads off each actual partitioned area. The volume boot sector is discussed in the next section.

Note that you easily can break the forward chaining at any one of the partition boot sectors by damaging the extended DOS partition table entry. When a forward link is broken, future DOS volumes are not addressed. If you damage or remove the extended partition table entry from the master partition boot sector, then on the next bootup, drives D through F cease to exist.

Now, troubleshooting problems with missing drives should be easier. If drives E and F disappear after you boot the system, the problem must be the partition boot sector located at cylinder 32, head 0, sector 1, or the partition at cylinder 64, head 0, sector 1. If either of these two sectors is damaged, the link between volumes D and E breaks, and later volumes such as E and F cease to exist to DOS. You can edit the partition table to correct the problem (see Chapter 9 for information on editing).

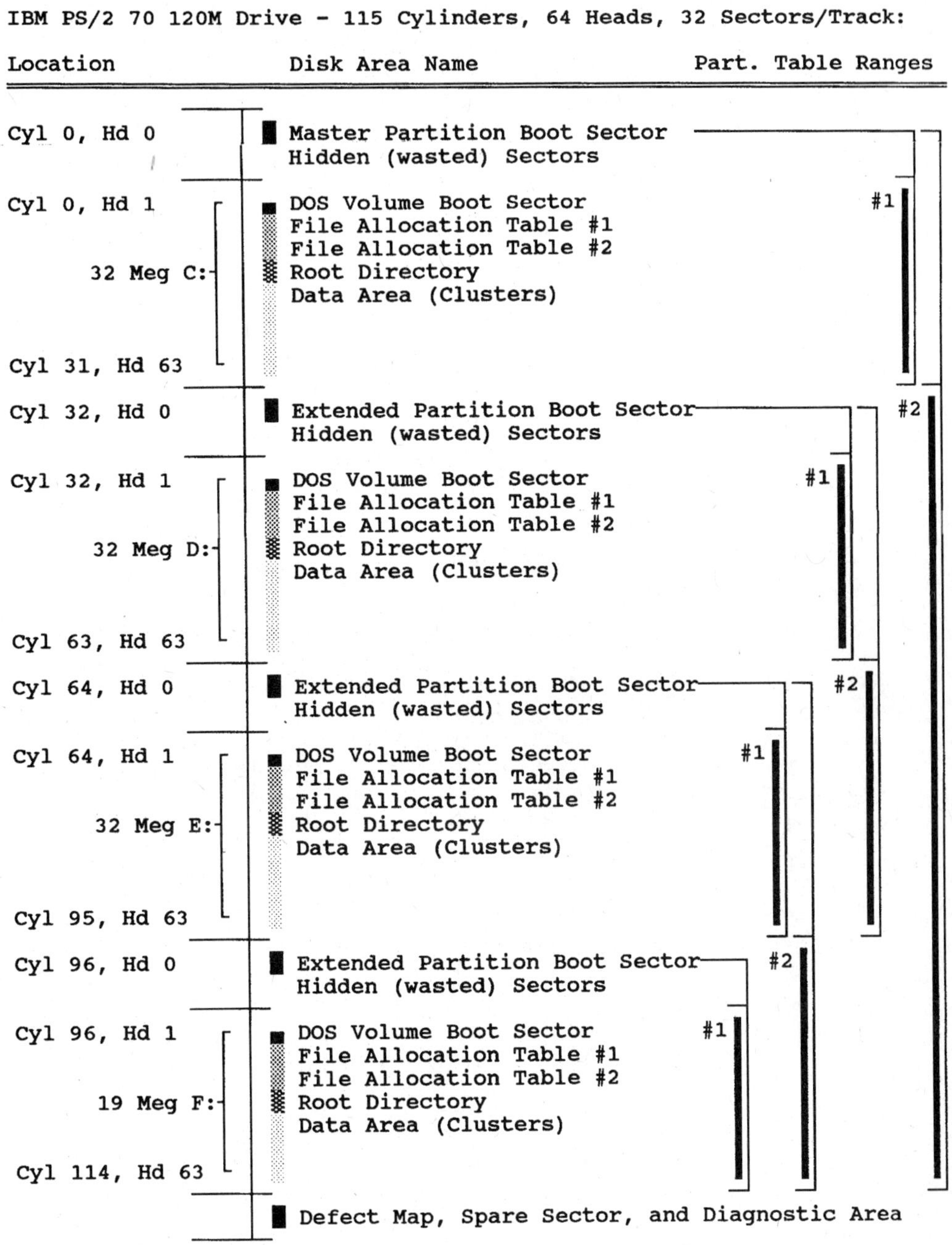

```
IBM PS/2 70 120M Drive - 115 Cylinders, 64 Heads, 32 Sectors/Track:

Location                Disk Area Name                        Part. Table Ranges

Cyl 0, Hd 0             Master Partition Boot Sector
                        Hidden (wasted) Sectors
Cyl 0, Hd 1             DOS Volume Boot Sector                          #1
                        File Allocation Table #1
                        File Allocation Table #2
        32 Meg C:       Root Directory
                        Data Area (Clusters)
Cyl 31, Hd 63
Cyl 32, Hd 0            Extended Partition Boot Sector                     #2
                        Hidden (wasted) Sectors
Cyl 32, Hd 1            DOS Volume Boot Sector                      #1
                        File Allocation Table #1
                        File Allocation Table #2
        32 Meg D:       Root Directory
                        Data Area (Clusters)
Cyl 63, Hd 63
Cyl 64, Hd 0            Extended Partition Boot Sector                 #2
                        Hidden (wasted) Sectors
Cyl 64, Hd 1            DOS Volume Boot Sector                  #1
                        File Allocation Table #1
                        File Allocation Table #2
        32 Meg E:       Root Directory
                        Data Area (Clusters)
Cyl 95, Hd 63
Cyl 96, Hd 0            Extended Partition Boot Sector             #2
                        Hidden (wasted) Sectors
Cyl 96, Hd 1            DOS Volume Boot Sector              #1
                        File Allocation Table #1
                        File Allocation Table #2
        19 Meg F:       Root Directory
                        Data Area (Clusters)
Cyl 114, Hd 63
                        Defect Map, Spare Sector, and Diagnostic Area
```

Fig. 7.10. Disk areas on a 120M disk.

As you can see from these examples, the decoding of partition tables can be complicated unless you understand where they are and what the values mean. In Chapter 9, you examine data recovery utility software and learn to assemble a toolkit with impressive capabilities.

The next section of this chapter discusses the DOS volume boot sector and its function.

The DOS Volume Boot Sector

The volume boot sector is the first sector on any area of any drive that is addressed as a volume or logical DOS disk. On a floppy disk, for example, the volume boot sector is the first sector on the disk. On a hard disk, the volume boot sectors are located as the first sector within any disk area allocated as a nonextended partition, which is an area recognizable as a DOS volume.

This special sector contains a program and some special data tables. The first volume boot sector on a disk is loaded by the system ROM BIOS for floppies or the master partition boot sector on a hard disk. This program receives control and attempts to load the first DOS system file (IBMBIO.COM). This sector is transparent to a DOS system—outside of the data area of the disk where files are stored. This sector is created by the DOS FORMAT command.

For hard disks, a volume boot sector exists at the beginning of every DOS logical drive area allocated on the disk—both in the primary and extended partitions. Although all the partitions will contain the program area as well as a data table area, only the program code from the volume boot sector in the active partition on a hard disk is ever executed. The other partition boot sectors are simply read by the DOS system files during boot to read their data table and determine the volume parameters.

Decoding the DOS Volume Boot Sector

The following listing shows a typical DOS volume boot sector—in this case, one from the 300M C partition used in the previous examples:

```
Hexadecimal Byte Values                                    ASCII Text

    0  1  2  3  4  5  6  7  8  9  A  B  C  D  E  F  0123456789ABCDEF

000 EB 3C 90 49 42 4D 20 20-34 2E 30 00 02 10 01 00 .<.IBM  4.0.....
010 02 00 02 00 00 F8 96 00-20 00 40 00 20 00 00 00 ........  .@.  ...
020 E0 5F 09 00 80 00 29 DC-12 54 14 33 32 30 4D 5F ._....)..T.320M_
030 53 43 53 49 20 20 46 41-54 31 36 20 20 20 FA 33 SCSI  FAT16   . 3
040 C0 8E D0 BC 00 7C 16 07-BB 78 00 36 C5 37 1E 56 .....¦...x.6.7.V
050 16 53 BF 3E 7C B9 0B 00-FC F3 A4 06 1F C6 45 FE .S.>¦.........E.
060 0F 8B 0E 18 7C 88 4D F9-89 47 02 C7 07 3E 7C FB ....¦.M..G...>¦.
070 CD 13 72 7C 33 C0 39 06-13 7C 74 08 8B 0E 13 7C ..r¦3.9..¦t....¦
080 89 0E 20 7C A0 10 7C F7-26 16 7C 03 06 1C 7C 13 ..¦..¦.&.¦...¦.
090 16 1E 7C 03 06 0E 7C 83-D2 00 A3 50 7C 89 16 52 ..¦...¦....P¦..R
0A0 7C A3 49 7C 89 16 4B 7C-B8 20 00 F7 26 11 7C 8B ¦.I¦..K¦.  ..&.¦.
0B0 1E 0B 7C 03 C3 48 F7 F3-01 06 49 7C 83 16 4B 7C ..¦..H....I¦..K¦
0C0 00 BB 00 05 8B 16 52 7C-A1 50 7C E8 87 00 72 20 ......R¦.P¦...r.
0D0 B0 01 E8 A1 00 72 19 8B-FB B9 0B 00 BE DB 7D F3 .....r........}.
0E0 A6 75 0D 8D 7F 20 BE E6-7D B9 0B 00 F3 A6 74 18 .u...  ..}.....t.
0F0 BE 93 7D E8 51 00 32 E4-CD 16 5E 1F 8F 04 8F 44 ..}.Q.2...^....D
100 02 CD 19 58 58 58 EB E8-BB 00 07 B9 03 00 A1 49 ...XXX.........I
110 7C 8B 16 4B 7C 50 52 51-E8 3A 00 72 E6 B0 01 E8 ¦..K¦PRQ.:.r....
120 54 00 59 5A 58 72 C9 05-01 00 83 D2 00 03 1E 0B T.YZXr..........
130 7C E2 E2 8A 2E 15 7C 8A-16 24 7C 8B 1E 49 7C A1 ¦.....¦..$¦..I¦.
140 4B 7C EA 00 00 70 00 AC-0A C0 74 29 B4 0E BB 07 K¦...p....t)....
150 00 CD 10 EB F2 3B 16 18-7C 73 19 F7 36 18 7C FE .....;..¦s..6.¦.
160 C2 88 16 4F 7C 33 D2 F7-36 1A 7C 88 16 25 7C A3 ...O¦3..6.¦..%¦.
170 4D 7C F8 C3 F9 C3 B4 02-8B 16 4D 7C B1 06 D2 E6 M¦........M¦....
180 0A 36 4F 7C 8B CA 86 E9-8A 16 24 7C 8A 36 25 7C .6O¦......$¦.6%¦
190 CD 13 C3 0D 0A 4E 6F 6E-2D 53 79 73 74 65 6D 20 .....Non-System.
1A0 64 69 73 6B 20 6F 72 20-64 69 73 6B 20 65 72 72 disk or disk err
1B0 6F 72 0D 0A 52 65 70 6C-61 63 65 20 61 6E 64 20 or..Replace and
1C0 70 72 65 73 73 20 61 6E-79 20 6B 65 79 20 77 68 press any key wh
1D0 65 6E 20 72 65 61 64 79-0D 0A 00 49 42 4D 42 49 en ready...IBMBI
1E0 4F 20 20 43 4F 4D 49 42-4D 44 4F 53 20 20 43 4F O  COMIBMDOS  CO
1F0 4D 00 00 00 00 00 00 00-00 00 00 00 00 00 55 AA M.............U.
```

Note some familiar landmarks—the standard signature bytes 55AAh at offset 1FEh, which are required for all boot sectors. Near the end of the sector at offset 195h, you can see the error message that this sector may display if a problem occurs from loading the system files:

```
Non-System disk or disk error
Replace and press any key when ready
```

After that error message, you can see the names of the system files that this sector attempts to load (IBMBIO.COM and IBMDOS.COM). The rest of this sector consists of program code to locate and load the system files and the special disk parameter block located near the beginning of the sector.

The single data table in this sector is called the *media parameter block*, or *disk parameter block*. DOS needs this information to read and verify the capacity of a disk volume as well as the location of important features such as the FAT. The format of this data is specific; errors can cause problems with booting from a disk or with accessing it. Some non-IBM OEM versions of DOS do not adhere to the standards set forth by IBM for the format of this data, which can cause interchange problems with disks formatted by different versions of DOS. The later versions can be more particular.

Fixing Problems with the DOS Volume Boot Sector

If you suspect that boot sector differences are causing your inability to access a disk, you can use a utility program such as DOS DEBUG or Norton Utilities to copy a boot sector from the newer version of DOS to the disk formatted by the older version. With the Norton Utilities DiskEdit program, for example, you can edit a sector on disk and replace corrupted information in the boot sector with correct information.

After you fix the boot sector, you may find that the old version of DOS interferes with the new version. Note that this problem has never existed with different DOS versions from the same OEM, but this problem may occur if you mix different OEM versions.

A good example of this problem in action was an obscure problem that occurred when one attempted to boot IBM DOS 4.0 on a hard disk that was originally formatted by a non-IBM OEM version of DOS. Versions of IBM DOS 4.0 prior to SYSLEVEL Version CSD UR25066 cannot read a disk that does not have “IBM ” as the first 4 bytes in the OEM name and version field in the boot sector.

Mapping the DOS Volume Boot Sector

Because the format and structure of the volume boot sector is so important to accessing the disk, table 7.7 lists the information in the sector. This information is useful when you need to edit the information on the boot sector to correct corrupted information.

Table 7.7
DOS Volume Boot Sector Format

Offset	*Length*	*Item*
00h 0	3 bytes	Jump instruction to boot program code
03h 3	8 bytes	OEM name and DOS version ("IBM 4.0")
0Bh 11	1 word	Bytes/sector (must be a power of 2)
0Dh 13	1 byte	Sectors/cluster (must be a power of 2)
0Eh 14	1 word	Reserved sectors (boot sectors—usually 1)
10h 16	1 byte	FAT copies (usually 2)
11h 17	1 word	Maximum root directory entries (usually 512)
13h 19	1 word	Total sectors (if partition <= 32M, else 0)
15h 21	1 byte	Media descriptor byte (F8h for hard disks)
16h 22	1 word	Sectors/FAT
18h 24	1 word	Sectors/track
1Ah 26	1 word	Number of heads
1Ch 28	1 dword	Hidden sectors (if partition <= 32M, 1 word only)
The following information is for DOS 4.0 and later versions, else 00h:		
20h 32	1 dword	Total 32-bit sectors (if partition >= 32M, else 0)
24h 36	1 byte	Physical drive number (00h or 80h)
25h 37	1 byte	Reserved (00h)
26h 38	1 byte	Extended boot record signature (29h)
27h 39	1 dword	Volume serial number
2Bh 43	11 bytes	Volume label ("NO NAME " stored if no label)
36h 54	8 bytes	File system ID ("FAT12 "or "FAT16 ")
The following information applies to all DOS versions:		
3Eh 62	450 bytes	Boot program code
1FEh 510	2 bytes	Signature bytes (55AAh)

In the first column of table 7.7, the two values represent the offset into the sector in hexadecimal and decimal notation, respectively. The next column indicates the field length and format, and the last column explains the meaning of each field. Remember that a word is two bytes read in reverse order; a dword is two words read in reverse order. The data from offset 03h (OEM name and version) through 36h is the data table area called the disk parameter block. This information is retrieved by IBMBIO during boot time for hard disks and when you change floppy disks.

Fixing Problems with the Disk Parameter Block

The accuracy of this block of data is critical because DOS bases its operations on these vital disk statistics. For example, if the information for reserved sectors or sectors/FAT gets corrupted, DOS may look in the wrong places on a disk to find the FAT tables. Corruption in the disk parameter block usually spells disaster for access to the disk. If the disk parameter block information or the program part of the sector gets corrupted, a nonbootable disk often results. In most cases, the system locks up during an attempted boot from that disk. Sometimes, however, you may see one of the following error messages:

- `Missing operating system`
- `Disk boot failure`
- `Non-system disk or disk error`
  `Replace and press any key when ready`

The `Missing operating system` message comes from the master partition boot sector. The message indicates that the volume boot sector in the active partition lacks the valid signature bytes 55AAh.

The `Disk boot failure` message indicates that some problem has occurred inside the volume boot sector or the system files, which are loaded normally by the volume boot sector.

The `Non-system disk or disk error` message indicates that the system files cannot be found or loaded for some reason. To respond to either problem, check the volume boot sector and the system files for possible corruption. In Chapter 10, you see some examples of volume boot sector corruption and possible repair procedures.

Decoding the Disk Parameter Block

The disk parameter block contains a great deal of information about the disk on which it resides. This information is critical for DOS to address the disk. If this information is corrupted, you may be unable to read the disk or you may encounter significant file system problems. For example, DIR commands showing crazy file names and improper bytes free may appear. CHKDSK may report massive problems with the disk. Usually, damaged disks in the volume boot sector become unbootable. Knowledge of the volume boot sector and disk parameter block comes in handy when problems arise.

Now you're going to decode the values stored in the disk parameter block from the example volume boot sector examined in the preceding section. The disk parameter block section of the volume boot sector follows:

```
Hexadecimal Byte Values                                ASCII Text

    0  1  2  3  4  5  6  7  8  9  A  B  C  D  E  F  0123456789ABCDEF

000 EB 3C 90 49 42 4D 20 20-34 2E 30 00 02 10 01 00 .<.IBM4.0......
010 02 00 02 00 00 F8 96 00-20 00 40 00 20 00 00 00 .........@....
020 E0 5F 09 00 80 00 29 DC-12 54 14 33 32 30 4D 5F . ....)..T.320M_
030 53 43 53 49 20 20 46 41-54 31 36 20 20 20 FA 33 SCSI  FAT16   .3
```

The actual disk parameter block bytes are underlined in this part of the beginning of the volume boot sector. Table 7.8 lists each field and the byte contents, as well as the meaning of each value.

Table 7.8
Field and Byte Contents

Offset	*Length*	*Item*	*Converted Byte Values*	*Translation*
03h	8 bytes	OEM name and DOS version	None	"IBM 4.0"
0Bh	1 word	Bytes/sector	0200h	512
0Dh	1 byte	Sectors/cluster	10h	16
0Eh	1 word	Reserved sectors	0001h	1
10h	1 byte	FAT copies	02h	2
11h	1 word	Max. root dir. entries	0200h	512
13h	1 word	Total sectors	0000h	0

continues

Table 7.8 *(continued)*

Offset	*Length*	*Item*	*Converted Byte Values*	*Translation*
15h	1 byte	Media descriptor byte	F8h	Hard disk
16h	1 word	Sectors/FAT	0096h	150
18h	1 word	Sectors/track	0020h	32
1Ah	1 word	Number of heads	0040h	64
1Ch	1 dword	Hidden sectors	00000020h	32
20h	1 dword	Total (32-bit) sectors	00095FE0h	614,368
24h	1 byte	Physical drive number	80h	Hard disk
25h	1 byte	Reserved	00h	0
26h	1 byte	Extended boot signature	29h	DOS 4.0+
27h	1 dword	Volume serial number	145412DCh	1454-12DC
2Bh	11 bytes	Volume label	None	"320M_SCSI"
36h	8 bytes	File system ID	None	"FAT16 "

An explanation of each field follows:

OEM name and DOS version. An ASCII text representation of the original equipment manufacturer of the DOS used to FORMAT or SYS the disk, as well as the version number.

Bytes/sector. The number of bytes per sector on the disk. This value is normally equal to 0002 (word) = 0200h = 512. This value must be a power of 2.

Sectors/cluster. The number of sectors per cluster or allocation unit on the disk. This value must be a power of 2.

Reserved sectors. The number of sectors on the disk preceding the FATs and therefore reserved for the volume boot sector. This value is almost always 1.

FAT copies. The number of copies of the FAT on the disk. This value usually is 2 except in the case of a VDISK, where the value is 1.

Maximum root directory entries. The maximum number of entries possible in the root directory. This value varies for floppy disks but is almost always equal to 0002 (word) = 0200h = 512 for a hard disk.

Total sectors. The total number of sectors in this volume. If the volume size is greater then 32M, however, this field is 0 and another field carries the total sectors information.

Media descriptor byte. A single byte that indicates the type of disk to DOS. Legal values are F0h through FFh; any values outside that range are not legal. Beginning with DOS 2.0, this byte's function has changed to the volume boot sector disk parameter block. In other words, DOS used to use this single byte to determine the characteristics of a disk but now reads the byte for the disk parameters. This byte varies for floppy disks; it is always F8h for hard disks. Table 7.9 lists the media descriptor bytes for DOS-supported disks.

Table 7.9
Media Descriptor Bytes

Disk Type	*Hard Disk*	*Floppy Disk*						
Disk size (in.)	-	3 1/2	3 1/2	5 1/4	5 1/4	5 1/4	5 1/4	5 1/4
Disk capacity (K)	-	1440	720	1200	180	360	160	320
Media descriptor byte	F8h	F0h	F9h	F9h	FCh	FDh	FEh	FFh
Sides (heads)	-	2	2	2	1	2	1	2
Tracks/side	-	80	80	80	40	40	40	40
Sectors/track	-	18	9	15	9	9	8	8
Bytes/sector	-	512	512	512	512	512	512	512

Sectors/FAT. The number of sectors that comprise each FAT.

Sectors/track. The number of sectors on each track of the disk.

Number of heads. The number of data heads per cylinder of the drive.

Hidden sectors. The number of sectors lost to the partition table boot sector for this volume. This value is almost always equal to the number of sectors per track on the drive. If the partition is less than or equal to 32M, this field is only 1 word rather than a dword.

Total (32-bit) sectors. The total number of sectors in the volume if the volume size is greater than or equal to 32M. If the volume size is less than 32M, this field is 0. If the disk was created by FORMAT or SYS from DOS 3.3 or an earlier version, then this field is 0.

Physical drive number. Indicates whether the disk is a floppy (00h) or a hard disk (80h). If the disk was created by FORMAT or SYS from DOS 3.3 or an earlier version, this field is 0.

Reserved. Always has a value of 00h. If the disk was created by FORMAT or SYS from DOS 3.3 or an earlier version, this field is 0.

Extended boot record signature. If the value 29h is present, indicates that this disk carries the extended DOS 4.0+ boot sector data. If the disk was created by FORMAT or SYS from DOS 3.3 or an earlier version, this field is 0.

Volume serial number. A special 32-bit number used as a serial number for the disk. This value is created by the DOS 4.0+ FORMAT or SYS commands by the use of a random number generator combined with the date and time as a seed value. Because more than four billion combinations are possible, you will not see two disks with the same numbers. A multitasking operating system can use this data to detect floppy disk changes during program operation. If the disk was created by FORMAT or SYS from DOS 3.3 or an earlier version, this field is 0.

Volume label. An ASCII text copy of the volume label on the disk. The volume label is still stored as a special case file on the disk. This field carries the text `NO NAME` if no label was specified during the format. If the disk was created by FORMAT or SYS from DOS 3.3 or an earlier version, this field is 0.

File system ID. Carries an ASCII text value indicating the type of file system on the disk. The currently supported values are either FAT12 or FAT16, indicating a disk with a 12-bit or 16-bit FAT, respectively. If the disk was created by FORMAT or SYS from DOS 3.3 or an earlier version, this field is 0.

Don't forget that the end of any volume boot sector also must contain the proper signature bytes (55AAh), or the disk is not bootable.

The next section focuses on the DOS directory system, including the root directory as well as subdirectories. The DOS directory structure, along with the FAT, represents the core of the DOS disk management system.

Directories

A *directory* is like a simple database containing information for DOS about the files stored on a disk. Each record in a directory is 32 bytes long, and no delimiters or separating characters exist between the fields or records. A directory stores a great deal of information about a file, including the name, attribute, time and date of creation, size, and where the beginning of the file is located on the disk.

Note a distinction in this last bit of information—the *beginning* of the file. A directory lacks information about where the file continues on the disk and whether the file is contiguous or fragmented. For such information, you need the FAT.

Two basic types of directories exist: the *root directory* and *subdirectories*. You can have only one root directory per volume. The root directory always is stored on a disk in a fixed location, following the two FAT copies. The type of disk and the disk's capacity determines the root directory's size. After the root directory is created, its length cannot be extended to hold more entries. A hard disk volume usually has a root directory with room for 512 entries. Subdirectories are stored as files in the data area of the disk, so they have no fixed length limits.

All directories are organized the same way. Essentially the directories are small databases with a fixed record length of 32 bytes. The directory information is linked to the FAT by the starting-cluster entry. In fact, if all files on a disk were no longer than one single cluster, the FAT would be useless. The directory stores all the information DOS needs to manage the file, with the exception of all the clusters the file occupies other than the first one. The FAT stores the remaining information about which other clusters the file uses.

To trace a file on the disk, you start with the directory entry and—using the information about the starting cluster of the file and its size—go to the FAT. From there, you can follow the "chain" of clusters that the file occupies until you reach the end of the file.

Decoding a Root Directory Entry

Following is an example showing the first sector from the root directory of a 720K 3 1/2-inch floppy disk with a few files on it. You can use this information to correct a corrupted disk by using a disk editor to replace the corrupted data on the disk.

```
Hexadecimal Byte Values                                  ASCII Text

    0  1  2  3  4  5  6  7  8  9  A  B  C  D  E  F  0123456789ABCDEF

000 49 42 4D 42 49 4F 20 20-43 4F 4D 27 00 00 00 00 IBMBIO  COM'....
010 00 00 00 00 00 00 00 60-9B 14 02 00 64 87 00 00 .......‘....d...
020 49 42 4D 44 4F 53 20 20-43 4F 4D 27 00 00 00 00 IBMDOS  COM'....
030 00 00 00 00 00 00 00 60-B5 14 24 00 90 91 00 00 .......‘..$.....
040 43 4F 4D 4D 41 4E 44 20-43 4F 4D 20 00 00 00 00 COMMAND COM ....
050 00 00 00 00 00 00 00 60-DD 14 49 00 85 93 00 00 .......‘..I.....
060 46 4C 4F 50 50 59 5F 44-49 53 4B 28 00 00 00 00 FLOPPY_DISK(....
070 00 00 00 00 00 00 47 1E-48 15 00 00 00 00 00 00 ......G.H.......
080 43 4F 4E 46 49 47 20 20-53 59 53 20 00 00 00 00 CONFIG  SYS ....
090 00 00 00 00 00 00 69 14-30 15 6E 00 AB 00 00 00 ......i.0.n.....
0A0 41 55 54 4F 45 58 45 43-42 41 54 20 00 00 00 00 AUTOEXECBAT ....
0B0 00 00 00 00 00 00 6E 6A-30 15 6F 00 CD 01 00 00 ......nj0.o.....
0C0 44 4F 53 20 20 20 20 20-20 20 20 10 00 00 00 00 DOS        .....
0D0 00 00 00 00 00 00 25 23-48 15 70 00 00 00 00 00 ......%#H.p.....
0E0 E5 45 53 54 49 4E 47 20-54 58 54 20 00 00 00 00 .ESTING TXT ....
0F0 00 00 00 00 00 00 29 23-48 15 71 00 10 00 00 00 ......)#H.q.....
100 00 00 00 00 00 00 00 00-00 00 00 00 00 00 00 00 ................
110 00 00 00 00 00 00 00 00-00 00 00 00 00 00 00 00 ................
120 00 00 00 00 00 00 00 00-00 00 00 00 00 00 00 00 ................
130 00 00 00 00 00 00 00 00-00 00 00 00 00 00 00 00 ................
140 00 00 00 00 00 00 00 00-00 00 00 00 00 00 00 00 ................
150 00 00 00 00 00 00 00 00-00 00 00 00 00 00 00 00 ................
160 00 00 00 00 00 00 00 00-00 00 00 00 00 00 00 00 ................
170 00 00 00 00 00 00 00 00-00 00 00 00 00 00 00 00 ................
180 00 00 00 00 00 00 00 00-00 00 00 00 00 00 00 00 ................
190 00 00 00 00 00 00 00 00-00 00 00 00 00 00 00 00 ................
1A0 00 00 00 00 00 00 00 00-00 00 00 00 00 00 00 00 ................
1B0 00 00 00 00 00 00 00 00-00 00 00 00 00 00 00 00 ................
1C0 00 00 00 00 00 00 00 00-00 00 00 00 00 00 00 00 ................
1D0 00 00 00 00 00 00 00 00-00 00 00 00 00 00 00 00 ................
1E0 00 00 00 00 00 00 00 00-00 00 00 00 00 00 00 00 ................
1F0 00 00 00 00 00 00 00 00-00 00 00 00 00 00 00 00 ................
```

This example has a volume label, five files, one subdirectory, and one deleted file. Each directory entry is 32 bytes long, which corresponds to two lines in this chart. Entries that are not allocated contain all 00h bytes. The structure of all directories is the same whether they are the root directory or a subdirectory.

The format and position of the data in each 32-byte directory entry are listed in table 7.10.

Table 7.10
DOS Directory Format

Offset	*Length*	*Item*
00h 0	8 bytes	File name
08h 8	3 bytes	Extension
0Bh 11	1 byte	File attributes
0Ch 12	10 bytes	Reserved
16h 22	1 word	Time of creation
18h 24	1 word	Date of creation
1Ah 26	1 word	Starting cluster
1Ch 28	1 dword	Size in bytes

In this table, the first column specifies the offset into the directory entry for each field. Do not confuse this with the offset into the sector. The length of each field is specified in the next column, and the last column contains the item of the field.

The File Name Field

The file name field contains the first eight characters of the file name. The first byte of the file name is specially treated by DOS, and certain values indicate the file status. The file status byte may contain the values listed in table 7.11.

Table 7.11
File Status Byte Values

Hex Value	*Decimal Value*	*ASCII Character*	*Description*
00h	0	-	Unused entry
05h	5	♣	Represents σ
2Eh	46	.	Subdirectory
E5h	229	σ	Deleted file

More detailed explanations of the descriptions follow:

- *Unused entry*. This description indicates that this directory entry has never been used. DOS refuses to examine further entries in the directory after encountering this byte as the first character in the file name field. In practical terms, this byte improves performance by limiting the length of directory searches. If the 00h byte is placed accidentally as the first character of a file name, however, access to additional files is prevented.

- *Represents* σ. The ♣ character (Ctrl-E) indicates that the first character of the file name is actually E5h or σ (a lowercase sigma). This value appears if you create a file in which the sigma character was the first character of the name—a rare occurrence.

- *Subdirectory*. If the first file name entry in a directory is a period, this value indicates that this is a subdirectory entry. If the second byte of the file name is also 2Eh—the file name for the second entry is two periods—the cluster field for that entry contains the cluster number of this directory's parent directory.

- *Deleted file*. The appearance of σ in the first position of the file name field indicates that the file entry has been used but the file has been deleted or erased. In the sample directory, the file TESTING.TXT had been deleted. As you can see, the directory entry is intact except for the first character, which is now the sigma character.

If any other character appears as the first character in the file name field, the character is treated as the first character of a file name. File names must be left justified and padded with blanks if they do not use the full 8 bytes.

The Extension Field

The extension field is three characters long and must be left justified and padded with blanks if it does not use the full 3 bytes. If no file extension exists, this field contains all blanks (20h).

The File Attributes Field

The file attributes field at offset 0Bh uses individual bits in a single byte to determine the characteristics of the file. By setting individual bits on or off, the individual attributes can be set or unset. To make a file a hidden file, for example, a program can change the third bit from a 0 to a 1. The complete attribute byte is mapped in table 7.12.

Table 7.12
DOS Directory File Attribute Byte

Bit Positions *7 6 5 4 3 2 1 0*	*Hex Value*	*Description*
0 0 0 0 0 0 0 1	01h	Read-only file
0 0 0 0 0 0 1 0	02h	Hidden file
0 0 0 0 0 1 0 0	04h	System file
0 0 0 0 1 0 0 0	08h	Volume label
0 0 0 1 0 0 0 0	10h	Subdirectory
0 0 1 0 0 0 0 0	20h	Archive (updated since backup)
0 1 0 0 0 0 0 0	40h	Reserved (normally set to 0)
1 0 0 0 0 0 0 0	80h	Reserved (normally set to 0)

Look at the following examples:

0 0 1 0 0 0 0 1	21h	Read only, archive
0 0 1 1 0 0 1 0	32h	Hidden, subdirectory, archive
0 0 1 0 0 1 1 1	27h	Read only, hidden, system, archive

You decode the attribute byte by converting the hexadecimal value of the byte to binary. The positions of the 1 bits determine which attributes are set on or off.

If none of the bits is set, the file is normal and can be read or written without restrictions. Files that are marked as read only cannot be opened for output with INT 21h function 3Dh; the operation fails, and an error code is returned. Of course the file or data still can be written through other INT functions, such as INT 26h or INT 13h functions. Setting a file to read only doesn't give you security from illegal writes but can prevent accidental writes to a file.

Files marked as hidden or system files are excluded from normal directory searches. If the volume label attribute is set, that entry contains the volume label in the file name and extension fields. Any other information in the entry is ignored, and this attribute may exist only in the root directory.

Files that have the subdirectory attribute set are treated like directories. These files are in directory format, with 32-byte entries containing directory information. The first two files in a subdirectory are . and .. (one period and two periods).

The archive bit is set to on whenever the file is written to and closed. This bit is used by the BACKUP and RESTORE commands.

The DOS ATTRIB command can manipulate some of the attribute bits for a file. ATTRIB can change only the read-only and archive bits. To set or unset any other bit, a more powerful utility is necessary. For example, you can use the FILEFIND command in Norton Utilities Version 5.0 or the FA command in Norton Utilities Version 4.5 to set all file attributes (see *Using Norton Utilities*, published by Que Corporation, for more information).

The Reserved Field

The next 10 bytes in a directory entry are reserved by DOS. These bytes are normally all 00h.

The Time Field

You encounter the time field at offset 16h. This information is stored as a word that contains the time when the file was created or last updated. The time is mapped into the individual time values by the conversion of the word value to a hexadecimal number, the conversion of the hexadecimal number to binary, and then the mapping of the bits as listed in table 7.13.

Table 7.13
Determining the Time

	Hours	*Minutes*	*Seconds/2*
Bit #	F E D C B	A 9 8 7 6 5	4 3 2 1 0
Bit Value	H H H H H	M M M M M M	S S S S S

In the table, H equals Hours, M equals Minutes, and S equals Seconds/2.

The Hours part of this field contains the binary number representing the hours from 0 through 23. The Minutes portion stores minutes in a binary representation of 0 through 59. The Seconds part of this field does not have enough digits to store the complete seconds value in binary, so you must divide the seconds by 2 and store the result as the binary number of 2-second increments. As a result, file times are stored to a maximum resolution of plus or minus 2 seconds.

Figure 7.11 shows an example. The time field is converted and translated from the CONFIG.SYS file entry in the directory sector. This figure shows how to get from the word value to the hour, minute, and second the file was last created or updated.

```
69 14 (word) = 1469h = 00010100 01101001b

00010100 01101001b
              └────► Seconds/2 = 01001b = 9 = 18/2
00010100 01101001b
      └──┴─────────► Minutes = 100011b = 35
00010100 01101001b
  └─────────────────► Hours = 00010b = 2

Time = 2:35:18
```

Fig. 7.11. Decoding the time.

The Date Field

The date field is stored at offset 18h as a word value. To determine the actual date, you must convert the word value to a hexadecimal number, convert the hexadecimal number to a binary number, and then map the bits as listed in table 7.14.

Table 7.14
Determining the Date

	Year-1980	*Month*	*Day*
Bit #	F E D C B A 9	8 7 6 5	4 3 2 1 0
Bit Value	Y Y Y Y Y Y Y	M M M M	D D D D D

In the table, Y equals Years-1980, M equals Months, and D equals Days.

The Years number is stored as the binary equivalent of 0 through 119 decimal. The year is interpreted as the number of years past 1980. For example, 1991 is stored as 11. The months are stored as the binary equal of 1 through 12, and the days are stored as the binary value representing 1 through 31.

Figure 7.12 shows an example. The date field is converted and translated from the same CONFIG.SYS file entry. This figure shows how to get from the word value to the year, month, and day the file was last created or updated.

```
30 15 (word) = 1530h = 00010101 00110000b

00010101 00110000b
            └──────► Days = 10000b = 16
00010101 00110000b
       └──┘─────────► Months = 1001b = 9
00010101 00110000b
   └────────────────► Years-1980 = 0001010b = 10 = 1990-1980

Date = 09/16/1990
```

Fig. 7.12. Decoding the date.

The Starting Cluster Field

The starting cluster field located at offset 1Ah is one of the most important fields in a directory entry. This number tells DOS the cluster or allocation unit where the file begins on the disk. This value is stored as a word, which means that it must be converted to a hexadecimal number for interpretation. The starting cluster value for the COMMAND.COM file entry in the example directory follows:

49 00 (word value) = 0049h = cluster 73

The word value 49 00 is equal to the hexadecimal number 0049h, which is equal to 73 decimal.

The Size Field

The size field is another important field in a directory entry. This number represents the file size in bytes. This value is stored as a dword value; you read the 4 bytes backward to convert the value to a hexadecimal number. Using the COMMAND.COM file as an example, you can figure out how big the file is by following these steps:

85 93 00 00 (dword value) = 00009385h = 37,765 bytes

Decoding a Complete Directory Entry

You can put this information together and translate a complete directory entry. If you examine the IBMDOS.COM file entry from the example directory, you find the following information:

```
Hexadecimal Byte Values                                        ASCII Text

    0  1  2  3  4  5  6  7  8  9  A  B  C  D  E  F  0123456789ABCDEF

000 49 42 4D 44 4F 53 20 20-43 4F 4D 27 00 00 00 00  IBMDOS COM'.....
010 00 00 00 00 00 00 00 60-B5 14 24 00 90 91 00 00  .......'..$.....
```

Table 7.15 lists the contents of the IBMDOS.COM from the example directory.

Table 7.15
Contents of IBMDOS.COM

Offset	*Length*	*Item*	*Converted Hex Values*	*Translation*
00h	8 bytes	File name		"IBMDOS "
08h	3 bytes	Extension		"COM"
0Bh	1 byte	File attributes	27h	R-O,Hid,Sys,Arc
0Ch	10 bytes	Reserved	00h	-
16h	1 word	Time of creation	6000h	12:00:00
18h	1 word	Date of creation	14B5h	05/21/1990
1Ah	1 word	Starting cluster	0024h	Cluster 36
1Ch	1 dword	Size in bytes	00009190h	37,264 bytes

Utility programs can translate the directory data into information like that found in the right column in this listing. Powerful disk editors enable you to make changes with the disk information formatted and displayed in a manner understandable by people.

Decoding a Subdirectory Entry

A subdirectory is a special kind of file with a structure matching that of the root directory. These files contain a set of two special entries that point to a parent directory and to the subdirectory itself. These pointers appear as the first two file entries in a subdirectory, the files named . and .. (one and two periods).

The . file entry represents the subdirectory file itself. The entry contains a starting cluster value indicating the starting cluster of the subdirectory file. The length entry for a subdirectory file name is always zero. The .. directory entry is a pointer to the parent directory of the subdirectory. The starting cluster field contains the starting cluster number for the parent directory or is filled with zeros if the parent directory is the root directory.

The first two file entries in the DOS subdirectory on the 720K disk used in the previous examples follow:

```
Hexadecimal Byte Values                                ASCII Text

    0  1  2  3  4  5  6  7  8  9  A  B  C  D  E  F 0123456789ABCDEF

000 2E 20 20 20 20 20 20 20-20 20 20 10 00 00 00 00 .          .....
010 00 00 00 00 00 00 25 23-48 15 70 00 00 00 00 00 ......%#H.p.....

000 2E 2E 20 20 20 20 20 20-20 20 20 10 00 00 00 00 ..         .....
010 00 00 00 00 00 00 25 23-48 15 00 00 00 00 00 00 ......%#H.......
```

For clarity, a space has been added to separate the two entries. The contents of those first two file entries are examined in table 7.16.

Table 7.16
Contents of the First Two Subdirectory Entries

Offset	*Length*	*Item*	*Converted Hex Values*	*Translation*
00h	8 bytes	File name		". "
08h	3 bytes	Extension		" "
0Bh	1 byte	File attributes	10h	Subdir
0Ch	10 bytes	Reserved	00h	-
16h	1 word	Time of creation	2325h	04:25:10
18h	1 word	Date of creation	1548h	10/08/1990
1Ah	1 word	Starting cluster	0070h	Cluster 112
1Ch	1 dword	Size in bytes	00000000h	Always 0 bytes

Offset	*Length*	*Item*	*Converted Hex Values*	*Translation*
00h	8 bytes	File name		".. "
08h	3 bytes	Extension		" "
0Bh	1 byte	File attributes	10h	Subdir
0Ch	10 bytes	Reserved	00h	-
16h	1 word	Time of creation	2325h	04:25:10
18h	1 word	Date of creation	1548h	10/08/1990
1Ah	1 word	Starting cluster	0000h	0 = parent is root
1Ch	1 dword	Size in bytes	00000000h	Always 0 bytes

As you can see from this example, the DOS directory is a first-level subdirectory; its parent directory is the root directory. The .. entry has a starting cluster value of zero. A nonzero starting cluster value indicates the location of the parent directory. Directory problems, such as circular chains or the inability to move back to a parent after entering a subdirectory, can result if these starting cluster values are corrupted. Remember that directory . and .. entries are zero bytes long. The actual length is irrelevant because directories allocate space one cluster at a time, managed by the FAT.

When a root directory is destroyed or damaged, the pointers to the subdirectories are lost. To fix this disaster, you can search the sectors of the disk for . with 10 spaces after the period or .. with 9 spaces after the two periods. If you find this pattern on a disk, it probably is a sector containing the beginning of a subdirectory. By locating these subdirectory files, you can restore most of the files on the disk, depending on how fragmented the files were (see Chapter 10 for details on data recovery problem solving).

The File Allocation Table

The *file allocation table (FAT)* is a table of number entries describing how each cluster is allocated on the disk. A single entry exists for each cluster in the data area of the disk. Sectors in the nondata area on the disk are outside the range of the disk controlled by the FAT. The sectors involved in the boot sectors, FAT, and root directory are outside the range of sectors controlled by the FAT.

The FAT does not manage every data sector. Instead, the FAT allocates space in groups of sectors called *clusters*. A cluster is one or more sectors designated by DOS as allocation units of storage. The smallest space a file can use on a disk is one cluster, and if the file is one byte larger than one cluster, two clusters are used. All files use space on the disk in integer cluster units. DOS determines the size of a cluster when you format the disk with the DOS FORMAT command.

Think of the FAT as a spreadsheet that controls the cluster usage of the disk. Each cell in the spreadsheet corresponds to a single cluster on the disk, and the number stored in that cell is a code telling whether that cluster is used by a file. If the cluster is used by a file, the code tells where the next cluster of that file is located.

The numbers stored in the FAT are hexadecimal numbers that are 12 or 16 bits long. The 16-bit FAT take 2 bytes of space and can be edited fairly easily. The 12-bit numbers, however, are 1.5 bytes long, which presents a problem because most disk sector editors show data in byte units. To edit the FAT, you must perform hexadecimal/binary math to convert the displayed byte units to FAT numbers. Fortunately, most tools and utility programs have a FAT editing mode that performs conversions automatically. Most utilities also show the FAT numbers in decimal form.

DOS determines whether a 12-bit or 16-bit FAT is placed on disk with the FDISK program, even though the FAT is written during the high-level format. Floppy disks use a 12-bit FAT. On hard disk volumes with more than 16M, DOS creates a 16-bit FAT; otherwise, DOS creates a 12-bit FAT.

DOS keeps two copies of the FAT; each one occupies contiguous sectors on the disk. The second FAT copy immediately follows the first. Unfortunately, DOS only uses the second copy as an occasional check for whether the copies compare. The first copy is the only one actually used. If the first copy is trashed, DOS cannot use the second one.

A final disappointment is that when the first FAT is updated by DOS, the first copy is copied immediately onto the second copy. If the first copy was corrupted, but was updated by DOS, the bad first FAT is copied over the previously good second copy. After the update, the second copy is a mirror image of the first one—complete with all its problems.

Because of these procedures, the usefulness of the second FAT copy is limited to manual repair operations. Even for manual repair, you must catch the problem before DOS has a chance to update the disk.

How DOS Allocates Space

Remember that a single cluster is the smallest unit of the disk that DOS can deal with when writing to or reading a file. A cluster is equal to one or more sectors, and although a cluster can be a single sector, a cluster is usually more than one. Having more than one sector per cluster reduces the size and processing overhead of the FAT and enables DOS to run faster by having fewer individual units of the disk to worry about. The trade-off is wasted disk space. Because DOS only can manage space in the cluster unit, every file consumes disk space in increments of one cluster.

Table 7.17 lists the default cluster sizes DOS uses for various disk formats.

Table 7.17
Default Cluster Sizes

Drive	*Type*	*Default Cluster Size*
5 1/4	360K	2 sectors or 1,024 bytes
5 1/4	1.2M	1 sector or 512 bytes
3 1/2	720K	2 sectors or 1,024 bytes
3 1/2	1.44M	1 sector or 512 bytes

High-density disks have smaller cluster sizes because they have many more individual sectors than low-density disks. The larger the FAT, the more entries that must be managed and the slower DOS runs. This slowness is due to the excessive overhead in managing many individual clusters. The trade-off is in the minimum allocation unit—the cluster size itself. With smaller clusters, you have less wasted space after the end of each file to the end of the cluster. With larger clusters, the wasted space grows larger. The high-density floppy drives are faster than the low-density counterparts, so IBM and Microsoft probably thought that the decrease in cluster size would be welcome because the drive's faster operation offsets the larger FAT.

For hard disks, the cluster size varies among the different versions of DOS and different disk sizes. Table 7.18 lists the cluster sizes that most DOS versions select.

Table 7.18
Selected Cluster Sizes

Hard Disk Volume Size	*Default Cluster Size*	*FAT Type*
0-15M	8 sectors or 4,096 bytes	12-bit
16-128M	4 sectors or 2,048 bytes	16-bit
129-256M	8 sectors or 4,096 bytes	16-bit
257-512M	16 sectors or 8,192 bytes	16-bit
513-1,024M	32 sectors or 16,384 bytes	16-bit
1,025-2,048M	64 sectors or 32,768 bytes	16-bit
2,049-4,096M	128 sectors or 65,536 bytes	16-bit

These cluster sizes are selected by the DOS FORMAT command and are the minimum possible for a given partition size in most cases. The 8K clusters are the smallest possible for a partition size greater than 256M. Although most non-IBM OEM versions of DOS work like the IBM version, some versions use different cluster sizes than this table indicates. For example, COMPAQ DOS shifts to larger cluster sizes earlier than IBM DOS. COMPAQ DOS shifts to 4K clusters at 64M partitions, 8K clusters at 128M partitions, and 16K clusters at 256M partitions.

The effect of these larger cluster sizes on disk use can be substantial. I currently have about 5,000 files on my hard drive, which usually wastes about half of the last cluster used for each file. In other words, my hard drive wastes 20M of file space. The equation is 5,000 x (.5 x 8)K. With COMPAQ DOS, this wasted space doubles to 40M for the same 5,000 files!

COMPAQ DOS does not use the most efficient (or smallest) cluster size possible because COMPAQ wants to improve the performance of the system at the expense of disk space. Larger cluster sizes get a smaller FAT with fewer numbers to manage. This result reduces the DOS overhead for storing and retrieving files, which makes the system faster.

How the FAT Is Organized

Expressed in normal hexadecimal notation, a 12-bit FAT number is three digits long, and a 16-bit number is four digits long. If the cluster that a cell is watching is empty, the number stored there is (0)000 in hexadecimal. If the cluster is a part of a file, the number stored in that cell entry is the next cluster that the file occupies. When a file is stored, the first cluster's cell entry points to the second cluster, the second cluster's cell entry points to the third cluster, and so on. The cluster numbers can be traced like a chain. The last cluster occupied by the file has a cell entry of (F)FFF, which indicates that this is the last cluster, not a pointer to another cluster.

Bad or unusable clusters have a special entry—(F)FF7—in the FAT that indicates that the clusters are never to be used.

The numeric entries in a FAT may be any of the entries listed in table 7.19.

Table 7.19
The Numeric Entries in a FAT

FAT Number	*Description*
(0)000	The cluster is unused (available).
(F)FF0 - (F)FF6	The cluster is reserved (not available).
(F)FF7	The cluster is bad (not available).
(F)FF8 - (F)FFF	The cluster is the last in a particular file.
(0)002 - (F)FEF	The cluster is in use by a file. The number itself indicates the next cluster occupied by this file.

Although DOS may use several different FAT numbers to indicate the last cluster of a file, I have seen only the (F)FFF number used. I never have seen the numbers indicating reserved clusters on any disk.

Note that a 16-bit FAT uses the full four-digit hexadecimal number, and a 12-bit FAT uses only the three-digit portion minus the leading digit in parentheses.

The following formula shows how a FAT is calculated. You can use this formula to derive other disk allocations as well:

$$SPF = \frac{TS - RS - \dfrac{D * BPD}{BPS}}{CF + \dfrac{BPS * SPC}{BPC}}$$

In the formula, the letters stand for the following items:

TS	The total sectors on disk.
RS	The number of sectors at the beginning of the disk that are reserved for the DOS volume boot sector. Normally 1 sector.
D	The number of directory entries in the root directory. Normally 512.
BPD	The number of bytes per directory entry. Always 32.
BPS	The number of bytes per logical sector. Usually 512, but you can specify a different number with VDISK.
CF	The number of FATS per disk. Usually 2; however, VDISK is 1.
SPF	The number of sectors per FAT. Maximum 64.
SPC	The number of sectors per allocation unit. Must be a power of 2.
BPC	The number of bytes per FAT entry. 1.5 for 12-bit FATs; 2 for 16-bit FATs.

The FAT is an organized list of numbers that can tell you what each cluster of the disk is "doing." By tracing the FAT entries, you can determine which clusters a file occupies, which clusters are available for new file storage, and which clusters are marked as bad. When a file has been erased or lost, you can use programs such as Norton Utilities to trace the parts of a file and put them back together to restore (unerase) a file.

The Data Area

The data area of a disk follows the boot sector, FATs, and root directory on a volume. This area is managed by the FAT and the root directory and is divided by DOS into allocation units that are sometimes called *clusters*. These clusters are where normal files are stored on a volume.

DOS 4.0 can handle sectors using a 32-bit numbering scheme. This scheme permits a maximum of 4,294,967,296 sectors (2 terabytes) of total disk space. But the FAT and cluster numbering scheme currently allow a maximum disk volume size of 4 gigabytes.

With 24 disk partitions of 4 gigabytes each, DOS 4 or later versions can support 96 gigabytes of disk space. Other limits, however, enter into this discussion. For example, the ROM BIOS has a limit of 1,024 maximum cylinders, 256 heads, and 64 sectors per track. With a controller that can translate the actual drive parameters to fit these limits, the maximum size for a single hard disk is 8 gigabytes. Because a partition cannot exceed 4 gigabytes, you split this disk into at least 2 partitions.

A *file* is a group of clusters containing data that is part of a single entity. The file is managed by a name and other information contained in a directory entry, as well as a chain of cluster numbers in the FAT indicating the actual clusters in use by the file.

You can inspect the entries for the file in the directory and the FAT to see whether damage has been done to the file itself or the management information used for controlling and locating the file. If the management information is damaged, you can correct it. If the file itself is damaged, you can recover the file except for the damaged clusters.

Some disk recovery programs, such as Norton Utilities Version 5.0, automate much of the disk recovery process. The Norton Disk Edit program, for example, automates searching for related parts (clusters) of a file, enabling you to reassemble the file and rewrite the corrected file to disk.

The Diagnostic Read and Write Cylinder

The FDISK partitioning program reserves the last cylinder of a hard disk for use as a special diagnostic read and write test cylinder. On systems with ESDI or SCSI disk interfaces, the drive and controller can allocate an additional area past the logical end of the drive for a bad track table and spare sectors for replacing bad sectors.

The diagnostics area permits diagnostics software to perform read and write tests on a hard disk without corrupting data. Low-level format programs for hard disks often use this cylinder as a scratch pad area for running interleave tests. Some low-level format programs use this cylinder to preserve data during nondestructive formats. This cylinder also is used as a head landing or parking cylinder on many hard disks that do not have an automatic parking facility.

Because this cylinder is reserved, FDISK reports fewer total cylinders for use than drive manufacturers claim. Operating systems do not use this cylinder for normal purposes because it lies outside the partitioned area of the disk.

Chapter Summary

In this chapter, you examined the structure of disks according to DOS. You learned about every area of floppy and hard disks, including data structures such as the master and extended partition boot sectors, volume boot sectors, directories, FATs, and so on. Many of these structures are complicated and can be difficult to decipher at first glance.

These structures are vital in allowing access to your disk. Small errors in these structures can render entire disks inaccessible and apparently lost. You can repair these areas and restore access to the data, which will make you look like a miracle worker to your associates!

This chapter's information is as detailed as possible so that it can serve as a reference in future data recovery situations. You can get to these areas, but to correct them you need to know how the areas are supposed to look.

Part II

Recovering Data

Includes

DOS Data Recovery Utilities
Special-Purpose Data Recovery Programs
Data Recovery Techniques
Virus Programs
Preventive Maintenance

8

DOS Data Recovery Utilities

DOS offers several rudimentary file management and recovery programs that often are sufficient for your data recovery efforts. The DOS commands useful for data recovery include COPY, CHKDSK, RECOVER, and DEBUG. These commands are crude and their effects sometimes drastic, but at times these commands are the only tools you have (or need) for data recovery. The RECOVER command is well known as a data recovery program, and most users know that they can use DEBUG to correct problems. The other commands, however, are not as well known for their data recovery capabilities. The CHKDSK command, for example, usually is used for simple inspection of file structure. Many users are not aware that they can use CHKDSK to repair a damaged file structure. In addition, you can use the COPY command for recovering from file or file system (file allocation table [FAT] and directory) damage.

Several new commands useful for data recovery were added in DOS Version 5.0, including the MIRROR, REBUILD, UNFORMAT, and UNDELETE commands. If you do not use DOS 5.0, you can find commands that perform these data recovery techniques in programs such as Norton Utilities and PC Tools.

This chapter examines the DOS commands and their capabilities in the data recovery process. DOS commands are, however, only a small selection of the tools you should have in your data recovery software toolbox. More sophisticated data recovery tools and advanced techniques are discussed in Chapters 9 and 10.

Using the COPY Command

The DOS COPY command is not to be considered as a powerful data recovery command. Some aspects of the command, however, will help you understand how data corruption or loss can take place. Because COPY is such a commonly used command and because it contains a few quirks and bugs, COPY can cause data loss. This section examines how COPY works and how it can create problems. You also learn how to use COPY correctly to prevent data loss and to recover data that is lost.

As you probably know, you use the DOS COPY command to copy a file (or group of files) to the same disk or another disk. The COPY command has not changed significantly since the release of DOS 2.0. The syntax for the COPY command, including optional parameters, is

> COPY [/A][/B] [*d:*][*path*]*filename*[/A][/B][*d:*][*path*]
> [*file name*][/A][/B][/V]

or

> COPY [/A][/B] [*d:*][*path*]*filename*[/A][/B] [+[*d:*][*path*]
> *file name*[/A][/B]] [*d:*][*path*][*filename*][/A][/B][/V]

The first file name usually specifies the *source* file, and the second file name specifies the *destination* file (except in *file concatenation*, in which two or more files are joined together). In file concatenation, if no destination file is listed, the first file name listed becomes the destination file and a source file at the same time. You can use wild-card characters within or in place of file names.

The /A (ASCII) parameter causes the file listed before the parameter and all remaining files (unless another parameter is indicated) to be treated as ASCII files. When you specify this parameter for source files, the data in the file is copied up to but not including the first end-of-file character (Ctrl-Z or 1Ah). Any remainder of the file is not copied. When used with a destination file, this parameter causes an end-of-file character (Ctrl-Z or 1Ah) to be added to the file as the last character. Use of this parameter in data recovery is discussed in the "What Ends a File?" section of this chapter.

The /B (binary) parameter causes the file listed before the parameter and all remaining files (unless another parameter is indicated) to be treated as binary files. When this parameter is specified for source files, the entire file is copied regardless of content. When used with a destination file, this parameter indicates that an end-of-file character (Ctrl-Z or 1Ah) should not be added as the last character in the file. The file contents simply are left "as is." Use of this switch in data recovery is discussed in the "What Ends a File?" section of this chapter.

The /V parameter verifies that the copied data is correct. This parameter prompts DOS to read and compare each sector after writing, and the additional step causes the COPY command to operate more slowly. Because hardware is usually reliable and because a sector failure normally would cause an error message to be displayed even without using /V, this parameter is usually not necessary. If your file is really important, however, you should use the /V switch to make sure that the copy is identical to the original.

The + symbol in the second version of the COPY command's syntax causes the command to concatenate, or combine, files as it copies. Concatenation is used when you want to combine two or more ASCII files quickly without having to use a text editor to perform the task.

Understanding the Problems with Concatenating Files

Using the COPY command to concatenate (add one file to the end of another file) can cause problems. This section alerts you to the possible problems resulting from concatenation and offers a method for avoiding these problems.

To copy the contents of FILE1 and FILE2 into FILE3, you can use the following command:

```
COPY FILE1 + FILE2 FILE3
```

You also can combine files (FILE1 and FILE2 in this example) by using the following command:

```
COPY FILE1 + FILE2
```

During the command's operation, DOS lists by name all files being appended. On termination of the process, DOS displays the following message:

```
1 File(s) copied
```

This screen message refers to the number of destination (or result) files created. By leaving off the destination file, you tell DOS to use the first source file as the destination. Thus, in this case, FILE1 will contain the same data that FILE3 did in the first example. This method of concatenation is more dangerous than the first method. If you make a mistake, one of your source files is altered.

You also can use wild cards when concatenating files, as in the following command:

COPY FILE*.TXT FILEALL.DOC

This command concatenates all files that match the FILE*.TXT criterion into a new file named FILEALL.DOC.

Notice that in this case the destination must be specified and should not be one of the files that would be matched by the source wild cards. If you do not specify a destination with this concatenation form, the following error message appears:

```
File cannot be copied onto itself
  0 File(s) copied
```

If you accidentally specify a source wild card that matches your destination file, and the destination file is not the first file matched by the source wild-card specification (or a directory entry is not open before the first file matched by the source wild-card specification), this error message appears:

```
Content of destination lost before copy
  1 File(s) copied
```

You also should know that the concatenation function is bugged (or is otherwise defective) in the DOS 3.3x supplied by most OEMs, including IBM and COMPAQ. If you use a wild-card specification on the source file, the files matching the wild cards are not appended properly. The first two files append correctly, but two embedded end-of-file (EOF) markers are placed in the destination after the second appended file, and one additional EOF marker is embedded in the destination following every other file after the second file. The embedded end-of-file markers then prevent the file from loading beyond the second file. DOS 3.3's defective concatenation function can be illustrated by the following example. If you type

COPY FILE?.TXT NEWFILE.TXT

at the `D:\>` prompt, you receive the following message:

```
FILE1.TXT
FILE2.TXT
FILE3.TXT
FILE4.TXT
  1 File(s) copied
```

This command results in a corrupted version of the NEWFILE.TXT file, in which two embedded EOF characters (and sometimes a few lines of garbage) appear after the FILE2.TXT data. A single EOF character then appears after the FILE3.TXT and FILE4.TXT data. If the concatenation had functioned correctly, one EOF would have been inserted after the FILE4.TXT data, and all other EOF characters would have been stripped from the ends of the individual files.

You can use several methods to work around the DOS 3.3x bug. The easiest way to avoid the bug is to upgrade to DOS 4.xx. DOS 4.xx (with corrective service applied—see Chapter 6) contains no significant bugs and requires only 11K to 17K more memory than Version 3.3, depending on whether you use disk partitions greater than 32M.

Two other methods enable you to work around the bug without changing DOS versions. The first method is to not use wild cards in the source specification and to list specifically all the files you want to concatenate, as in the following example:

```
COPY FILE1.TXT+FILE2.TXT+FILE3.TXT+FILE4.TXT NEWFILE.TXT
```

Another work-around involves simply adding one more file to the source list, as illustrated in the following example:

```
COPY FILE?.TXT+NUL: NEWFILE.TXT
```

The NUL: file name is a dummy name that DOS understands as an empty file. It adds nothing to the copy; NUL: is merely a place holder for the EOF marker.

By using these work-around methods, you can circumvent the concatenation problem in DOS Version 3.3x.

Comparing ASCII and Binary Files

Understanding the operation of the /A and /B switches is important to using the COPY command and can give you insight into how these command options can cause data loss problems. The emphasis in this section is on preventing data loss by understanding how DOS processes files.

COPY defaults to the /B (binary) operation unless one of the following conditions exists:

- You specify /A in the command.
- File concatenation is being performed.
- You are copying to or from a DEVICE name.

In these cases, COPY defaults to /A (ASCII) operation. To understand the use of the /A and /B switches, you need to know more about what causes a file to end. The following section discusses the conditions that cause DOS to determine the end of a file.

What Ends a File?

When reaching what DOS determines to be the end of a file, DOS stops any further processing on that file. If the DOS-determined end of the file does not correspond to the actual end of the file, you have a problem. You may copy a file, for example, and discover that only part of the file was copied because improper file termination occurred.

An incorrect termination may have been caused by an improper use of the COPY command. To be able to solve file termination problems, you need to understand the conditions that prompt DOS to determine the end of a file. You then can avoid creating partial files.

Three conditions cause DOS to decide that a file has ended. All three conditions can (and often do) apply to a single file at the same time. When processing a file, DOS searches for all three conditions simultaneously. When any of the conditions appear, the file is ended. (In other words, the condition that appears first takes precedence over the other conditions and causes processing on the file to stop.)

The following two end-of-file conditions apply to all files:

- Reaching the number of bytes specified in the directory listing of the file
- Running into a FAT end-of-chain marker

If and only if the file is being interpreted as an ASCII file (for example, on a COPY with the /A parameter), the following condition also applies:

- Running into an end-of-file marker (Ctrl-Z or 1Ah)

Because files most commonly are treated as binary files, condition 3 often does not apply. The situation most likely to be encountered first is condition 1. If, for example, a file is listed in the directory as using 150 bytes, the file will end at 150 bytes. The FAT end-of-chain marker for that file would not appear until later. (If the file was stored on a 720K floppy, the cluster size would be 2 sectors, or 1,024 bytes; therefore, as long as the file size was less than or equal to 1,024 bytes, the FAT chain-end cluster condition would not come into play.)

In the FAT, the directory entry size always falls within the range of bytes allocated by the last cluster in the file. You can take a 150-byte text file stored on a 720K floppy disk, for example, and use a disk editor to manually change the directory to 1,024 bytes before any allocation errors result. Allocation errors basically are discrepancies between what the FAT has allocated for the file on the disk and the size of the file in the directory.

Many system operations treat an ASCII text file as if it were a binary file. You can use WordStar Professional Release 4.0, for example, to create and save a nondocument ASCII file named TEST1.TXT that contains one line: ***This is a test.*** After saving the file to disk, you can run a DIR command. At the `D:\>` prompt, type

DIR TEST?.TXT

You get the following result:

```
Volume in drive D has no label
Volume Serial Number is 2E63-0BDE
Directory of  D:\

TEST1            TXT          128 10-12-90      7:12a
                 1 File(s)        5160960 bytes free
```

Interestingly, the file that required only 15 keystrokes contains 128 bytes. Running a couple of COPY commands may give you some insight into what is happening. At the `D:\>` prompt, type

COPY TEST1.TXT TEST2.TXT

You see the message `1 File(s) copied.`

At the `D:\>` prompt, type

COPY /A TEST1.TXT TEST3.TXT

You see the message `1 File(s) copied.`

At the `D:\>` prompt, type

DIR TEST?.TXT

You see the message

```
Volume in drive D has no label
Volume Serial Number is 2E63-0BDE
Directory of D:\

TEST1    TXT    128 10-12-90 7:12a
TEST2    TXT    128 10-12-90 7:12a
TEST3    TXT     17 10-12-90 7:12a
  3 File(s)    5152768 bytes free
```

The first COPY command treated the source and destination files as binary, the default mode of COPY. The copy procedure was executed, therefore, according to the directory size or the FAT end-of-chain marker, and no EOF (Ctrl-Z) character was added to the end of the destination. Because the directory entries and FAT chains in this example were not corrupted, the directory size determined the actual end-of-file condition, and the full 128 bytes were copied. The 128 bytes are the number of bytes allocated to the file. Even though only 17 bytes are used, 128 bytes are available, leaving 111 bytes of "wasted" space.

The second COPY command used the /A switch, which caused the source and destination files to be treated as ASCII files. The /A switch on the source file caused the COPY operation to stop when the first EOF (Ctrl-Z) character was seen, when the directory size was reached, or when the FAT chain ended. In this case, a Ctrl-Z character was found at an offset of 16 bytes (at the 17th byte in the file). This character and any subsequent characters were ignored, and the first 16 bytes were written to the destination file. Because the destination file also was treated as an ASCII file, the 16 bytes were written and a single Ctrl-Z character was added to the end of the file, for a total size of 17 bytes.

> ***Note:*** If you don't understand how 15 keystrokes can equal 17 bytes, the following explanation may help. The text (*This is a test*) accounts for 14 keystrokes. Pressing Enter to end the line accounts for a single keystroke but places two bytes in the file. These bytes are the carriage return (Ctrl-M or 0Dh) and line feed (Ctrl-J or 0Ah) characters, which are used for moving the cursor to the beginning of the line and then to the next line, respectively. These characters are the 15th and 16th bytes. The final Ctrl-Z or EOF character is the 17th byte, finishing off the file.

Some programs (WordStar, for example) "pad" the end of a file (like the TEST1.TXT file) with extra characters. Most often these characters are additional Ctrl-Z characters, as in the preceding example using WordStar. You can use the TYPE command on any of the three files that resulted from this example, and the files appear to be exactly the same. If you load the files back into WordStar or any other text editor (such as DOS EDLIN), all three files appear identical because these programs treat all files as ASCII text files.

You now should know that no special way exists for any program (including COPY) to know implicitly whether a file is supposed to be treated as ASCII or binary. In the case of COPY, as you can see from the example, the way in which a file is treated can produce different (and interesting) results.

Knowing how programs copy and save files can be helpful when you are investigating information loss. If, for example, you do not know about the end-of-file marker, you can be confused about the seemingly different lengths of files that have equivalent contents. For example, you may be able to recover a file created by a DOS 3.3 concatenation (that used a wild card) by removing extra EOF markers from the file with a disk editor such as Norton DiskEdit (see Chapter 9 for more information).

Knowing what you can expect to find in sectors after a file ends also can be helpful in data recovery situations.

What Comes After the End of a File?

When a file is copied or written to a disk, the data is stored up to the file's end. As discussed previously, several interpretations of the end-of-file condition exist. A file is written until a given end condition, based on the interpretation, is reached. What you may not know, however, is what happens on the disk after the end of the file is reached. What happens, for example, between the end of a file and the end of a sector? What happens in the space from the end of the sector to the end of the cluster? The answers to these questions are relevant to data security and data recovery. The following discussion provides you with insight into how you can recover erased and encrypted information from a disk. You sometimes can recover information that never has been written to a file!

A bit of experimentation may help answer the questions posed in the preceding paragraph. Suppose, for example, that you format a 720K 3 1/2-inch disk as follows:

```
FORMAT A: /F:720 /V:FLOPPY_DISK
```

This FORMAT command uses the high-density drive (drive A in this experiment) to format the 720K disk. The /F:720 parameter indicates to the FORMAT command that the disk is 720K. Without this parameter, the FORMAT command would default to 1.44M, the default capacity of the high-density drive. The /V:FLOPPY_DISK parameter creates a volume label on the disk. (Note that neither parameter works as specified with DOS versions earlier than 3.3x.) The disk now contains a volume boot sector, a blank FAT, a root directory with only a volume label entry, and a data area consisting of 2-sector clusters, which contain the following data:

```
Hexadecimal Byte Values                                       ASCII Text
     0  1  2  3  4  5  6  7  8  9  A  B  C  D  E  F           0123456789ABCDEF

000 F6 F6 F6 F6 F6 F6 F6 F6-F6 F6 F6 F6 F6 F6 F6 F6           ÷÷÷÷÷÷÷÷÷÷÷÷÷÷÷÷
010 F6 F6 F6 F6 F6 F6 F6 F6-F6 F6 F6 F6 F6 F6 F6 F6           ÷÷÷÷÷÷÷÷÷÷÷÷÷÷÷÷
020 F6 F6 F6 F6 F6 F6 F6 F6-F6 F6 F6 F6 F6 F6 F6 F6           ÷÷÷÷÷÷÷÷÷÷÷÷÷÷÷÷
030 F6 F6 F6 F6 F6 F6 F6 F6-F6 F6 F6 F6 F6 F6 F6 F6           ÷÷÷÷÷÷÷÷÷÷÷÷÷÷÷÷
040 F6 F6 F6 F6 F6 F6 F6 F6-F6 F6 F6 F6 F6 F6 F6 F6           ÷÷÷÷÷÷÷÷÷÷÷÷÷÷÷÷
050 F6 F6 F6 F6 F6 F6 F6 F6-F6 F6 F6 F6 F6 F6 F6 F6           ÷÷÷÷÷÷÷÷÷÷÷÷÷÷÷÷
060 F6 F6 F6 F6 F6 F6 F6 F6-F6 F6 F6 F6 F6 F6 F6 F6           ÷÷÷÷÷÷÷÷÷÷÷÷÷÷÷÷
070 F6 F6 F6 F6 F6 F6 F6 F6-F6 F6 F6 F6 F6 F6 F6 F6           ÷÷÷÷÷÷÷÷÷÷÷÷÷÷÷÷
080 F6 F6 F6 F6 F6 F6 F6 F6-F6 F6 F6 F6 F6 F6 F6 F6           ÷÷÷÷÷÷÷÷÷÷÷÷÷÷÷÷
090 F6 F6 F6 F6 F6 F6 F6 F6-F6 F6 F6 F6 F6 F6 F6 F6           ÷÷÷÷÷÷÷÷÷÷÷÷÷÷÷÷
0A0 F6 F6 F6 F6 F6 F6 F6 F6-F6 F6 F6 F6 F6 F6 F6 F6           ÷÷÷÷÷÷÷÷÷÷÷÷÷÷÷÷
0B0 F6 F6 F6 F6 F6 F6 F6 F6-F6 F6 F6 F6 F6 F6 F6 F6           ÷÷÷÷÷÷÷÷÷÷÷÷÷÷÷÷
0C0 F6 F6 F6 F6 F6 F6 F6 F6-F6 F6 F6 F6 F6 F6 F6 F6           ÷÷÷÷÷÷÷÷÷÷÷÷÷÷÷÷
0D0 F6 F6 F6 F6 F6 F6 F6 F6-F6 F6 F6 F6 F6 F6 F6 F6           ÷÷÷÷÷÷÷÷÷÷÷÷÷÷÷÷
0E0 F6 F6 F6 F6 F6 F6 F6 F6-F6 F6 F6 F6 F6 F6 F6 F6           ÷÷÷÷÷÷÷÷÷÷÷÷÷÷÷÷
0F0 F6 F6 F6 F6 F6 F6 F6 F6-F6 F6 F6 F6 F6 F6 F6 F6           ÷÷÷÷÷÷÷÷÷÷÷÷÷÷÷÷
100 F6 F6 F6 F6 F6 F6 F6 F6-F6 F6 F6 F6 F6 F6 F6 F6           ÷÷÷÷÷÷÷÷÷÷÷÷÷÷÷÷
110 F6 F6 F6 F6 F6 F6 F6 F6-F6 F6 F6 F6 F6 F6 F6 F6           ÷÷÷÷÷÷÷÷÷÷÷÷÷÷÷÷
120 F6 F6 F6 F6 F6 F6 F6 F6-F6 F6 F6 F6 F6 F6 F6 F6           ÷÷÷÷÷÷÷÷÷÷÷÷÷÷÷÷
130 F6 F6 F6 F6 F6 F6 F6 F6-F6 F6 F6 F6 F6 F6 F6 F6           ÷÷÷÷÷÷÷÷÷÷÷÷÷÷÷÷
140 F6 F6 F6 F6 F6 F6 F6 F6-F6 F6 F6 F6 F6 F6 F6 F6           ÷÷÷÷÷÷÷÷÷÷÷÷÷÷÷÷
150 F6 F6 F6 F6 F6 F6 F6 F6-F6 F6 F6 F6 F6 F6 F6 F6           ÷÷÷÷÷÷÷÷÷÷÷÷÷÷÷÷
160 F6 F6 F6 F6 F6 F6 F6 F6-F6 F6 F6 F6 F6 F6 F6 F6           ÷÷÷÷÷÷÷÷÷÷÷÷÷÷÷÷
170 F6 F6 F6 F6 F6 F6 F6 F6-F6 F6 F6 F6 F6 F6 F6 F6           ÷÷÷÷÷÷÷÷÷÷÷÷÷÷÷÷
180 F6 F6 F6 F6 F6 F6 F6 F6-F6 F6 F6 F6 F6 F6 F6 F6           ÷÷÷÷÷÷÷÷÷÷÷÷÷÷÷÷
190 F6 F6 F6 F6 F6 F6 F6 F6-F6 F6 F6 F6 F6 F6 F6 F6           ÷÷÷÷÷÷÷÷÷÷÷÷÷÷÷÷
1A0 F6 F6 F6 F6 F6 F6 F6 F6-F6 F6 F6 F6 F6 F6 F6 F6           ÷÷÷÷÷÷÷÷÷÷÷÷÷÷÷÷
1B0 F6 F6 F6 F6 F6 F6 F6 F6-F6 F6 F6 F6 F6 F6 F6 F6           ÷÷÷÷÷÷÷÷÷÷÷÷÷÷÷÷
1C0 F6 F6 F6 F6 F6 F6 F6 F6-F6 F6 F6 F6 F6 F6 F6 F6           ÷÷÷÷÷÷÷÷÷÷÷÷÷÷÷÷
1D0 F6 F6 F6 F6 F6 F6 F6 F6-F6 F6 F6 F6 F6 F6 F6 F6           ÷÷÷÷÷÷÷÷÷÷÷÷÷÷÷÷
1E0 F6 F6 F6 F6 F6 F6 F6 F6-F6 F6 F6 F6 F6 F6 F6 F6           ÷÷÷÷÷÷÷÷÷÷÷÷÷÷÷÷
1F0 F6 F6 F6 F6 F6 F6 F6 F6-F6 F6 F6 F6 F6 F6 F6 F6           ÷÷÷÷÷÷÷÷÷÷÷÷÷÷÷÷

     0  1  2  3  4  5  6  7  8  9  A  B  C  D  E  F           0123456789ABCDEF

000 F6 F6 F6 F6 F6 F6 F6 F6-F6 F6 F6 F6 F6 F6 F6 F6           ÷÷÷÷÷÷÷÷÷÷÷÷÷÷÷÷
010 F6 F6 F6 F6 F6 F6 F6 F6-F6 F6 F6 F6 F6 F6 F6 F6           ÷÷÷÷÷÷÷÷÷÷÷÷÷÷÷÷
020 F6 F6 F6 F6 F6 F6 F6 F6-F6 F6 F6 F6 F6 F6 F6 F6           ÷÷÷÷÷÷÷÷÷÷÷÷÷÷÷÷
030 F6 F6 F6 F6 F6 F6 F6 F6-F6 F6 F6 F6 F6 F6 F6 F6           ÷÷÷÷÷÷÷÷÷÷÷÷÷÷÷÷
040 F6 F6 F6 F6 F6 F6 F6 F6-F6 F6 F6 F6 F6 F6 F6 F6           ÷÷÷÷÷÷÷÷÷÷÷÷÷÷÷÷
050 F6 F6 F6 F6 F6 F6 F6 F6-F6 F6 F6 F6 F6 F6 F6 F6           ÷÷÷÷÷÷÷÷÷÷÷÷÷÷÷÷
060 F6 F6 F6 F6 F6 F6 F6 F6-F6 F6 F6 F6 F6 F6 F6 F6           ÷÷÷÷÷÷÷÷÷÷÷÷÷÷÷÷
```

```
070 F6 F6 F6 F6 F6 F6 F6 F6-F6 F6 F6 F6 F6 F6 F6 F6     ÷÷÷÷÷÷÷÷÷÷÷÷÷÷÷÷
080 F6 F6 F6 F6 F6 F6 F6 F6-F6 F6 F6 F6 F6 F6 F6 F6     ÷÷÷÷÷÷÷÷÷÷÷÷÷÷÷÷
090 F6 F6 F6 F6 F6 F6 F6 F6-F6 F6 F6 F6 F6 F6 F6 F6     ÷÷÷÷÷÷÷÷÷÷÷÷÷÷÷÷
0A0 F6 F6 F6 F6 F6 F6 F6 F6-F6 F6 F6 F6 F6 F6 F6 F6     ÷÷÷÷÷÷÷÷÷÷÷÷÷÷÷÷
0B0 F6 F6 F6 F6 F6 F6 F6 F6-F6 F6 F6 F6 F6 F6 F6 F6     ÷÷÷÷÷÷÷÷÷÷÷÷÷÷÷÷
0C0 F6 F6 F6 F6 F6 F6 F6 F6-F6 F6 F6 F6 F6 F6 F6 F6     ÷÷÷÷÷÷÷÷÷÷÷÷÷÷÷÷
0D0 F6 F6 F6 F6 F6 F6 F6 F6-F6 F6 F6 F6 F6 F6 F6 F6     ÷÷÷÷÷÷÷÷÷÷÷÷÷÷÷÷
0E0 F6 F6 F6 F6 F6 F6 F6 F6-F6 F6 F6 F6 F6 F6 F6 F6     ÷÷÷÷÷÷÷÷÷÷÷÷÷÷÷÷
0F0 F6 F6 F6 F6 F6 F6 F6 F6-F6 F6 F6 F6 F6 F6 F6 F6     ÷÷÷÷÷÷÷÷÷÷÷÷÷÷÷÷
100 F6 F6 F6 F6 F6 F6 F6 F6-F6 F6 F6 F6 F6 F6 F6 F6     ÷÷÷÷÷÷÷÷÷÷÷÷÷÷÷÷
110 F6 F6 F6 F6 F6 F6 F6 F6-F6 F6 F6 F6 F6 F6 F6 F6     ÷÷÷÷÷÷÷÷÷÷÷÷÷÷÷÷
120 F6 F6 F6 F6 F6 F6 F6 F6-F6 F6 F6 F6 F6 F6 F6 F6     ÷÷÷÷÷÷÷÷÷÷÷÷÷÷÷÷
130 F6 F6 F6 F6 F6 F6 F6 F6-F6 F6 F6 F6 F6 F6 F6 F6     ÷÷÷÷÷÷÷÷÷÷÷÷÷÷÷÷
140 F6 F6 F6 F6 F6 F6 F6 F6-F6 F6 F6 F6 F6 F6 F6 F6     ÷÷÷÷÷÷÷÷÷÷÷÷÷÷÷÷
150 F6 F6 F6 F6 F6 F6 F6 F6-F6 F6 F6 F6 F6 F6 F6 F6     ÷÷÷÷÷÷÷÷÷÷÷÷÷÷÷÷
160 F6 F6 F6 F6 F6 F6 F6 F6-F6 F6 F6 F6 F6 F6 F6 F6     ÷÷÷÷÷÷÷÷÷÷÷÷÷÷÷÷
170 F6 F6 F6 F6 F6 F6 F6 F6-F6 F6 F6 F6 F6 F6 F6 F6     ÷÷÷÷÷÷÷÷÷÷÷÷÷÷÷÷
180 F6 F6 F6 F6 F6 F6 F6 F6-F6 F6 F6 F6 F6 F6 F6 F6     ÷÷÷÷÷÷÷÷÷÷÷÷÷÷÷÷
190 F6 F6 F6 F6 F6 F6 F6 F6-F6 F6 F6 F6 F6 F6 F6 F6     ÷÷÷÷÷÷÷÷÷÷÷÷÷÷÷÷
1A0 F6 F6 F6 F6 F6 F6 F6 F6-F6 F6 F6 F6 F6 F6 F6 F6     ÷÷÷÷÷÷÷÷÷÷÷÷÷÷÷÷
1B0 F6 F6 F6 F6 F6 F6 F6 F6-F6 F6 F6 F6 F6 F6 F6 F6     ÷÷÷÷÷÷÷÷÷÷÷÷÷÷÷÷
1C0 F6 F6 F6 F6 F6 F6 F6 F6-F6 F6 F6 F6 F6 F6 F6 F6     ÷÷÷÷÷÷÷÷÷÷÷÷÷÷÷÷
1D0 F6 F6 F6 F6 F6 F6 F6 F6-F6 F6 F6 F6 F6 F6 F6 F6     ÷÷÷÷÷÷÷÷÷÷÷÷÷÷÷÷
1E0 F6 F6 F6 F6 F6 F6 F6 F6-F6 F6 F6 F6 F6 F6 F6 F6     ÷÷÷÷÷÷÷÷÷÷÷÷÷÷÷÷
1F0 F6 F6 F6 F6 F6 F6 F6 F6-F6 F6 F6 F6 F6 F6 F6 F6     ÷÷÷÷÷÷÷÷÷÷÷÷÷÷÷÷
```

Notice that both sectors in this cluster are filled completely with the ÷ (F6h or division sign) character. These characters are written into the data area of each sector when a disk is low-level formatted. Actually, all sectors on the disk are written in this manner. When the low-level format phase of the floppy FORMAT command is finished, the program returns the heads to the beginning area of the disk and writes the volume boot sector, the FAT, and root directory on the disk. Every sector on the disk then contains the F6h character—except the volume boot sector, the FAT, and the root directory, which already have been overwritten.

Note that the FORMAT command performs the low-level and high-level format operations for a floppy disk. For a hard disk, the operations are separate and are performed by separate programs. On a hard disk, many different fill characters are used by the various low-level format programs; therefore, you may see a different character or set of characters filling every sector of a hard disk that has just been low-level formatted. You should become familiar with the fill characters used by your program. When you see these characters in a sector, you know that the sector has not been written to since the last low-level format was performed. This knowledge can be important when you are looking for data on a hard disk in data recovery situations. When you are searching a disk for lost information (using a disk editor), for example, you will be able to tell quickly the difference between data and fill characters.

Suppose that you want to write a file to the disk and then verify that the file exists. Type the following at the `A:\>` prompt (create the ^Z at the end of the sentence by pressing Ctrl-Z and then pressing Enter; this keystroke produces an end-of-file [EOF] marker):

COPY CON: TEST01.TXT

This is a test of a direct copy from
the CONSOLE device to a file called TEST01.TXT.

This file ends after the period
at the end of this sentence. ^Z

The following message appears:

```
1 File(s) copied
```

Then type *dir* at the `A:\>` prompt. The following message appears:

```
Volume in drive A has no label
Volume Serial Number is 2722-0DC8
Directory of A:\

TEST01         TXT          150 10-11-90          7:47a
               1 File(s)      729088 bytes free
```

At the `A:\>` prompt, type the following:

TYPE TEST01.TXT

You then see the following:

```
This is a test of a direct copy from
the CONSOLE device to a file called TEST01.TXT.

This file ends after the period
at the end of this sentence.
```

The first COPY command creates the TEST01.TXT file by writing data directly from the keyboard (the CON: device) to the TEST01.TXT file. When you type the last line in the file, press Ctrl-Z to enter an EOF character before you press the Enter key. The DIR command then shows that the file exists and contains exactly 150 bytes. The TYPE command verifies that the contents of the file are no more or no less than what you entered initially.

Because this file is the first file saved on the freshly formatted disk, the file is in cluster 2—the first cluster available on the disk. (Remember that all cluster numbering starts with 2.) The cluster size on a 720K floppy disk is 2 sectors (1,024 bytes), which represents the amount of space that has been taken from the disk by this file. This file occupies 150 bytes, which requires at least one whole cluster—1,024 bytes. The listing that follows represents the information in this disk's cluster 2:

```
Hexadecimal Byte Values              ASCII Text
    0  1  2  3  4  5  6  7  8  9  A  B  C  D  E  F   0123456789ABCDEF

000 54 68 69 73 20 69 73 20-61 20 74 65 73 74 20 6F  This is a test o
010 66 20 61 20 64 69 72 65-63 74 20 63 6F 70 79 20  f a direct copy
020 66 72 6F 6D 0D 0A 74 68-65 20 43 4F 4E 53 4F 4C  from..the CONSOL
030 45 20 64 65 76 69 63 65-20 74 6F 20 61 20 66 69  E device to a fi
040 6C 65 20 63 61 6C 6C 65-64 20 54 45 53 54 30 31  le called TEST01
050 2E 54 58 54 2E 0D 0A 0D-0A 54 68 69 73 20 66 69  .TXT.....This fi
060 6C 65 20 65 6E 64 73 20-61 66 74 65 72 20 74 68  le ends after th
070 65 20 70 65 72 69 6F 64-0D 0A 61 74 20 74 68 65  e period..at the
080 20 65 6E 64 20 6F 66 20-74 68 69 73 20 73 65 6E   end of this sen
090 74 61 6E 63 65 2E 00 00-00 00 00 00 00 00 00 00  tence..........
0A0 00 00 00 00 00 00 00 00-00 00 00 00 00 00 00 00  ................
0B0 00 00 00 00 00 00 00 00-00 00 00 00 00 00 00 00  ................
0C0 00 00 00 00 00 00 00 00-00 00 00 00 00 00 00 00  ................
0D0 00 00 00 00 00 00 00 00-00 00 00 00 00 00 00 00  ................
0E0 00 00 00 00 00 00 00 00-00 00 00 00 00 00 00 00  ................
0F0 00 00 00 00 00 00 00 00-00 00 00 00 00 00 00 00  ................
100 E8 30 32 D8 00 51 DA 55-8B EC 55 E9 00 00 83 EC  .02..Q.U..U.....
110 07 2E A1 B1 2D A3 17 0C-B8 01 00 88 46 FD C4 3E  ....-.......F..>
120 7F 18 26 8A 45 62 32 E4-0B C0 75 03 E9 8A 00 4C  ..&.Eb2...u....L
130 C4 06 7F 18 8C C2 52 50-E8 6A F5 75 03 E9 54 00  ......RP.j.u..T.
140 C4 06 7F 18 8C C2 89 46-F9 89 56 FB C4 3E 7F 18  .......F..V..>..
150 26 8B 45 7B 89 46 F7 8B-46 F7 50 C4 7E F9 58 26  &.E{.F..F.P.~.X&
160 3B 45 7B 74 03 E9 0A 00-C4 7E F9 B8 01 00 26 88  ;E{t.....~....&.
170 45 62 8D 7E F9 16 57 E8-6D 53 C4 46 F9 8C C2 52  Eb.~..W.mS.F...R
180 50 C4 06 7F 18 8C C2 5B-59 E8 19 3B 75 03 E9 C6  P......[Y..;u...
190 FF E9 25 00 4C 83 EC 51-B8 06 00 50 E8 0A 6F B1  ..%.L..Q...P..o.
1A0 50 E8 05 37 E8 70 FD 88-46 FD A0 F6 18 32 E4 0B  P..7.p..F....2..
1B0 C0 75 03 E9 03 00 E9 1B-00 8A 46 FD 32 E4 0B C0  .u........F.2...
1C0 75 03 E9 0F 00 E8 D5 6D-E8 95 FA 4C E8 C7 FD 75  u......m...L...u
1D0 03 E9 00 00 E9 00 00 8B-E5 5D C3 00 00 00 00 00  .........]......
1E0 00 00 00 00 00 00 00 00-00 00 00 00 00 00 00 00  ................
1F0 00 00 00 00 00 00 00 00-00 00 00 00 00 00 00 00  ................
```

```
     0  1  2  3  4  5  6  7  8  9  A  B  C  D  E  F    0123456789ABCDEF

000 F6 F6 F6 F6 F6 F6 F6 F6-F6 F6 F6 F6 F6 F6 F6 F6   ÷÷÷÷÷÷÷÷÷÷÷÷÷÷÷÷
010 F6 F6 F6 F6 F6 F6 F6 F6-F6 F6 F6 F6 F6 F6 F6 F6   ÷÷÷÷÷÷÷÷÷÷÷÷÷÷÷÷
020 F6 F6 F6 F6 F6 F6 F6 F6-F6 F6 F6 F6 F6 F6 F6 F6   ÷÷÷÷÷÷÷÷÷÷÷÷÷÷÷÷
030 F6 F6 F6 F6 F6 F6 F6 F6-F6 F6 F6 F6 F6 F6 F6 F6   ÷÷÷÷÷÷÷÷÷÷÷÷÷÷÷÷
040 F6 F6 F6 F6 F6 F6 F6 F6-F6 F6 F6 F6 F6 F6 F6 F6   ÷÷÷÷÷÷÷÷÷÷÷÷÷÷÷÷
050 F6 F6 F6 F6 F6 F6 F6 F6-F6 F6 F6 F6 F6 F6 F6 F6   ÷÷÷÷÷÷÷÷÷÷÷÷÷÷÷÷
060 F6 F6 F6 F6 F6 F6 F6 F6-F6 F6 F6 F6 F6 F6 F6 F6   ÷÷÷÷÷÷÷÷÷÷÷÷÷÷÷÷
070 F6 F6 F6 F6 F6 F6 F6 F6-F6 F6 F6 F6 F6 F6 F6 F6   ÷÷÷÷÷÷÷÷÷÷÷÷÷÷÷÷
080 F6 F6 F6 F6 F6 F6 F6 F6-F6 F6 F6 F6 F6 F6 F6 F6   ÷÷÷÷÷÷÷÷÷÷÷÷÷÷÷÷
090 F6 F6 F6 F6 F6 F6 F6 F6-F6 F6 F6 F6 F6 F6 F6 F6   ÷÷÷÷÷÷÷÷÷÷÷÷÷÷÷÷
0A0 F6 F6 F6 F6 F6 F6 F6 F6-F6 F6 F6 F6 F6 F6 F6 F6   ÷÷÷÷÷÷÷÷÷÷÷÷÷÷÷÷
0B0 F6 F6 F6 F6 F6 F6 F6 F6-F6 F6 F6 F6 F6 F6 F6 F6   ÷÷÷÷÷÷÷÷÷÷÷÷÷÷÷÷
0C0 F6 F6 F6 F6 F6 F6 F6 F6-F6 F6 F6 F6 F6 F6 F6 F6   ÷÷÷÷÷÷÷÷÷÷÷÷÷÷÷÷
0D0 F6 F6 F6 F6 F6 F6 F6 F6-F6 F6 F6 F6 F6 F6 F6 F6   ÷÷÷÷÷÷÷÷÷÷÷÷÷÷÷÷
0E0 F6 F6 F6 F6 F6 F6 F6 F6-F6 F6 F6 F6 F6 F6 F6 F6   ÷÷÷÷÷÷÷÷÷÷÷÷÷÷÷÷
0F0 F6 F6 F6 F6 F6 F6 F6 F6-F6 F6 F6 F6 F6 F6 F6 F6   ÷÷÷÷÷÷÷÷÷÷÷÷÷÷÷÷
100 F6 F6 F6 F6 F6 F6 F6 F6-F6 F6 F6 F6 F6 F6 F6 F6   ÷÷÷÷÷÷÷÷÷÷÷÷÷÷÷÷
110 F6 F6 F6 F6 F6 F6 F6 F6-F6 F6 F6 F6 F6 F6 F6 F6   ÷÷÷÷÷÷÷÷÷÷÷÷÷÷÷÷
120 F6 F6 F6 F6 F6 F6 F6 F6-F6 F6 F6 F6 F6 F6 F6 F6   ÷÷÷÷÷÷÷÷÷÷÷÷÷÷÷÷
130 F6 F6 F6 F6 F6 F6 F6 F6-F6 F6 F6 F6 F6 F6 F6 F6   ÷÷÷÷÷÷÷÷÷÷÷÷÷÷÷÷
140 F6 F6 F6 F6 F6 F6 F6 F6-F6 F6 F6 F6 F6 F6 F6 F6   ÷÷÷÷÷÷÷÷÷÷÷÷÷÷÷÷
150 F6 F6 F6 F6 F6 F6 F6 F6-F6 F6 F6 F6 F6 F6 F6 F6   ÷÷÷÷÷÷÷÷÷÷÷÷÷÷÷÷
160 F6 F6 F6 F6 F6 F6 F6 F6-F6 F6 F6 F6 F6 F6 F6 F6   ÷÷÷÷÷÷÷÷÷÷÷÷÷÷÷÷
170 F6 F6 F6 F6 F6 F6 F6 F6-F6 F6 F6 F6 F6 F6 F6 F6   ÷÷÷÷÷÷÷÷÷÷÷÷÷÷÷÷
180 F6 F6 F6 F6 F6 F6 F6 F6-F6 F6 F6 F6 F6 F6 F6 F6   ÷÷÷÷÷÷÷÷÷÷÷÷÷÷÷÷
190 F6 F6 F6 F6 F6 F6 F6 F6-F6 F6 F6 F6 F6 F6 F6 F6   ÷÷÷÷÷÷÷÷÷÷÷÷÷÷÷÷
1A0 F6 F6 F6 F6 F6 F6 F6 F6-F6 F6 F6 F6 F6 F6 F6 F6   ÷÷÷÷÷÷÷÷÷÷÷÷÷÷÷÷
1B0 F6 F6 F6 F6 F6 F6 F6 F6-F6 F6 F6 F6 F6 F6 F6 F6   ÷÷÷÷÷÷÷÷÷÷÷÷÷÷÷÷
1C0 F6 F6 F6 F6 F6 F6 F6 F6-F6 F6 F6 F6 F6 F6 F6 F6   ÷÷÷÷÷÷÷÷÷÷÷÷÷÷÷÷
1D0 F6 F6 F6 F6 F6 F6 F6 F6-F6 F6 F6 F6 F6 F6 F6 F6   ÷÷÷÷÷÷÷÷÷÷÷÷÷÷÷÷
1E0 F6 F6 F6 F6 F6 F6 F6 F6-F6 F6 F6 F6 F6 F6 F6 F6   ÷÷÷÷÷÷÷÷÷÷÷÷÷÷÷÷
1F0 F6 F6 F6 F6 F6 F6 F6 F6-F6 F6 F6 F6 F6 F6 F6 F6   ÷÷÷÷÷÷÷÷÷÷÷÷÷÷÷÷
```

In this listing, all data that is part of the file is underlined. As you can see, the file ends at offset 95h (149 decimal)—the intersection of row 90 and column 5—which is the 150th byte. All data up to the 150th byte is the file, and any data after that point is not part of the file.

Note that when it saves a file, DOS does not write simply the number of characters that are in the file. DOS adds data to the end of a file to pad out the last sector. The information from offset 96h to 1FFh in the first sector of the preceding listing, for example, was added by DOS to fill out the sector. (The ROM BIOS writes to a disk in minimum increments of one sector, and DOS uses the ROM BIOS.)

The data DOS uses to pad out the sector comes from memory (wherever the file data was stored temporarily in RAM). When a sector is called out to be written, any data found in RAM immediately following the file is written to the disk (along with the file) to pad out the last sector. Many data elements are written to the disk in this manner, including portions of subdirectories that were loaded into DOS buffers, pieces of programs that were run prior to the write operation, and portions of data that were entered using programs run before the write occurred. Almost anything can be written to the disk to pad out a sector.

If security is an issue, for example, you may be interested to know that part of a private note you typed into your system and encrypted before storing may be stored on the disk in unencrypted form (because you had to enter the data into memory before the data could be encrypted). The amount of data affected is small—fewer than 512 bytes each time. DOS pads out the remaining bytes in a sector.

Although the information found at the end of a sector usually is not a complete file, you can recover the pieces by using a disk editor (see Chapters 9 and 10 for details).

The data that follows the last sector used in the last cluster of a file is particularly interesting. Although DOS works with disks in cluster increments, you can see that the last sector of cluster 2 in the preceding example has never been written to. Whatever data already exists in the final sectors of the last cluster of a written file remains undisturbed. If, for example, you delete a file that used both sectors in cluster 2, and if you then write a new file (such as the file in the preceding example) on that disk, you would see that the first sector contains the new file and the data to pad out the end of a sector. Any other cluster sectors remain unused and therefore contain whatever data they previously contained. In other words, any unused sectors in the last cluster of a file may contain data that you thought you had erased a long time ago.

A solution to this security problem is to back up all the files on the hard disk, low-level format the disk, partition it, high-level format it, and restore the files. This procedure ensures that the ending cluster sectors are initialized to the same byte pattern across the disk. If you are worried about security, check your backup program to see how it saved the files. Some backup programs save entire clusters—not just sectors or the file itself. Also, the Norton Utilities WIPEINFO command with the /E option wipes out all erased files and unused space on disk, deleting any residual information at the ends of files.

You also should note that every file stored on your disk uses (on average) only half the sectors in the last cluster of the file. Suppose, for example, that you have a 315M hard disk partition with a cluster size of 16 sectors (8,192 bytes). If you currently have about 5,000 files, you are wasting 5,000 x 16/2 sectors, or 40,000 sectors. 40,000 sectors x 512 bytes/sector equals 20,480,000 bytes, or nearly 20M. You therefore have approximately 20M of old data from files that supposedly had been erased floating around on your hard disk in these "wasted" sectors. Some of this data may be temporary files or even memory remnants of unencrypted, supposedly secure information. If you were worried about security rather than data recovery, this situation would be a problem.

Using the CHKDSK Command

The DOS CHKDSK command is useful, powerful, and generally misunderstood. At first glance, the CHKDSK command's primary functions appear to be reporting how disk space is allocated for a given volume and reporting DOS memory allocation. Although the CHKDSK command performs these (and other) functions, the program's principal value lies in discovering, defining, and repairing problems with the DOS directory and file allocation table system. CHKDSK is rather crude and simplistic when compared to some aftermarket utilities; however, the command is a valuable tool in handling data recovery problems with minimum overhead.

Many users are not aware that the CHKDSK command can inform you about how fragmented a given file has become. Fragmentation of files can cause your hard disk to work slower and less efficiently. Excessive fragmentation can cause loss of information. The CHKDSK command also can produce a list of all files (including hidden and system files) on a particular volume—performing like a super-DIR command. By far the most important capabilities of CHKDSK are the detection and correction of problems with the DOS file management system.

The name of the program is misleading, because CHKDSK seems to be a contraction of CHECK DISK. CHKDSK does not check a disk's integrity or file nor can the command show, mark, or locate the bad sectors on a disk. The real function of CHKDSK is to inspect directories and FATs to determine whether they correspond or contain discrepancies. The CHKDSK program does not detect (or report) any damage in a file itself; only the disk's FAT and directory areas (the "table of contents") are checked. In addition, the command's name gives no indication of the program's capacity to repair problems with the directory and FAT structures.

Examining the CHKDSK Command Syntax

When you run the CHKDSK command, use the following syntax:

CHKDSK [*d:*][*path*][*filename*] [/F][/V]

The [*d:*] parameter specifies the disk volume to be analyzed. The [*path*] and [*filename*] options specify files to be checked for fragmentation. The drive, path, and file specifiers are optional. If you do not specify parameters, the CHKDSK command processes the default volume or drive and does not check files for contiguity. If you do specify the path and file name parameters, CHKDSK checks the files to see whether they are stored contiguously on the disk.

When specifying files to be checked for fragmentation, you can use wild cards to include all the files in a given directory. One limitation of the fragmentation analysis is that you can check for fragmentation only within a given directory, not across directory boundaries.

The /F (fix) parameter enables repairs to be performed if problems are discovered in the directories and FATs. If the /F parameter is not specified, the program is prevented (by default) from writing to the disk, and all repairs are performed in a "mock" fashion.

The /V (verbose) parameter causes the program to list all entries in all disk directories and to give more detailed information when errors are encountered.

Knowing When To Use CHKDSK

The primary function of CHKDSK is to compare the directory and FAT to see whether they agree with one another—if all the data in the directory for files, such as the starting cluster and the size information, corresponds to what is found in the FAT as far as chains of clusters with end-of-chain indicators. CHKDSK also checks subdirectory file entries and the special . and .. entries used for tying the subdirectory system together. If you were given a directory and a FAT to examine, you easily could spot errors in the same manner as CHKDSK does but probably not as quickly.

The second function of CHKDSK is to implement repairs to the disk structure. That is, CHKDSK "patches" the disk such that the directory and FAT are in alignment and agreement. From a repair standpoint, understanding CHKDSK is fairly easy. CHKDSK almost always modifies the directories on a disk to correspond to what is found in the FAT.

CHKDSK is not a "smart" repair program and often can do more damage "repairing" the disk than if it were left alone. In many cases, the original information in the directories is correct, and you can use this information to help repair the FAT tables. But, if you have run CHKDSK with the /F parameter, the original directory information no longer exists, and a good FAT repair is then impossible.

For this reason, you must never run CHKDSK with the /F parameter without first running the program in read-only mode (without the /F parameter) to determine whether damage exists and to what extent. (If you do not specify the /F parameter when running CHKDSK, the program is prevented from making any corrections to the disk.) Carefully examine any disk damage and determine just how CHKDSK would "fix" the problems (as discussed in the following section on CHKDSK use). Run the program in the /F mode only after deciding that CHKDSK in fact will make the correct assumptions about the damage.

One of the most dangerous things you can do is place a CHKDSK /F command in your AUTOEXEC.BAT file. If your disk directories and FAT system become damaged one day, attempting to load a program whose directory and FAT entries are messed up can lock the system. On rebooting, you will find CHKDSK "fixing" the problem without proper study of the situation on your part. You can lose an entire disk structure to CHKDSK in one incident. And you have no easy way to undo the CHKDSK "repair." If you want to include CHKDSK in your AUTOEXEC.BAT file, leave off the /F parameter.

Note that problems reported by CHKDSK usually are problems with the software and not the hardware. Although the situation is certainly possible, you rarely (if ever) will see a case in which lost clusters, allocation errors, or cross-linked files were caused directly by a hardware fault. The cause is usually a defective program or a program that has been stopped before it can close files or purge buffers.

You should run CHKDSK at least once a day on any hard disk system. Finding out about file structure errors as soon as possible is important. Placing a CHKDSK command in your AUTOEXEC.BAT file therefore can be a good idea; just do not use the /F parameter. You also should run CHKDSK anytime you suspect that directory or FAT damage may have occurred. Anytime a program terminates abnormally or the system crashes for some reason, for example, run CHKDSK to see whether any file system damage has occurred.

Knowing CHKDSK's Limitations

In several instances, the CHKDSK command operates only partially or not at all. The CHKDSK command does not process volumes or portions of volumes created as any of the following:

- SUBST command volumes
- ASSIGN command volumes
- JOIN command subdirectories
- Network volumes

The SUBST command creates a *virtual volume*, which is an existing volume's subdirectory using another volume specifier (drive letter) as an alias. To analyze the files in the subdirectory created with the SUBST command, you must give the *true name*—the actual path name to the files. TRUENAME is an undocumented command in DOS Version 4.0 and later versions that shows you the actual path name for a volume created with the SUBST command.

You also can use the SUBST command to find the true name of a particular volume, as in the following example:

```
C:\>SUBST E: C:\AUTO\SPECS

C:\>E:

E:\>CHKDSK *.*

Cannot CHKDSK a SUBSTed or ASSIGNed drive

E:\>SUBST

E:\>C:\AUTO\SPECS

E:\>TRUENAME E:

C:\AUTO\SPECS

E:\>CHKDSK C:\AUTO\SPECS\*.*

Volume 320M_SCSI       created 09-05-1990 11:22a
Volume Serial Number is 1454-12DC

  314384384 bytes total disk space
      81920 bytes in 4 hidden files
    2342912 bytes in 286 directories
  147865600 bytes in 4822 user files
  164093952 bytes available on disk
```

```
       8192 bytes in each allocation unit
      38377 total allocation units on disk
      20031 available allocation units on disk

     655360 total bytes memory
     562224 bytes free

All specified file(s) are contiguous
```

In this example, the SUBST command is used for creating the E volume from the C:\AUTO\SPECS directory. After you change to the E volume and execute a CHKDSK of the volume and files, the following error message appears:

```
Cannot CHKDSK a SUBSTed or ASSIGNed drive
```

To run the CHKDSK command on virtual volume E's files, you have to determine the actual path that the volume represents. As you can see, you can accomplish this task by using the SUBST command with no parameters or the TRUENAME command (DOS Version 4.0 and later versions only). After determining the actual path to the files, you can specify the appropriate CHKDSK command to check the volume and files.

The CHKDSK command also does not process a disk drive that you have altered using the ASSIGN command. If, for example, you have specified the command ASSIGN A=B, you cannot analyze drive A unless you unassign the drive (again by using the ASSIGN command at the DOS prompt with now options).

The CHKDSK command is not capable of processing a directory tree section that has been created with the JOIN command, which joins two disk drives together as if they were one drive. Note that upon encountering volumes on which you have used the JOIN command, CHKDSK processes the actual portion of the volume (the disk you're currently logged on to) and then displays the following warning message:

```
Directory is joined
tree past this point not processed
```

This message indicates that CHKDSK cannot process the directory on which you have used the JOIN command. CHKDSK continues to process the rest of the volume and displays the requested volume information.

The CHKDSK command is not capable of processing a networked (shared) disk from a server or workstation. At the file server, you cannot use the CHKDSK command on a volume that has any portion accessible to other remote network stations. At a workstation, you cannot run CHKDSK on a volume that is not physically on the remote station. If you are using a server or a workstation and attempt to run CHKDSK on a volume that is shared on a network, the following error message appears:

```
Cannot CHKDSK a network drive
```

If you want to run CHKDSK on the networked volume, remember that you can run CHKDSK only on the system in which the volume is located physically and only if sharing of the volume has been suspended or disabled.

Understanding CHKDSK Output

If you run the CHKDSK command on a typical hard drive, you are likely to see output similar to the following example. At the `C:\>` prompt, type

CHKDSK

The following message appears:

```
Volume 120M_MFM created 10-07-1990 5:13a
Volume Serial Number is 1017-0CD3

  117116928 bytes total disk space
      73728 bytes in 3 hidden files
     614400 bytes in 272 directories
  112644096 bytes in 4516 user files
     143360 bytes in bad sectors
    3641344 bytes available on disk

       2048 bytes in each allocation unit
      57186 total allocation units on disk
       1778 available allocation units on disk

     655360 total bytes memory
     565344 bytes free
```

As you can see, the CHKDSK command usually displays the following information about a disk volume:

- Volume name and creation date
- Volume serial number
- Number of bytes in total disk space
- Number of files and bytes in hidden files
- Number of files and bytes in directories
- Number of files and bytes in user files
- Number of bytes in bad sectors (deallocated clusters)
- Number of bytes available on disk

- Number of bytes in total memory (RAM)
- Number of bytes in free memory
- Error messages if disk errors are encountered

> ***Note:*** If a volume name or volume serial number does not exist on a particular volume, that information simply is not displayed. Also, if no clusters in the volume's FAT are marked as bad, no display of bytes in bad sectors appears.

DOS 4.01's version and later versions of CHKDSK also tell how large each allocation unit (or cluster) is, how many total allocation units are present, and how many of them currently are not being used.

At the end of the report, you can see that CHKDSK counts up the total amount of DOS usable RAM memory, which in this case is 640K or 655,360 bytes. (Remember that 1K is equal to 1,024 bytes.) Then CHKDSK displays the number of bytes of memory currently unused or free. This figure basically tells you the size of the largest executable program you can run.

Note that CHKDSK with DOS 3.3 or earlier versions does not recognize the PS/2 Extended BIOS Data Area, which is located in memory such that it uses the highest 1K of addresses in contiguous conventional memory. Thus, for most systems with 640K of contiguous memory addressed before the "video wall," the Extended BIOS Data Area occupies the 640th kilobyte. DOS 3.3 and earlier versions do not recognize this memory because the PS/2 BIOS "steals" it from DOS, so CHKDSK under 3.3 or earlier versions reports only 639K, or 654,336 bytes of total memory. If you upgrade to DOS 4.0 or later versions, you get the correct 640K report.

Note the line that reads `143360 bytes in bad sectors`. Although this line looks like a problem or an error message, it is not. Many people think that this report means something is wrong with the disks, but CHKDSK simply is telling you that a certain number of clusters is marked as bad in the FAT and that DOS will never use these clusters.

Suppose, for example, that you have just formatted a new 720K floppy disk and have run the CHKDSK command, which reported no bad clusters. Next, suppose that you use a utility program to mark clusters 150 and 151, consisting of 2,048 bytes, as bad in the FAT. CHKDSK then produces this report:

```
Volume FLOPPY_DISK created 10-21-1990 3:57p
Volume Serial Number is 2563-16FF

   730112 bytes total disk space
    72704 bytes in 3 hidden files
    37888 bytes in 1 user files
     2048 bytes in bad sectors
   617472 bytes available on disk

     1024 bytes in each allocation unit
      713 total allocation units on disk
      603 available allocation units on disk

   655360 total bytes memory
   562224 bytes free
```

As you can see, CHKDSK now reports 2,048 bytes in bad sectors, which exactly corresponds to the two clusters just marked as bad. Even if these clusters are perfectly good, if they are marked as bad in the FAT, the clusters show up as bad in the CHKDSK report.

> ***Caution:*** Using disk editor utility programs like those supplied with the Norton Utilities or Mace Utilities, you can alter the FAT in just about any way you want. Be warned, however, that playing around with the contents of the FAT can lead to data loss. Experiment on a "disposable" disk and then only after reading Chapters 9 and 10.

Because nearly all hard disks are manufactured and sold with defective areas, seeing the "bytes in bad sectors" message is not uncommon at all. In fact, using the manufacturer defect list that is shipped with each drive and that indicates all known defective spots, you could probably prove that most of the higher quality hard disks on the market today have more bad sectors than do the lesser quality drives. You should note that many of the newest controllers allow for *sector and track sparing*, in which the defects are mapped out of the DOS readable area so that DOS never has to deal with them. This feature is almost standard in drives with embedded controllers, such as the IDE (Integrated Drive Electronics) or SCSI (Small Computer Systems Interface) drives.

Although the "bad sectors" message should not be cause for alarm, some of CHKDSK's output can contain warnings of potential or actual data loss. The CHKDSK command can alert you to lost allocation units, cross-linked files, and other problems. And, when you specify optional parameters, CHKDSK can show the following data elements:

- Names and number of fragments in noncontiguous files
- Names of all directories and files on disk, including hidden files

The following paragraphs describe how you can use CHKDSK to check for fragmented files and hidden files and how you can respond to problems revealed in the CHKDSK report.

Using CHKDSK To Check for Fragmented Files

If you specify the [*path*] and [*filename*] parameters, CHKDSK checks all specified files to see whether they are stored contiguously on the disk. Wild cards are allowed in the file name specification to include some or all of the files in a given directory for fragmentation analysis. One flaw with the fragmentation analysis is that you cannot check for fragmentation across directory boundaries—only within a given directory.

Files that are loaded into contiguous tracks and sectors of the floppy disk are naturally more efficient. If files are spread over wide areas of the disk, access operations take longer. Fragmented files are much more difficult to recover than contiguous files if any kind of problem is found with the FAT or directory system on the disk. Also, even though DOS can use pointer numbers in the FAT to find the locations of all a file's fragments, sometimes, for various reasons, these pointers may be lost or corrupted. DOS then no longer can locate some portion of a file. (CHKDSK can alert you to this condition and even can reclaim this unused file space for use by another file by freeing space in the FAT that is no longer being used by a file.)

When you check for contiguity, CHKDSK displays one of two messages:

```
All specified file(s) are contiguous
```

or

```
[filename] contains xxx non-contiguous blocks
```

For each fragmented file on the disk, the second message displays how many fragments the file is in.

Utility programs that can unfragment files on a disk are featured in Chapter 9, but even if you have only DOS, you can accomplish a full defragmentation in several ways. For floppy disks, you can defragment files by formatting a new replacement disk and using COPY or XCOPY to copy all the files from the fragmented disk to the replacement. For a hard disk, you have to back up completely, format, and then restore the disk. Needless to say, this operation on a hard disk is time-consuming and dangerous, which is why so many defragmenting utilities are on the market today.

Using CHKDSK To Check for Hidden Files

You also can use CHKDSK as a super-DIR command. As an example, consider a disk that was formatted with DOS 4.01 with the following command at the `C:\>` prompt:

```
FORMAT A: /F:720 /S /V:FLOPPY_DISK
```

The following message appears:

```
Insert new diskette for drive A:
and press ENTER when ready...

Format complete
System transferred

  730112 bytes total disk space
  110592 bytes used by system
  619520 bytes available on disk

    1024 bytes in each allocation unit
     605 allocation units available on disk

Volume Serial Number is 2563-16FF

Format another (Y/N)?n
```

The status report at the end of the format operation is similar to the output of the CHKDSK command. Run CHKDSK on this disk by typing the following command at the `C:\>` prompt:

```
CHKDSK A:
```

The following message appears:

```
Volume FLOPPY_DISK created 10-21-1990 3:57p
Volume Serial Number is 2563-16FF

  730112 bytes total disk space
   72704 bytes in 3 hidden files
   37888 bytes in 1 user files
  619520 bytes available on disk

    1024 bytes in each allocation unit
     713 total allocation units on disk
     605 available allocation units on disk

  655360 total bytes memory
  562224 bytes free
```

Notice that in this case CHKDSK shows the volume name and serial number information. The reason is that the FORMAT command placed a volume label on the disk with the /V:FLOPPY_DISK parameter, and FORMAT with DOS 4.0 and later versions automatically places the volume serial number on a disk. You also should notice that this disk contains four total files with three of them having the hidden attribute set. If you want to see the names of these hidden files, you need to reexecute the CHKDSK command with the /V parameter. At the `C:\>` prompt, type the following:

CHKDSK A: /V

The following message appears:

```
Volume FLOPPY_DISK created 10-21-1990 3:57p
Volume Serial Number is 2563-16FF
Directory A:\
        A:\IBMBIO.COM
        A:\IBMDOS.COM
        A:\COMMAND.COM
        A:\FLOPPY_D.ISK

  730112 bytes total disk space
   72704 bytes in 3 hidden files
   37888 bytes in 1 user files
  619520 bytes available on disk

    1024 bytes in each allocation unit
     713 total allocation units on disk
     605 available allocation units on disk

  655360 total bytes memory
  562224 bytes free
```

The /V parameter causes CHKDSK to list the names of all directories and files across the entire disk, which in this case is only four total files. Although CHKDSK does not identify exactly which of the listed files are hidden and which are not, you know that COMMAND.COM is the only user (normal) file on the disk, so the other three listed must be marked as hidden. The first two are the DOS system files, and the third hidden file is the volume label, which is stored in the root directory as a normal directory entry just as any other file would be.

You may be particularly interested in determining the name of a hidden file if it has appeared "out of the blue." Although some legitimate programs may create such files, you should check them out to make sure that they are not part of a computer virus program's doing (see Chapter 11 for more information on viruses).

After listing how many bytes are used up by the hidden and user files, CHKDSK lists how much total space is available on the disk.

> *Note:* During the format of this particular disk, the FORMAT program did not find any unreadable sectors, so no clusters were marked in the FAT as bad or unusable. CHKDSK thus did not display the `xxxxxxxxx bytes in bad sectors` message. Even if the disk had developed bad sectors since the FORMAT operation, CHKDSK still would not display any bytes in bad sectors. The reason is that CHKDSK does not test for and count up bad sectors but instead simply reads the FAT and reports on whether the FAT says that bad sectors exist. Also, you should note that CHKDSK does not count sectors at all but clusters or allocation units instead, because that is how the FAT system operates.

Interpreting CHKDSK Error Messages

Although having bytes in bad sectors does not constitute an error or problem, CHKDSK does report problems on a disk volume with a variety of error messages. When discovering an error in the FAT or directory system, CHKDSK reports the error with one of several descriptive messages.

The messages vary to fit the particular error; however, sometimes they can be cryptic or misleading. Also, CHKDSK does not tell you exactly how you should handle an error. That is, CHKDSK does not tell you whether the program itself can repair the problem, whether you have to resort to some other utility, or what the consequences of the error and the repair will be. Neither does CHKDSK tell you what caused the problem in the first place and how you can avoid a repeat of the problem. This section examines the errors that CHKDSK can catch, what the messages indicate, how to correct the problems, and perhaps what caused the problems in the first place.

Because all CHKDSK can do is compare the directory and FAT structures to see whether they support or comply with one another, CHKDSK can detect only certain types of problems. When discrepancies between the directory and the FAT structures are discovered by CHKDSK, the problems almost always fall into one of these categories:

- Lost allocation units (clusters)
- Allocation errors
- Cross-linked files

Although these problems are the most common errors you see with CHKDSK, the program can detect additional problems. The following paragraphs first examine these common problems and then look at other problems that occur much less frequently.

To start, suppose that you have a typical 720K disk that has been formatted with DOS 4.01 and that contains eight data files in the root directory. When the disk was formatted, no volume label was added to the disk, so the eight data files are the only items in the directory list. Because the data files were added all at the same time right after the format, they are contiguous and begin in the first usable cluster (cluster 2). During the format, clusters 75 and 76 were marked as bad; however, these bad clusters are far enough into the disk so as not to interfere with your eight data files.

Note that although having a hard disk end up with marked-as-bad clusters (due to marking bad tracks in the low-level format) is normal, this situation is not considered normal for floppy disks. You probably should throw away any floppy disk formatted with bad clusters.

Typing *dir* at the `B:\>` prompt results in the following CHKDSK report on this 720K disk:

```
Volume in drive B has no label
Volume Serial Number is 2563-16FF
Directory of B:\

90CCAM      TXT       7541   02-25-90    9:43a
90CVETT     TXT       6528   02-25-90    9:40a
90FSHO      TXT       8940   10-26-89   11:52a
90MECLPS    TXT       1531   10-10-89   11:18p
90N300TT    TXT       2763   02-25-90    9:44a
90PFORM     TXT       7744   02-25-90   11:55a
90PGTA      TXT       6070   02-25-90   11:56a
90PTA       TXT       7552   02-25-90   11:56a
            8 File(s) 675840 bytes free
```

Typing *chkdsk* at the `B:\>` prompt results in the following message:

```
Volume Serial Number is 2563-16FF

   730112 bytes total disk space
    52224 bytes in 8 user files
     2048 bytes in bad sectors
   675840 bytes available on disk

     1024 bytes in each allocation unit
      713 total allocation units on disk
      660 available allocation units on disk

   655360 total bytes memory
   556800 bytes free
```

Now examine the contents of the directory and FAT for this disk. A translated representation of the *beginning* portions of the root directory and FAT follows:

Root Directory

File Name	*Ext.*	*Size*	*Date*	*Time*	*Cluster*	*Attributes*
90CCAM	TXT	7541	2-25-90	9:43 a.m.	2	Arc
90CVETT	TXT	6528	2-25-90	9:40 a.m.	10	Arc
90FSHO	TXT	8940	10-26-89	11:52 a.m.	17	Arc
90MECLPS	TXT	1531	10-10-89	11:18 p.m.	26	Arc
90N300TT	TXT	2763	2-25-90	9:44 a.m.	28	Arc
90PFORM	TXT	7744	2-25-90	11:55 a.m.	31	Arc
90PGTA	TXT	6070	2-25-90	11:56 a.m.	39	Arc
90PTA	TXT	7552	2-25-90	11:56 a.m.	45	Arc

File Allocation Table

Cluster	*0*	*1*	*2*	*3*	*4*	*5*	*6*	*7*	*8*	*9*
0	-	-	3	4	5	6	7	8	9	END
10	11	12	13	14	15	16	END	18	19	20
20	21	22	23	24	25	END	27	END	29	30
30	END	32	33	34	35	36	37	38	END	40
40	41	42	43	44	END	46	47	48	49	50
50	51	52	END	0	0	0	0	0	0	0
60	0	0	0	0	0	0	0	0	0	0
70	0	0	0	0	0	BAD	BAD	0	0	0
80	0	0	0	0	0	0	0	0	0	0
90	0	0	0	0	0	0	0	0	0	0
100	0	0	0	0	0	0	0	0	0	0
110	0	0	0	0	0	0	0	0	0	0
120	0	0	0	0	0	0	0	0	0	0
130	0	0	0	0	0	0	0	0	0	0
140	0	0	0	0	0	0	0	0	0	0
150	0	0	0	0	0	0	0	0	0	0

These directory and FAT images have been translated to show a representation of their contents that is easy to understand. Note that the raw sector content in hexadecimal would look different from the translated examples presented here. Also understand that these translated examples are only the first half sector or so of both the root directory and FAT 1. The remainder of both areas would be filled with 00h in reality.

Now, with this example in place, with a directory and FAT that currently have no errors or problems whatsoever, you can see how CHKDSK reports problems as damage is created. The following sections examine how CHKDSK responds to a variety of damage in both the directory and the FAT. Focus first on FAT damage and how CHKDSK reports and corrects these problems.

Dealing with Lost Allocation Units (Clusters)

If somehow an extra FAT chain were written to the disk without an appropriate directory entry, the root directory and FAT may look like this:

Root Directory

File Name	*Ext.*	*Size*	*Date*	*Time*	*Cluster*	*Attributes*
90CCAM	TXT	7541	2-25-90	9:43 a.m.	2	Arc
90CVETT	TXT	6528	2-25-90	9:40 a.m.	10	Arc
90FSHO	TXT	8940	10-26-89	11:52 a.m.	17	Arc
90MECLPS	TXT	1531	10-10-89	11:18 p.m.	26	Arc
90N300TT	TXT	2763	2-25-90	9:44 a.m.	28	Arc
90PFORM	TXT	7744	2-25-90	11:55 a.m.	31	Arc
90PGTA	TXT	6070	2-25-90	11:56 a.m.	39	Arc
90PTA	TXT	7552	2-25-90	11:56 a.m.	45	Arc

File Allocation Table

Cluster	*0*	*1*	*2*	*3*	*4*	*5*	*6*	*7*	*8*	*9*
0	-	-	3	4	5	6	7	8	9	END
10	11	12	13	14	15	16	END	18	19	20
20	21	22	23	24	25	END	27	END	29	30
30	END	32	33	34	35	36	37	38	END	40
40	41	42	43	44	END	46	47	48	49	50
50	51	52	END	0	0	0	0	0	0	0
60	0	0	0	0	0	0	0	0	0	0
70	0	0	0	0	0	BAD	BAD	0	0	0
80	0	0	0	0	0	0	0	0	0	0
90	0	0	0	0	0	0	0	0	0	0
100	0	0	113	114	END	0	0	0	0	0
110	0	0	0	0	0	0	0	0	0	0
120	0	0	0	0	0	0	0	0	0	0
130	0	0	0	0	0	0	0	0	0	0
140	0	0	0	0	0	0	0	0	0	0
150	0	0	0	0	0	0	0	0	0	0

If you typed *chkdsk* at the `B:\>` prompt now, the report would be as follows:

```
Volume Serial Number is 2563-16FF
Errors found, F parameter not specified
Corrections will not be written to disk

3 lost allocation units found in 1 chains.
Convert lost chains to files (Y/N)?y

  730112 bytes total disk space
   52224 bytes in 8 user files
    3072 bytes would be in 1 recovered files
    2048 bytes in bad sectors
  672768 bytes available on disk

    1024 bytes in each allocation unit
     713 total allocation units on disk
     657 available allocation units on disk

  655360 total bytes memory
  556800 bytes free
```

This error is one of the most common ones that CHKDSK finds. Chains of *lost clusters*—or *lost allocation units*—are basically files that have been stored on the disk but do not have any directory entry that claims "ownership" of them. In this example, you can see that the problem starts in the FAT entry for cluster 112. In this position is the number 113, which indicates that cluster 112 is in use and that the file using it continues in cluster 113. In the entry for cluster 113 the problem continues, where the chain is linked forward to cluster 114. Finally, at cluster 114, a FAT end-of-chain indicator tells DOS that the "file" ends at this cluster. This FAT chain involves three clusters—hence the CHKDSK error message.

As you can see, when CHKDSK runs, it checks to see that each cluster indicated as being in use is "owned" by a particular directory entry or file name.

Notice that the report announces that because the command was not invoked with the /F parameter (normal on a first run), any corrections that can be made will not be written to the disk. This method is a read-only or safe mode of operation and enables you to see what CHKDSK may do about the problem without having the program actually do anything. After the `F parameter not specified` warning, you get to the error message itself, which is in the following form:

```
xxx lost allocation units found in yyy chains.
Convert lost chains to files (Y/N)?
```

At this point, CHKDSK is telling you how many lost clusters or allocation units were found in total, as well as how many chains they are in. Remember that a chain is a group of clusters linked together by FAT pointers. If none of the lost clusters pointed to any others that were in use, the number of lost clusters would equal the number of total chains, because each cluster would be a chain of only one cluster.

After the `lost allocation units` error message, CHKDSK asks whether you want to convert the lost chains to files. What CHKDSK means is that it would be willing to create new directory entries that match the locations of the lost chains, thus giving them an "owner" and making them "legal." Each chain is assigned a file name in this fashion: FILE0000.CHK, FILE0001.CHK, FILE0002.CHK, and so on.

Because in the example only a single chain is lost, pressing Y to answer yes to the `Convert lost chains to files` question causes CHKDSK to create a directory entry, named FILE0000.CHK, to match the lost chain. Then you can use the TYPE command or other utility or applications programs to inspect the file's contents. You may find, for example, that the file contains missing records from a database file. Usually, however, you will find that the file contains garbage characters or what seems to be a copy of a piece of a file that is currently intact and has no problems. In other words, the lost clusters are often a portion of a temporary file created by some applications program while it was working.

The problem of lost clusters is probably the most benign error that CHKDSK will ever report to you. Lost clusters almost never are caused by a hardware problem and almost always are caused by a problem with one or more applications or utility programs. While running, many applications programs extensively use disk or memory buffers or temporary files to store data. If a program is not exited properly, which enables the application to clean up the temporary files and purge any disk buffers, these open files and buffers are likely to be left on the disk. Because DOS does not update the directory entry for a file until it is closed, the directory entry may not reflect the true status of the file.

> ***Note:*** When a new file is written to a disk with DOS interrupts and function calls, DOS starts by allocating space for the file in the FAT. As more data is written to the open file, additional FAT clusters are allocated and a chain is built. If the system is interrupted before DOS is used to close the file, a directory entry for that file has never been written and the file is nothing but a collection of lost clusters.

Anything that can interrupt a system while it is processing therefore can increase the propensity for lost clusters. One of the biggest causes is users who exit applications with the Ctrl-Alt-Del reboot sequence or the reset switch. This type of activity should be discouraged, even though CHKDSK easily can correct the problem by assigning any lost clusters a real file name and thus giving you access to the data.

In this sample CHKDSK report, if you answer yes to the question about converting the lost allocation units to files, the final report indicates that only 3,072 bytes would be in 1 recovered file. The reason is that CHKDSK initially was not run with the /F parameter, so any corrections are inhibited. If you rerun CHKDSK with the /F parameter, the report changes to 3,072 bytes are in 1 recovered file, and the FILE0000.CHK file is created on the disk and placed in the root directory.

The following listing shows what the root directory and FAT of the disk would look like if you ran CHKDSK /F and answered yes to the question about converting lost allocation units to files:

Root Directory

File Name	*Ext.*	*Size*	*Date*	*Time*	*Cluster*	*Attributes*
90CCAM	TXT	7541	2-25-90	9:43 a.m.	2	Arc
90CVETT	TXT	6528	2-25-90	9:40 a.m.	10	Arc
90FSHO	TXT	8940	10-26-89	11:52 a.m.	17	Arc
90MECLPS	TXT	1531	10-10-89	11:18 p.m.	26	Arc
90N300TT	TXT	2763	2-25-90	9:44 a.m.	28	Arc
90PFORM	TXT	7744	2-25-90	11:55 a.m.	31	Arc
90PGTA	TXT	6070	2-25-90	11:56 a.m.	39	Arc
90PTA	TXT	7552	2-25-90	11:56 a.m.	45	Arc
FILE0000	CHK	3072	11-01-90	3:00 a.m.	112	Arc

File Allocation Table

Cluster	*0*	*1*	*2*	*3*	*4*	*5*	*6*	*7*	*8*	*9*
0	-	-	3	4	5	6	7	8	9	END
10	11	12	13	14	15	16	END	18	19	20
20	21	22	23	24	25	END	27	END	29	30
30	END	32	33	34	35	36	37	38	END	40
40	41	42	43	44	END	46	47	48	49	50
50	51	52	END	0	0	0	0	0	0	0
60	0	0	0	0	0	0	0	0	0	0
70	0	0	0	0	0	BAD	BAD	0	0	0
80	0	0	0	0	0	0	0	0	0	0

Cluster	*0*	*1*	*2*	*3*	*4*	*5*	*6*	*7*	*8*	*9*
90	0	0	0	0	0	0	0	0	0	0
100	0	0	113	114	END	0	0	0	0	0
110	0	0	0	0	0	0	0	0	0	0
120	0	0	0	0	0	0	0	0	0	0
130	0	0	0	0	0	0	0	0	0	0
140	0	0	0	0	0	0	0	0	0	0
150	0	0	0	0	0	0	0	0	0	0

Note the new FILE0000.CHK directory entry. The starting cluster value matches the beginning of the lost chain, and the size of the file was calculated simply by the multiplication of the number of allocation units or clusters in the chain by the cluster or allocation unit size (3 x 1,024 = 3,072). The date and time fields are simply filled in with the date and time at which the CHKDSK command was run.

If you answer no to the question about converting the lost allocation units to files, the FAT chain is simply zeroed and the directory is left unmodified. The directory and FAT in this case look just like they looked before this problem occurred. This approach is basically (but not exactly) the same as answering yes to the question and then immediately deleting any of the FILE*xxxx*.CHK files that result.

Although you rarely will find anything of use in the lost cluster files, you should convert them to files so that at least you can inspect their contents to identify what they are and perhaps what program created them. If you are sure that you will find nothing of interest in the file, go ahead and answer no. If from experience you know that the lost allocation units are a result of a premature ending of a program compile, for example, and you know that the data consists only of unusable machine code, then you comfortably can skip the creation of the FILE*xxxx*.CHK files by answering no.

Dealing with Allocation Errors

The next most common error that you find in a CHKDSK report is an *allocation error*. The following chart shows a case in which the example disk has a problem with one of the directory entries:

Root Directory

File Name	*Ext.*	*Size*	*Date*	*Time*	*Cluster*	*Attributes*
90CCAM	TXT	7541	2-25-90	9:43 a.m.	2	Arc
90CVETT	TXT	0	2-25-90	9:40 a.m.	10	Arc
90FSHO	TXT	8940	10-26-89	11:52 a.m.	17	Arc

File Name	*Ext.*	*Size*	*Date*	*Time*	*Cluster*	*Attributes*
90MECLPS	TXT	1531	10-10-89	11:18 p.m.	26	Arc
90N300TT	TXT	2763	2-25-90	9:44 a.m.	28	Arc
90PFORM	TXT	7744	2-25-90	11:55 a.m.	31	Arc
90PGTA	TXT	6070	2-25-90	11:56 a.m.	39	Arc
90PTA	TXT	7552	2-25-90	11:56 a.m.	45	Arc

File Allocation Table

Cluster	*0*	*1*	*2*	*3*	*4*	*5*	*6*	*7*	*8*	*9*
0	-	-	3	4	5	6	7	8	9	END
10	11	12	13	14	15	16	END	18	19	20
20	21	22	23	24	25	END	27	END	29	30
30	END	32	33	34	35	36	37	38	END	40
40	41	42	43	44	END	46	47	48	49	50
50	51	52	END	0	0	0	0	0	0	0
60	0	0	0	0	0	0	0	0	0	0
70	0	0	0	0	0	BAD	BAD	0	0	0
80	0	0	0	0	0	0	0	0	0	0
90	0	0	0	0	0	0	0	0	0	0
100	0	0	0	0	0	0	0	0	0	0
110	0	0	0	0	0	0	0	0	0	0
120	0	0	0	0	0	0	0	0	0	0
130	0	0	0	0	0	0	0	0	0	0
140	0	0	0	0	0	0	0	0	0	0
150	0	0	0	0	0	0	0	0	0	0

The directory entry for the 90CVETT.TXT file has been damaged. Specifically, the size entry for the file has been zeroed. You should know that because the original size of the file was listed as 6,528 bytes and the file occupies 7 clusters on the disk, an allocation error would be caused by this directory entry if the size was changed to anything outside the range of 6,145 to 7,168 bytes. The reason is that if 7 1K-sized clusters are in use by the file, the smallest the file could be is 6,145 bytes (6K plus 1 byte), and the largest it could be is 7,168 bytes (7K exactly). Any size more or less, and a discrepancy must exist between the size listed in the directory entry for the file and the number of clusters used by the file. If you type ***chkdsk*** at the `B:\>` prompt for this example, you receive the following response:

```
Volume Serial Number is 2563-16FF
Errors found, F parameter not specified
Corrections will not be written to disk

B:\90CVETT.TXT
   Allocation error, size adjusted
```

```
730112 bytes total disk space
 52224 bytes in 8 user files
  2048 bytes in bad sectors
675840 bytes available on disk

  1024 bytes in each allocation unit
   713 total allocation units on disk
   660 available allocation units on disk

655360 total bytes memory
556800 bytes free
```

If you type ***chkdsk /f*** at the `B:\>` prompt, you see the following response:

```
Volume Serial Number is 2563-16FF

B:\90CVETT.TXT
  Allocation error, size adjusted

  730112 bytes total disk space
   52224 bytes in 8 user files
    2048 bytes in bad sectors
  675840 bytes available on disk

    1024 bytes in each allocation unit
     713 total allocation units on disk
     660 available allocation units on disk

  655360 total bytes memory
  556800 bytes free
```

Typing ***dir*** at the `B:\>` prompt results in the following message:

```
Volume in drive B has no label
Volume Serial Number is 2563-16FF
Directory of  B:\

   90CCAM    TXT  7541  02-25-90   9:43a
   90CVETT   TXT  7168  02-25-90   9:40a
   90FSHO    TXT  8940  10-26-89  11:52a
   90MECLPS  TXT  1531  10-10-89  11:18p
   90N300TT  TXT  2763  02-25-90   9:44a
   90PFORM   TXT  7744  02-25-90  11:55a
   90PGTA    TXT  6070  02-25-90  11:56a
   90PTA     TXT  7552  02-25-90  11:56a
                  8 File(s)  675840 bytes free
```

As you can see from these command examples, the first report is a result of running CHKDSK without the /F parameter so that corrections are not written to the disk. Here is where you first see the allocation error reported.

CHKDSK then is run with the /F parameter, which shows the same error message but this time corrects the problem. The final DIR command shows just how CHKDSK corrected the problem, which is by modifying the directory entry to match what is found in the FAT. Therefore, the size of the file has been changed from 0 to 7,168, which corresponds to the 7 clusters found in use by the file. If you discover a problem of this nature, the CHKDSK program is sufficient for solving the problem.

Note that the original size of this file was 6,528 bytes. CHKDSK has no way of knowing what the actual or original size of the file was, so the program always figures the largest number possible given the number of clusters used. CHKDSK basically multiplies the number of clusters used by the file times the size of a single cluster to arrive at the file size.

The fact that the size in bytes is now slightly larger than it used to be isn't a problem, regardless of the type of file you are dealing with. Remember that the contents of the clusters involved with the file have not changed—only the size as listed in the directory entry for the file. If the file is a text file (as this one is), it probably has an end-of-file (Ctrl-Z) character defining the end of the file so that the "filler" bytes up to the end of the last cluster aren't included in any uses of the file. If the file is a binary file, these filler bytes between the former end of the file and the end of the last cluster in use by the file now seem to be included and essentially have become part of the file. This situation still isn't a problem, however, because these extra bytes after the end of the file marker (Ctrl-Z) are ignored whether the file is a binary program file or even a data file.

If the file is a binary data file, in many cases you can restore it to its original size by loading the file into the application that was used originally for creating the file and then saving the file back out to disk. This method works because most binary data file formats use a special end-of-file sequence recognized only by the application that created them.

Other conditions besides an incorrect directory entry size number can cause an allocation error when you're running CHKDSK. Because the directory size and FAT chain for each file are compared, FAT damage can cause this problem to occur as well. If the FAT chain were to become corrupted, an allocation error (among other errors) probably would result. If for any reason the FAT chain believed to be representing the file doesn't agree in length with the number of bytes in the directory entry for the file, an allocation error results.

Because CHKDSK always believes the FAT chain in these situations, CHKDSK almost never can restore the file to normalcy if the FAT is damaged. CHKDSK "fixes" the error by changing the directory to match the FAT, which may not repair the file. If the FAT rather than the directory truly is damaged, usually other error messages accompany the allocation error when CHKDSK is run. Therefore, if you see a file allocation error plus other errors, do not use the CHKDSK program to solve the problem. In these cases, a complete recovery of the damaged files is more difficult and involved than just running CHKDSK. For those situations, recovery may be possible with a program such as Norton Disk Doctor (see Chapters 9 and 10, which cover various recovery programs and techniques).

Dealing with Cross-Linked Files

If CHKDSK reports *cross-linked files* on your disk, you have a more serious problem than those situations already discussed. A finding of cross-linked files almost always means that you have damage in the FAT rather than the directory. FAT damage is much more difficult to repair than directory damage because the FAT is much more complicated. In fact, CHKDSK can report but cannot repair this type of damage at all.

When files are reported as being cross-linked, the following error message appears:

```
d:\path\file1.txt
  Is cross linked on allocation unit xx

d:\path\file2.txt
  Is cross linked on allocation unit xx
```

The meaning of cross-linkage is simple: files that are cross-linked claim the same areas of the disk as their own. In other words, several files claim one or more of the same clusters or allocation units on a disk, which cannot be true. Only one file can "own" any given cluster on a disk. Cross-linkage usually comes in pairs but must involve at least two files. Having only a single file reported as cross-linked is not possible, but you may have *many* files cross-linked. The CHKDSK report gives you a list of each file involved and reports the precise cluster where the cross-linkage begins.

The following chart provides a snapshot of the critical areas of the sample disk and lists how cross-linked files may appear:

Root Directory

File Name	*Ext.*	*Size*	*Date*	*Time*	*Cluster*	*Attributes*
90CCAM	TXT	7541	2-25-90	9:43 a.m.	2	Arc
90CVETT	TXT	6528	2-25-90	9:40 a.m.	10	Arc
90FSHO	TXT	8940	10-26-89	11:52 a.m.	17	Arc
90MECLPS	TXT	1531	10-10-89	11:18 p.m.	26	Arc

File Name	*Ext.*	*Size*	*Date*	*Time*	*Cluster*	*Attributes*
90N300TT	TXT	2763	2-25-90	9:44 a.m.	28	Arc
90PFORM	TXT	7744	2-25-90	11:55 a.m.	31	Arc
90PGTA	TXT	6070	2-25-90	11:56 a.m.	39	Arc
90PTA	TXT	7552	2-25-90	11:56 a.m.	45	Arc

File Allocation Table

Cluster	*0*	*1*	*2*	*3*	*4*	*5*	*6*	*7*	*8*	*9*
0	-	-	3	4	5	6	7	8	9	END
10	11	12	13	14	15	16	END	18	19	20
20	21	22	23	24	25	26	27	END	29	30
30	END	32	33	34	35	36	37	38	END	40
40	41	42	43	44	END	46	47	48	49	50
50	51	52	END	0	0	0	0	0	0	0
60	0	0	0	0	0	0	0	0	0	0
70	0	0	0	0	0	BAD	BAD	0	0	0
80	0	0	0	0	0	0	0	0	0	0
90	0	0	0	0	0	0	0	0	0	0
100	0	0	0	0	0	0	0	0	0	0
110	0	0	0	0	0	0	0	0	0	0
120	0	0	0	0	0	0	0	0	0	0
130	0	0	0	0	0	0	0	0	0	0
140	0	0	0	0	0	0	0	0	0	0
150	0	0	0	0	0	0	0	0	0	0

Typing ***chkdsk*** at the `A:\>` prompt results in the following report:

```
Volume Serial Number is 2563-16FF
Errors found, F parameter not specified
Corrections will not be written to disk

A:\90FSHO.TXT
   Allocation error, size adjusted

A:\90FSHO.TXT
   Is cross linked on allocation unit 26

A:\90MECLPS.TXT
   Is cross linked on allocation unit 26

   730112 bytes total disk space
    52224 bytes in 8 user files
     2048 bytes in bad sectors
   675840 bytes available on disk
```

```
   1024 bytes in each allocation unit
    713 total allocation units on disk
    660 available allocation units on disk

 655360 total bytes memory
 564400 bytes free
```

Now you should be able to see that the FAT chain for the 90FSHO.TXT file has been corrupted. Specifically, the FAT entry for cluster 25 should have been an END indicator but instead has been changed to point to cluster 26. This situation causes several problems. First of all, cluster 26 is already in use by the file 90MECLPS.TXT. In other words, the file 90MECLPS.TXT "owns" cluster 26, which is specifically pointed to by the directory entry for that file. Now, however, the file 90FSHO.TXT also claims ownership of cluster 26; thus, the files are cross-linked on allocation unit 26.

Another problem caused by this corrupted FAT entry is the allocation error. In other words, the 90FSHO.TXT file seems to use more clusters on the disk than the directory entry indicates should be used. According to the directory entry, only 9 clusters should be in use by the file, but the corrupted FAT entry causes the FAT chain to extend for 11 clusters.

Note that the cross-linkage error messages almost never are alone in the CHKDSK report. CHKDSK almost always reports other problems, also, such as allocation errors or lost clusters. In these cases, the other problems reported are usually a result of the cross-linkage itself, so repairing these other problems would be improper. Instead, you should attend to the cross-linkage first; then you can focus on handling any other remaining problems.

The preceding example shows why you should *never* run CHKDSK with the /F parameter without first examining the problem at hand. In fact, you should not run CHKDSK /F at all if cross-linked files are reported. If you were to run CHKDSK with the /F parameter on this sample disk, for example, you would do more damage than good. At this point, only a single entry in the FAT is corrupted, and the directory is perfectly intact. CHKDSK /F would succeed in modifying the directory to match the damaged FAT chain, which is hardly the result you want. In other words, the size of the 90FSHO.TXT file would be modified improperly from the current correct size of 8,940 bytes to 11,264 bytes.

When CHKDSK reports cross-linkage, you have several ways to attack the problem. CHKDSK cannot repair cross-linked files at all, but some simple DOS commands can. Without knowing exactly what has been damaged, you normally would work at dealing with the remnants of the damage one piece at a time. If you want to recover the data in the files as well as repair the DOS structures, follow these steps:

Note: The following procedure works on ASCII text files. You may not be able to recover other kinds of files with this method.

1. Use the COPY command to copy the cross-linked files to another disk.
2. Use the DEL or ERASE command to delete the cross-linked files from their original locations. The DEL command marks the directory entry as being deleted and also returns all the clusters in the FAT chain to "available" status by placing zeros in the FAT entries for those clusters. If two files are involved in the cross-linkage and you delete only one of them, you further damage the FAT chain for the other file because the chain then has some zero entries in it. Thus, you must delete *all* the files involved. If as many as 10 files are cross-linked, you must delete all 10 files.
3. Run CHKDSK /F and assign any lost clusters as files.
4. Examine the copies of the cross-linked files to determine which are correct (usually only one). If these files are ASCII text files, you can examine them with a text editor. If these files are program files such as WKS files, use the appropriate software to examine them.
5. Examine the FILE*xxxx*.CHK files with a text editor to determine to which of the remaining copies of the cross-linked files they belong.
6. Using a text editor, delete the portion of the incorrect cross-linked file copies and add the correct FILE*xxxx*.CHK fragment(s). If you cannot find missing fragments of the file, you may be able to use a disk editor such as Norton DiskEdit to locate and recover the lost portions of the file (see Chapter 10).

Another way is to see whether you can discover the "explosion" itself and undo it at the source. The following steps explain how you may go about determining the cause of the damage and undoing it directly:

1. Using a disk editor such as Norton DiskEdit, examine the FAT chains of all files reported as cross-linked.
2. By examining the contents of each cross-linked file with the disk editor, determine which chains are incorrect and patch in correct values. For example, parts of file 1 may be cross-linked with file 2. In order to know which parts belong to which file, you need to know something about the contents of files.
3. Run CHKDSK to see whether any lost clusters remain. If so, determine to which of the cross-linked files they belong and modify the FAT chains of those files to include the appropriate lost clusters.

In either procedure, any problems reported by CHKDSK in addition to the cross-linkage usually indicate which files are the ones with the FAT chain defects. Any resultant lost clusters usually belong to one or more of the files listed as being cross-linked. By combining the data in the raw copies of the original cross-linked files with any lost cluster data, you usually can be successful in re-creating the files as they were before any damage to the FAT occurred. Finally, by deleting the cross-linked files, you place the directory and FAT structures back into harmony with one another, thus eliminating the structure errors by zeroing the FAT chains that were involved.

Examining Less Common Error Messages

This section describes some of the less common error messages you may see when using the CHKDSK command. Following each message is an explanation of what it means and pointers on how to address the problem.

Problem:

```
Probable non-DOS disk
Continue (Y/N)?
```

Solution: If you used the /F switch, answer no. Use Norton Disk Doctor to diagnose and possibly fix this problem.

Problem:

```
d:\path\filename.txt
Allocation error for file, size adjusted
```

Solution: The file *filename* has an invalid sector number in the FAT. CHKDSK truncates the file at the end of the last valid sector. Check this file to ensure that all information in the file is correct. If you find a problem, use your backup copy of the file. This message usually is displayed when the problem is in the FAT, not in the file. Your file should still be good.

Problem:

```
Cannot CHDIR to root
```

CHKDSK could not return to the root directory during its scan of the disk's subdirectories. When this message appears, CHKDSK aborts.

Solution: Try running the command again. If the message reappears, restart DOS and try CHKDSK again. If the message appears yet again, the disk is damaged and CHKDSK cannot fix the damage. Try to copy as many files as possible to another disk; then reformat or retire the damaged disk.

Problem:

```
directoryname
Cannot recover direntry
entry, processing continued
```

CHKDSK cannot recover *direntry*, which is either the current directory entry (.) or the parent directory entry (..) in the named subdirectory, *directoryname*. This subdirectory may be so badly damaged that CHKDSK cannot recover the directory.

Solution: If possible, copy all the files from this subdirectory to another disk or subdirectory. Then erase the files in the original subdirectory and remove the subdirectory (using the RD command). Most likely, you have lost the files in the subdirectory that CHKDSK reported to be faulty. You may need to restore the files from backup copies.

If the problem is in a floppy disk's subdirectory, copy all the files from the offending disk to another floppy. Either reformat or retire the offending disk.

Problem: `CHDIR .. failed trying alternate method`

CHKDSK is confused and does not know how to return to a parent directory. This error is internal to CHKDSK or DOS (or both) and does not mean that your disk drive or floppy disk is bad.

Solution: The best approach is to restart DOS and rerun CHKDSK. If you see this message a second time, get another copy of CHKDSK from your DOS master disk. The copy of CHKDSK you are using probably is bad. Restart DOS and run CHKDSK a third time. If you still get this error, your disk has a serious flaw. Copy whatever files you can from the disk. Retire or reformat the floppy disk; reformat the hard disk.

Problem:

```
filename
Contains invalid cluster, file truncated
```

The file *filename* has a bad pointer to a section in the FAT on the disk. If you used the /F switch, CHKDSK truncates the file at the last valid sector. If you didn't use the /F switch, CHKDSK takes no action.

Solution: Check the *filename* file to see whether all information is intact. If it is, usually CHKDSK can correct this problem without any loss of information in the file.

Problem:

```
directoryname
Convert directory to file (Y/N)?
```

The directory ***directoryname*** contains so much bad information that the directory is no longer usable as a directory. If you respond by pressing Y at this prompt, CHKDSK converts the directory into a file so that you can use DEBUG or some other tool to repair the directory. If you answer by pressing N, CHKDSK takes no action.

Solution: Respond by pressing N the first time you see this message. Try to copy any files you can from this directory to another disk. Check the copied files to see whether they are usable. Then rerun CHKDSK to convert the directory into a file and try to recover the rest of the files.

Problem: `Disk error reading FAT n`

CHKDSK encountered a disk error while attempting to get information from FAT 1 or FAT 2 (indicated by the number *n*). The probable cause is a premature shutdown while the computer was trying to write to the disk (for example, a power failure, a system lockup, or removal of the floppy disk from the drive too soon).

Solution: If this message appears for FAT 1 or FAT 2 on a floppy disk, copy all the files to another disk. Then retire or reformat the bad disk. If the message appears for both FAT 1 and FAT 2, the floppy disk is unusable. Copy the files to another disk and retire or reformat the bad floppy after you have removed all the information you can.

If the message appears for your hard disk, use the BACKUP command to back up all files on the disk. Then reformat and use the RESTORE command on the hard disk.

Problem: `Disk error writing FAT n`

CHKDSK encountered a disk error while attempting to put information into FAT 1 or FAT 2 (shown by the number *n*).

Solution: If this message appears for FAT 1 or FAT 2 on a floppy disk, copy all the files to another disk. Then retire or reformat the bad disk. If the message appears for both FAT 1 and FAT 2, the floppy disk is unusable. Copy the files to another disk and retire or reformat the bad disk after you have removed all the information you can.

If the message appears for the hard disk, back up all files on the disk, reformat it, and then restore it.

Problem: . or

```
..

Entry has a bad attribute or
Entry has a bad size or
Entry has a bad link
```

The link to the parent directory (..) or the current directory (.) has a problem.

Solution: If you used the /F switch, CHKDSK attempts to repair the problem by correcting the link to the parent or current directory. This procedure is normally a safe one and doesn't carry the risk of losing files.

Problem:

```
filename
First cluster number is invalid, entry
truncated
```

The file *filename*'s first entry in the FAT refers to a nonexistent portion of the disk. If you used the /F switch, the file becomes a zero-length file (truncated).

Solution: Try to copy this file to another floppy disk before CHKDSK truncates the file. You may not get a useful copy, however, and the original file is lost.

Problem:

```
filename
has invalid cluster, file truncated
```

A part of the file *filename*'s chain of FAT entries points to a nonexistent part of the disk. If you used the /F switch, the file is truncated at its last valid sector. If you did not use the /F switch, no corrective action is taken.

Solution: Try to copy this file to a different disk and then rerun CHKDSK with the /F switch. You may lose part of the file.

Problem:

```
filename1
Is cross linked on cluster x

filename2
Is cross linked on cluster x
```

Two files—*filename1* and *filename2*—have an entry in the FAT that points to the same area (cluster) of the disk. In other words, the two files think that they own the same piece of the disk.

Solution: Having cross-linked files is a serious problem—basically an error in the FAT pointer structure that has several file fragments pointing to the same individual cluster on the disk. Only one file can own the cluster, so to recover from this problem, simply make a copy of each of the files listed as cross-linked and then delete the original cross-linked versions from the disk. The delete action cleans up the FAT entries for these files by zeroing them out, and the cross-linking problem is taken care of. Next, examine each of the files you just copied. At best, only one of all the files linked together is intact and correct. The other contains garbage at the point where the cross-linking had taken place; that file will probably have to be restored from a backup or re-created.

CHKDSK takes no action on this problem. You must correct the problem yourself by completing the following steps:

1. Copy both files to another floppy disk.
2. Delete the files from the original disk.
3. Edit the files as necessary. Both files may contain some garbage.

Problem:

```
Insufficient room in root directory
Erase files from root and repeat CHKDSK
```

CHKDSK has recovered so many lost clusters from the disk that the root directory is full. CHKDSK aborts at this point.

Solution: Examine the FILE*xxxx*.CHK files. If you find nothing useful, delete them. Then rerun CHKDSK with the /F switch to continue recovering lost clusters.

Problem:

```
directoryname
Invalid current directory
```

The directory ***directoryname*** has invalid information in it. CHKDSK attempts to repair this directory.

Solution: For more specific information about the problem with the directory, do one of the following:

- Type ***chkdsk /v*** and then press Enter.

  or

- Move into the faulty directory if possible. Type ***chkdsk *.* /v*** and then press Enter.

The verbose mode tells you more about what is wrong.

Problem:

```
directoryname
Invalid sub-directory entry
```

The directory ***directoryname*** has invalid information in it. CHKDSK attempts to repair this directory.

Solution: For more specific information about the problem with the directory, do one of the following:

- Type and ***chkdsk /v*** and press Enter.

  or

- Move into the faulty directory if possible. Type ***chkdsk *.* /v*** and press Enter.

The verbose mode tells you more about what is wrong. If you need to, copy the files from this directory and repeat CHKDSK with the /F switch to fix the problem.

Problem:

```
Probable non-DOS disk
Continue (Y/N)?
```

The special byte in the FAT indicates that your disk is a DOS disk but was not formatted, was formatted under a different operating system, or is badly damaged.

Solution: If you used the /F switch, answer by pressing N. Recheck the disk without the /F switch and then answer by pressing Y in response to the prompt. See what action CHKDSK takes. Then, if your disk is a DOS disk, run CHKDSK again with the /F switch.

If you did not use the /F switch, press Y at the `Continue (Y/N)?` prompt and watch what action CHKDSK takes. Then decide whether you want to rerun CHKDSK /F to correct the disk.

Problem: `Processing cannot continue,`
`message`

This error message indicates that CHKDSK is aborting because of an error; *message* tells you exactly what the problem is.

Solution: The likely culprit is a lack of enough random-access memory to check the floppy disk. This message occurs most often with 64K systems. Because most systems have 256K or more, users should see the message infrequently. If DOS returns this message, you may have to increase the amount of memory in your computer or borrow another computer to check the floppy disk.

Problem: `Tree past this point not processed`

CHKDSK cannot continue down the indicated directory path because the system has found a bad track or the subdirectory is a disk on which you have used the JOIN command.

Solution: If you have not used the JOIN command, copy all files from the disk to another floppy. The original disk may not be usable anymore, and you may have lost some files.

Problem: `xxxxxxxxxx bytes disk space freed`

CHKDSK regained some disk space that was improperly marked as in use. *xxxxxxxxxx* tells you how many additional bytes are now available.

Solution: To free this disk space, review and delete any FILE*xxxx*.CHK file that does not contain useful information.

Problem: `xxx lost clusters found in yyy chains`
`Convert lost chains to files (Y/N)?`

Although CHKDSK has found *xxx* blocks of data allocated in the FAT, no file on the disk is using these blocks. They are lost clusters, which CHKDSK normally frees safely if no other error or warning message is given.

A lost cluster is a unit of storage with a pointer indicating that the file is in use, but no directory entry claims ownership of that cluster. Basically, you can think of a chain of these lost clusters as a file fragment with no name. These fragments usually are created by programs that are terminated before they can finish an operation. A program usually writes to clusters on the disk while saving information and then finishes the operation by closing the file, which enables DOS to create the directory entry for the file. If the program is terminated before any open files are closed, lost clusters are a likely result.

Solution: If you answer by pressing N at the `Convert lost chains to files` question, CHKDSK simply zeroes the lost cluster pointers to indicate that these clusters are now available for other files to use. If you answer by pressing Y at the prompt, CHKDSK gives the fragment a directory entry or name. The first name used is FILE0000.CHK, and if any more fragments exist, they are given the name FILE0001.CHK, and so forth.

Also, if any lost clusters are noted, you are given the opportunity to recover these units. Suppose, for example, that you see the following message:

```
2 lost Clusters found in 1 chains.
Convert lost chains to files (Y/N)?
```

If you reply by pressing Y, you then see the same messages that were generated in your first use of CHKDSK. But one new line appears:

```
xxxxx bytes in 1 recovered file
```

If you then check the directory, you find that a new file has been added. Because only one bad chain exists, you find FILE0000.CHK. Had more chains been noted in the error message, you would have seen a correspondingly larger number of these new files listed in sequence. Now that DOS has stored this data for you, you can check the file to see what data it contains. If you want to retain this data, you can rename the file as necessary and go on to better things. If not, erase the file, thus reclaiming the disk space for later use.

If you have given the /F switch and answer by pressing Y, CHKDSK joins each set of lost chains into a file called FILE0000.CHK, placed in the root directory of the disk. Examine the file and delete any portions that do not contain useful information.

If you answer by pressing N and have used the /F switch, CHKDSK simply frees the lost chains so that the disk space can be reused by other files. No files are created.

If you answer by pressing Y but have not given the /F switch, CHKDSK displays the actions it *would* take but does not take any action.

Using the RECOVER Command

The DOS RECOVER command is designed to mark clusters as bad in the FAT. When a file cannot be read properly because of a bad sector on the disk, the RECOVER command marks the FAT so that those particular clusters are not used by another file. Essentially, they are barricaded off so that another file will never occupy those clusters. This program is highly dangerous. If you use this program without a knowledge of what it will do, you may lose information from your disk.

Many users have a misunderstanding of how this program operates. Many think that the RECOVER program is used for recovering the file or the data within the file in question. What happens in reality is that the command recovers only the portion of the file before the location of the defect. The defective portion is marked off in the FAT as bad, and all data after the defect is returned to available status. You always should make a copy of the file to be recovered because the COPY command can get all the information, including the data following the defect.

The recovery operation has two phases:

1. Preserve as much of the data in the file as possible—all the data in a file up to the point of the defect.

2. Mark the FAT so that these bad sectors or clusters of the disk are not used again.

Preserving the Data

Suppose that you tell your word processing program to load a file called DOCUMENT.TXT. The hard disk has developed a defect in a sector that is used by this file, and in the middle of loading it, you see this message appear on-screen:

```
Sector not found error reading drive C
Abort, Retry, Ignore, Fail?
```

You normally should attempt to retry by pressing R. You may be able to read the file on a retry, so you should make this attempt several times. If you can load the file by retrying, simply save the loaded version to a file with a different name, and the data in the file is then preserved. If, after 10 or so retries, you still cannot read the file, press A for Abort. The data will be more difficult to recover.

To recover the data in the file, use the DOS COPY command to make a copy of the file under a different name. For example, you may use this command:

COPY DOCUMENT.TXT DOCUMENT.NEW

In the middle of the copy, you see the `Sector not found` error message again. The key to this operation is to answer by pressing I for the Ignore option so that the bad sectors are ignored and the copy operation can continue to the end of the file. This process produces a copy of the file with the entire file intact—both before and after the error location. The bad sectors themselves appear as gibberish or garbage in the new copied file, but at least the entire copy is completely readable. You probably need to use your word processor to load this new copy and remove or retype the garbled sectors because they are permanently lost.

If the file is a binary file, such as part of a program, you probably have to consider the whole thing a total loss because you do not have the option of retyping the bytes that make up a program file. Your only hope in this situation is to have a backup of the file, which you should have anyway.

At this point, you have completed phase 1, which was to recover as much of the data as possible. Now you're ready to move on to phase 2, which is to mark the disk so that these areas are not used again.

Marking the Disk

Marking the disk is accomplished with the RECOVER command itself. After making the attempted recovery of the data (phase 1), you can mark the sectors as bad in the FAT by using the RECOVER command as follows:

RECOVER *filename*

Continuing with the example used in the preceding section, you would type

RECOVER DOCUMENT.TXT

Press any key to begin recovery of the specified file. You can use wild cards in the file name (such as DOCUMENT.*), but RECOVER will recover only the first file that matches.

RECOVER reports the following information:

```
xxxxx of yyyyy bytes recovered
```

xxxxx is the number of bytes of the original length of the file (*yyyyy*) that has been recovered.

The recovered file (DOCUMENT.TXT in this example) is still on the disk after this operation, but the file has been truncated at the location of the error. Any sectors that the RECOVER command could not read are marked as bad sectors in the FAT. These sectors show up the next time you run a CHKDSK command. You may want to run CHKDSK before and after running the RECOVER command to see the effect of the additional bad sectors.

Your final step is to delete the original bad file (DOCUMENT.TXT) because you already have created a copy of it with as much good data as you can recover.

> ***Warning:*** Remember to be careful when using the RECOVER program. When used improperly, RECOVER can do a great deal of damage to your files and the FAT. If you enter the RECOVER command without a file name for it to work on, the program assumes that you want *every file on the disk* recovered. The program then proceeds to operate on every file and subdirectory on the disk. All subdirectories are converted to files, and all file names are placed in the root directory and given the names FILE0000.REC, FILE0001.REC, and so on. This procedure essentially wipes out the file system on the entire disk. *Do not* use the RECOVER command accidentally without providing a file name! This program is so dangerous when misused that you may want to delete it from the hard disk in order to prevent accidentally invoking the program.

Using the SYS Command

The SYS command is designed to transfer the two hidden system files from one disk to another. This command is provided because these files have to be placed in a specific location on disk and cannot simply be copied to the disk. SYS also updates the volume boot sector so that it is correct for the new version of DOS. Boot volumes, like other areas on disk, are subject to information loss caused by gradual loss of the magnetic image on the disk or overwriting of the information by another program. For this reason, you can use SYS to rebuild a volume boot sector when no backup is available.

The syntax of the command is

SYS [*d:*][*path*] *d:*

[*d:*][*path*] specifies an optional source drive and path for the system files. If omitted, the current default drive is used. IBM DOS 4.0 and later versions support this parameter, but it may not be supported by some non-IBM OEM versions of DOS and did not exist prior to Version 4.0 in any OEM version. *d:* specifies the drive to which you want to transfer the system files.

SYS properly rebuilds the boot sector of a disk only if the command is convinced that no boot sector is present. To convince SYS that no valid volume boot sector is present on the destination disk, you must place 00h bytes in the OEM Name and Version field and the signature bytes field. These fields on the disk identify the licensee of DOS. This procedure is best done with one of the disk editors such as those included in the Norton Utilities or Mace Utilities. By placing 00h bytes in the 8-byte OEM Name and Version field and the 2-byte signature bytes field and then rebooting the system from a DOS floppy, you make DOS believe that no valid volume boot sector exists on the disk. Then you can run the SYS command to rebuild the boot sector and copy the system files to the disk.

When you use SYS, the system files already may exist on the disk. If so, they are overwritten as a part of the SYS procedure. As long as the system files already on the disk are the same as what you are adding, you will experience no problems from the overwrite. Just be sure that you have the same version and revision level of DOS on your bootable floppy that you have on the hard disk.

If the volume originally did not have any system files on it, you unnecessarily add them as part of the SYS procedure. You can use one of the disk editors from Norton Utilities or Mace Utilites to unhide and delete the system files after the procedure is complete.

Using the DEBUG Command

If you don't have access to a disk editor such as that from Norton Utilities or Mace Utilities, DEBUG can serve as a crude editor to help you correct information on disk. The DEBUG program included with your DOS distribution disk is a powerful debugging tool for programmers who develop programs in assembly language. Some of the activities you can perform with DEBUG follow:

- Display data from any memory location.
- Display or alter the contents of the CPU registers.
- Display the assembly source code of programs.
- Enter data directly into any memory location.

- Input from a port.
- Move blocks of data between memory locations.
- Output to a port.
- Perform hexadecimal addition and subtraction.
- Read disk sectors into memory.
- Trace the execution of a program.
- Write disk sectors from memory.
- Write short assembly language programs.

With more powerful programs available in the marketplace for debugging and assembling code, these days the most common use for DEBUG is patching assembly language programs to correct problems or to change an existing program feature, or sometimes patching disk sectors directly. Unless you are experienced at using the DEBUG command, you should use one of the disk editors, such as Norton's DiskEdit program, to patch disk sectors. Refer to Chapters 9 and 10 for more information on these programs.

The documentation for the DEBUG program is no longer found in the standard DOS manual. If you are serious about using the DEBUG program, you need to purchase the *DOS Technical Reference Manual*, which contains the information you need in order to use this program.

Because some program patches refer to the use of DEBUG as the tool for correcting problems, this section includes information about DEBUG that you can use as a reference for those tasks.

To use the DEBUG program, make sure that DEBUG.COM is in the current directory or in the current DOS PATH. Then type the following command and press Enter:

DEBUG [*d:*][*path*][*filename*] [*arglist*]

[*filename*] specifies the file to be debugged. [*arglist*] consists of parameters and switches that will be passed to the program. You may specify the *arglist* parameter if the *filename* parameter is present. When *filename* is loaded into memory, it is loaded as if it had been invoked with the following command:

[d:][path]filename arglist

When the DEBUG prompt "-" is displayed, you can enter a debugging command.

Using DOS 5.0 Data Recovery Tools

Several additional commands that you can use in data recovery have been added to DOS beginning with Version 5.0. These commands include the MIRROR, UNFORMAT, and UNDELETE commands. You may be familiar with similar commands in Norton Utilities and PC Tools. With these commands, you can protect your disk from unintentional formatting and erasure of files and directories. This section discusses the use of these new DOS commands.

Using the MIRROR Command

You use the MIRROR command to cause DOS to store system information on disk for the purpose of using that information to recover data. This system information—the FAT contents, the boot record information, and information about the root directory—is stored in a file named MIRROR.FIL in the root directory of the disk. The MIRROR.FIL information helps the UNFORMAT and UNDELETE commands recover erased files, formatted disks, and corrupted partition tables. (For more on how MIRROR uses this information to recover data, see the discussion of the UNDELETE and UNFORMAT commands later in this chapter.)

For the MIRROR command to be useful, however, it must be used *before* the loss of data occurs. For this reason, you usually will want to place the MIRROR command in your AUTOEXEC.BAT file to make sure that the command is invoked often, at least each time you boot your computer.

The syntax for the MIRROR command is

MIRROR [*drive*] [...] [/T*drive*[-*entries*]][/L]

or

MIRROR /U

or

MIRROR /PARTN

The [*drive*] argument in the MIRROR command indicates for which drive you want to save system information. If you do not specify a drive, MIRROR uses the current drive. To cause the MIRROR command to save information about drive C, for example, you use this command:

MIRROR C:

The [...] argument indicates that you can include more than one drive name in the command. To cause MIRROR to save system information about drives C and D, for example, you use the command

MIRROR C: D:

The [/T*drive*[-*entries*]] option, when included in the command line, causes MIRROR to load a memory-resident program that keeps track of information about deleted files. The ***drive*** parameter indicates which drive the MIRROR command "watches." Note that this option requires the drive letter without the normal colon (:) following the drive name. To cause MIRROR to monitor drive C, for example, you use the command

MIRROR /TC

The ***entries*** option is a number between 1 and 999 that specifies the maximum number of files for which information is kept. If you specify 1, for example, MIRROR keeps up with information only on the last file erased. If you specify 2, MIRROR keeps up with the last 2 files erased, and so on. If you use a large number, the tracking file (PCTRACK.DEL) will become large. If you do not specify the number of files to track, MIRROR defaults to a number that depends on the disk size type. Unless you have experience in this area, using the default is best.

Table 8.1 reports the default number of entries that will be tracked for each disk size.

Table 8.1
MIRROR File-Tracking Information

Disk Size	*Number of Entries*	*File Size*
360K	25	5K
720K	50	9K
1.2M	75	14K
1.44M	75	15K
20M	101	18K
32M	202	36K
More than 32M	303	55K

If you want MIRROR to keep track of the last 10 files erased on disk C, for example, you use this command:

MIRROR /TC-10

The /L switch causes MIRROR to keep only the latest copy of the MIRROR file. If you do not include this option when you run the MIRROR program, and if the MIRROR.FIL file already exists, MIRROR copies the old MIRROR.FIL to a file named MIRROR.BAK and then creates a new MIRROR.FIL file with the current information.

The /U switch unloads the memory-resident erased file-tracking program. If you have loaded other memory-resident programs since the MIRROR memory-resident program was loaded, however, this command cannot unload the program from memory. In this case, you must unload all programs loaded after the MIRROR program before you successfully can use the /U option.

The /PARTN switch instructs the MIRROR program to save in a file named PARTNSAV.FIL information about how a hard disk is partitioned. When you include this switch, the MIRROR command prompts you to place a disk in your floppy drive so that the information can be saved to that disk. The information needs to be on a floppy disk because if the hard disk partition is lost, a file containing the information on the hard disk is of no use. Therefore, you need to keep the floppy disk handy in case you need to use it (with the UNFORMAT command) to rebuild the partitions on your hard disk.

Using the MIRROR command gives the commands UNDELETE and UNFORMAT vital information when you need those commands to help recover data. Therefore, you need to place the MIRROR command in your AUTOEXEC.BAT file with options to save system information about all hard disk drives on your computer and to track erased files. Additionally, you need to use the /PARTN switch to create a floppy disk that contains information about your hard disk partitions. The following sections discuss how the MIRROR information is used for helping other DOS commands recover information on your disk.

Using the UNDELETE Command

Accidentally erasing files on your disk is an easy thing to do. If your fingers operate faster than your brain at times, for example, you may enter a command like DEL *.WP when you mean to use DIR *.WP. The result of this mistake is an accidental deletion of files. But all is not lost. The Norton Utilities and similar programs have provided ways of unerasing files for years. Now, with DOS 5.0, this capability is built into the operating system.

When a file is "erased," the contents of the file on disk are not changed. The erasing process simply informs DOS that the space previously used by that file is now available for storing another file, and the name of the deleted file is removed from the directory. (Actually, only the first character of the file name is changed to the ASCII character 229, which appears as the Greek letter sigma on-screen, telling DOS that the file is deleted.)

DOS can undelete that file if you instruct the system to do so before information is written over the space containing the deleted file. You must undelete a file as quickly as possible before information is written over the deleted data. Therefore, do not run any programs (except UNDELETE) to ensure your maximum chances of recovering the file. If you have run programs that create files, you still may be able to recover the file if none of the programs has overwritten the erased data.

The syntax of the UNDELETE command is

UNDELETE [*filespec*][/LIST][/ DT]

or

UNDELETE [*filespec*][/ LIST][/ DOS]

or

UNDELETE [*filespec*][/ LIST][/ ALL]

The *filespec* option specifies the location and the file to be undeleted. To undelete files with the extension DBF on drive C in the \KWIKSTAT directory, for example, you use the command

UNDELETE C:\KWIKSTAT*.DBF

The /LIST switch tells the UNDELETE command to list the names of files available to be deleted (specified by the *filespec* option).

The /DT switch tells UNDELETE to undelete only those files that are recorded in the tracking file produced by the MIRROR command. You are prompted to confirm the undelete for each possible file.

Note that you can delete files that are not in MIRROR.FIL, but the probability of successful deletion will not be as high.

The /DOS switch tells UNDELETE to undelete only those files listed internally by DOS as deleted—that is, they have an ASCII character 229 as the first character of the file name in the directory. You are prompted to confirm the undelete for each possible file.

The /ALL switch suppresses the confirming prompt. This switch causes all files in the delete tracking file to be undeleted (if that file is present). If the delete tracking file is not present, this command undeletes all deleted files in the DOS directory, using the # character as the first character of the undeleted file. If a file with the same name already exists on disk, another character is supplied to make the undeleted file name unique.

You can use only one of the switches /DT, /ALL, or /DOS in the UNDELETE command line at a time. If you do not use any of these switches, UNDELETE uses the information in the delete tracking file if that information is available. If the delete tracking file is not available, UNDELETE attempts to delete files that are marked for delete in the DOS directory.

If the information in a deleted file has been overwritten, that file cannot be undeleted. You may, however, be able to recover some portions of the file by using a disk edit program such as Norton's DiskEdit (see Chapters 9 and 10 for more information).

Using the UNFORMAT Command

Many people lose important information because of an accidental disk format. Before DOS 5.0 was released, the only way to recover from an unintentional format was by using an unformat utility program from packages such as Norton Utilities or PC Tools. Now DOS contains an unformat utility.

Before learning how the UNFORMAT command works, you need to be aware of some changes in the DOS 5.0 FORMAT command. In older versions of FORMAT, when you formatted a hard disk, the information in the FAT and root directory was erased, but the information on the hard disk was not erased. Therefore, if you could rebuild the FAT and the directory, you could recover the information on the hard disk. This approach is precisely how an unformat process works. When you formatted a floppy disk, however, the data on the disk was erased and you had no way to recover the data with an unformat. DOS Version 5.0 formats a previously formatted floppy disk by erasing only the information in the FAT and root directory. (The FORMAT 5.0 command also scans the disk for bad sectors but does not destroy the data on the disk in the process.) Therefore, DOS 5.0 enables you to unformat floppy disks (that were formatted under the default mode of the DOS 5.0 FORMAT command).

This default mode of formatting that does not erase the information on the disk is called a *safe format*. To format a disk and erase all the information on it, use the /U (unconditional) switch in the FORMAT command.

When a disk has been "safely" formatted, you often can use the UNFORMAT command to rebuild the disk to its former state. But UNFORMAT may not be capable of restoring all files correctly. To give UNFORMAT the best chance of performing a thorough rebuilding of your disk, you need to run the MIRROR command often, at least each time you boot the computer and *before* the accidental format takes place. See the section titled "Using the MIRROR Command" for more information.

In addition to being capable of unformatting a disk, the UNFORMAT command also can restore a corrupted disk partition table. The processes of using UNFORMAT to unformat a disk—with and without the MIRROR command—and of rebuilding a disk partition table are explained in the following sections.

The syntax for the UNFORMAT command is

UNFORMAT *drive:* [/J]

or

UNFORMAT *drive:* [/P][/L][/TEST]

or

UNFORMAT [/PARTN][/P][/L]

The *drive:* option specifies the disk you want to unformat.

The /J switch tells the UNFORMAT command to verify that the information in files created by the MIRROR command matches the system information on the disk. This command does not unformat the disk, but you may run it prior to the unformatting process to verify that the unformat probably will work.

The /P switch tells the UNFORMAT command to send information about the unformatting process to the printer. If you use this switch, UNFORMAT attempts to rebuild the disk only with information in the root directory and system files and does not use the MIRROR information even if it is available (see the discussion on unformatting without a MIRROR file for more information).

The /L switch (when used without the /PARTN switch) lists all files and subdirectories found by the unformat process. If you use this switch, UNFORMAT attempts to rebuild the disk only with information in the root directory and system files and does not use the MIRROR information even if it is available (see the discussion on unformatting without a MIRROR file for more information).

When you use the /L switch with the /PARTN switch, a report on the current drive's partition table is generated, based on 512K sectors.

When you use the /TEST switch, a report on what information the unformat process will be capable of rebuilding is generated. If you use this switch, UNFORMAT produces the report only with information in the root directory and system files and does not use the MIRROR information even if it is available (see the discussion on unformatting without a MIRROR file for more information).

When you use the /PARTN switch, the UNFORMAT command attempts to rebuild the partition table of the hard disk drive. For this command to be successful, you must have used the MIRROR command previously to create the file PARTNSAV.FIL (see the section "Using the MIRROR Command" for more details).

Using the MIRROR File in the Unformatting Process

The unformatting process has the best chance of succeeding if you have used the MIRROR command recently to capture information about the disk's FAT and root directory. To prepare for the possibility of needing to unformat your hard disk, make sure that you perform these steps:

1. Make sure that the MIRROR command is in your AUTOEXEC.BAT file to capture your FAT and root directory information often. If you leave your computer on nearly all the time, you may want to get into the habit of entering the MIRROR command at least daily.

2. Create an emergency boot disk (a floppy disk) containing the same version of DOS that is on your computer. Place the UNFORMAT command and any relevant drivers necessary to boot your computer and access your hard disks. You can use this disk to run the UNFORMAT command if you cannot use your hard disk. Thus, if your drive C (your hard disk) is formatted accidentally, you can use the floppy disk to unformat it.

After taking care of these preliminary steps, you are ready to run the UNFORMAT command when necessary. To unformat drive C, for example, use this command:

```
UNFORMAT C:
```

If you are unsure whether a MIRROR file exists, you can run the UNFORMAT command first with the /J switch to verify that the MIRROR information exists and that it agrees with the system information on disk.

When you enter the UNFORMAT command, it searches for the latest MIRROR information, displays that information's date and time, and asks whether you want to use the information to unformat the disk. Press Y to proceed.

If for some reason the latest MIRROR file is bad—perhaps it was created accidentally *after* your disk had been formatted—press N. Then UNFORMAT looks for the backup MIRROR file and asks whether you want to use it.

Press Y to proceed with the unformat. If you press N, you are asked whether you want to attempt an unformat without the MIRROR information. If you press Y, the unformat proceeds (for more information, see the next section, "Unformatting Without the MIRROR File"). If you press N, the disk is not unformatted.

> ***Warning:*** If you format the disk with the /U option, the UNFORMAT program cannot unformat the disk. Also, if you run the FDISK program on your hard disk before using UNFORMAT, you may not be able to unformat the disk.

Unformatting without the MIRROR File

If you have not created a MIRROR file, or if your MIRROR file is not usable, you still may be able to unformat much of your disk by using the UNFORMAT command. You may want to use the /TEST and /P switches first to determine to what extent the UNFORMAT command will work. If you have Norton Utilities Version 5.0 or 6.0, you may find that its UNFORMAT program can perform a better job. In either case, you probably cannot restore the hard disk to exactly the same shape it was in before the format.

To unformat your hard disk without a MIRROR file, enter the UNFORMAT command. You may use the /P, /L, or /TEST switches in the same way as described earlier. UNFORMAT will attempt the recovery by using file information in the root directory and FAT.

If UNFORMAT finds a file that is fragmented, for example, the command may not be capable of recovering the entire file. The program asks whether you want to recover a portion of the file. If the file is a text file, a partial recovery may be helpful. If the file is a program file (such as an EXE or a COM file), a partial restoration is of no use. For files that cannot be recovered with the DOS UNFORMAT command, you may be able to reconstruct by using a disk editor such as Norton's DiskEdit (see Chapters 9 and 10).

Using UNFORMAT To Restore Disk Partition Information

If the disk partition information on your hard disk becomes corrupted, you may be able to recover with the UNFORMAT command. For the partition to be recovered, you must have used the MIRROR command previously to create the file PARTNSAV.FIL. You should place this file on the same boot floppy disk on which you have stored the UNFORMAT command—for emergency use. To recover a corrupted partition table, use this command:

```
UNFORMAT /PARTN
```

The program asks you to enter the name of the disk drive that contains the file PARTNSAV.FIL (usually A:). UNFORMAT then uses that information to rebuild your partition table. You are prompted to place a boot disk in drive A (your recover disk) and reboot. You then may need to use the UNFORMAT command (without the /PARTN switch) to restore the directories and files on your hard disk.

All the recovery features of DOS 5.0 depend on your foresight to use the MIRROR command periodically to capture information about your disk that can help DOS restore the disk's information.

Chapter Summary

This chapter covered the use of the DOS commands CHKDSK, COPY, RECOVER, and DEBUG in their relationship to data recovery. Also, new data recovery commands available in DOS Version 5.0—MIRROR, UNDELETE, and UNFORMAT—were examined. If used correctly, these commands can help you correct some data problems. This chapter described both problems and solutions associated with these DOS commands. An informed understanding of how the commands work can help you avoid some data problems and solve others.

Now turn to the next chapter, which contains information about other programs that can provide you with a powerful set of tools to help you in your data recovery quest.

9

Special-Purpose Data Recovery Programs

Although you may take every precaution to prevent something from going wrong with your system, on occasion systems do crash, data is lost, and data recovery attempts get under way. This chapter describes the capabilities of several popular data recovery tools. These programs are widely acclaimed as excellent disaster recovery programs; however, they are not the only such programs available. Most data recovery programs provide a variety of features and capabilities beyond those discussed in the following sections. You should select programs according to your own needs.

Assembling a Utility Library

When assembling a cost-effective utility library, three major players (Norton Utilities, Mace Utilities, and PC Tools) control most of the data recovery utility market, but several smaller companies have excellent products that are often overlooked.

Norton Utilities is perhaps the most popular file and disk recovery and inspection program on the market. Norton Utilities is powerful and is perhaps the single most comprehensive package available today. This software has been around in one form or another since the early days of the IBM PC. Norton Utilities qualifies as a standard in its own right because of the popularity and power in these utilities. The best features of this program are the sector-editing capabilities and some of the disk information that the program can display. The newer versions include data encryption, a nondestructive low-level formatter/reinterleaver, Lotus/dBASE file fix, and several other improvements.

Although a relative latecomer compared with Norton Utilities, Mace Utilities has actually been around for several years and has achieved a following for itself. Mace Utilities offers an alternative to Norton software and performs many functions in an easier-to-use fashion than does Norton Utilities. One of the great features of this program is the Mace Utilities Sector Editor (MUSE). MUSE contains an excellent directory and FAT editor system. The MUSE package also includes a dBASE file fix and text file fix program. MUSE, however, does not include the word processing file repair capabilities that Mace has.

Although PC Tools from Central Point Software, Inc., is a total set of front-end system utilities, the program is often viewed in competition with Norton Utilities and Mace Utilities for data recovery. PC Tools can maintain backups of the FAT and directory systems on the hard disk, enabling recovery from an accidental format. The disk defragmenter is suitable for smaller disks, and the sector editor is weak compared with others. An excellent unerase function is available that uses the FAT backups created by the program to work more accurately in cases where the deleted file had been fragmented.

When you assemble a utility library, you need the following computer capabilities:

- Low-level formatting
- INT 13h (physical) sector editing
- FAT and directory repair
- DOS sector (INT 25/26h) sector editing
- Binary file editing (INT 21h)
- Text file editing
- File unerasing
- File defragmenting
- Application-specific file recovery (Lotus, dBASE, etc.)

Although you need to know how to operate most of these programs, many of them automate the recovery procedure and do much of the work for you. To be fully capable in all data recovery situations, your computer system should include one or more hard disk utility programs that work in each of these categories.

Examining Types of Low-Level Format Programs

One of the most basic utilities you need in your technician's toolkit is a low-level format program. This program is used for performing the initial (and any subsequent) formatting of a hard disk. This process can involve many complicated specifications to tailor the operation to the type of controller and drive being used. Basically, two main operational types of low-level format programs are available: those that access the disk controller directly through CCB or SCB commands sent out through the particular I/O port addresses used by the controller or those that operate the format by using INT 13h BIOS commands.

INT 13h BIOS Interface

An INT 13h disk sector editor is the most powerful tool available for major data recovery operations. This tool is essential for recovery operations because it enables you to view and modify literally any data in any sector on the disk.

Programs that use INT 13h functions enable the BIOS interface to translate the INT 13h BIOS commands into the direct controller CCB or SCB commands. Unfortunately, only a few BIOS commands are associated with formatting, and programs that use these commands miss out on a great deal of additional capabilities at the direct controller level. Essentially, programs that format by using INT 13h BIOS functions take the easy way out and are therefore much less effective in tough situations or where a high level of customization or control is wanted by the technician.

Two subcategories of low-level format programs are available that use the INT 13h interface: general-purpose low-level format programs and simple reformatters.

The simplest way to write a general-purpose low-level format program is to use the INT 13h BIOS interface. This method enables the program to run on a variety of different controllers and offers the easiest way to do a quick and easy type of format. Most commonly available format programs work in this manner.

Many of these programs also are capable of performing a nondestructive format on a drive already formatted and that contains live data. Nondestructive programs pick the information off the hard drive, reformat, and lay the information back down as refreshed information in proper alignment. The program in this case formats a single track at a time, backing up and restoring the data before and after formatting each track. In fact, almost every good formatting program available today offers this feature.

The second main type of INT 13h format program offers the nondestructive reformat. The reformat program cannot be used for the initial format of a drive; the program is good only for refreshing the data on a drive already formatted. (*Refreshing* the data means that the nondestructive format program picks the information off the hard drive and lays it back down in full strength, or "refreshed.") This program offers the lowest level of functionality in format programs and usually is not desirable when more powerful utilities are available.

Examples of good programs for reformatting drives already formatted are SpinRite II and Disk Technician Advanced. These programs are designed to be used by end users, not technicians or PC managers.

CCB or SCB Interface

The second type of formatters that work directly at the controller CCB or SCB level are more powerful than those that work through INT 13h. CCB- or SCB-level formatters have access to features and capabilities that vary from controller to controller. Because programs that work at this level need to know the exact controller being used, few programs at this level run on multiple different controllers. This situation means that these formatters are usually dedicated to a specific controller. Often, these formatters are built directly into the controller as a part of the controller's own ROM BIOS. When a formatter is built into the controller, the format program is written specifically for the controller the program is installed on and therefore can use features that other programs cannot know about. Be sure to back up your hard drive before using one of these low-level formatters built into the ROM BIOS.

This type of program is almost always required where the controller is being used in a translation mode, where the actual physical characteristics of the drive are being modified when reported to the system. Translation is often used on RLL (ST-506/412), IDE, ESDI, and SCSI drives. Because these drives often have more cylinders or sectors than standard software recognizes, they are set up to cut the number of cylinders or sectors down by increasing one of the other parameters.

If you were installing an ESDI drive with 1,500 cylinders, 9 heads, and 32 sectors per track, for example, this situation creates a problem. The standard IBM BIOS and DOS only accept a 10-bit number for cylinders, which places the maximum limit at 1,024. Because this drive has 1,500 cylinders, you either must forget about all the cylinders above number 1,023 or put the ESDI controller into translation mode. In translation mode, the controller fools the system into thinking that the number of cylinders is cut in half, to 750, while also doubling the number of heads to 18. This procedure results in the same number of sectors accessible, but the system is being fooled.

Translation presents a problem for any INT 13h low-level format program because it also is fooled. Therefore, any attempt at formatting the drive with this translation enabled results in the wrong sector header ID information being written to the disk, as well as defect mapping becoming wildly incorrect. A format program that works directly with the controller at the register level can see through the translation and can format the drive correctly.

Another problem is that many controllers have the capability of writing the drive table parameters directly on the drive to circumvent an inadequate ROM BIOS drive table. These controllers write the user-supplied parameters directly on the disk, usually in a hidden extra sector. Any conventional low-level format program that lacked specifics about this type of controller actually can end up overwriting this information, destroying access to the entire disk.

Several alternatives are available, but some are better than others.

Low-Level Format Programs

This section examines various brands of low-level format programs.

IBM Advanced Diagnostics

The IBM Advanced Diagnostics is the standard low-level format program in the IBM world. This program is powerful and works directly at the controller register level, but lacks features and functions that many other programs offer.

The Advanced Diagnostics software is available from IBM in the Hardware Maintenance Service (HMS) manual. This book/disk combination package is sold by IBM and used by technicians for service and troubleshooting.

Anyone can purchase this package; users don't have to be dealers or authorized service centers. Many other computer companies do not sell their service manuals or diagnostics software to anybody except authorized dealers. IBM sells a separate HMS package for XT/AT and PS/2 MicroChannel Architecture systems.

Note that although you can purchase the Advanced Diagnostics and HMS manuals for PS/2 systems, the Advanced Diagnostics is actually hidden on the standard Reference disk that comes with each MCA-based PS/2 (Model 50 and later models). This Advanced Diagnostics program contains a special low-level format program that works directly with the IBM ST-506/412 MFM, RLL, IDE, ESDI, and SCSI drives. The program also does automatic defect mapping and surface analysis. This program is the only program you should use for low-level formatting on PS/2 systems.

Note: To access this special hidden diagnostics, press Ctrl-A at the Reference disk main menu, and the diagnostics appears.

For the PS/2 systems with AT-bus slots (Model 40 and earlier models), you need to purchase the XT/AT HMS manual and PS/2 supplements to get the Advanced Diagnostics. The Advanced Diagnostics for the XT and PC systems is lacking in several important features, so you may not want to use it for these systems. The interleave is fixed at 6 to 1 during the format, and manufacturer defect mapping is not done at all. This drawback is inexcusable and mandates that another program be used. The interleave should be adjustable by the end user from 1 to 1 to 8 to 1. Having the interleave fixed at 6 to 1 is not the most efficient way to re-create information from most hard drives.

The AT version of the program, however, is capable of performing defect mapping and enables the interleave to be adjusted from the default of 3 to 1. The only problem is that 2 to 1 is the lowest allowable interleave selection, so if you have upgraded to a faster controller, you need another program that will enable you to change the interleave all the way up to 1 to 1.

Warning: The IBM format programs do not support a nondestructive reformat option, so backups and restores are mandatory.

All in all, for PC or XT systems, the IBM low-level format programs on the Advanced Diagnostics are lacking. The programs are OK for older AT systems, and they are the only way to go for PS/2 systems.

Htest/Hformat

The Htest/Hformat program is one of the most powerful and capable low-level format programs available anywhere. This package, from Mace Utilities, is a library of programs that operates at the controller register level and the BIOS level.

To improve operation at the controller register level, the package includes many drivers that support different controllers. Drivers are included for virtually the entire Western Digital controller line. Because many other controller manufacturers make controllers based on the Western Digital designs and even use Western Digital chipsets, the drivers work with a number of other makes and models.

This program gives you precise control over the formatting and surface analysis operations. For example, the interleave test that the program performs not only shows the results of different interleave settings but also shows the effects of variations of skew. *Skew* is the offset in sectors between the sides of the platters to allow time for the heads to be selected electronically. Precise control of formatting and surface analyses means that these programs give you a choice of choosing the interleave value instead of being stuck with a preset value.

After determining the best interleave and skew, you can perform a destructive (as in initial) format or a nondestructive reformat operation on the drive, to set the desired interleave and skew factors. The program can be run interactively through a complicated command interface or can be driven by scripts, which enable you to automate the process. The price of the program is in the complexity of the package and the large number of options over which you have control.

This program also includes several programs designed for data recovery, such as a replacement for the DOS FDISK program, which does not destroy data on the drive. This FDISK program can mimic all the capabilities of FDISK in DOS but limits the write operations to only the master and extended partition boot sectors and does not damage any other sectors as does the real FDISK. This enhanced FDISK program can be used for rebuilding a hard disk partition table without disturbing any information in the partitions themselves. This FDISK utility enables you to restore a blown partition table boot sector without doing damage to the FATs, root directory, or other areas of the disk.

This program is recommended for its power and capabilities and is definitely not for the end user; the tool is complex and not easy to use. For many users, this program represents the heavy artillery used for light duty or standard formatting, especially where users need the power of direct register access to the controller.

Disk Manager

Disk Manager is a set of disk utilities that offers several capabilities. In this chapter, however, you learn only the program functions regarding low-level formatting. Ignore the functions of this program for supporting drives not in the BIOS drive tables or for any sort of partitioning.

Aside from the partitioning and drive table capabilities that you should not use, this program is a good low-level format program. The program works at the register level for the standard ST-506/412 Western Digital types of controllers and can work at the BIOS level for others. The program enables you to adjust interleave, skew, and proper entry of manufacturer defect information.

The program can deal with translating controllers but cannot run the controller format if the drive parameters are stored on the drive. The on-line help in the newer versions of the program is good and has essentially evolved into the complete manual for the program.

> ***Warning:*** This program runs in a destructive mode when formatting and cannot reformat a disk nondestructively.

One notable feature about Disk Manager is that Seagate, the nation's largest manufacturer of hard drives, has shipped a customized version of this program with most Seagate drives sold during the past several years. This widespread shipping program means that you already may own a copy of this program. If you do, you may want to use the program as a low-level format program. Remember, however, that you always should run the program in Manual mode (/M) to disable the automatic drive table setting, partitioning, and high-level formatting operations. These other operations should be done with your System Setup program, and DOS should do the partitioning and high-level formatting.

HDtest

HDtest is a capable, user-supported, easy-to-use, low-level format program. HDtest is available in the IBM Hardware Special Interest Group on CompuServe, in user-supported software libraries such as the Public Software Library, or direct from the author, whose address is provided in this chapter.

This program has a nice menu system and is easy to use. The program is an INT 13h BIOS-level formatter, so it does not work in some cases where a disk has been damaged magnetically in a severe fashion; in normal instances, however, it works well. The program supports virtually any drive that has a BIOS interface but does not work on most ESDI or SCSI systems, including PS/2s. The program is ideal for standard formatting of XT and AT systems with ST-506/412 controllers, both MFM and RLL.

Because the program works at the BIOS level, translation or dynamic configuration of drive tables is not supported. In that case, you either must disable the translation or use programs that work at the controller register level.

The program has a surprising number of features including interleave testing and selection, a reformat capability, surface analysis, and manufacturer defect mapping by cylinder and head. This program is ideally suited when you are using standard ST-506/412 controllers and want an effective, simple, fast, low-level format program.

This program is available from the following address:

HDtest
Jim Bracking
967 Pinewood Drive
San Jose, CA 95129
(408) 725-0628

Disk Reformatter Programs

Disk reformatter programs are stripped low-level format programs that work in a nondestructive fashion. The programs back up each track before formatting it and restore the data when the track format is complete. The main purpose of these utilities is to give you an easy way to do something simple such as change the interleave of a drive, without undertaking the complete repartitioning and restore operations. These programs are geared more for the end user, handle BIOS and CCB operations automatically, and require little user interaction. SpinRite II fits in this category.

> ***Warning:*** Don't forget to back up your system before you use one of these programs.

These programs still require that a backup be performed. Any problem that occurs during the reformat operation results in a loss of at least the track being operated on during the format and possibly others as well. In fact, many users have found that because of incompatibilities with their systems, the operation ended up scrambling the entire disk.

A fringe benefit of these programs is the refreshing of the sector headers and trailers, which is a by-product of any low-level format operation.

You may not want to use these programs because they cannot be used for initial formats of drives and they operate at the INT 13h level (precluding access to many special features of different controllers). These programs are designed more for the end user rather than a data recovery specialist.

Norton Utilities (Calibrate)

Of all the reformat programs available today, the Norton Utilities Calibrate program is among the top sellers. The program is a straightforward package with all the capabilities you want in a program of this type. The program enables simple testing of the controller and drive, checks the interleave, and resets it if you want.

> ***Warning:*** Although the nondestructive format operations work well for most systems, remember to make a backup just in case.

Calibrate works well with other full-blown, low-level format programs. Calibrate leaves the manufacturers' defect information marked by other programs intact and effectively performs a refresh and surface analysis around any already recorded defects. Like most reformatters, the program does not touch the first track on the disk (where the partition table resides). The program works through the BIOS and cannot be sure that the controller is doing dynamic configuration with a special sector on that track. Items like skew also are not adjustable by this program because that requires register-level access to the controller.

Calibrate enables testing to be done at a level you control. What you are controlling is the number of different patterns repetitively written to each track as the reformat takes place. If the program cannot actually perform the reformat, as is the case with most of the more advanced disk interfaces, then read-and-write testing still takes place.

This program also works on more types of drives and controllers than do most reformatters. It even operates on a PS/2 SCSI adapter with cache but only does read-and-write testing and not an actual format. This situation is the case with most controllers not of the standard ST-506/412 type. If you need a simple reformat program that works on the majority of disks—and does not affect the manufacturers' defect information you so carefully laid out during the initial low-level format—you may want to try the Calibrate program, which comes with Norton Utilities 5.0 and later.

SpinRite

SpinRite, by Gibson Research Corporation, is a reformat utility. This program performs a read-and-write test on disk drives, evaluates and optimizes disk interleave, and refreshes the low-level format. All its various functions are carried out nondestructively, without altering the content of disk files.

The program is menu driven and easy to use. The quick scan works well. The program offers different levels of pattern testing. If the controller is of the basic ST-506/412 design, the program can do only read-and-write testing and not actual formatting.

When the program is in the format mode, the first track is automatically skipped to avoid problems with dynamically configured controllers. This feature means that the track containing the master partition boot sector can never be reformatted by SpinRite.

In normal operation, SpinRite also evaluates disk performance and tests for the optimum interleave.

One annoying aspect of this program is that it defaults to a mode that wipes out the manufacturers' defect information, which was written during the last low-level format. Although this situation can be overridden with a /leavebad parameter, most users do not know that they should complete this step.

The problem with this program is that any low-level format program, no matter how sophisticated, cannot uncover marginal areas in the same manner that the manufacturer of the drive can. If you have a drive with 27 manufacturer-marked defects, for example, few low-level format programs (SpinRite included) find more than 5 of these as actual defects. This situation means that the other 22 locations were not bad enough to be picked up by a simple digital read-and-write test but were bad enough to be found marginal by the manufacturer's sophisticated analog testing. Nothing should conflict with the manufacturer-indicated defects if you want trouble-free operation of the drive.

The SpinRite program is perhaps the most popular of the reformatter programs; generally, it operates well, especially in the later versions of the program. Just remember to ensure that the program leaves the manufacturers' defect marks alone, by using the /leavebad parameter.

Reviewing INT-13h Sector Editors

A sector or disk sector editor that works at the INT 13h level is an absolute requirement for a data recovery specialist. These programs enable you access to a drive regardless of the condition of partition tables, boot sectors, FATs, directories, etc. This capability means that because the programs work directly with the BIOS interface to the drive, they literally can read and write any sector anywhere on the drive.

This type of access is needed when the drive is not recognized as a volume by DOS. In other words, if you cannot access the drive letter (C, D, etc.), this is the type of utility you need. For direct access to areas that reside outside the partition boundaries themselves, such as the master and extended partition boot sectors and hidden sectors on the drive, you also need an editor that works in INT 13h BIOS mode.

Many popular programs you have heard about—PC Tools Deluxe, Mace Utilities, and most others—do not enable you to edit a disk at this level. In fact, only three programs are known to function as disk editors in this mode: Norton Utilities (NU or DiskEdit), DiskMinder from Westlake Data, and an editor in the DOSUTILS package from Ontrack. DiskEdit from Norton Utilities and DiskMinder from Westlake Data are superior and are discussed in this chapter.

Norton Utilities (NU and DiskEdit)

The Norton Utilities NU editor is available in Version 4.5 and earlier releases of the program. Version 5 and later versions now include DiskEdit. The new editor is greatly improved. The NU and DiskEdit editors have become the standard data recovery programs because of their success in the marketplace. More copies of these programs have been sold than any other.

The older editor is still useful because it puts a single sector on a single screen. This capability means that when you scroll forward or backward through the disk, you are moving one sector at a time, and each byte in the sector falls in the same place on the screen according to its offset in the sector.

The DiskEdit utility displays either less than a single sector on-screen or more than one, depending on the video mode of your video adapter hardware. DiskEdit adapts to your video hardware to fill the screen whether you are in a 25-, 43-, or 50-line mode. Although an improvement in general, the display no longer conforms to a single sector per screen, and scrolling forward or backward a given number of sectors is not as simple anymore.

DiskEdit also includes dynamic linking capabilities, which the older editor lacks. This capability means that when you are editing a directory entry for a file, you can jump right to the chain of entries in the FAT for that file with a single keystroke. From there you can jump to the sectors of the file with another keystroke. Because much data recovery involves jumping between the directory and FAT, this capability makes the job much easier. Other editors—the Mace Utilities editor and DiskMinder—have had this linking capability before, but now Norton Utilities has it as well.

Because of the INT 13h mode of operation (absolute sector mode), the dynamic linking between disk structures like the directory and FAT areas, and the overall success of this program in the marketplace, you may want to use this editor over the others.

DiskMinder

The DiskMinder program from Westlake Data is exclusively a disk/sector editor. Unlike Norton Utilities or other programs, DiskMinder doesn't try to be a jack of all trades; instead, it does one job well.

DiskMinder enables you to edit INT 13h BIOS sectors, DOS sectors, files, FAT tables, directories, and partition tables in comprehensible formats. In addition, DiskMinder offers dynamic linking between related information before Norton Utilities and others. This capability is handy for reconstructing damaged disks.

DiskMinder also offers full search and replace, with scope limited by the current mode (current file, disk, etc.). DiskMinder has automatic FAT-building capabilities, enabling you to view the contents of a cluster with a single key and then add it to the FAT chain you're building with another single key.

This program has a simple, intuitive user interface that in many ways is cleaner than the DiskEdit program. DiskMinder specializes in one area (disk editing) and does it well. If you are serious about data recovery, you may want to take a close look at this program.

Reviewing Automatic Disk Diagnostic and Repair Programs

This category includes the automatic do-it-all utility program that has become popular in the past few years. This utility program checks the FAT and directory structures and then tests the data area containing files where it looks for unreadable sectors. Add to this a check for validity on the DOS volume boot sector as well as the master partition boot sector, and you can easily see the versatility of this program.

The trend to this type of program was started by Norton Utilities with its DiskTest program in the earlier versions. This program was designed as a replacement for the DOS RECOVER command and evolved into the Norton Utilities Disk Doctor program, which included the capabilities of the DOS CHKDSK command and some other functions as well.

Disk diagnostic and repair programs claim to test every area of the disk. They make sure that not only are the sectors readable but also that the data structures contained within them are valid. This capability seems to be a tall order for a mere program. These programs have to be capable of understanding what they see, and if what they see is wrong, they correct the problem.

These programs are good at handling simple problems on completely standard systems but fall short when the problem is complex or the system configuration is abnormal.

The three main players in this field are Disk Doctor from Norton Utilities, Emergency Room from Mace Utilities, and Diskfix from PC Tools Deluxe.

Suppose that you are testing a disk and the program reports that both copies of the FAT are not the same. The program then offers to correct the problem. What does the program do? Copy the contents of FAT #1 over FAT #2? Copy FAT #2 over FAT #1? Or does the program merge the two copies together into an average of the two? You don't know what the program may do. What do you do?

One response is to thank the program for pointing out the problem and then tell the program to stay out of it and leave the disk alone. You then can call up your disk editor and examine the two FATs yourself. After that, you can make an informed, intelligent decision about what to do. If you decide that FAT #1 is trashed but FAT #2 is intact, then you can use the disk editor to copy FAT #2 over FAT #1.

The most dangerous of these automatic utilities is the Disk Doctor from Version 4.5 of the Norton Utilities. This program makes changes to your disk without saving as a form of backup the portions of the disk it changes. The newer Disk Doctor II included with Version 5.x and later, as well as Emergency Room and Diskfix, have this capability. These newer programs therefore have an undo capability in case the repairs they make are incorrect.

These automatic programs are not suited for the data recovery technician. They are designed for the end user who does not want to know how DOS stores information on a disk. Users who know this information, however, are far more intelligent than even the smartest of these automatic programs and generally may be able to make repairs by using a disk editor more effectively.

Automatic programs work well fulfilling the purpose for which they were designed: as a replacement for the DOS RECOVER and CHKDSK commands. The programs also do an admirable job of replacing the SYS command. This capability means that for simple cases of unreadable sectors in files, for which you normally use the RECOVER command to patch the FAT chain around the defective area, you should use one of these programs instead. In the case of substituting for RECOVER, you may find that these programs can work right down to the sector level, where RECOVER only works with whole clusters. This capability means that more of the file is available after the job is done than if RECOVER is used.

Also, the RECOVER command has bugs in every version of DOS tested up to but not including 5.0. Yet to be verified is whether the problems with RECOVER have been fixed in DOS 5. But, even if they have, other programs work down to the sector level, whereas RECOVER costs you portions of your file in cluster increments.

These utility programs also work better than CHKDSK at repairing problems with the FAT areas and directories. Also, these programs generally work better than the SYS command, which normally is used for correcting problems with the DOS system files and the DOS volume boot sector. These automatic programs can fix the types of problems you normally may have used SYS for and generally are more effective than SYS, especially when compared with the SYS command in DOS Version 3.3 and earlier.

Be careful when you use these programs. Make sure that you can undo any changes that these programs make if they perform an incorrect repair.

Norton Utilities (Disk Doctor and Disk Tool)

Norton Disk Doctor examines several aspects of hard and floppy disks, checking the integrity of the master partition boot sector, DOS volume boot sector, FATs, and data area.

Note that Version 4.5 of this utility is dangerous and should not be used because it lacks the undo capability. Also, various releases of 4.5 have been shipped, and some of them have a few nasty bugs, especially when dealing with nonstandard types of partitions or disks. If you have Version 4.5 and the time stamp does not read 4:51 p.m., then you do not have one of the later versions. You may want to upgrade to Version 5.x or later, which has added the undo capability, as well as fixed the problems of the earlier versions.

Versions 5.x and later have a new companion program, Disk Tools. This program contains some of the functions found in Version 4.5 of Disk Doctor, such as the make-a-disk-bootable operation (equivalent to SYS), and includes the capacity to undo the damage from incorrectly running the DOS RECOVER command across an entire disk rather than on a single file.

Several releases have been made of Version 5.x of Norton Utilities. You may have noted that date and time stamps show the following two releases so far:

- 07-17-90 5:00p
- 09-25-90 5:00p

If you have the first release, call the manufacturer, Symantec, and obtain the necessary maintenance release, which is sent at no cost to you.

Mace Utilities (Emergency Room)

Mace Utilities from Fifth Generation Systems Inc. includes a disk diagnostic and repair program, the Emergency Room, which is similar to the Norton Utilities Disk Doctor.

One notable feature of this program is its capacity to create a backup of the areas of the disk it repairs, enabling you to undo these repairs if they are done incorrectly. This valuable feature was missing from the competition.

PC Tools (Diskfix)

PC Tools from Central Point Software Inc. includes the program Diskfix, which is basically equivalent to the Norton Utilities Disk Doctor and the Mace Utilities Emergency Room. This program works like the others and notably has the undo capability.

Reviewing Unerase or Undelete Utilities

One of the simplest data recovery operations is the unerasure of a deleted or erased file. This operation is possible because DOS does not actually erase the file. Instead, DOS writes zeros in the FAT chain for the file and overwrites the first letter in the file's name with a lowercase Greek Sigma (σ) character. Because the directory entry still has information indicating the starting cluster of the file as well as the length of the file, unerasing the entry usually is a simple operation.

Unerasing a file can be more complicated under certain circumstances, however. If the original file had been fragmented, for example, the free clusters following where the file had started may no longer belong to that file. Also, DOS reuses a directory entry at the earliest opportunity, but the actual disk space occupied by the file may be reused at a later time. This feature results in files that actually can be unerased but that have no available directory information from which to start. In these situations, powerful unerase programs can be helpful.

The Norton Utilities, Mace Utilities, and PC Tools packages include powerful unerase programs. The simplest unerase program is Quick Unerase (QU), found in older versions of Norton Utilities. The older QU program handled fragmented files with difficulty and was incapable of unerasing a file where the directory entry had been reused. This program has been enhanced greatly by the newer Unerase program found in Versions 5.x and later. Most newer unerase programs can work in these tougher situations.

These three packages come with programs used for making backups of the FAT and directory areas of a disk in special hidden files recognizable to the particular programs making the backups. These FAT and directory backup capabilities originally were designed to unformat an accidentally high-level-formatted hard disk. Now these backups have an even more important use: They can be used for more effectively unerasing files.

Each of these utility packages includes an unerase program that looks for the system area backup made by the package's companion program. Normally you put the system area backup command into your AUTOEXEC.BAT file to ensure that such a backup is made during every boot operation. When the corresponding package's unerase program is activated, the program looks on the disk for the special hidden backup of the system area, which—if found—can greatly aid the unerase procedure.

With a copy of the FAT and directory areas of the disk at hand, the unerase program easily can handle fragmented files correctly and even unerase a file where the directory entry has been reused.

In tough cases, where no system area backup is available, these unerase programs enable you to scan the free clusters of a disk, looking for the contents of the erased file. When (and if) you find the file data in question, the programs help you rebuild the FAT chain and directory entries for the file, cluster by cluster.

You may want to use one of these packages to back up your system areas frequently. Then, when a difficult unerase operation arises, your system area backups enhance the capabilities of the unerase programs.

Reviewing File Defragmenting Utilities

Many users today defragment the files on their hard disks. If you ask users why they defragment their files, many indicate that as files become fragmented, the read-and-write performance of the disk begins to suffer because of the additional movements required by the disk mechanism to access the files. After defragmenting, the files are all in one piece on the disk, and unnecessary movement is eliminated. This capability results in a speedier system.

Speed is only a secondary concern, however. You should be more concerned with a major system area disaster, where the FATs and root directory are damaged or overwritten. A complete rebuild of these areas may be easy if the files on the disk were recently defragmented. If the files are extremely fragmented, however, you may be in for a messy job in reconstructing the fragmented and split FAT chains.

Periodic defragmenting makes future data recovery operations, whether simple ones such as unerasing files (deleted *after* the defragmenting operation) or complex ones such as rebuilding a completely trashed FAT system, become straightforward and even routine. A fringe benefit is the increased disk performance and reduced wear and tear on the drive actuator mechanism.

Norton Utilities, Mace Utilities, and PC Tools

Each of the three major disk utility packages includes a defragmentation utility program, and for the most part they work well. The Norton Utilities Speed Disk program offers the greatest level of control, enabling you to select the order of file and directory placement on the disk. The Mace Utilities Unfragment program does not offer that level of control but does work well.

The PC Tools Compress (really a misnomer) utility works but does not adequately handle larger hard disk partitions well. In fact, the PC Tools program runs out of memory if you have more than approximately 2,000 files on your disk. You normally have that many files on a 100M drive, so the program may not work on drives much larger unless they are relatively empty.

You should not run any defragmenting utility without a recent backup.

The Norton Utilities and Mace Utilities programs work regardless of the number of files or disk size, as long as the operating system is DOS. The only problem with these programs is that they take time to operate. On a 30M drive approaching maximum storage capacity, for example, the programs usually take from 30 to 60 minutes to complete the job.

Vopt

One of the best defragmenting programs available is Vopt by Golden Bow Systems, Inc. This program excels in speed of operation. The same 30M disk that the other defragmenting disks need a minimum of 30 minutes to clear takes Vopt 2 to 5 minutes to defragment. In fact, under normal operation, you may find that the program rarely takes more than 1 to 2 minutes to work.

Vopt is faster because it's smarter than most of the other programs; by being more intelligent, it does less overall work. Vopt treats the hard disk like a giant jigsaw puzzle, looking for the best way to fit files on the disk in a defragmented fashion and with the disk files packed to the beginning of the disk. As the program operates, defragmentation takes place first, with the fragmented files being copied to free areas of the disk in a contiguous fashion. Then the program goes into packing mode, which works by moving files from the end of the disk that fit holes near the beginning of the disk. The end result is a disk completely defragmented and packed in record time. Unlike with the Norton Utilities Speed Disk program, you have no control over where files and directories end up on the disk, but that is not important.

If you have been using other defragmenting utility programs, you may want to take a look at Vopt. The package also includes several other small utility programs, such as an improved version of CHKDSK, a disk mapping utility, a memory usage map, system and disk performance tests, and floppy diagnostic utilities. All programs are command driven, but they prompt the user for needed input.

Reviewing File and Sector Editing Utilities

To edit files, you need several editors that work in different modes of operation. The INT 13h editors previously mentioned (NU, DiskEdit, and DiskMinder) also work in other modes, which makes them useful in a variety of situations.

Normally, you do not want to access a disk in INT 13h mode, because doing so requires a three-coordinate approach to everything. You must specify areas of the disk by cylinder, head, and sector. Normally this mode is used only in severe cases of disk corruption or when the partition tables have been damaged.

For standard disk editing, you may want to work in DOS Sector (INT 25/26h) mode or even DOS File (INT 21h) mode. Each of these editors works well in all three modes of operation.

Mace Utilities comes with a good disk editor, Mace Utilities Sector Editor. This program lacks an INT 13h mode but works well in the other two modes. In fact, it works well in these modes and supports linking between structures such as the FAT chain of a file and the file's directory entry and data. This feature enables easy movement through the disk during recovery operations.

A binary editor you may want to consider is Hexcalibur, a user-supported product. This program offers a unique feature that virtually no other binary editor has: a high-quality editor designed for examining, modifying, or manipulating disk files in their raw, or binary, format. Hexcalibur enables you to examine and change any part of a file by using either hexadecimal characters or standard ASCII characters. This program is especially useful for examining and editing files that standard ASCII editors either do not read or do read but display in a nonusable format.

Hexcalibur has another unique feature: an Insert mode. This capability means that as you type new characters or hex values into the file, all subsequent data is shifted to the right and the file length is extended. This feature is especially useful when you're correcting corrupted application program binary files, such as database files, where alignment of fields is important.

The program costs about $30 and is available from the following address:

Hexcalibur
Gregory Publishing Company
333 Cobalt Way, Suite 107
Sunnyvale, CA 94086
(408) 727-4660

> ***Warning:*** Hexcalibur is intended as a general-purpose editor. The program wasn't written to be used for fixing damaged disk directories or for performing other low-level repair operations. The program doesn't provide any instructions to assist in such activities, which should be performed by experts only. Serious, irreparable damage to the disk directory can result if such repair is attempted—with Hexcalibur or a similar program—by untrained people. Such damage can mean the irrecoverable loss of data.

Finally, you need some sort of ASCII text file editor for modifying text files and for general-purpose work. Many people suffer with the DOS EDLIN program, but you may want to purchase one of the commercially available editors or obtain one of the many high-quality user-supported editors on the market. The choice of editor seems to be a personal one among computer users. You need to try a few before you find one to your liking. Following are two that you may want to consider:

QEdit Advanced
SemWare
4343 Shallowford Road, Suite C-3
Marietta, GA 30062-5003
Voice: (404) 641-9002
Fax: (404) 640-6213
BBS: (404) 641-8968

and

EDWIN
by Kim Kokkonen
TurboPower Software
(719) 260-6641

Reviewing Application-Specific Data Recovery Tools

Many applications programs save their data to specially formatted files. Often these files are of a binary type, which means that they consist of data other than ASCII characters. These files can be edited only with a binary editor, and the format of the files is not intuitive and in fact is normally incomprehensible. Recovery of these types of files can be difficult. If the structure of the file does not follow what the applications program expects, the application either may not load any part of the file past the damaged area (such as 1-2-3) or may misinterpret the data past the damaged area (such as dBASE).

In these cases, several companies have written specialized recovery programs tuned to a particular application that knows the special format required by that application. These utilities rework the structure of the file until the applications program that originally created it fully loads and correctly interprets the file.

Unfortunately, only the most popular applications programs have found a market for this type of utility. The most common examples are the numerous utility programs designed to rebuild or restore damaged 1-2-3-, dBASE-, or WordPerfect-compatible files. Fortunately, because these programs are generally the most popular in their respective areas, most other applications read and write these types of files as well. For example, most other spreadsheet programs can be made to read and write Lotus-compatible files. This capability sometimes can be used for helping reconstruct a damaged file even if that format is not the application's own format.

General File Repair

The newer versions of Norton Utilities include recovery programs for Lotus and dBASE files. Mace Utilities includes recovery utilities for dBASE and word processing files. Although these utilities work well, this is a perfect example of where specialization improves the breed. Several Lotus and dBASE file repair programs are available from other manufacturers, and they work better than the ones included with Norton Utilities and Mace Utilities.

Lotus File Repair

For Lotus-compatible files, you may want to consider the RESCUE Plus program from Intex Solutions. This program is unequaled in its capacity to reconstruct damaged Lotus files quickly and accurately. The program automatically constructs a bridge area between the good portions of the file across the damaged area, thus enabling the Lotus program to load the complete file. All you lose is the actual sector or sectors that were damaged; the rest of the file is visible.

DBF File Repair

For dBASE-compatible files, nothing works as well as the dSALVAGE program from Comtech Publishing Ltd. This program can diagnose and recover damaged dBASE, FoxBASE, Clipper, and dBXL files that conform to the DBF file standards. The program also features a built-in editor for file header and data portions of dBASE files. Another feature is that the newest version of the program, dSALVAGE Professional, includes a free copy of the latest version of the DiskMinder editor from Westlake Data.

For More Information

The names, addresses, and phone numbers of the data recovery utilities discussed in this chapter follow:

Disk Manager and DOSUTILS
OnTrack Computer Systems Inc.
6321 Bury Drive
Eden Prairie, MN 55346
(612) 937-1107
(800) 752-1333

DiskMinder
Westlake Data Corp.
P.O. Box 1711
Austin, TX 78767
(512) 328-1041

dSALVAGE (includes DiskMinder from Westlake Data)
Comtech Publishing Ltd.
P.O. Box 456
Pittsford, NY 14534

Mace Utilities 1990
Fifth Generation Systems Inc.
11200 Industriplex Blvd.
Baton Rouge, LA 70809
(504) 291-7221
(800) 873-4384

Norton Utilities
Peter Norton Computing Inc.
100 Wilshire Blvd., Ste. 900
Santa Monica, CA 90401
(213) 319-2000 (tech support)

OPTune
GAZELLE
42 N. University Ave.
Provo, UT 48601
(800) 233-0383

PC Tools Deluxe 7.0
Central Point Software Inc.
15220 N.W. Greenbrier Parkway, Ste. 200
Beaverton, OR 97006
(503) 690-8090

SpinRite II
Gibson Research Inc.
Laguna Hills, CA
(714) 830-2200

Vopt
Golden Bow Systems Inc.
842 E. Washington St., Ste. B
San Diego, CA 92103
(800) 284-3269 (sales)
(619) 298-9349 (tech support)

For other programs, you should contact the manufacturers of the particular applications in question to learn whether they have their own data recovery utilities or whether they know of any utilities commercially available that support their products. You should follow the guidelines of the technical support staff of the applications program manufacturer.

Chapter Summary

Even when adequate precautions are taken, hard disk disasters do occur. This chapter showed you how to use commercial disaster recovery programs to maintain duplicate copies of the partition table, FAT, and root directory to assist in file and format recovery; undelete files; repair specific binary files such as spreadsheets and databases; recover from an accidental disk format; and revive a nonbootable or dead disk. Of course, even the best error recovery programs are not foolproof. The simplest and best safeguard is to maintain frequent disk backups.

10

Data Recovery Techniques

In this chapter, you examine various problems and errors that can occur on a hard disk and techniques for recovering hard disk data that has been lost or damaged. You learn the difference between a physically damaged sector, an unreadable sector, and a corrupted sector, and from which you can recover data. Also covered in this chapter are DOS bugs, various error messages, how to recover data by using general utility programs, and special utility recovery programs for various applications programs.

Defining Data Recovery Problems

When a problem requiring data recovery occurs, several levels of disk or data damage may exist. In the most elemental sense, however, only the following primary levels require data recovery techniques:

- Unreadable sectors
- Corrupted sectors

Unreadable sectors are caused by *physical* damage, which is irreversible, or by *magnetic* damage, which is reversible through a fresh low-level format. Although you can reverse the damage caused by magnetic damage and avoid using physically damaged sectors, you still have lost data in these sectors.

Corrupted sectors are sectors with corrupted data that you can attempt to restore to original condition by using one of the utility programs or techniques described in this chapter.

Examining Physically Damaged Sectors

Physically damaged sectors are unreadable sectors that cannot be salvaged through a low-level format. This damage, the most severe level possible, generally means that something has happened to the surface of the disk that prevents the disk from reading or writing information. The damage can be a nick or scratch on the disk from one of the heads or even a bad head or head actuator (positioner). These sectors cannot be made readable again, so they must be identified as defective sectors during a new low-level format and never used again.

After you discover damaged disk sectors, you should read or back up the remaining readable sectors to another disk, either as files or as track and sector images, and then redo the low-level format. When you redo the format, be sure to mark off the physically damaged areas as defective. This low-level format enables the disk to remain in service with the bad sectors mapped out. Essentially, this is a variation on the unreadable sectors and still may result in files with missing or corrupted sectors after the reformat. In these cases, proceed to handle the corrupted sectors in the appropriate manner.

Two ways are available to determine bad sectors on a hard drive and take them out of service:

- Use the manufacturer's defect list, which is provided with new hard drives, to enter defects during a low-level reformat just before a low-level format. No disk drive is perfect, and all manufacturers provide this list.

- Use a third-party program, such as Disk Technician, which automatically seeks out and finds that sector's end and maps out the bad sectors for you. This kind of format is especially useful after the hard drive is in service and is full of information and you don't want to back up and restore a time-consuming job.

Examining Unreadable Sectors

An *unreadable sector* represents the second level of disk damage. This kind of damage means that the disk drive and controller cannot get a good read of the sector even when invoking the Error Correction Code capabilities found in the controller. This type of problem is caused by magnetic image damage in the sector header or address area, or possibly even the data or Cyclic Redundancy Check (CRC) bytes.

This type of damage can cause several consequences. One is that if you do not reformat the track containing the offending sector(s), the problem rarely goes away. A possible exception to this consequence are tracks and sectors rendered unreadable because of dimensional changes in the disk from thermal expansion and contraction. In such a case, the disk dimensions and tolerances may change, enabling the sector(s) to become readable without reformatting. Even if the disk becomes readable, however, you should still reformat the drive to refresh the sector headers, trailers, and data areas so that they are in line with the current physical head positions.

When you have the drive restored so that you can read the information, immediately perform a backup. Then you can run a program such as Disk Technician or SpinRite II, both of which do a low-level nondestructive reformat of the entire drive. Remember to get that information off the hard drive and onto a backup medium. Running these programs should bring the disk back to a normal condition. If not, you probably need to do a low-level format by using the built-in BIOS. This procedure destroys all information on the drive.

Unreadable sectors often are caused by magnetic damage in the sector header area. This area is important because it contains the address information that enables the drive and controller to know at which positions they are reading and writing information. The only way to restore the header and trailer information is by reformatting the track containing the offending sectors.

If only a few sectors on the track are unreadable, save the readable sectors to another disk, reformat the track containing the unreadable sectors, and then restore the saved information from the readable sectors. Saving does not totally complete the recovery job, however. The unreadable sectors are now readable but have no real information in them other than the pattern of bytes used by the particular low-level format program involved. You now can restore these sectors as if they had been corrupted originally.

> ***Warning:*** If you're using a program such as Hexcalibur to save and restore data, be careful. Hexcalibur and programs like it are intended as general-purpose hex editors. Hexcalibur was not written to be used for fixing damaged disk directories or for performing other low-level repair operations. The program doesn't provide instructions to assist users in such activities, which should be performed by experts only. Serious, irreparable damage to the disk directory can result if such repair is attempted by untrained people. Such damage can mean the irrecoverable loss of data.

Examining Corrupted Sectors

A *corrupted sector* is the simplest level of disk or data damage. A corrupted sector occurs when the 512 data bytes have been altered in some fashion from their original or desired state. In a single sector, the alteration can be anything from a single bit change to an overwrite of the entire 512 bytes. Unreadable sectors that were made readable also are considered corrupted sectors. You need to restore the data that had been there originally.

The corrupted sector is by far the most common data recovery problem. The consequences of this type of data alteration are from severe to mild. If data bytes are randomly altered in the areas that the BIOS and DOS use to manage the disk, for example, the results can range from a total system lockup to an inaccessible disk. In a second example, if the master partition boot sector is overwritten with 00h bytes, then on the next system boot, DOS volumes C through Z may cease to exist. If the damage is to other important areas such as the DOS volume boot sector or the file allocation tables (FATs), DOS may lose track of one or possibly all the files on the disk. If this type of damage occurs within a program file, the system may attempt to execute the random bytes as if they were a program, perhaps locking up the system.

If sectors are corrupted in a data file, some programs (1-2-3, for example) refuse to load the file past the damaged sector. Other programs enable you to load the entire file, but the damaged area may appear garbled. Finally, if this type of damage occurs in a sector not directly used by DOS to manage the disk data area, and not currently in use by any file, then no consequences from the damage may occur and no repairs may be necessary.

The solution to corrupted sectors is to replace the altered data with a copy of the original data. Of course, doing so is easier said than done. If the damage is in a DOS management area such as a partition boot sector, volume boot sector, FAT, or directory, techniques are available to reconstruct these areas. Reconstruction is possible because the format and construction of these areas on the disk are documented and interrelated. Often, you can reconstruct one of these areas by reading information from other, nondamaged areas of the disk and reverse-engineering.

If the corruption occurs in an area for which no backup or documented existing structure such as a program or data file is available, the job of restoration is much more difficult. If two sectors in the middle of a client database file are overwritten with garbage, for example, then 1,024 bytes of client information are lost. If each database record has 256 bytes, then clearly information from at least four records has been lost. Although recovery of the lost records is impossible, the corrupted sectors can be altered to make the database program think that they were records. This technique, the best possible fix for this type of situation, enables the program to look past these sectors and read the remainder of the file in proper fashion.

Programs designed to reconstruct database records automatically or semi-automatically put together files that eliminate the bad cluster so that the program thinks the record is complete when it is pulled up under the program.

If the damage occurs in the middle of an executable program file, you cannot reconstruct the missing or altered bytes. Your only recourse is to delete the program file and reload it from an original copy.

As you can see, depending on the location and severity of sector corruption, restoration of missing or altered information can range from easy to impossible. Restoration of areas with a known structure is straightforward, and much of this chapter deals with this type of data recovery.

Discovering Unreadable or Damaged Sectors

You usually discover unreadable sectors by reading or writing to the disk and getting in response the error message `Abort, Retry, Ignore, Fail?` This DOS message indicates that the sector in question has become unreadable or unwritable. As you can see in the following DOS-generated error messages, the message itself often provides a clue to the nature of the problem:

- `Data error`. Indicates an error or magnetic defect in the sector data field. The CRC following this field does not verify the data as being correct. Most data in the sector is probably still readable, but the contents cannot be trusted. Make a note of which file contains this sector and use a disk editor to read each sector of the file individually. When the defective sector is located, copy the entire cluster containing the bad sector to a free cluster and reroute the FAT chain appropriately.

- `Seek error`. Indicates severe damage to the disk format or failing disk hardware. Attempt a complete backup of the disk. Perform a fresh low-level format and surface analysis. (The surface analysis can be done by programs such as SpinRite and Desk Technician, which check the disk and look for surface defects that result in cluster failures.) Run FDISK, then run FORMAT, and restore the saved data.

- `Invalid media type`. Indicates that the DOS volume boot sector is invalid for this volume. Use an editor in INT 13h mode, locate the DOS volume boot sector, and make necessary corrections. As an easier alternative, use one of the automatic repair utilities such as Norton Disk Doctor, Mace Emergency Room, or PC Tools Diskfix.

- `Sector not found`. Indicates damage in the sector header containing the addressing information. Data from this sector most likely cannot be read. Note the file involved and recover by following the same procedures indicated for `Data error`. The resultant file will be missing data from this sector.

- `General failure`. Usually indicates damage to a portion of the sector header; however, the address area appears to be readable. Most if not all of the data from this sector can be recovered. Note the file involved and follow the procedures indicated for `Data error`.

In each of these examples, you need to determine whether the sectors are physically damaged or magnetically damaged. Unfortunately, the only way to do so is to low-level format the disk and perform a surface analysis. For this kind of job, you may want a real low-level format utility such as the one built into your hard disk controller ROM BIOS. Additional low-level format utilities you may want to use include the Htest/Hformat package from Kolod Research, the IBM Advanced Diagnostics, the PS/2 Systems, and the Advanced Diagnostics found on the Reference disk. These low-level format programs run at the controller register level and completely reformat all tracks of a disk. Light-duty programs such as SpinRite and Disk Technician run at the INT 13h level.

Some ST-506/412 controllers (particularly RLL versions) write special hidden or reserved sectors usually on the first track of the disk. These sectors can only be refreshed by the appropriate ROM BIOS-based format program, which destroys all data in the process. In these cases, you need to perform a complete disk backup, reformat, run FDISK, run FORMAT, and restore all the data. If you can use Htest/Hformat, you can run a nondestructive format that enables you to eliminate the FDISK, FORMAT, and restore portions of the job. You still should perform a backup before any low-level format, whether or not it claims to be nondestructive. Note that the IBM low-level format programs are always destructive, and for the PS/2 systems, perform automatic defect mapping and a surface analysis. The other formatters usually have a surface analysis as a separate operation. In these cases, you should perform a surface analysis.

When you run the low-level format, be sure to mark the tracks the manufacturer has identified as being bad. Then use the surface analysis to test the remaining good tracks. You should perform the low-level format immediately before the surface analysis so that the sector headers and data areas are refreshed to current head positions. This step prevents the surface analysis from incorrectly identifying sectors with mistracking errors caused by thermal compensation problems or other forms of magnetic damage as real hard flaws in the disk media. Good surface analysis programs like those from IBM or Kolod Research interface directly to the controller at the register level and bypass DOS and the BIOS. This direct interface enables these programs to detect when controller retries or ECC retries are occurring and correctly mark these tracks as bad. Programs that worked through the BIOS or DOS cannot receive this information, and these subtle errors being corrected by the controller are masked. This masking may enable marginal areas to be put into service.

Do not enable any low-level format or surface analysis program to restore to good status any tracks identified as being bad. Doing this procedure is asking for problems.

Fixing Unreadable or Damaged Sectors

Disk sectors become unreadable because of some physical or magnetic defect. When sectors are physically damaged, they become unreadable because of a physical, or *hard*, defect rather than a magnetic, or *soft*, defect with the drive at that location. With hard defect damage, a reformat operation cannot restore the sectors to working condition. In some cases, if the physical damage is not severe, a reformat may restore the sectors to usability, but this procedure is not recommended. Instead, these sectors should be identified and marked as bad at the sector level and in the FAT.

You can restore sectors that are soft damaged, or magnetically flawed, to operability by reformatting the tracks on which they reside. To preserve data, make backups of any areas to be reformatted so the data can be restored afterward.

Recovering a File with Physical Defects

If you have a file with unreadable sectors, several programs are available that virtually automate the data recovery process. You can do your own recovery by using disk editors such as the NU or DiskEdit programs from Norton Utilities, but an easier way may exist.

Each of the three utility packages discussed in Chapter 9 comes with a program designed to automate data recovery. These programs are the all-in-one autopilot programs from Norton Utilities, Mace Utilities, and PC Tools. In the Norton line, you may want to use Disk Doctor II in Norton Utilities 5.0 or later releases. The Mace Utilities Emergency Room program came out after the Norton Utilities program and reflects many improvements over the original Disk Doctor. The same can be said for the PC Tools Diskfix program. Each of these packages performs a general health check of your disk, examining the partition boot sectors, volume boot sectors, FATs, root directory, and subdirectories, and scans every sector and cluster for readability.

When a bad sector is found, the file straddling the cluster with the bad sector is identified and repaired. The repair technique involves locating the cluster with the bad sector, copying its contents into a good cluster, pointing the FAT chain for the file to follow the change, and marking the bad cluster in the FAT.

Although this step enables the file to become readable again, it does not mark the sectors as bad at the low level. You can mark sectors in two ways: by using a low-level format program and typing in the location of the entire track containing the defective sector or the individual sector itself, or by a surface analysis.

With the utilities that work at the DOS level, the bad sector marks are just bad cluster marks in the FAT. This procedure works well as a temporary fix, but the real fix is to redo the low-level format and mark the sectors at both levels: the sector header itself as well as the FAT. This step can be done easily after the DOS-level utility has made the file completely readable so that what is left of it can be backed up, copied, or loaded.

Rebuilding DOS Disk Management Areas

Rebuilding the areas DOS uses to manage a disk and keep track of programs and data is the primary function of data recovery. Reconstructing these areas is an essential skill made possible because these areas have a consistent and documented structure, and several tools exist that greatly aid reconstruction.

The areas in question for a given disk follow:

- Master partition boot sector
- Extended partition boot sectors
- DOS volume boot sectors
- FATs
- Root directory
- Subdirectories

This section discusses how to rebuild each of these areas by using a variety of tools and techniques.

Fixing Master and Extended Boot Sectors

The master and extended partition boot sectors are essential structures on a hard disk. If these sectors are altered or become unreadable, entire volumes of the drive become inaccessible. Damage to these sectors may be indicated by an inability to access a given DOS volume. Note that these structures are not present on floppy disks.

The master and extended partition boot sectors are originally created on your hard disk by the DOS FDISK utility. That is the utility you should have used to create them. DOS FDISK is preferred because other utilities such as

Disk Manager or SpeedStor create nonstandard partition boot sectors and use undocumented structures and information. Damaged undocumented structures are extremely difficult to restore.

Using DOS FDISK

Although you can use the DOS FDISK utility to rebuild a damaged partition boot sector, you may experience some problems. The most significant problem occurs after writing the master or extended partition boot sectors: FDISK fills the DOS volume boot sector for the given volume with F6h bytes (thus totally destroying it) and then writes random garbage to the next 8 to 16 tracks following the DOS volume boot sector on the disk. These tracks are precisely where the FATs and root directory reside. In fact, FDISK trashes the DOS volume boot sector, both FAT copies, the root directory, and some of the first few files on the disk.

This trade is hardly an even trade. FDISK gives you the master partition boot sector if you give it up to 16 tracks on the disk. A trading analogy may go something like "I'll give you one dollar if you give me a $20 bill."

These tracks are overwritten to enable FDISK to test the tracks so that the program knows that the disk is usable with DOS. DOS cannot manage defective sectors in the area occupied by the volume boot sector, FATs, or root directory.

You can use FDISK for this repair. Simply copy to another disk the 16 tracks starting with the DOS volume boot sector of the affected volume and then restore these sectors after FDISK is done. You then have a perfect repair. Just to be safe, you may want to copy more than 16 tracks—perhaps 25 to 30.

This backup or copy of sectors to files can be done with several utilities, such as NU or DiskEdit from Norton Utilities, DiskMinder from Westlake Data, or SECCOPY from Htest/Hformat. Each of these utilities functions in the INT 13h mode necessary to read and write sectors through the BIOS and circumventing DOS.

The XFDISK or KFDISK programs from Mace Utilities do everything that the standard DOS FDISK does except write to any other sectors other than the partition boot sectors. The programs write the partition boot sectors and leave everything else alone. These programs make rebuilding sectors an easy job.

Editing the Sector Directly

Another way to rebuild a partition boot sector is to access the desired sector directly with an editor such as NU or DiskEdit from Norton Utilities or DiskMinder from Westlake Data. These editors enable you to bypass DOS and see and edit sectors as they function in INT 13h mode. To restore anything, however, you need to know the exact structure of a correct example of the sector.

Note that this sector consists of a program portion, the partition tables themselves, and signature bytes at the end. The program portion is generic and transportable from system to system, which means that you can borrow a copy of this sector from another disk and then redo the partition table portion. Appendix C provides an example of the master partition boot sector program written by the FDISK program included with IBM DOS 3.3 or 4.0. These bytes can be copied into a sector where the program has been damaged.

> ***Warning:*** Because the programs from different FDISK versions vary slightly, do not attempt to mix different versions and be sure to copy all of the new program.

After copying or entering the program portion of the sector, you should be able to reconstruct the data fields. By using the Norton editors, for example, you can invoke the partition table lens, which formats the 16 raw hexadecimal bytes for each partition table entry into understandable decimal and English form. Then you can enter the partition starting and ending locations, system indicator byte, boot ID byte, and relative and total sector fields.

Restoring from a Backup

One final reconstruction technique is the simplest: restore the defective partition boot sector from a previously made backup. Several programs perform this type of backup and restore operation. Of course, this procedure may include doing the backup and restore directly with the INT 13h disk editors such as the NU or DiskEdit program or the DiskMinder package.

Other programs may automate the procedure, such as the Format Recover or IMAGE program from Norton, the XFDISK or KFDISK program from Kolod Research, and the RXBACK or PC Tools MIRROR program from Mace. These utilities can take copies of the partition boot sectors and other important areas and store them either on another disk or in a hidden file on the hard disk itself. The program then can find this file when the need for restoration arises.

These utility programs usually are installed as part of the AUTOEXEC.BAT file and are executed each time the computer is booted. If a problem occurs during the course of the day, you can use these hidden snapshots to restore the hard disk to the condition it was when the snapshot was taken.

As long as the system is left on and is not rebooted, you can use these special files to restore the information. If the system is turned off and restarted, the AUTOEXEC.BAT file again takes a snapshot. This time the snapshot is taken of the corrupt situation, rendering these special files useless.

The two solutions to this problem follow:

- Leave the system on and start the recovery process immediately.
- Insert a DOS system disk into drive A before turning on the computer so that the computer boots from this floppy disk. This action prevents the AUTOEXEC.BAT file from running, leaving this special file alone. After booting from the floppy, use the utility program (also from the floppy) to recover the information in the special hidden file to restore the hard drive.

Fixing the Volume Boot Sector

The DOS volume boot sector is important to DOS's understanding of the layout of a disk. This sector keeps information about where the FATs and root directory are, as well as other important items. If this information ever becomes corrupted or unreadable, DOS isn't capable of making sense out of the disk. If DOS trusts the wrong information in a damaged sector, it becomes unbootable and misinformed as to the locations of the FATs and root directory.

After booting from a floppy, you may see garbage characters after running the DIR command on the damaged disk. This condition normally indicates that the volume boot sector has been damaged. In this case, a little damage actually can do more harm than a great deal of damage: If the sector is not completely damaged, DOS may believe information that is incorrect. If the sector is totally overwritten, DOS normally does not believe that the sector has been created yet and offers tools to recreate it. In fact, DOS goes by only two of the fields in the sector, the OEM name and DOS version field and signature byte field. If these two fields contain correct information, DOS trusts the rest of the DOS volume boot sector and misinterprets the disk.

If you think the DOS volume boot sector is defective, causing DOS to misread the locations of the FATs and root directory, make a copy of the one present now. Then go in with an editor and destroy it further. In other words, use a disk editor to zero out at least the portions of the sector designated as the 8-byte OEM name and version field as well as the 2-byte signature byte field. You can zero out more of the sector than just these two fields. In fact, you can write 00h to the entire sector. Then reboot the system, enabling DOS to reread the DOS volume boot sector.

Note: After making changes to either partition boot sectors or DOS volume boot sectors, you must reboot the system for the changes to be recognized by DOS.

On rebooting, DOS no longer knows how large the FATs should be or the location of the root directory. In this case, DOS performs on-the-fly calculations for these areas based on the size of the partition. The locations calculated for the FATs and root directory are the same as DOS had made when originally formatting the disk, provided that DOS was used when you formatted the disk. If you used Disk Manager to format the volume, little chance exists that DOS may calculate the same values for the FAT and root directory locations. By using DOS to run FDISK and FORMAT on a given volume, you give yourself a measure of safety when the time comes to use DOS to reconstruct these areas.

After DOS calculates a copy of the DOS volume boot sector, you should be able to log on to the volume and perform a DIR command to verify whether the root directory is still intact. You may be surprised to find all the data still readable and intact. Of course, at this time, a good idea is to back up all files and then reformat the disk and restore the files.

Consider that the DOS FORMAT command originally placed this sector on the disk after FDISK had originally overwritten it with F6h characters. Because the DOS FORMAT command wrote this sector in the first place, it certainly can rewrite it. But here again it seems an unfair trade, because the DOS FORMAT command initializes or blanks both FATs and the root directory in the process. On a typical 30M disk, this procedure takes 122 sectors for both FATs and 32 sectors for the root directory.

If you saved these areas before the FORMAT operation, you can restore them immediately after. This restoration can be done easily with the NU or DiskEdit editors but not so easily with any of the other products.

The DOS SYS command also is ideal for correcting the DOS volume boot sector. This command writes or updates the DOS volume boot sector as well as writes out the system files. If the disk did not originally contain system files, however, SYS may not work because the first two directory entries and cluster 2 on the disk must be available. Unless you are using DOS Version 4.0 or later, in which case SYS locates the files occupying these areas and moves them, write the DOS volume boot sector and system file copies on the disk.

Note that unless the OEM name and signature byte fields are cleared (overwritten with something like F6h or 00h), SYS trusts the current copy of the DOS volume boot sector and does not actually correct any data values stored within it. SYS still, however, updates the sector to contain any features that were added by newer DOS versions. For example, SYS may add the volume boot sector fields unique to DOS 4.0 and later, if they were not already present, but may not correct any data in the fields that were already there.

To use either the DOS FORMAT or SYS command to repair a damaged DOS volume boot sector, you first must convince DOS that no DOS volume boot sector is present. To convince DOS, overwrite the OEM name and signature byte fields in the sector with some byte value such as 00h or F6h. Then reboot, make backups of either all the files on the disk or just the critical areas such as the FATs and root directory, and then use either the FORMAT or SYS command to restore the DOS volume boot sector. Finally, restore the backed up sectors or files, and the job is complete.

Other utilities such as the Norton Disk Doctor, Mace Emergency Room, or PC Tools Diskfix also can reconstruct a damaged DOS volume boot sector. These programs know enough about how a good one should look in order to reconstruct one when required.

Recovering from a Death Disk

In most systems you have encountered, a catastrophic and disturbing bug is present that you may not have known how to deal with. A good name for this problem is the *death disk*, and few people have ever recovered successfully from this problem without replacing the hard disk damaged in this way.

The death disk bug displays the following symptom: When you attempt to reboot your system from the hard disk, the system locks during the early portion of the boot and no error messages appear—just a flashing cursor. This symptom can be caused by a variety of corruption problems in the master partition boot sector, the DOS volume boot sector, the system files, or COMMAND.COM.

If your system locks up during a reboot attempt, try to reboot from a bug-free, write-protected floppy disk. The floppy should be write-protected because some virus programs, frequently found in floppies, create the same symptom you're trying to fix. The only way to guarantee that the floppy remains bug free is to write-protect it. Think of it as insurance.

As you reboot the system from your floppy disk, the following actions occur:

- The power-on self test (POST) runs and drive A is tested. Drive A's access light comes on, and you hear the drive heads move.
- Drive B (if installed) is tested. The access light comes on, and you hear the drive heads move.
- The diagnostic cylinder or area from drive C is tested. You see a brief flicker of the hard disk access light while this area is read. You then hear a single beep, which indicates successful completion of the POST (two beeps for COMPAQ systems).

Now the boot process is started and drive A is accessed again, but this time with the intention of booting. Because you have a bootable disk in drive A, all seems to be going well and DOS appears to be loading from the disk. A few seconds into the disk boot, IBMBIO.COM is read into memory and takes control of the system. From your previous look at the boot process in earlier chapters, you know that IBMBIO.COM now scans installed devices and attempts to establish the system configuration.

IBMBIO scans the hard disk while you are booting from the floppy. One or two seconds after the hard disk is polled by IBMBIO, the whole process comes to a sudden halt. A flashing cursor appears on-screen, but no disk activity, and the system has entered an infinite loop. You can verify that the system is looping somewhere and not totally locked up by pressing the Caps Lock, Num Lock, or Scroll Lock key. The keys still toggle their respective lights on the keyboard (AT types of systems only). In fact, a Ctrl-Alt-Del still resets the system, only to have the same process repeat, including the infinite loop lockup.

As long as that hard disk remains connected to the system in its current state, you may never boot from the hard disk and you may not even be able to boot from a floppy.

What specifically is this death disk problem, and exactly how do you fix it? The bug in most versions of IBMBIO.COM (or IO.SYS as the case may be) is linked to the byte field at offset 13 (or 0Dh) in the DOS volume boot sector. This field stores a value indicating the number of sectors per cluster for the volume. The death disk bug is activated if this value is set to a 00h. No other value can invoke the bug, and the bug is present only if IBMBIO decides to trust the DOS volume boot sector, which may be the case if the OEM name and signature byte fields are left intact. Hard disk partitions between 16M and 128M capacity normally may have a 04h for this field, indicating 4 sectors per cluster or 2,048 byte clusters.

To repair the problem, use your INT 13h editor to get to the DOS volume boot sector and change the byte at offset 13 to the appropriate value based on the partition size. See Appendix C for the complete map to the DOS volume boot sector, as well as a chart showing the correct cluster size for any sized partition.

If you are thinking about unplugging the hard disk and then booting from a floppy, you are on the right track. Assume that you remove the hard disk from the system, the system is running and has booted off your floppy, and you now are looking at an `A:\>` prompt. What next? If you plug in the drive with the power on, you still cannot gain access because the controller cannot find a drive connected to it. When no hard drive is visible during the POST operation, most systems' BIOS do not install the INT 13h interface to the hard disk. This situation means that you are effectively locked out of the drive even if you do plug it back in.

You have a way to get the job done, but it varies depending on the kind of hard disk interface and system you are using.

In most IBM AT-compatible systems, if you indicate the drive type in CMOS Setup, even if the disk is disconnected during POST, the BIOS still installs an INT 13h interface to the drive. After reconnecting all the cables, you then can access the disk by using any of the editors that function in INT 13h mode such as Norton's NU or DiskEdit. No other mode can work, as DOS was incapable of reading the partition tables or volume boot sector because you had the disk disconnected.

When plugging in cables from a drive to a running system, exercise extreme caution or you can destroy the circuitry on the drive and controller. For ST-506/412 or ESDI drives, you may want to plug in the control (34-pin) cable first, the data (20-pin) cable second, and the power cable last. For IDE or SCSI drives, you want to plug in the single drive interface cable first and the power cable last. The rule of thumb is that all other cables must be connected before plugging in the power. Also, be sure to plug the cables in with the correct orientation.

Cables usually have polarizing pins that prevent you from plugging the cables in backward. Marking the cable connector with a felt-tip pen, however, helps to ensure correct installation. The power plug is polarizing and is extremely difficult if not impossible to plug in incorrectly.

Unplugging the drive completely to enable the system to boot presents problems. Many power supplies do not function properly without a 12-volt load, which you remove when you unplug the drive. COMPAQ systems, among others, cannot install the INT 13h BIOS interface to the drive if any of the cables are disconnected during the POST, no matter what CMOS says. Most systems also show a 1780 POST error code, which indicates that the controller cannot cause the drive to seek. A better technique is to keep the drive completely connected during the POST, but immediately after the POST finishes, unplug one of the cables to render the drive unreadable during the floppy boot operation. This operation is slightly trickier because timing is important. If you are too slow in disabling the drive after the POST, then IBMBIO, which is loading from drive A, has a chance to read drive C and cause the system to lock. To resolve this problem, you may want to pursue one of the following recommendations:

- For ST-506/412 or ESDI drives, unplug the data (20-pin) cable from the controller immediately after the beep, which shows that the POST has been completed successfully. This step renders the drive unreadable in a safe manner, while enabling power connections to remain intact.

- For IDE or SCSI drives, you have to pull the power connector. Loosen it first with the system off; then immediately after the POST quickly and cleanly unplug it from the drive. The drive then spins down and becomes unreadable. In this case, leave the single interface cable connected. After the system has completed booting from the floppy, reconnect the power cable to the drive and the drive spins back up.

- For PS/2 systems with IDE drives (whether they are ST-506/412 MFM, RLL, or ESDI internally) you are in a tougher situation. These drives carry all the control, data, and power signals in a single connection usually between a drive and interposer board or cable. If you plug this drive into a system with the system powered up, you destroy the drive circuitry and possibly the motherboard. Therefore, unplugging the drive is not a solution to this problem with such a system. Note that PS/2 systems with SCSI or standard ST-506/412 or ESDI drives still can use the preceding techniques to regain access to the system and drive.

Users of PS/2 Models 25, 30, 25-286, 30-286, 50, 50Z, and 70 would be in a tough situation. Fortunately, for owners of PS/2 Models 25, 30, 286, 386, 50, 50z, and 70, another alternative exists to solve this problem instead of disconnecting the drive.

You may recall that on non-PS/2 systems, you normally cannot boot DOS from either the hard disk or floppy while the disk is connected. You can boot the IBM Advanced Diagnostics, however. These diagnostics do not run under a normal DOS but have their own custom diagnostics DOS on the disk. The death disk problem therefore has to be a DOS bug rather than a ROM BIOS bug. That situation is good because you can replace DOS easier than the ROM BIOS. Although you can boot a system afflicted with the death disk problem by using IBM Advanced Diagnostics, without disconnecting the hard disk, the only thing you can do with the diagnostics is to low-level format the drive.

This step removes the death disk problem but also may remove all data. Note also that you cannot drop to a regular DOS prompt when running the Advanced Diagnostics, nor can you use the diagnostics to format only a single track. The Advanced Diagnostics low-level format program formats the entire disk and starts from the back of the disk (highest cylinder) and works forward. The death disk problem is normally in the first sector on the second track (the DOS volume boot sector).

By now you know that the bug is in IBMBIO.COM. The next task is to find other DOS versions with the bug. After you run every version of IBM and Microsoft DOS released to date, and several other OEM versions as well, you discover the following results: All versions of DOS other than IBM DOS 4.0 with CSD UR25066 or later have the bug. All OEM versions of 3.3 have it, and so far, all OEM versions of 4.x have it except IBM DOS. As of this writing, IBM has released no fewer than six versions of DOS 4.0, and only the past three do not have the bug. IBM DOS 4.0 versions are summarized in table 10.1.

Note that only the last three versions do not have the death disk bug and may boot to the floppy even if the death disk problem is present. Because the disk has remained connected, the INT 13h interface is installed, and you can access the disk with a disk editor to make repairs. You may not be able to access the disk directly through DOS because you immediately receive an `Invalid media type` error message with `Abort, Retry, Ignore?` An INT 13h editor becomes your only means of access to the disk at this point.

The latest versions of PS/2 Reference disks are based on DOS 4.0 CSD UR25066 or later, thus avoiding the bug if you boot from these disks. But like the Advanced Diagnostics, you cannot drop to a regular DOS prompt from the Reference disk menus.

> ***Note:*** No other OEM version of DOS has corrected this bug, including the 4.01a release from Microsoft. IBM releases more fixes to their versions of DOS than most other OEMs.

The death disk problem has not been tested with DOS 5.x.

Table 10.1
IBM DOS 4.x Versions

File Name	*Size*	*Date*	*Version*	*SYSLEVEL*	*Comments*
IBMBIO.COM	32810	06/17/88	4.00		Original release
IBMDOS.COM	35984	06/17/88			
COMMAND.COM	37637	06/17/88			
IBMBIO.COM	32816	08/03/88	4.01	CSD UR22624	EMS fixes
IBMDOS.COM	36000	08/03/88			
COMMAND.COM	37637	06/17/88			
IBMBIO.COM	32816	08/03/88	4.01	CSD UR24270	Date change fixed
IBMDOS.COM	36000	11/11/88			
COMMAND.COM	37652	11/11/88			
IBMBIO.COM	33910	04/06/89	4.01	CSD UR25066	"Death disk" fixed
IBMDOS.COM	37136	04/06/89			
COMMAND.COM	37652	11/11/88			
IBMBIO.COM	34660	03/20/90	4.01	CSD UR29015	SCSI support
IBMDOS.COM	37248	02/20/90			
COMMAND.COM	377650	03/20/90			
IBMBIO.COM	34660	04/27/90	4.01	CSD UR31300	HPFS fixes
IBMDOS.COM	37264	05/21/90			
COMMAND.COM	377650	6/29/90			

Summary of Bug Problem

Because most users do not have the IBM DOS 4.0 CSD version, they may think that their systems are severely damaged and that they may be locked out completely. Most technicians who troubleshoot this problem replace the hard disk and toss the old one because the computer cannot boot as long as the drive is connected. These technicians mistakenly believe that the drive has suffered some sort of physical or electrical damage. This is not a physical or electrical problem, but it is a software bug that you can correct by using a 13h text editor.

Unerasing Data Files

On most disks, DOS keeps a pointer to the disk indicating the next cluster to use for any file operations. This condition means that even if a file is deleted and more files are written to the disk, the original deleted file still may be recoverable. DOS always uses the first available directory entry, which may have contained the name of the desired deleted file, but the file data itself remains on the disk in what now are available clusters.

When a file is deleted, the first character of the file name in the directory is replaced with a Greek lowercase sigma (σ) character. This sign is DOS's clue that the file is erased. Also, the FAT chain in use by the file is zeroed, making the clusters available for use.

If you need to undelete a file, and data has been written to the disk after the file has been deleted, you first should try the conventional method of using one of the undelete utilities such as Quick Unerase from Norton Utilities. If the utility can find the former directory entry for the file, replace the sigma character with a valid character and then enable the utility to retype the FAT chain. If the directory entry points to a cluster already in use, you are too late and the file space already has been reused by another file.

If the unerase utility does not or cannot find the file you want to unerase as a deleted file, that means the directory entry for the erased file has been reused but the disk space likely has not. This situation means that you should begin searching the unused clusters on the disk for the data in the erased file. This procedure may take awhile on a large hard disk. Also, you must know what the contents of the file look like so that you recognize the data when you see it.

When (and if) you find an available cluster with data from your deleted file, begin looking in subsequent clusters for the rest of the file. Note the number of each cluster that contains the file data. Then retype the FAT chain by using the disk editor and either enable CHKDSK to create a directory entry for you (as your chain looks like lost clusters to CHKDSK) or create the entry yourself.

Handling Damaged Directories and FATs

When either the DOS directory or FAT system is damaged, access to files through programs that use DOS are compromised. Normally, this type of damage first is discovered by the DOS CHKDSK command, and most of this type of damage can be repaired by CHKDSK as well.

CHKDSK is a directory and FAT checker and reports problems in these areas in a consistent manner. CHKDSK checks each chain of clusters in the FAT to ensure that it starts with a directory entry pointing to it and ends with a proper end of chain marker. The length of the chain is compared to the size of the file in the directory, and each chain is checked to see that all clusters pointed to are unique to a single chain. Chains also are checked for invalid values such as cluster pointers beyond the range of available clusters on the disk or that point to clusters marked as bad. A summary of the basic DOS CHKDSK-reported problems follows:

- `Allocation error`. Indicates that the FAT chain length and directory size for the given file do not agree. CHKDSK can fix this problem if you use the /F parameter but always sides with the FAT chain and alters the directory size to match. This step may not actually be correct, so do not run CHKDSK /F unless you are sure the directory entry is at fault.

- `xx lost clusters in yy chains`. Indicates one or more FAT chains without directory entries pointing to them. CHKDSK can assign a directory entry to each chain when run with the /F parameter. Alternatively, CHKDSK /F zeros each of the clusters in each chain, making them available for storage if you answer *no* to the `Convert lost chains to files` message.

- `Invalid cluster`. Indicates that a chain contains a pointer to a cluster either higher or lower in value than is possible based on the disk capacity. Alternatively, the pointer can be to a cluster already marked as bad. CHKDSK /F replaces the errant pointer with an end of chain indicator, truncating the file at that point. If the chain points to a bad cluster, the bad cluster indicator is changed to an end of chain indicator, thus involving the bad cluster in a file and unmarking it in the process. You may need to use another utility such as Disk Doctor, Emergency Room, or Diskfix to remark the cluster as bad.

- `Probable nonDOS disk`. Indicates that the first byte in the first FAT table is not correct. This byte is the media identification byte, and if you place the correct value back in this position, the error is solved. Alternatively, you can live with the error message, and CHKDSK ignores the problem if you tell it to continue anyway. Note that this is one of the most benign and simple data recovery problems to solve.

The preceding problem has been encountered on several users' disks. By using a disk editor and placing the correct media ID byte in the first position of the first FAT table, users have solved this problem easily and quickly. Most users want to know how the problem occurs. Often the only way to determine how a particular problem occurs is to watch users in operation. One possible cause of the `Probable nonDOS disk` error is a user who has partitioned a drive but has not performed a high-level DOS FORMAT before using the disk. This step certainly may result in that message when you run CHKDSK and may end up causing other problems as well.

CHKDSK also can discover and fix various other problems, but one problem CHKDSK reports on but doesn't fix is cross-linked files. This problem indicates that the files listed claim ownership of the same cluster on the disk. This situation is a more serious form of damage, and CHKDSK is incapable of repairing the problem. Frequently, you may think that the better procedure is to use a disk editor and look at the FAT directly. You often can see the errant chain and correct the problem right at the source. This procedure is the best way to repair the problem.

One problem that CHKDSK cannot help with, nor even detect, is when the two FAT copies are not the same. DOS normally makes every attempt to keep the two FAT copies identical. When a problem occurs, however, you may find that one of the copies is damaged and the other is valid. Be careful about using utilities such as Disk Doctor, Emergency Room, or Diskfix in a situation such as this. These products detect the problem and decide on their own about which copy is better than the other.

In this case, use a disk editor and examine each of the FAT copies to determine the correct one. As a safeguard, copy both of them to another disk. Then use the editor to copy the sectors of the good FAT over to the bad one.

This procedure is not necessary if FAT#1 is the good one, because FAT#2 is not used by DOS and is corrected automatically during subsequent disk writes when DOS copies FAT#1 onto FAT#2. FAT#1 is the copy that DOS uses. If FAT#1 is damaged, you can use a disk editor to copy the sectors of FAT#2 onto FAT#1.

The only time that DOS ever uses FAT#2 is if FAT#1 develops unreadable sectors. If the sectors are merely corrupted, then DOS uses only FAT#1.

Recovering a Formatted Disk

Unformatting a hard disk that has been DOS high-level reformatted is possible because the DOS high-level format operation initializes only the DOS volume boot sector, FAT copies, and root directory. All data following the root directory remain intact. Note that some non-IBM or non-Microsoft OEM DOS versions actually write to the disk during the high-level format, rendering any recovery impossible.

Most of the data recovery utility packages on the market today come with unformat programs. These programs have the following three basic functions:

- A primary function of all of these programs is to take a snapshot of the DOS volume boot sector, FATs, and root directory and write it as a special hidden file on the disk. You normally may put a command invoking this function in the AUTOEXEC.BAT file on the hard disk, causing this type of backup to be performed on every boot.
- If a problem arises in which FAT and directory restoration are needed, such as recovering from an accidental DOS FORMAT, you can use the second function of the program, which is to restore the saved snapshot copy of these areas.
- Recovery becomes much tougher if you have no snapshot of these areas to work with, as may be the case when purchasing the unformat utility after the problem has arisen. In this case, you can recover most files on the disk by a straightforward operation, which is the third function of these unformat programs: to unformat a disk in which no such snapshot backup can be found. Treat subdirectories as files in the data area of the disk that have escaped alteration during a high-level format. The subdirectories are like buried treasure waiting to be uncovered and, when they are found, contain a complete list of file directory entries showing file names, starting clusters, and lengths.

In a sense, you now have a situation in which you are doing a massive unerase operation on each subdirectory that you find. This procedure is better than an actual unerase because you have the full directory entry for each file, including the first character intact. If all the files were not fragmented on the disk, recovery may be complete except for files that were in the root directory, in which case all record of them has been lost. But you do not have many (if any) important files in the root directory, except perhaps the DOS files, which can be restored from an original DOS disk.

This condition is an excellent argument for unfragmenting your disk periodically: recovery from a FAT disaster becomes a piece of cake. Running a program such as Optune or Vopt is helpful in trying to recover from a FAT disaster. You can recover a hard drive that has contiguous clusters more easily than one that is fragmented. You should note that many of the utility packages make use of the snapshot files for several other functions, such as unerasing fragmented files automatically with perfect success. You may want to use the snapshot utilities in the Norton Utilities, Mace Utilities, or PC Tools packages to avail yourself of these features.

Understanding DOS Error Messages

Whenever DOS detects an unrecoverable error during reading or writing to any of the devices on your system, DOS pauses the system and displays an error message in the following format:

```
<type> error reading <device>

Abort, Retry, Ignore, Fail?
```

or

```
<type> error writing <device>

Abort, Retry, Ignore, Fail?
```

In these messages, *<type>* is the type of error that has occurred, and *<device>* is the name of the device having the problem, such as C or PRN. Following is a list of error types that may be reported:

Extended Errors:

```
Invalid function
File not found
Path not found
Too many open files
Access denied
Invalid handle
Memory control blocks destroyed
Insufficient memory
Invalid memory block address
Invalid environment
Invalid format
Invalid function parameter
Invalid data
Invalid drive specification
Attempt to remove current directory
Not same device
```

```
No more files
Write protect error
Invalid unit
Not ready
Invalid device request
Data error
Invalid device request parameters
Seek error
Invalid media type
Sector not found
Printer out of paper error
Write fault error
Read fault error
General failure
Sharing violation
Lock violation
Invalid disk change
FCB unavailable
System resource exhausted
Code page mismatch
Out of input
Insufficient disk space
File exists
Cannot make directory entry
Fail on INT 24
Too many redirections
Duplicate redirection
Invalid password
Invalid parameter
Network data fault
Function not supported by network
Required system component not installed
```

Parse Errors:

```
Too many parameters
Required parameter missing
Invalid switch
Invalid keyword
Parameter value not in allowed range
Parameter value not allowed
Parameter format not correct
Invalid parameter
Invalid parameter combination
```

To recover from an `Abort, Retry, Ignore, Fail?` error prompt, consider your responses carefully. If possible, correct the cause of the error condition before responding to the prompt. When responding to the error prompt, you pick a selection by typing the first letter of the choice. In most cases, you should make your choices in the following order:

- Retry the operation because the error may not occur again. The system tries the read or write operation again.
- Abort the program. The system terminates the program that requested the read or write operation that failed.
- Fail the current DOS system call and continue processing the program. The application is notified that the call was returned in error.
- Ignore the error condition and continue processing the program. The application is not notified that the call was returned in error.

The Fail and Ignore responses should be used carefully. Many applications do not pick up the error-reporting by Fail. In that case, the Fail selection is converted to Abort. Some applications may not allow Ignore; in that case, the operation is converted to Fail. If Retry is denied by a program, the Retry selection is converted to Fail.

A dangerous situation exists when these types of errors occur on a floppy disk. You must not change the disk in any drives while the system is at the error prompt. Because the system is in a paused state, it is unaware that the disk has been changed and you may corrupt the disk you just inserted. You can remove and replace the same disk in a drive—just do not change any.

Solving Corruption in Data or Program Files

When sector or file corruption takes place in a program file, the recovery is simple: just restore the file from an original copy. A program with even one bit out of place is useless and may lock up the system. A data file, however, is not so rigid. If a data file has a sector that is corrupted, although you may lose some information from the file, the remainder of the file is useful. In some cases, you just have a small amount of garbage somewhere in the file. With a text file, you can delete the garbage characters or replace them with something benign, such as spaces.

Some programs expect their data files to be in a rigid format and syntax. If the file deviates from the accepted standard, some of these programs refuse to load any of the file past the point where the structure is damaged or recognize the file as one of their own and therefore resist loading any of it. This condition means that a large portion of a file can be rendered useless even by a small flaw in the structure. This section focuses on how to massage the structure of a file to make it recognizable by the program that originally created it and to enable that program to load the entire file.

Fixing a 1-2-3 File

As an example, assume that you are loading a copy of a 1-2-3 Loan Amortization spreadsheet file, which has developed an unreadable sector. Assume that the sector is physically damaged and has been since the disk was new; however, the user who installed and formatted the file originally did not mark the manufacturer defect tracks on the disk. This situation enabled the tracks to be low-level formatted as good tracks (which they were because none of them was bad enough to be detected by any low-level format or surface analysis), which must run at the digital level by using the disk controller. You load your Loan spreadsheet. After a few seconds of disk activity you hear a beep, and you see one of these messages on-screen:

- `Part of file is missing`
- `Not a valid worksheet file`
- `Disk error`

In this case, with a physical defect, the message may likely be the `Disk error` message. You then exit the 1-2-3 program and attempt to read the file from the disk with the DOS COPY command as follows:

```
COPY LOAN.WK1 NUL:
```

This command tests the file for readability by reading the contents of the file and copying it to the nul device or garbage can. This step results in the following message:

```
Data error reading drive C
Abort, Retry, Ignore, Fail?
```

This command verifies that the file contains an unreadable sector. The next thing to do is copy this file to another disk.

```
COPY LOAN.WK1 A:
```

When the `Data error` message appears again, first try the Retry option several times to see whether you can get a good read. You can retry the operation at least 10 times. To help in the case of disk-positioning errors, you may reboot the hard disk and try the preceding command again. After you see that the Retry option does not help you, use Ignore to enable the remainder of the file to be copied to the destination. One problem with this copy is that when DOS has a sector read error and you use the Ignore option, more than just one sector becomes lost. DOS may corrupt many sectors in the destination file beginning with sectors immediately following the original bad sector. Although you are making a copy of the file, this is not the actual repair.

You have two ways to proceed. The first and most difficult may involve using a disk editor to read each sector of the file to locate the unreadable one. When the unreadable sector is found, use the disk editor to determine where that sector is exactly, in cluster terms, as well as INT 13h terms, or cylinder, head, and sector numbers. After locating the cluster that contains the bad sector, use the editor to copy that cluster to another cluster that is free according to the FAT. Next, edit the FAT chain for the file to point to the new cluster copy and back to the remainder of the chain. Go back to the original cluster of the file with the bad sector and mark the cluster as bad in the FAT.

A simpler way to proceed may be to use a program such as Norton Disk Doctor II to perform the same steps as in the preceding paragraph, except the program may do it virtually automatically. No matter which method you choose, the result is the same. After exiting the utility or editor, you have a completely readable file, but at least one sector in the destination does not contain the same data as it had originally. In some cases, it may contain all 00h bytes or perhaps just some random garbage bytes.

Now when you copy the file to nul, no error message appears that verifies the file is readable. When you attempt to load the spreadsheet into 1-2-3 again, however, the following error message appears:

```
Part of file is missing
```

Also, virtually none of the file is loaded, and certainly nothing after the location of the original defective sector in the file. The problem is that the data is not in the rigid format that 1-2-3 expects. You need a utility designed just for this purpose.

Although several utilities are designed specifically for reconstructing damaged portions of 1-2-3 files, you may want to consider the Rescue Plus program from Intex Solutions. After running that program on this file and enabling it to patch the damaged sector, you may have a file that is completely loadable to 1-2-3 with no error messages. Do understand that the program cannot magically re-create your missing sector of data, but it can make that sector look like an empty portion of a correct spreadsheet file. After loading the corrected file, you should study the file for problems or errors in formulas and rekey the missing information.

Rebuilding Applications Program Data Files

Many different types of applications programs are on the market today. Not all of them are popular and used by many people. Unfortunately, not all of them have sold well enough to incite a programmer to create a recovery tool specifically for many applications. But for the most popular packages, these types of programs abound. This section contains recommendations of some of the best programs available.

Using 1-2-3 Spreadsheet Files

For 1-2-3 spreadsheet files, or even Symphony, the Rescue Plus program from Intex Solutions is the most capable recovery program for these types of files. Rescue Plus is almost uncanny in its capacity to massage a corrupted portion of a file to make it loadable to the Lotus products. Although a Lotus spreadsheet file repair program currently comes with the Norton Utilities, the Intex product has yet to be beat.

Using dBASE III and IV Data Files

A wealth of products is available for dBASE data file repairs. Because these products have been around for a while, and because the structure of a dBASE data file is well documented and fairly simple, these products have a great deal of success in dealing with file dBASE problems.

A dBASE file consists of a special 512-byte header, and the remainder of the file contains the file data, with each record taking up the same space in the file. Because the file has fixed-length records consistent throughout the file, the recovery of problems is easy. Most of the recovery programs have no problem patching the dBASE file header because the structure is well documented. Most of the programs also are capable of realigning fields or records that have become out of sync with the rest of the file. And all the programs also are capable of removing improperly placed end-of-file markers (Ctrl-Z) so that the remainder of a file may be loaded.

Of all the programs available for dBASE file recovery, you may want to try the dSALVAGE program from Comtech Publishing. The program can handle any versions of dBASE that have been available and may recover from more problems than any of the other packages. dSALVAGE was designed and should be used exclusively for dBASE file recovery. As a bonus, if you purchase the dSALVAGE Professional product, you may receive a copy of Westlake Data's DiskMinder disk editor.

Using Word Processing Files

Word processing files are among the easiest to fix because their format is much like a regular ASCII text file. The structure is loose and most editors can handle their files. Some are more difficult than others, however, such as the popular WordPerfect program. Several possibilities are available for recovering files like these.

For fixing word processing files, the Mace Utilities includes the program TEXTFIX. This program can deal specifically with the following file formats:

- ASCII
- WordStar
- DisplayWrite
- MultiMate
- Microsoft Word
- WordPerfect

The program does an excellent job with any of these types of files, and many other word processors use similar file formats, making the program adaptable to others.

Another alternative in fixing damaged word processing documents is one of the many file converters available to convert one type of word processing file to another. You can run a file through the conversion utility to fix it. Because the conversion utilities usually are much less picky about what they read, you can take a damaged WordPerfect file, for example, and convert it to a WordStar file and then convert the result back to a WordPerfect file again. You then have a file now loadable by WordPerfect.

Using Other File Formats

Because as many different file formats exist as applications programs, you normally may not find a fancy utility designed for your particular package. What you should do is call the technical support people at the company that makes the application. They usually are aware of a utility program that may perform file restoration for their product. In some cases, they may even make or offer one specifically for their own product.

In the case of file formats for which no products are available, you still should contact the technical support department to see whether it has any documentation on the application file format that it can release. If not, then a couple of books are available that contain helpful file format information for a variety of applications. The following books are available:

PC File Formats and Conversions
Author: Ralf Kussman
Abacus
5370 52nd St. SE
Grand Rapids, MI 49512

More File Formats for Popular PC Software
Author: Jeff Walden
Wiley Press
605 3rd Ave.
New York, NY 10158

These books contain a wealth of information about application file formats. The first book was published more recently and documents the Lotus and dBASE file formats from the newer versions of those products. This book also comes with a sample disk containing software.

Chapter Summary

In this chapter, you examined the different levels of data recovery possible and learned some guidelines on how to proceed to solve a particular problem. You learned that in data recovery disk sectors can become permanently unreadable because of physical damage, unreadable because of magnetic damage, or just corrupted.

You learned different techniques for recovering or restoring information necessary for DOS to manage the disk. These areas include the partition boot sectors, volume boot sectors, FATs, and directory sectors. An essential tool in performing virtually any data recovery job is an excellent disk editor.

Be sure that the editor you use can work in the INT 13h or BIOS mode of operation. This feature enables you to bypass DOS when DOS cannot make sense of the disk.

Finally, this chapter discussed the restoration of files with special formats, such as applications program data files. If your application is a popular one, such as 1-2-3 or dBASE, then you have excellent recovery software available for the purchase. If your package is less popular, you need to contact the company selling the product to see what it recommends for recovery software or whether any extra documentation on file formats is available.

True data recovery may be possible only if you have a real understanding of the disk hardware and the way that DOS works with it. After that, getting a feel for navigating around the disk areas is important. Understanding the structure of the various data areas of the disk is necessary. At the end of this book are appendixes with the most useful information available about disks and data recovery.

11

Virus Programs

A recent scare in the PC world is due to a new type of malicious software called a *virus*. Viruses often are attached to other programs; viruses spread themselves from system to system and then wait for a time to spring to life and cause problems. A great deal of hype in the press follows viruses, but these types of programs are rare. Many people conveniently blame viruses for mysterious computer problems.

This chapter examines viruses by defining them and then giving guidelines on how to protect yourself from infection.

Defining Virus Programs

Although most people call all malicious or devious programs *viruses*, several terms—*worm* and *Trojan horse*, for example—can categorize such programs. In a strict definition, the term *virus* is specific and indicates one category of these programs. However, because the term *virus* has become generic, describing any type of destructive, devious, or malicious program, this book uses the term *virus* in a general sense and the term *true virus* to refer to the specific category.

True Virus

A *true virus* is a program that can embed itself into other programs or otherwise infect other programs by modifying them to include the virus. When the infected programs are executed, the true virus spreads itself to still other programs. Not all true viruses are malicious; some merely perform a prank, such as sending the user a nasty message. However, some true virus programs destroy data by erasing files and formatting disks. A true virus is dangerous because it can spread to virtually any executable file. Recovery is difficult. If you miss just one copy of a true virus, it can spread to reinfect the entire system.

Although new virus programs are discovered all the time, a few existing viruses continue to crop up. Some of the more well known viruses include Brain, Friday the 13th (Black Friday), Ogre, Ping Pong, Jerusalem, PLO, and Golden Gate.

Some of these viruses, such as Ping Pong, are more aggravating than destructive. Ping Pong attaches itself to the boot sector and causes a bouncing ball to appear on-screen. The ball wipes out information on your screen but does no apparent damage to files.

Other viruses aren't so nice. The Golden Gate virus determines when it has replicated itself 500 times, and then it formats drive C.

Worm

A *worm* is a stand-alone program that, when executed, spreads to other users and systems by sending copies of itself. Some types of worm programs are designed to exhaust system resources—CPU time, disk space, spool space, and so on—by replicating themselves endlessly. Worm programs differ from true viruses in that worms are complete programs in themselves; they are not embedded into other programs.

A special type of worm program spreads copies of itself through network-attached computers. The famous Internet Worm by Robert Morris that transmitted itself among UNIX systems is the classic example of this type of program. The IBM Christmas Card Worm that transmitted a chain letter of Christmas cards over IBM's internal network is another example. Network worms are security threats; they use networks to spread themselves against the wishes of the system owners and disrupt networks by overloading them.

Trojan Horse

A *Trojan horse* is a program designed to do things that the user of the program did not intend to do. An example of a Trojan horse is a program that copies a password or user ID file to another file. Many Trojan horses have been uploaded to bulletin board systems, which enables the perpetrator to download the normally protected password files and gain total access to the system. Another common Trojan horse purports to be a graphics display program, but when you run it, the program formats your hard disk and displays obscenities on the screen.

This type of program is common, because Trojan horses are easier to write than other types of viruses. Some of the simplest Trojan horse programs are really just other dangerous programs that have been renamed so people will run them accidentally.

One of the best-known Trojan horse programs is the AIDS Information program distributed by the fictitious PC Cyborg Corporation. This Trojan horse is examined in more detail in the section "Determining Where Viruses Originate" later in this chapter.

Another form of Trojan horse program is the logic bomb, a Trojan horse that remains dormant within a computing system until some condition occurs. The bomb can be triggered by a change in a file, an input sequence to the program, or a time or date. Logic bombs that are triggered or activated at a certain time or date usually are called time bombs.

Suppose that an embezzler writes a program that transfers odd cents from clients' accounts into his own account. However, the embezzler knows that if he is caught, this program may be found on the computer as evidence of his work. Therefore, he designs a logic bomb that watches for him to log on to the computer each day. If he does not log on, the bomb explodes, erasing evidence of his malicious work.

Some Trojan horse programs are set to perform their destruction (such as erasing files or formatting your disk) on certain dates, such as Friday the 13th or Halloween. Therefore, you may carry a Trojan horse program on your computer for months without knowing of its existence—until it strikes.

Defective Software

Bug-ridden, poor program code can lock up your system and damage data just as easily as a virus. Early programs that readjusted your hard disk interleave sometimes terminated abnormally, leaving the hard disk wiped out. The innocent user who ran this type of program without having a backup of the hard disk was asking for a problem. Many people thought that they had been the victim of a virus attack, but the real cause was simply bad programming and bugs; no malicious intent existed. The opposite also may be true. That is, victims of a virus attack may think that they simply are having hardware problems. Whatever the cause, the best solution is to have a viable backup of your important information.

Hardware Problems

Many users find a scapegoat in the virus hype—blaming viruses for hardware problems. If the hard disk fails or refuses to boot, for example, people often blame a virus with no evidence to back up their charges. Most likely, the hard disk or controller has failed.

Determining Where Viruses Originate

Viruses come from a variety of sources. The most malicious programs tend to come from persons with scores to settle. To get revenge for mistreatment, for example, a disgruntled employee may write a program that infects company computers. Some virus programs, such as the PLO and IRA viruses, are attributed to political organizations.

One of the most publicized Trojan horse attacks was with a program that demanded that a certain amount of money be sent—or else the data on the computer would be destroyed. The person who sent out this program (under the guise of a health organization) spent as much as $100,000 pulling off this effort. The professional-looking disk package was sent to major corporations and PC user groups around the world, purporting to contain a database of AIDS information. Enclosed with the disk was a professional flier with the title "AIDS Information - An Introductory Diskette" and a license that included the following excerpt:

> In case of breach of license, PC Cyborg Corporation reserves the right to use program mechanisms to ensure termination of the use of these programs. These program mechanisms will adversely affect other program applications on microcomputers.
>
> Warning: Do not use these programs unless you are prepared to pay for them.

> PC Cyborg Corporation does not authorize you to distribute or use these programs in the United States of America. If you have any doubt about your willingness or ability to meet the terms of this license agreement or if you are not prepared to pay all amounts due to PC Cyborg Corporation, then do not use these programs.

This program thoroughly trashed hard disks. Fortunately, programs such as the Norton Utilities were capable of recovering most of the erased files and directories.

Other viruses are the result of experiments by computing students or computer enthusiasts. Cases exist where virus programs actually came from course assignments in computer programming classes. Even though many of the virus programs originally were written "innocently," some escaped into networks and onto personal computers.

A number of virus programs seem to have their origins in the Middle East or Asia. In many of these places, pirated versions of software are widespread—not just pirated disks but illegally reproduced programs including disks and manuals. A number of pirated software products contain viruses. Be wary of using any illegal or pirated software, particularly if it was purchased by a friend who just came home from Hong Kong, India, the Middle East, or other third-world countries.

Some virus programs give you hints of their presence. The Pakistani Brain virus relabels your disk volume label to *BRAIN*. When you perform a DIR or CHKDSK command, you notice that the volume label is BRAIN.

Unfortunately, not every virus program gives warnings. However, methods exist to detect viruses' presence. For more information, see the section "Protecting Against Viruses" later in this chapter.

Understanding How a Virus Is Passed

The name *virus* is appropriate for these types of programs because like biological viruses, the programs attach themselves to a host—another computer program (usually an EXE or COM file). Depending on the type of virus, it may replicate itself by searching for and attaching to EXE or COM files on disk. After a virus integrates itself into a program, each time the program is run the virus may be capable of taking control—often invisibly—and replicating itself again or causing destruction.

When you copy a virus-contaminated file to a floppy disk, the virus goes with the file. The person who uses the floppy disk unknowingly allows the virus to pass on to his or her computer. In a network, the program actually may send itself to other locations via the network.

Protecting Against Viruses

The simplest, best way to protect your computer against all types of destructive programs is to back up your disks frequently. You also can "quarantine" new software on a certain system to see whether the programs operate without errors and with no hidden surprises. Some companies run a new program on a nonnetworked computer to verify that the program does not contain a virus.

You cannot completely protect a computer system from virus attacks, but the strategies examined in this section decrease the risks.

Make Backups

Make frequent backups of critical data and programs and keep several versions. In your backup strategy, do not just overwrite one backup with another. For example, keep a backup that is a week old, a month old, two months old, and so on.

Back up new software immediately after installation. Retain original distribution disks in a safe location. You should use copies of the original distribution disks to load software to your disks, to prevent any possibility of contaminating the original distribution disks with a virus from your computer. You also should write-protect disks used for installing a program; doing so prevents any virus from being copied to the floppies.

Remember that backups are not a panacea for virus protection. Although necessary for recovery, backups also present a place for a virus to hide. When you stop a virus attack and remove the virus from software on the system, the obvious way to recover altered or lost files is by restoring them from backups. Care must be taken not to reintroduce the virus into the system in the process. After information is restored from the backup, you should inspect the disk to ensure that the virus is not present in any file.

Control System Access

Control access to systems by limiting access to specific users. Do not let other people run or load software onto your system without your consent. You should even be careful about letting technical support people work on your computer. One piece of research suggested that many virus attacks in companies result from an unknowing support person who loads infected software onto several computers. You can control access to your computer by locking it or placing a password program on it.

Use Only Software from Reliable Sources

Use only software obtained from reputable sources. Access software from bulletin boards or public networks only if you are confident in their virus-screening methods. Well-known public access sources such as CompuServe and Genie carefully check software before permitting it to be downloaded. After all, if these sources permitted infected software on their networks, they would go out of business quickly. You can feel comfortable accessing information from these sources.

However, you should be more careful about downloading a program from a bulletin board run by a hobbyist. Many bulletin board operators, aware of this concern, take great pains to check the software that is available on their networks. Judge each source for yourself.

Each year disk vendors sell thousands (perhaps millions) of disks of public domain and shareware programs. You can find them at flea markets, through ads in magazines or newspapers, and so on. Again, you should consider the reliability of the company selling the disks. Many reputable disk vendors belong to professional organizations, such as the Association of Shareware Professionals (ASP). If you order shareware or public domain disks, I recommend that you verify that the dealer is a member of ASP.

Some people have become overly concerned about using bulletin boards, public access networks, or disk vendors. However, the people whose livelihood depends on these forms of information transmission are fanatical about keeping their software free of virus programs. Many operators of these systems and their respective professional organizations are actively prosecuting people who attempt to place infected programs in the public arena.

However, virus programs crop up in even the most protected software packages. Several commercial packages for the PC and Macintosh have been recalled because they were contaminated "at the factory."

Limit Mail

Limit electronic mail communication to nonexecutable files. Separate electronic mail from communication that must move executable files so that they can be controlled separately. Never run a program that you receive from an unknown source. One recent Thanksgiving message was sent to people on an educational network. The program was named Turkey and produced a cute *Happy Thanksgiving* message, but the program actually was a Trojan horse that erased files.

Take Precautions When Exchanging Software

Use care when exchanging software between computers at work or between your home computer and your office computer. Other people may not be as careful about protecting their computers. Also, you may be more lax in loading software at home and may have a time bomb waiting to go off that you unknowingly can pass to your office computer by copying software from home to the office.

Develop a Plan

Learn about the system and the software used to distinguish between normal and abnormal activity. A program with excessive disk access may be erasing files or formatting a disk. If such a problem occurs, stop the program quickly. Then examine your disk to see whether you can detect any problems.

Deal with viruses before a problem occurs. If you control software for a company, for example, you can publish guidelines about loading software. You may want to provide a test system for trying out software.

Several commercial programs can help detect and get rid of virus programs. Having tools to prevent and deal with the virus problem will help you recover more quickly if an attack occurs. A brief list of the tools available follows:

BOMBSQAD and **CHK4BOMB**
Andy Hopkins
526 Walnut Lane
Swarthmore, PA 19081

These programs read the contents of a program and attempt to find dangerous code. These programs can intercept calls from a program, warn you that something suspicious is about to happen, and give you an opportunity to cancel the program.

CHECKUP
Levin and Associates
9405 Bustleton Ave.
P.O. Box 14546
Philadelphia, PA 19115

This program detects viral infections in a file by comparing file sizes to baseline values (usually stored on a floppy disk). A file's size changing may be evidence of a virus attack.

DPROTECT
GEE WIZ Software Company
10 Manton Ave.
East Brunswick, NJ 08816

This program watches the calls made by programs running on your system and warns you if data on a protected disk is about to be changed.

Flu_Shot+
Software Concepts Design
594 Third Ave.
New York, NY 10016

This program was one of the first memory-resident virus-protection software programs available. With Flu_Shot+, you select a class of files—such as all COM, EXE, and BAT files—to protect. The program watches your system and detects when one of the protected files is changed. When a detection is made, a window appears on-screen and you are informed of the problem. You then must choose to allow the activity to continue or to disable it.

Norton AntiVirus
Symantec
1-800-343-4714

This program contains both detection and prevention components. AntiVirus operates as a memory-resident program to detect when a possible virus activity is launched. The program warns you and gives you an opportunity to stop the activity or allow it to continue (if the activity is a normal program function rather than a virus attack). With this package, Symantec also provides access to a 24-hour newsline that will help you keep up to date on the latest viruses.

Virusafe
Comnetco Inc.
29 Olcott Sq.
Bernardsville, NJ 07924

This program contains a virus diagnostics program and a program integrity checker that scans your programs for possible infection.

VIRUSCAN
McAfee Associates
4423 Chenney
Santa Clara, CA 95054

This program scans your program files to determine whether they have been tampered with. CLEANUP, a companion program, attempts to salvage any virus damage.

Virus Guard
IP Technologies
1575 Corporate Dr.
Costa Mesa, CA 92626

This program prevents corrupted programs from running. A program that has been tampered with does not run, which prevents the viral infection from continuing.

Vir-X
Microcraft
P.O. Box 1652
Richmond, IN 47374

Vir-X consists of three programs: Protek, Detek, and DiskLoc. Protek enables you to choose files to protect. Detek examines a selected program for possible viral infection. DiskLoc is a memory-resident program that monitors your system for attempts to access your disk's boot sector.

Analyzing the effectiveness of these programs is difficult because new virus programs are discovered all the time and because new versions of these programs continually change their capacities to deal with virus attacks. If you are in charge of data protection and recovery for an organization, you probably will want to have a selection of these programs handy to help you deal with whatever situation arises.

Check for Viruses

Run periodic checks for viral infections. One simple test is to compare the COMMAND.COM file on your boot disk to a copy of the file. Many virus programs attach themselves to COMMAND.COM. If COMMAND.COM has been changed, virus activity may be afoot. To perform this test, copy COMMAND.COM from your original DOS disk to your boot disk under a new name, such as TESTCOPY.XXX. Then use the COMP command to compare the copy with the COMMAND.COM on your boot disk. Here is an example:

```
COMP COMMAND.COM TESTCOPY.XXX
```

If the two files differ, you should begin looking for the source of the difference. You can enter a version of this command in your AUTOEXEC.BAT file so that this test is performed automatically each time you boot your computer. For example, type the following:

```
ECHO N|COMP COMMAND.COM TESTCOPY.XXX
```

The difference in this version is the ECHO N| prefix. This prefix automatically answers the question `Compare Another?` with an N (No) so you don't have to answer the question yourself. By placing this line in your AUTOEXEC.BAT file, you can perform the COMMAND.COM comparison each time your computer is booted.

Quarantine Infected Computers

Develop procedures to contain an infection after it is detected. When you find a virus on a computer, do not allow information from that computer to be copied to any other computer until the problem is solved. Quarantine any backup disks from that computer. If the person that uses this computer also uses other computers (such as a home computer or a traveling laptop), quarantine these computers until they are free of infection.

Chapter Summary

The computer virus problem is somewhat like the proliferation of a biological viral disease. To prevent biological disease, you must stay away from the source of the disease. You must abstain from activities that bring you into contact with the disease. And you must protect yourself in case you are exposed to the disease and become infected—have some sort of prescription available, for example.

In the same way, protect your computer against contact with programs that may be carriers of computer virus programs: true viruses, Trojan horses, or worms. Periodically check for the existence of virus programs on your disk. Finally, plan to deal with a virus attack if it occurs. With a reasonable amount of caution, the virus problem is controllable.

12

Preventive Maintenance

The old saying "An ounce of prevention is worth a pound of cure" applies to the safe maintenance of your data. Although this book has covered different methods for recovering data, you should try to prevent the loss to begin with. Generally, the amount of time and energy you use to prevent data loss is far less than the energy you have to expend to recover lost information. Therefore, taking basic steps that prevent data loss or enable you to overcome data loss as easily as possible is prudent. For example, although you may not be able to avoid losing data if a natural disaster occurs, you can have a disaster recovery plan that helps you get your information back on-line quickly.

This chapter discusses several simple procedures for preventing data loss, including backing up your data, avoiding dangerous commands, not using mixed DOS versions, and controlling resident software.

Backing Up Your Data

No matter how hard you try, you are likely to lose data at some point—because of a natural disaster, fire, massive hard disk breakdown, virus, or some other disaster. Therefore, you need to prepare yourself for this eventuality according to the importance of the information on your computer.

If your computer keeps real-time records of financial transactions or other vital, expensive information, you need to have a thorough backup procedure in place to minimize data loss. If you use your computer only to write term papers, however, your requirements for current backups are less stringent. In other words, you need to determine the level of backup required so that if your computer blows up right now, you can recover the information in a reasonable amount of time.

Creating a Backup Strategy

To analyze your need for a backup strategy, you need to consider the risk factors involved. You can categorize the value of your data in the following way, as an example:

- *The data is vital.* Loss of more than 3 hours' worth of data would create a costly and critical situation.
- *The data is important.* Loss of more than 24 hours' worth of data would create a costly and critical situation.
- *The data can be re-created easily.* Loss of up to one week's worth of data would not be critical.

Thus, if your computer contains vital data, follow an incremental backup schedule that captures new information every three hours. If the most critical data on your computer falls in the second category, a daily backup will suffice. If your computer contains data in the last category, a weekly backup is sufficient. You should determine the frequency of backups according to the importance of your most critical data.

Performing a backup of information is only one part of a data maintenance plan. If you keep backup copies of your data in your desk drawer and your building burns down, what good is the backup?

The following steps provide a backup plan you can institute to ensure that your periodic backups are protected:

1. To begin the backup process, make two backup copies of your hard disk. Take one copy of the backup to a safe place outside the office (your home, for example).
2. Every day, perform an incremental backup to the backup copy you keep at the office. That is, add to the backup the files that have changed that day. A daily incremental backup usually takes less than 15 minutes.

3. On Friday, bring the backup that has been at the safe location back to the office and perform a full backup at the end of the day. Take the backup with the week's incremental backups to the safe location.

4. On Monday, start with the new full backup that you did the previous Friday for performing the incremental backup.

This process gives you a daily backup at the office as well as a backup that is at most one week old in a safe location. Thus, if a minor disaster (such as a hard disk crash) occurs, you have at hand information that is at most one day old; if a major disaster occurs (the place burns down), you can restore information that is at most one week old.

Again, you should determine the frequency of your backups according to how much information you are willing to lose—a day's, week's, or month's worth, for example.

Another part of your backup strategy concerns which files you should back up. You usually do not need to back up all files on your hard disk. If you lose program files (such as WordPerfect), you can reload the program from the original files if you have kept them in a safe location. Eliminating files you do not have to back up makes the backup quicker and requires fewer disks (or tape). However, because some programs may take hours to install, you may want to include them in your backup. You need to judge which technique is best for your situation.

Another part of your backup strategy concerns the type of medium you should use for the backup. Every PC can use floppy disks for backups. However, other methods with additional advantages are available.

Tape backups, for example, are popular. Some PCs come with optional built-in tape backup units. With the tape backup method, you use a cartridge similar to a VCR tape that can contain 20M, 30M, 40M, or more. You can perform a tape backup on one PC or a network. Many advantages exist for network backups. In many work places, PC users simply don't take the time to back up on a regular basis. If a user's data is on a network system, the network administrator may take over the backup burden. That way, the backups are performed on a timely basis, and the backups probably are stored off-site in a safe location.

Another backup method you can use is a removable hard disk, such as a Bernoulli disk. In this case, a permanent hard disk can be backed up to one or more removable disks that may hold 10M to 20M each. This method is like backing up to big floppy disks.

A less common method is backing up to optical disks (silver platters similar to the compact disks used for music). As the technology improves for this method, it will become more common. On some optical disks, you can store almost a gigabyte (1,000M) of information.

Of the methods mentioned, the tape backup is the most common used (besides floppies). Backing up to disks can be time-consuming. If you can afford to do so, purchasing a tape backup system may make the backup chore easier to perform and may help you avoid data loss in the future.

Using the BACKUP and RESTORE Commands

The DOS BACKUP and RESTORE commands have been notorious ever since they appeared with Version 2.0. Because BACKUP must be issued at the command line, many users have had difficulty determining the exact syntax to use for the program to work properly. Also, BACKUP in earlier versions of DOS expected disks to be formatted. If you ran out of formatted disks in the middle of a backup, you were in trouble.

This user unfriendliness is only part of the problem. A number of bugs have caused problems with BACKUP in several versions of DOS, including 2.0, 3.0, and 3.3. In Version 3.0, for example, BACKUP occasionally has problems creating the BACKUP.@@@ file, which contains header information about the backup. If you perform a backup and notice that the size of this file is 0, then BACKUP has goofed and you have to repeat the backup, which may take hours. In addition, if you have backed up using DOS 3.3 or a later version, earlier versions of the DOS RESTORE command cannot read the backup.

Because of the poor performance of these DOS programs, you should consider obtaining more reliable software for performing backups. Several recommended programs are Fastback (from Fifth Generation Systems), DS Backup (from Design Software), the PC Tools Deluxe built-in backup software (from Central Point Software), and Norton Backup (from Symantec). See "Using Other Backup Programs" later in this chapter for information on using these utilities.

Remember that regardless of the software you use, backups to floppy disks are generally not acceptable with today's larger hard drives, simply because of the sheer number of floppy disks required (see the preceding section for information on alternative backup methods).

Using BACKUP

Even with its problems, the DOS BACKUP command may be sufficient for your needs. Before using BACKUP, you should estimate the number of disks you will need. You can run CHKDSK to determine how much disk space is currently being used on your hard disk.

For example, when I enter the CHKDSK command on my computer, I get the following report:

```
Volume Serial Number is 3E22-0EEC

  60663808 bytes total disk space
    225280 bytes in 9 hidden files
    204800 bytes in 66 directories
  59285504 bytes in 2931 user files
    948224 bytes available on disk

      2048 bytes in each allocation unit
     29621 total allocation units on disk
       463 available allocation units on disk

    656384 total bytes memory
    455392 bytes free
```

If you have 20M of information on your hard disk, for example, and you are backing up to 360K disks, you need

$$20{,}000{,}000 \div 360{,}000 = 55.5$$

or about 56 disks. If you are only using 15M of the disk, you need

$$15{,}000{,}000 \div 360{,}000 = 41.7$$

or about 42 disks. Table 12.1 gives the approximate number of disks needed to back up some common hard disk sizes, assuming that the disks are full.

Table 12.1
Approximate Number of Disks Needed for Backup

Hard Disk Size	*Number of Floppy Disks According to Size*				
	360K	*720K*	*1.2M*	*1.44M*	*2.88M*
10M	29	15	9	8	4
20M	59	29	18	15	8
30M	83	44	27	22	11
40M	116	58	35	29	15
70M	200	100	60	50	25
80M	229	115	69	59	30

After you determine how many disks you need, you should format that number of disks plus 1. If you are using DOS 3.3 or later, BACKUP formats an unformatted disk before backing up information to it. Thus, if you run out of formatted disks (using DOS 3.3 or later), you still can continue with the backup by using unformatted disks.

The BACKUP command for backing up your entire drive C to floppy disks in drive A follows:

```
BACKUP C:\ A: /S
```

This command indicates that the backup begins with the root directory of drive C and continues with all subdirectories (/S) to the A drive. Generally, the BACKUP command takes the following form:

BACKUP *source destination /switch(es)*

In this command, *source* is the drive and file specifications of your hard disk; *destination* is the name of the floppy disk drive to which you are backing up. In addition, a number of switches are available for specifying which files should be backed up—according to the date and time the files were created, for example. The switch specified in the example is /S, which creates all the subdirectories from the hard drive onto the floppy drive. For more detailed information on the BACKUP command, refer to your DOS manual or *Using PC DOS*, published by Que Corporation.

Using RESTORE

You should use the RESTORE command from the same version of DOS that you used to back up your system; however, note that the rules require only that you use a RESTORE command from a version equal to or later than the version whose BACKUP you used. Thus, you can back up files with the DOS 3.3 BACKUP command and restore them with the DOS 4.0 RESTORE command, because all versions of RESTORE are designed to be compatible with earlier versions of BACKUP. Still, you should try to use the most recent version of BACKUP and RESTORE. And, if at all possible, you definitely should use the same version of DOS for your backup and restore.

The RESTORE command for restoring all files from a backup set of disks is

```
RESTORE A: C:\*.* /S
```

A: is the drive containing the backed up floppy disks; C:*.* specifies that all files should be restored, beginning at the root directory. The /S switch specifies that all subdirectories from the root also should be restored, making the backup complete.

At times, a single file may be lost or corrupted, and you will want to restore only that file. Suppose, for example, that the file BUDGET.WK1 in your C:\LOTUS directory has been trashed. You have a backup that is a few days old, and you want to restore the file from the backup disks. To restore the file, first make the C:\LOTUS directory your default directory by typing *cd \lotus*; then issue the following command to restore the single file:

RESTORE A: C:BUDGET.WK1

You are prompted to enter the backup disks into drive A one at a time until the file is located from the stack of backup disks. Then RESTORE copies the file from the backup disk into your \LOTUS directory. The general form of the RESTORE command is

RESTORE *source destination /switch(es)*

In this command, *source* is the name of the disk drive containing the backup floppy disks; *destination* specifies where to put the restored files. A number of switches are available for specifying the files to restore—according to the date and time the files were created, for example. For more detailed information on the RESTORE command, refer to your DOS manual or *Using PC DOS*, published by Que Corporation.

Using Other Backup Programs

A number of third-party backup programs are available. Most of these programs are menu driven and provide more options than the DOS BACKUP and RESTORE commands. With these programs, you do not have to worry about mixing versions of the DOS BACKUP command because they are usually independent of any DOS version.

The purpose of this section is to give you basic information about available programs—not to review them. Some of the more popular programs follow:

- Norton Backup (from Symantec). This program operates from a series of pull-down menus and supports the use of a mouse. With Norton Backup, you can select which files to back up by choosing to include or exclude them from a backup list. You can define several lists. For example, you may have a monthly backup list, a weekly list, and a daily list. Your weekly or daily backup can be incremental—only backing up files that have changed since the last backup. Norton Backup formats disks as you back up, so you don't need to preformat disks. Norton tells you how many disks are needed and gives an estimate of the time required for the backup. Also, after you perform a backup, you can perform a verify procedure to check the reliability of the backup disks. Norton Backup also examines your computer to determine the maximum speed at which it can back up to disks. You get a much quicker backup by using this program rather than DOS BACKUP. Norton Backup is examined in detail in Que Corporation's *Using Norton Utilities*.

- PC Tools Deluxe (from Central Point Software). This program provides a backup procedure (Central Point Backup) as a part of its utilities package. This backup program operates from a well-designed menu system. You can choose to back up your entire drive, a directory, or a selected number of files. You are given an estimate of the number of disks required for the backup and the amount of time required (this program is faster than DOS BACKUP). This backup program supports file compression and incremental backups; therefore, you don't need as many disks as with DOS BACKUP, and you can back up only those files that have changed since the last backup. After you back up your disk, you can choose to compare the backup to the current data. You should perform this function to check the validity of your backup. PC Tools Deluxe's Central Point Backup is examined in detail in Que Corporation's *Using PC Tools Deluxe*.

- Fastback Plus (from Fifth Generation). This program is one of the first and most popular backup programs available. Fastback Plus operates from a menu that gives you many options for including or excluding files from a backup list. Fastback Plus gives you an estimate of the backup time, formats disks as needed, and optionally compresses data so that fewer disks are needed than with DOS BACKUP. As with any backup program, you always should verify that a backup is valid by testing it immediately after the backup is performed.

Each program mentioned here uses its own backup format. Therefore, you cannot back up with Norton Backup and then restore the files to disk with PC Tools or DOS RESTORE. You must use the same program to restore the files that you used to back up the files.

You can use a number of other backup programs in lieu of DOS BACKUP. These programs include Back-It, COREfast, BackEZ, DS Backup+, Take Two Manager, SY-STORE, Intelligent Backup, and BAKUP. When you choose a backup program, keep the following questions in mind:

- Does the program enable you to include and exclude specific files and global files (for example, *.COM) from the backup?

- Does the program allow automatic disk formatting during the backup?

- Does the program give you an estimate of the number of disks needed as well as a time estimate? Is it faster to use than DOS BACKUP?
- Does the program provide a way for verifying the validity of the backup? This point is important. Even if the backup program is good, problems with disk drives and disks can make a backup worthless. Always verify your backups. Keep multiple copies of backups if possible. For example, don't back up to the same disks every time. Keep several daily, weekly, or monthly backups for a period of time before reusing the disks for another backup.

All these backup tools, as well as others, are easier and faster to use than the DOS BACKUP and RESTORE commands. My recommendations are Norton Backup, DS Backup+, and Fastback Plus.

Handling Copy Protection

The nemesis of copy protection often prevents users from backing up software properly. Some software makers require users to run their original copies of programs on a day-to-day basis, sometimes requiring that disks be placed in a floppy drive for validation even though the system may contain an expensive hard disk.

I am opposed to any form of copy protection. My response to copy protection is to boycott whenever possible any software company engaged in this practice. You always can find alternatives to a program, and you even may discover that the unprotected alternative is a better program. Fortunately, copy protection schemes are declining, particularly in mass-marketed software. However, some special-use programs still use these protection schemes.

A copy protection scheme usually consists of writing a code to disk in a hidden directory or at a location not accessible through normal DOS use. When the protected program starts, it looks for this code on the disk. If the program does not find the code, the program does not run.

If you must use protected software, you can use CopyWrite from Quaid Software, Ltd., and Copy II PC from Central Point Software to back up most copy protected programs. You even can remove copy protection with these programs.

Remember that you have the legal right to back up your own software—a right guaranteed under U.S. copyright laws.

Avoiding Problems

Backing up your disk is one preventive measure for protecting the information on your disk. This section discusses several DOS commands that you should use carefully. This section also discusses mixing DOS versions and dealing with memory-resident software. Paying attention to these dangers can help you avoid losing important information.

Avoiding Dangerous Commands

Several DOS commands can be dangerous when issued by a beginning user. Most users agree that FORMAT can be a dangerous program, but the RECOVER and FDISK commands can be even more dangerous. Even COPY and XCOPY, when issued with improper arguments, can cause serious damage to your data. With these commands, the potential for disaster is only a few keystrokes away.

The FORMAT command, particularly on early versions of DOS, easily can destroy information on your hard disk. To prevent this problem, make sure that your hard disk is protected with the Norton Utilities IMAGE program or the PC Tools or DOS 5.0 MIRROR programs. These programs place a duplicate copy of important file information on your disk so that if an accidental FORMAT takes place, you can use the UNFORMAT command to recover the file information.

To prevent FORMAT from being issued, you can give the file FORMAT.COM another name, such as XXFORMAT.COM. Renaming FORMAT.COM prevents another user from issuing the FORMAT command. You also can replace the FORMAT command with the Norton Utilities Safe Format command. This version of FORMAT warns you when you are about to format a disk that contains files.

The DOS RECOVER command is poorly named. Many users assume that this command can recover lost files; in fact, this command recovers files that have a defective sector. If you run RECOVER without understanding how it operates, you risk losing all the files on your disk. You can, of course, use programs such as Norton Utilities' Disk Tools to recover from most of the damage done by the RECOVER command. However, you should consider erasing this command from your hard disk or renaming it as XRECOVER.COM, for example. If you are responsible for public access personal computers, you should remove this command in order to prevent an unknowing user from causing a great deal of damage.

You should run the FDISK program only when you install a hard disk. If you run the FDISK program on a current hard disk that contains information, you risk losing the data. Again, particularly for public access PCs, you should remove the FDISK command.

COPY and XCOPY are commands you use frequently, but they do have potential for creating problems. When DOS performs a copy, the file being copied may overwrite an existing file. Suppose, for example, that you have a file named REPORT.WP5 on your hard disk and that you copy the files *.WP5 from a floppy disk to your hard disk. If your floppy disk also contains a file named REPORT.WP5, it overwrites the REPORT.WP5 file on your hard disk. You usually cannot recover the original REPORT.WP5 file unless you have a backup of the file.

Because COPY and XCOPY are commonly used commands, you cannot easily prevent them from being issued. However, keeping backups of your hard disk enables you to recover important files if they are lost through an inadvertent copy.

Mixing DOS Versions

If you ever upgrade or downgrade a hard disk from one DOS version to another, make sure that you clean off all the DOS files that do not belong to the version you plan to run. For example, when you upgrade to a new version of DOS, you usually issue the command

```
SYS C:
```

to place a new copy of the system on drive C. However, this command does not copy all DOS files to your hard disk. You need to copy the other DOS files to your hard disk to be sure that you do not mix DOS versions.

To complete changing the DOS version, erase all your old DOS commands. Many users keep these commands in a directory, such as \DOS, so they easily can erase the entire directory. You also need to make sure that COMMAND.COM in the root directory is for the version being installed. If you have any DOS-related files in your root directory (such as ANSI.SYS), make sure that they are upgraded to the new DOS version. Copy all the new DOS files into your \DOS directory.

After you make all the upgrades, reboot your computer to verify that it is booting properly with the new DOS version. You can issue the VER command to display the DOS version that booted the computer. You also can test external DOS commands such as CHKDSK, FORMAT, and PRINT to verify that the new commands are working properly.

You can encounter some strange problems if you mix commands and programs from different versions of DOS. Many times, DOS simply indicates that you are using a command with an incorrect DOS version. Usually, newer versions of DOS have built-in protection; most commands check for the correct running version when invoked, but this protection may not always operate properly (especially when you are downgrading to an earlier version of DOS). Chapter 5 provides more information on using SYS to install new versions of DOS.

Controlling Resident Software

Many users get into trouble with *resident software*, software that loads itself into memory and waits for an activation key, usually a keystroke combination. Programs that can be activated by a key combination sometimes are called *pop-up*, *memory-resident*, or *TSR* (terminate-and-stay-resident) utilities or programs.

Resident programs often can conflict with each other as well as with applications programs or even DOS. For example, one program may overwrite the memory area already occupied by another program, causing the program whose memory area has been corrupted to act strangely, crash, or damage important information in memory or on disk. Resident programs can cause many different problems that appear consistently or intermittently. As a general rule, avoid using resident software unless absolutely necessary.

If you have traced a problem to a resident program conflict, the usual solution is to eliminate one of the conflicting programs. You also can change the load order of the programs. Certain programs may need to be first or last; you often can determine the preferred order only by trial and error.

Finally, remember that device drivers are also a form of resident software; therefore, loading these drivers in CONFIG.SYS may cause problems. Again, eliminating troublesome driver programs or changing the load order may solve the problem.

Unfortunately, resident program problems are likely to continue as long as we use DOS because DOS has no established rules for how resident programs should interact among one another as well as with the rest of the system. OS/2, however, is designed to handle many multitasking, memory-resident programs. This operating system will put an end to the problems with conflicting resident programs.

Chapter Summary

This book examined ways of recovering from data loss. However, an important part of data safety is preventing data loss. This chapter described some ways to avoid accidental data loss.

Backing up data is an essential part of the data recovery formula. You should implement a backup scheme that reflects the importance of your data. You also should be cautious when using dangerous DOS commands, mixing DOS versions, and working with resident software.

With a reasonable amount of foresight, you can provide a high level of safety for your computer data. First, try to prevent data loss. If data loss does occur, however, you can be prepared with a backup of the data and with your knowledge of the restoration techniques covered in this book.

Statistics for Floppy Disk Drives

This appendix provides information regarding the physical properties of floppy disks and drives. This information shows how one type of disk or drive differs from the others in operation and use. The charts in this appendix explain the differences among floppy disk formats, how data actually is written to the disk, and how one type of media differs from the others. Knowing this information can help you avoid improper use and formatting of disks, thereby preventing unnecessary data loss in the future.

Floppy Disk Formats

The following listing indicates the physical geometry of each of the standard floppy disk formats. From this information, you can see how the storage capacity of each type of disk is derived.

5 1/4-Inch Disk	*Double Density*	*High Density*
Bytes per sector	512	512
Sectors per track	9	15
Tracks per side	40	80
Sides	2	2
Capacity (kilobytes)	360	1,200

3 1/2-Inch Disk	*Double Density*	*High Density*	*Extra-High Density*
Bytes per sector	512	512	512
Sectors per track	9	18	36
Tracks per side	80	80	80
Sides	2	2	2
Capacity (kilobytes)	720	1,440	2,880

Floppy Disk Drive Track Widths

The following listing indicates the width of the magnetic track written by each standard floppy drive type. Understanding the implications of this information helps you recognize when you should not exchange disks between two different drives.

Drive Type	*Number of Tracks*	*Track Width*
5 1/4-inch 360K	40 per side	0.330 mm
5 1/4-inch 1.2M	80 per side	0.160 mm
3 1/2-inch 720K	80 per side	0.115 mm
3 1/2-inch 1.44M	80 per side	0.115 mm
3 1/2-inch 2.88M	80 per side	0.115 mm

For example, from this chart, you can see that because the 360K drive writes a track that is 0.330 millimeter wide, overwriting such a track using a 1.2M drive probably would result in a problem. This problem is due to the fact that when a wider track is overwritten by a narrower one, the overwrite is not complete. Usually, the 360K drive no longer can read a disk written on in such a manner. You also should be able to deduce that full read and write interchangeability exists between *all* the 3 1/2-inch drives. That is, a 2.88M drive can write perfectly on 720K or 1.44M formatted disks with no problems. This interchangeability is due to the fact that the written track widths are the same for all the standard 3 1/2-inch drives.

Floppy Disk Media Specifications

This following listing shows the physical differences among the various standard disk media. Many users share the common misconception that double-density (DD) and high-density (HD) disks are actually the same, especially in the 3 1/2-inch size. This idea is absolutely incorrect! Many users who believe this myth are improperly formatting DD disks as if they were HD disks. In fact, thc disks are very different physically and magnetically, as outlined here.

5 1/4-Inch Disk

Media Parameters	*Double Density (DD)*	*Quad Density (QD)*	*High Density (HD)*
Tracks per inch (tpi)	48	96	96
Bits per inch (bpi)	5,876	5,876	9,646
Media doping agent	Ferrite	Ferrite	Cobalt
Coercivity (oersteds)	300	300	675
Thickness (microinches)	100	100	50
Recording polarity	Horiz.	Horiz.	Horiz.

3 1/2-Inch Disk

Media Parameters	*Double Density (DD)*	*High Density (HD)*	*Extra-High Density (ED)*
Tracks per inch (tpi)	135	135	135
Bits per inch (bpi)	8,717	17,434	34,868
Media doping agent	Cobalt	Cobalt	Barium
Coercivity (oersteds)	660	700	750
Thickness (microinches)	78	35	80
Recording polarity	Horiz.	Horiz.	Vert.

This information should discourage use of "hole punchers" or other devices designed to enable you to "fool" a drive into believing that a double-density disk is really a high-density disk. Improper formatting and use of such disks cause data loss after the disk has been stored for a period of time (usually six months to a year later) due to the inability of the lower coercivity media to hold the magnetic patterns stable. Use of devices or techniques to improperly format disks in this fashion should be discouraged!

FORMAT Command Parameters

You use the FORMAT command to format floppy disks (low- and high-level) and hard disks (high-level only).

The syntax for the command is

FORMAT *d*: *parameters*

where *d* stands for the letter of the drive you want formatted and *parameters* stands for any optional parameters you want to add.

Using Standard Parameters

Standard parameters include the following:

/S	Copies the DOS system files (IBMBIO.COM and IBMDOS.COM) and COMMAND.COM from the boot drive to the new disk.
/V:*label*	Creates a volume label on the new disk. The label can be up to 11 characters long.
/F:*nnnn*	Specifies the format of the disk. For 5 1/4-inch drives, the size can be 160K, 180K, 320K, 360K, or 1.2M. For 3 1/2-inch drives, valid sizes are 720K, 1.44M, and 2.88M.
/4	Formats a 5 1/4-inch, 360K, double-sided, double-density disk in a high-capacity (1.2M) drive.
/T:*nn*	Specifies the number of tracks on the disk to format.

/N:*nn*	Specifies the number of sectors on the disk to format.
/Q	Performs a quick format. This parameter prevents the normal scan for unreadable sectors during formatting, and any existing bad cluster marks in the FAT are preserved.
/U	Performs an unconditional format. This parameter prevents the saving of UNFORMAT information. Additionally, the /U parameter forces a low-level format on a floppy disk. On a hard disk, this parameter only prevents the saving of UNFORMAT information; previous data is not overwritten.

Examining Obsolete Parameters

Obsolete parameters include the following:

/1	Formats single-sided disks (5 1/4-inch only).
/8	Formats eight sectors per track (5 1/4-inch only).
/B	Creates dummy system files, reserving room for any DOS version's SYS command to copy actual files later.

Using Undocumented Parameters

Undocumented parameters (disks only) include the following:

/H	**Skips the** `Insert new diskette for drive X: and press ENTER when ready` **message.**
/BACKUP	**Skips the** `Insert new diskette for drive X: and press ENTER when ready...` **message.**
/SELECT	**Skips the** `Insert new diskette for drive X: and press ENTER when ready...` **message. Also suppressed are the disk space report, the** `Format another (Y/N)?` **message, and any error messages.**

/AUTOTEST	Skips the `Insert new diskette for drive X: and press ENTER when ready...` message. Also suppressed are the disk space report, the `Format another (Y/N)?` message, and any error messages. In addition, the `Volume label (11 characters, ENTER for none)?` message is suppressed.

Using Parameters with Various DOS Versions

Some general notes about FORMAT's parameters follow:

/S looks for system files on the default drive in DOS 3.3 and earlier versions. The boot drive is searched in DOS 4.0 and later versions.

/V is assumed in DOS 4.0 and later versions if /V:*label* is not specified. DOS 3.3 and earlier versions do not support the *:label* extension for /V.

/F operates in DOS 4.0 and later versions only. The 2.88M drive is supported in DOS 5.0 and later versions only.

/T and /N are supported in DOS 3.3 and later versions only. /T defaults to 80 and /N defaults to 9 in DOS 3.3 only. No defaults are assumed in DOS 4.0 and later versions; therefore, if one of the parameters is specified, then the other must be specified as well.

/Q operates in DOS 5.0 and later versions only. The default is to perform a scan for unreadable sectors and to ignore any previous bad cluster marks.

/U operates in DOS 5.0 and later versions only. The default is to save UNFORMAT information except for new disks or in cases where the formatted capacity is being changed.

/H operates in DOS 3.3 only.

/BACKUP, /SELECT, and /AUTOTEST operate in DOS 4.0 and later versions only.

Formatting Low-Density Disks in High-Density Drives

To format 360K disks in a 1.2M drive, use the following commands:

With DOS 3.0+, use *FORMAT A: /4*.

With DOS 3.2+, use *FORMAT A: /N:9 /T:40*.

With DOS 4.0+, use *FORMAT A: /F:360*.

To format 720K disks in a 1.44M or 2.88M drive, use the following commands:

With DOS 3.3+, use *FORMAT A: /N:9 /T:80*.

With DOS 4.0+, use *FORMAT A: /F:720*.

To format 1.44M disks in a 2.88M drive, use the following commands:

With DOS 5.0+, use *FORMAT A: /N:18 /T:80* or use *FORMAT A: /F:144*.

B

Hard Disk Parameter Tables

When a hard disk drive is installed in the system, the computer must have some method of informing the system BIOS about the physical geometry of the drive in order for the INT 13h functions to work. This task usually is accomplished through a fixed table that is contained in the motherboard or in the controller BIOS and that has entries defining various drive geometries. The disk installer then selects the entry that matches the drive being installed and usually informs the BIOS through the system's SETUP utility. After entering the drive type through SETUP, the type information usually is maintained in CMOS RAM by virtue of a long-life lithium battery. With XT systems, you should note that the INT 13h BIOS support is usually found directly on the hard disk controller itself in a built-in BIOS. In this case, selection of a particular drive type usually is done by moving jumpers on the controller card.

In the case of the battery-maintained CMOS memory, this SETUP procedure usually is performed only under the following conditions:

- The system is new and has not yet been set up.
- A new peripheral is installed. CMOS normally only stores information about the following items:

  Floppy drive types

  Hard drive types

  Base and extended memory

  Video display adapter and mode

Whether math coprocessor is installed

Date and time

The battery is dead or dying

The SETUP program comes on a disk for systems made by IBM or COMPAQ, but most compatibles made after 1987 have the SETUP program built directly into the BIOS itself. This arrangement eliminates the need for the disk and is very convenient to use. Usually, these BIOS-based SETUP programs are activated by a particular keystroke sequence either at any time or only during the power-on self test (POST). Three popular compatible BIOS manufacturers use the following keystrokes to activate SETUP:

Phoenix BIOS uses Ctrl-Alt-S.

AMI BIOS uses the Del key during the POST.

Award BIOS uses Ctrl-Alt-Esc.

In the case of the Phoenix or Award BIOS, you must hold the three keys down simultaneously to invoke SETUP. AMI simply has you press the Del key during the POST.

In order to select the correct hard disk type, you first need to know your own drives' physical characteristics. You can find this information in the technical reference documentation that came with your drive or system. If you did not receive this documentation, then call your vendor and demand it. After you know the parameters for your drive, you need to find a table entry in your particular BIOS that matches the drive parameters. If none is an exact match, then in some cases you can use an entry that is close, as long as the entries for cylinders, heads, or sectors per track are not more than the drive's capability. Also, you should match as closely as possible the write precompensation starting cylinder value for reliable operation on the drive's inner cylinders. See Chapters 3 and 4 for more information on hard drives.

Because a variety of BIOS manufacturers are in the marketplace today, your systems may contain different tables. Each BIOS manufacturer has defined its own drive tables, usually starting with entries that are the same as IBM's. Most BIOS drive tables are similar to IBM's for the first 15 or 23 entries, but from that point on they vary from manufacturer to manufacturer. This variance is the reason that a drive manufacturer cannot simply stamp the drive type on the drive itself. For example, the correct drive type used for a Seagate ST-251 drive varies according to the BIOS manufacturer as follows:

The IBM BIOS uses Type 8.

The COMPAQ BIOS uses Type 5.

The AMI BIOS uses Type 40.

The Award BIOS uses Type 40.

The Phoenix BIOS uses Type 44.

If Seagate wanted to put the drive type on the drive itself, which number should be used? Clearly, the company cannot put the drive type on the drive, and the installer or data-recovery specialist must make the correct selection.

The following charts show the contents of the disk tables for a variety of BIOS manufacturers, including IBM, COMPAQ, Phoenix, AMI, and Award. This information is helpful in determining the correct drive type for a particular drive and system combination. Note also that some BIOS vendors now provide user-definable entries in their tables, which means that the values in the table can be typed directly from the keyboard, thereby allowing for virtually infinite customization without having to actually modify the BIOS itself.

Also included in this appendix are tables for IBM's XT controllers, whose table format differs slightly from the tables found in AT systems.

IBM XT Hard Disk Controller Drive Tables

IBM sold XT systems with two different controllers. Actually, the controllers were the same, but the BIOS chip on the controllers was different. They differed primarily in the drive table information. Both controllers really were made for IBM by Xebec Corporation and also were sold by Xebec as the Model 1210 controller. Tables B.1 and B.2 list the drive tables included in the IBM-specific Xebec 1210 controllers.

Table B.1
IBM 10Mb Fixed-Disk Controller (Xebec 1210) Drive Table

Table	*Type*	*Cyls*	*Heads*	*WPC*	*Ctrl*	*LZ*	*S/T*	*Meg*	*Mb*
0	N/A	306	2	0	00h	N/A	N/A	5.08	5.33
1	N/A	375	8	0	05h	N/A	N/A	24.90	26.11
2	N/A	306	6	256	05h	N/A	N/A	15.24	15.98
3	N/A	306	4	0	05h	N/A	N/A	10.16	10.65

Table B.2
IBM 20Mb Fixed Disk Controller (Xebec 1210) Drive Table

Table	*Type*	*Cyls*	*Heads*	*WPC*	*Ctrl*	*LZ*	*S/T*	*Meg*	*Mb*
0	1	306	4	0	05h	305	17	10.16	10.65
1	16	612	4	0	05h	663	17	20.32	21.31
2	2	615	4	300	05h	615	17	20.42	21.41
3	13	306	8	128	05h	319	17	20.32	21.31

Note: Entry = Controller table position.

Table B.3 lists the Xebec 1210 drive table selection.

Table B.3
Xebec 1210 Drive Table Selection (Jumper W5)

	Controller Table Entry			
Jumper Pins	*#0*	*#1*	*#2*	*#3*
1	o≡o	o≡o	o o	o o
2	o≡o	o o	o≡o	o o
3	o≡o	o≡o	o o	o o
4	o≡o	o o	o≡o	o o

Note: Jumper pins 1 and 2 define drive 0 (C:); pins 3 and 4 define drive 1 (D:). By setting these jumpers, a particular drive table entry is selected. For example, to select table entry #1 for drive C, you would jumper pins 1 and 2.

Notes:

Type = Corresponding AT drive type number

Cyls = Total number of cylinders

Heads = Total number of heads

WPC = Write precompensation starting cylinder

Ctrl = Control byte, values determined according to the following list:

Bit #		*Hex*		*Meaning*
Bit 0	=	01h	=	Drive step rate (see table that follows)
Bit 1	=	02h	=	Drive step rate
Bit 2	=	04h	=	Drive step rate
Bit 3	=	08h	=	More than 8 heads
Bit 4	=	10h	=	Embedded servo drive
Bit 5	=	20h	=	OEM defect map at (cyls + 1)
Bit 6	=	40h	=	Disable ECC retries
Bit 7	=	80h	=	Disable disk access retries

Xebec 1210 Drive Step Rate Coding (Control Byte)

Hex Value	*Definition*
00h	3 millisecond step
04h	200 microsecond buffered step
05h	70 microsecond buffered step
06h	30 microsecond buffered step
07h	15 microsecond buffered step

LZ = Landing zone cylinder for head parking

S/T = Number of sectors per track

Meg = Drive capacity in megabytes

Mb = Drive capacity in millions of bytes

Note: The landing zone and sectors-per-track fields were not used in the 10Mb controller and are zero-filled in that case.

IBM AT and PS/2 BIOS Hard Disk Table

Table B.4 is the IBM motherboard ROM BIOS hard disk parameter table for AT or PS/2 systems using ST-506/412 (STD or IDE) controllers.

Table B.4
IBM AT and PS/2 ROM BIOS
Hard Disk Table

Type	*Cyls*	*Heads*	*WPC*	*Ctrl*	*LZ*	*S/T*	*Meg*	*Mb*
1	306	4	128	00h	305	17	10.16	10.65
2	615	4	300	00h	615	17	20.42	21.41
3	615	6	300	00h	615	17	30.63	32.12
4	940	8	512	00h	940	17	62.42	65.45
5	940	6	512	00h	940	17	46.82	49.09
6	615	4	65535	00h	615	17	20.42	21.41
7	462	8	256	00h	511	17	30.68	32.17
8	733	5	65535	00h	733	17	30.42	31.90
9	900	15	65535	08h	901	17	112.06	117.50
10	820	3	65535	00h	820	17	20.42	21.41
11	855	5	65535	00h	855	17	35.49	37.21
12	855	7	65535	00h	855	17	49.68	52.09
13	306	8	128	00h	319	17	20.32	21.31
14	733	7	65535	00h	733	17	42.59	44.66
15	0	0	0	00h	0	0	0	0
16	612	4	0	00h	663	17	20.32	21.31
17	977	5	300	00h	977	17	40.55	42.52
18	977	7	65535	00h	977	17	56.77	59.53
19	1024	7	512	00h	1023	17	59.50	62.39
20	733	5	300	00h	732	17	30.42	31.90

Type	*Cyls*	*Heads*	*WPC*	*Ctrl*	*LZ*	*S/T*	*Meg*	*Mb*
21	733	7	300	00h	732	17	42.59	44.66
22	733	5	300	00h	733	17	30.42	31.90
23	306	4	0	00h	336	17	10.16	10.65
24	612	4	305	00h	663	17	20.32	21.31
25	306	4	65535	00h	340	17	10.16	10.65
26	612	4	65535	00h	670	17	20.32	21.31
27	698	7	300	20h	732	17	40.56	42.53
28	976	5	488	20h	977	17	40.51	42.48
29	306	4	0	00h	340	17	10.16	10.65
30	611	4	306	20h	663	17	20.29	21.27
31	732	7	300	20h	732	17	42.53	44.60
32	1023	5	65535	20h	1023	17	42.46	44.52
33	614	4	65535	20h	663	25	29.98	31.44
34	775	2	65535	20h	900	27	20.43	21.43
35	921	2	65535	20h	1000	33	29.68	31.12
36	402	4	65535	20h	460	26	20.41	21.41
37	580	6	65535	20h	640	26	44.18	46.33
38	845	2	65535	20h	1023	36	29.71	31.15
39	769	3	65535	20h	1023	36	40.55	42.52
40	531	4	65535	20h	532	39	40.45	42.41
41	577	2	65535	20h	1023	36	20.29	21.27
42	654	2	65535	20h	674	32	20.44	21.43
43	923	5	65535	20h	1023	36	81.12	85.06
44	531	8	65535	20h	532	39	80.89	84.82
45	0	0	0	00h	0	0	0.00	0.00
46	0	0	0	00h	0	0	0.00	0.00
47	0	0	0	00h	0	0	0.00	0.00

Notes: Table entry 15 is reserved to act as a pointer to indicate that the actual type is greater than 15. Most IBM systems do not have every entry in this table. The maximum usable type number varies for each particular ROM version. The maximum usable type for each IBM ROM is indicated in table B.10 at the end of this appendix. If you have an IBM-compatible system, this table may be inaccurate for many of the entries beyond Type 15. Most compatibles follow the IBM table for at least the first 15 entries.

Most IBM PS/2 systems now come with hard disk drives that have the defect map written as data on the cylinder that is one cylinder beyond the highest reported cylinder. This special data is read by the IBM PS/2 Advanced Diagnostics low-level format program. This arrangement automates the entry of the defect list and eliminates the chance for human error, as long as you use only the IBM PS/2 Advanced Diagnostics for hard disk low-level formatting.

This type table does not apply to IBM ESDI or SCSI hard disk controllers, host adapters, and drives. Because the ESDI and SCSI controllers or host adapters query the drive directly for the required parameters, no table entry selection is necessary. Note, however, that the table for the ST-506/412 drives currently still can be found in the ROM BIOS of all the PS/2 systems, even if the model came standard with an ESDI or SCSI disk subsystem.

COMPAQ BIOS Hard Disk Table

Table B.5 is the COMPAQ motherboard ROM BIOS hard disk parameter table for the 286e version dated 03/22/89.

Table B.5
COMPAQ ROM BIOS (286e Version 03/22/89)
Hard Disk Parameters

Type	*Cyls*	*Heads*	*WPC*	*Ctrl*	*LZ*	*S/T*	*Meg*	*Mb*
1	306	4	128	00h	305	17	10.16	10.65
2	615	4	128	00h	638	17	20.42	21.41
3	615	6	128	00h	615	17	30.63	32.12
4	1024	8	512	00h	1023	17	68.00	71.30
5	805	6	65535	00h	805	17	40.09	42.04

Type	*Cyls*	*Heads*	*WPC*	*Ctrl*	*LZ*	*S/T*	*Meg*	*Mb*
6	697	5	128	00h	696	17	28.93	30.33
7	462	8	256	00h	511	17	30.68	32.17
8	925	5	128	00h	924	17	38.39	40.26
9	900	15	65535	08h	899	17	112.06	117.50
10	980	5	65535	00h	980	17	40.67	42.65
11	925	7	128	00h	924	17	53.75	56.36
12	925	9	128	08h	924	17	69.10	72.46
13	612	8	256	00h	611	17	40.64	42.61
14	980	4	128	00h	980	17	32.54	34.12
15	0	0	0	00h	0	0	0	0
16	612	4	0	00h	612	17	20.32	21.31
17	980	5	128	00h	980	17	40.67	42.65
18	966	5	128	00h	966	17	40.09	42.04
19	754	11	65535	08h	753	17	68.85	72.19
20	733	5	256	00h	732	17	30.42	31.90
21	733	7	256	00h	732	17	42.59	44.66
22	524	4	65535	00h	524	40	40.94	42.93
23	924	8	65535	00h	924	17	61.36	64.34
24	966	14	65535	08h	966	17	112.26	117.71
25	966	16	65535	08h	966	17	128.30	134.53
26	1023	14	65535	08h	1023	17	118.88	124.66
27	832	6	65535	00h	832	33	80.44	84.34
28	1222	15	65535	08h	1222	34	304.31	319.09
29	1240	7	65535	00h	1240	34	144.10	151.10
30	615	4	128	00h	615	25	30.03	31.49
31	615	8	128	00h	615	25	60.06	62.98
32	905	9	128	08h	905	25	99.43	104.26
33	832	8	65535	00h	832	33	107.25	112.46

continues

Table B.5 *(continued)*

Type	*Cyls*	*Heads*	*WPC*	*Ctrl*	*LZ*	*S/T*	*Meg*	*Mb*
34	966	7	65535	00h	966	34	112.26	117.71
35	966	8	65535	00h	966	34	128.30	134.53
36	966	9	65535	08h	966	34	144.33	151.35
37	966	5	65535	00h	966	34	80.19	84.08
38	611	16	65535	08h	611	63	300.73	315.33
39	1023	11	65535	08h	1023	33	181.32	190.13
40	1023	15	65535	08h	1023	34	254.75	267.13
41	1630	15	65535	08h	1630	52	620.80	650.96
42	1023	16	65535	08h	1023	63	503.51	527.97
43	805	4	65535	00h	805	26	40.88	42.86
44	805	2	65535	00h	805	26	20.44	21.43
45	748	8	65535	00h	748	33	96.42	101.11
46	748	6	65535	00h	748	33	72.32	75.83
47	966	5	128	00h	966	25	58.96	61.82

Note: Table entry 15 is reserved to act as a pointer to indicate that the actual type is greater than 15.

AMI BIOS Hard Disk Table

Table B.6 is the AMI motherboard ROM BIOS hard disk parameter table for the 286 version dated 04/30/89.

Table B.6
AMI ROM BIOS (286 BIOS Version 04/30/89)
Hard Disk Parameters

Type	*Cyls*	*Heads*	*WPC*	*Ctrl*	*LZ*	*S/T*	*Meg*	*Mb*
1	306	4	128	00h	305	17	10.16	10.65
2	615	4	300	00h	615	17	20.42	21.41

Type	Cyls	Heads	WPC	Ctrl	LZ	S/T	Meg	Mb
3	615	6	300	00h	615	17	30.63	32.12
4	940	8	512	00h	940	17	62.42	65.45
5	940	6	512	00h	940	17	46.82	49.09
6	615	4	65535	00h	615	17	20.42	21.41
7	462	8	256	00h	511	17	30.68	32.17
8	733	5	65535	00h	733	17	30.42	31.90
9	900	15	65535	08h	901	17	112.06	117.50
10	820	3	65535	00h	820	17	20.42	21.41
11	855	5	65535	00h	855	17	35.49	37.21
12	855	7	65535	00h	855	17	49.68	52.09
13	306	8	128	00h	319	17	20.32	21.31
14	733	7	65535	00h	733	17	42.59	44.66
15	0	0	0	00h	0	0	0	0
16	612	4	0	00h	663	17	20.32	21.31
17	977	5	300	00h	977	17	40.55	42.52
18	977	7	65535	00h	977	17	56.77	59.53
19	1024	7	512	00h	1023	17	59.50	62.39
20	733	5	300	00h	732	17	30.42	31.90
21	733	7	300	00h	732	17	42.59	44.66
22	733	5	300	00h	733	17	30.42	31.90
23	306	4	0	00h	336	17	10.16	10.65
24	925	7	0	00h	925	17	53.75	56.36
25	925	9	65535	08h	925	17	69.10	72.46
26	754	7	526	00h	754	17	43.81	45.94
27	754	11	65535	08h	754	17	68.85	72.19
28	699	7	256	00h	699	17	40.62	42.59
29	823	10	65535	08h	823	17	68.32	71.63
30	918	7	874	00h	918	17	53.34	55.93

continues

Table B.6 *(continued)*

Type	*Cyls*	*Heads*	*WPC*	*Ctrl*	*LZ*	*S/T*	*Meg*	*Mb*
31	1024	11	65535	08h	1024	17	93.50	98.04
32	1024	15	65535	08h	1024	17	127.50	133.69
33	1024	5	1024	00h	1024	17	42.50	44.56
34	612	2	128	00h	612	17	10.16	10.65
35	1024	9	65535	08h	1024	17	76.50	80.22
36	1024	8	512	00h	1024	17	68.00	71.30
37	615	8	128	00h	615	17	40.84	42.82
38	987	3	805	00h	987	17	24.58	25.77
39	987	7	805	00h	987	17	57.35	60.14
40	820	6	820	00h	820	17	40.84	42.82
41	977	5	815	00h	977	17	40.55	42.52
42	981	5	811	00h	981	17	40.72	42.69
43	830	7	512	00h	830	17	48.23	50.57
44	830	10	65535	08h	830	17	68.90	72.24
45	917	15	65535	08h	918	17	114.18	119.72
46	1224	15	65535	08h	1223	17	152.40	159.81
47	0	0	0	00h	0	0	0.00	0.00

Note: Table entry 15 is reserved to act as a pointer to indicate that the actual type is greater than 15. This BIOS uses Type 47 as a user-definable entry.

Award BIOS Version 3.05 Hard Disk Table

Table B.7 is the Award motherboard ROM BIOS hard disk parameter table for the Modular 286, 386SX, and 386 BIOS Version 3.05.

Table B.7
Award ROM BIOS
(Modular 286, 386SX, and 386 BIOS Version 3.05)
Hard Disk Parameters

Type	*Cyls*	*Heads*	*WPC*	*Ctrl*	*LZ*	*S/T*	*Meg*	*Mb*
1	306	4	128	00h	305	17	10.16	10.65
2	615	4	300	00h	615	17	20.42	21.41
3	615	6	300	00h	615	17	30.63	32.12
4	940	8	512	00h	940	17	62.42	65.45
5	940	6	512	00h	940	17	46.82	49.09
6	615	4	65535	00h	615	17	20.42	21.41
7	462	8	256	00h	511	17	30.68	32.17
8	733	5	65535	00h	733	17	30.42	31.90
9	900	15	65535	08h	901	17	112.06	117.50
10	820	3	65535	00h	820	17	20.42	21.41
11	855	5	65535	00h	855	17	35.49	37.21
12	855	7	65535	00h	855	17	49.68	52.09
13	306	8	128	00h	319	17	20.32	21.31
14	733	7	65535	00h	733	17	42.59	44.66
15	0	0	0	00h	0	0	0	0
16	612	4	0	00h	663	17	20.32	21.31
17	977	5	300	00h	977	17	40.55	42.52
18	977	7	65535	00h	977	17	56.77	59.53
19	1024	7	512	00h	1023	17	59.50	62.39
20	733	5	300	00h	732	17	30.42	31.90
21	733	7	300	00h	732	17	42.59	44.66
22	733	5	300	00h	733	17	30.42	31.90
23	306	4	0	00h	336	17	10.16	10.65
24	977	5	65535	00h	976	17	40.55	42.52
25	1024	9	65535	08h	1023	17	76.50	80.22

continues

Table B.7 *(continued)*

Type	*Cyls*	*Heads*	*WPC*	*Ctrl*	*LZ*	*S/T*	*Meg*	*Mb*
26	1224	7	65535	00h	1223	17	71.12	74.58
27	1224	11	65535	08h	1223	17	111.76	117.19
28	1224	15	65535	08h	1223	17	152.40	159.81
29	1024	8	65535	00h	1023	17	68.00	71.30
30	1024	11	65535	08h	1023	17	93.50	98.04
31	918	11	65535	08h	1023	17	83.82	87.89
32	925	9	65535	08h	926	17	69.10	72.46
33	1024	10	65535	08h	1023	17	85.00	89.13
34	1024	12	65535	08h	1023	17	102.00	106.95
35	1024	13	65535	08h	1023	17	110.50	115.87
36	1024	14	65535	08h	1023	17	119.00	124.78
37	1024	2	65535	00h	1023	17	17.00	17.83
38	1024	16	65535	08h	1023	17	136.00	142.61
39	918	15	65535	08h	1023	17	114.30	119.85
40	820	6	65535	00h	820	17	40.84	42.82
41	1024	5	65535	00h	1023	17	42.50	44.56
42	1024	5	65535	00h	1023	26	65.00	68.16
43	809	6	65535	00h	808	17	40.29	42.25
44	820	6	65535	00h	819	26	62.46	65.50
45	776	8	65535	00h	775	33	100.03	104.89
46	0	0	0	00h	0	0	0.00	0.00
47	0	0	0	00h	0	0	0.00	0.00

Note: Table entry 15 is reserved to act as a pointer to indicate that the actual type is greater than 15.

Award BIOS Version 3.10 Hard Disk Table

Table B.8 is the Award motherboard ROM BIOS hard disk parameter table for the Modular 286, 386SX, and 386 BIOS Version 3.1.

Table B.8
Award ROM BIOS (Modular 286, 386SX, and 386 BIOS Version 3.1) Hard Disk Parameters

Type	*Cyls*	*Heads*	*WPC*	*Ctrl*	*LZ*	*S/T*	*Meg*	*Mb*
1	306	4	128	00h	305	17	10.16	10.65
2	615	4	300	00h	615	17	20.42	21.41
3	615	6	300	00h	615	17	30.63	32.12
4	940	8	512	00h	940	17	62.42	65.45
5	940	6	512	00h	940	17	46.82	49.09
6	615	4	65535	00h	615	17	20.42	21.41
7	462	8	256	00h	511	17	30.68	32.17
8	733	5	65535	00h	733	17	30.42	31.90
9	900	15	65535	08h	901	17	112.06	117.50
10	820	3	65535	00h	820	17	20.42	21.41
11	855	5	65535	00h	855	17	35.49	37.21
12	855	7	65535	00h	855	17	49.68	52.09
13	306	8	128	00h	319	17	20.32	21.31
14	733	7	65535	00h	733	17	42.59	44.66
15	0	0	0	00h	0	0	0	0
16	612	4	0	00h	663	17	20.32	21.31
17	977	5	300	00h	977	17	40.55	42.52
18	977	7	65535	00h	977	17	56.77	59.53
19	1024	7	512	00h	1023	17	59.50	62.39
20	733	5	300	00h	732	17	30.42	31.90

continues

Table B.8 *(continued)*

Type	*Cyls*	*Heads*	*WPC*	*Ctrl*	*LZ*	*S/T*	*Meg*	*Mb*
21	733	7	300	00h	732	17	42.59	44.66
22	733	5	300	00h	733	17	30.42	31.90
23	306	4	0	00h	336	17	10.16	10.65
24	977	5	65535	00h	976	17	40.55	42.52
25	1024	9	65535	08h	1023	17	76.50	80.22
26	1224	7	65535	00h	1223	17	71.12	74.58
27	1224	11	65535	08h	1223	17	111.76	117.19
28	1224	15	65535	08h	1223	17	152.40	159.81
29	1024	8	65535	00h	1023	17	68.00	71.30
30	1024	11	65535	08h	1023	17	93.50	98.04
31	918	11	65535	08h	1023	17	83.82	87.89
32	925	9	65535	08h	926	17	69.10	72.46
33	1024	10	65535	08h	1023	17	85.00	89.13
34	1024	12	65535	08h	1023	17	102.00	106.95
35	1024	13	65535	08h	1023	17	110.50	115.87
36	1024	14	65535	08h	1023	17	119.00	124.78
37	1024	2	65535	00h	1023	17	17.00	17.83
38	1024	16	65535	08h	1023	17	136.00	142.61
39	918	15	65535	08h	1023	17	114.30	119.85
40	820	6	65535	00h	820	17	40.84	42.82
41	1024	5	65535	00h	1023	17	42.50	44.56
42	1024	5	65535	00h	1023	26	65.00	68.16
43	809	6	65535	00h	852	17	40.29	42.25
44	809	6	65535	00h	852	26	61.62	64.62
45	776	8	65535	00h	775	33	100.03	104.89
46	684	16	65535	08h	685	38	203.06	212.93
47	615	6	65535	00h	615	17	30.63	32.12

Note: Table entry 15 is reserved to act as a pointer to indicate that the actual type is greater than 15. This BIOS uses Types 48 and 49 as user-definable entries.

Phoenix BIOS Hard Disk Table

Table B.9 is the Phoenix motherboard ROM BIOS hard disk parameter table for the 286 BIOS Plus Version 3.10.

Table B.9
Phoenix ROM BIOS (286 BIOS Plus Version 3.10)
Hard Disk Parameters

Type	*Cyls*	*Heads*	*WPC*	*Ctrl*	*LZ*	*S/T*	*Meg*	*Mb*
1	306	4	128	00h	305	17	10.16	10.65
2	615	4	300	00h	615	17	20.42	21.41
3	615	6	300	00h	615	17	30.63	32.12
4	940	8	512	00h	940	17	62.42	65.45
5	940	6	512	00h	940	17	46.82	49.09
6	615	4	65535	00h	615	17	20.42	21.41
7	462	8	256	00h	511	17	30.68	32.17
8	733	5	65535	00h	733	17	30.42	31.90
9	900	15	65535	08h	901	17	112.06	117.50
10	820	3	65535	00h	820	17	20.42	21.41
11	855	5	65535	00h	855	17	35.49	37.21
12	855	7	65535	00h	855	17	49.68	52.09
13	306	8	128	00h	319	17	20.32	21.31
14	733	7	65535	00h	733	17	42.59	44.66
15	0	0	0	00h	0	0	0	0
16	612	4	0	00h	663	17	20.32	21.31
17	977	5	300	00h	977	17	40.55	42.52

continues

Table B.9 *(continued)*

Type	*Cyls*	*Heads*	*WPC*	*Ctrl*	*LZ*	*S/T*	*Meg*	*Mb*
18	977	7	65535	00h	977	17	56.77	59.53
19	1024	7	512	00h	1023	17	59.50	62.39
20	733	5	300	00h	732	17	30.42	31.90
21	733	7	300	00h	732	17	42.59	44.66
22	733	5	300	00h	733	17	30.42	31.90
23	306	4	0	00h	336	17	10.16	10.65
24	0	0	0	00h	0	0	0.00	0.00
25	615	4	0	00h	615	17	20.42	21.41
26	1024	4	65535	00h	1023	17	34.00	35.65
27	1024	5	65535	00h	1023	17	42.50	44.56
28	1024	8	65535	00h	1023	17	68.00	71.30
29	512	8	256	00h	512	17	34.00	35.65
30	615	2	615	00h	615	17	10.21	10.71
31	989	5	0	00h	989	17	41.05	43.04
32	1020	15	65535	08h	1024	17	127.00	133.17
33	0	0	0	00h	0	0	0.00	0.00
34	0	0	0	00h	0	0	0.00	0.00
35	1024	9	1024	08h	1024	17	76.50	80.22
36	1024	5	512	00h	1024	17	42.50	44.56
37	830	10	65535	08h	830	17	68.90	72.24
38	823	10	256	08h	824	17	68.32	71.63
39	615	4	128	00h	664	17	20.42	21.41
40	615	8	128	00h	664	17	40.84	42.82
41	917	15	65535	08h	918	17	114.18	119.72
42	1023	15	65535	08h	1024	17	127.38	133.56
43	823	10	512	08h	823	17	68.32	71.63
44	820	6	65535	00h	820	17	40.84	42.82

Type	*Cyls*	*Heads*	*WPC*	*Ctrl*	*LZ*	*S/T*	*Meg*	*Mb*
45	1024	8	65535	00h	1024	17	68.00	71.30
46	925	9	65535	08h	925	17	69.10	72.46
47	699	7	256	00h	700	17	40.62	42.59

Note: Table entry 15 is reserved to act as a pointer to indicate that the actual type is greater than 15. This BIOS uses Types 48 and 49 as user-definable entries.

Notes: For AT-class system drive tables,

Type = Drive type number

Cyls = Total number of cylinders

Heads = Total number of heads

WPC = Write precompensation starting cylinder

65535 = None

0 = All cylinders

Ctrl = Control byte, values according to the following list:

Bit #		*Hex*		*Meaning*
Bit 0	=	01h	=	Not used (XT = drive step rate)
Bit 1	=	02h	=	Not Used (XT = drive step rate)
Bit 2	=	04h	=	Not Used (XT = drive step rate)
Bit 3	=	08h	=	More than 8 heads
Bit 4	=	10h	=	Not used (XT = embedded servo drive)
Bit 5	=	20h	=	OEM defect map at (cyls + 1)
Bit 6	=	40h	=	Disable ECC retries
Bit 7	=	80h	=	Disable disk access retries

LZ = Landing zone cylinder for head parking

S/T = Number of sectors per track

Meg = Drive capacity in megabytes

Mb = Drive capacity in millions of bytes

IBM ROM BIOS Versions and Their Maximum Usable Hard Disk Type

Table B.10 shows the IBM ROM BIOS versions and date codes indicating the maximum usable drive type value for hard disk support. Refer to the IBM ROM BIOS hard disk drive table (see table B.4) to see the parameters for each type.

Table B.10
IBM ROM BIOS Versions and
Their Maximum Usable Hard Disk Type

System Description	*ROM BIOS Date*	*Maximum Usable Type*
PCjr	06/01/83	N/A
PC	04/24/81	N/A
PC	10/19/81	N/A
PC	10/27/82	N/A
PC Convertible	09/13/85	N/A
PC XT	11/08/82	N/A
PC XT	01/10/86	N/A
PC XT	05/09/86	N/A
PC AT	01/10/84	14
PC AT	06/10/85	23
PC AT	11/15/85	23
PC XT Mod. 286	04/21/86	24
PS/2 Mod. 25	06/26/87	26
PS/2 Mod. 30	09/02/86	26
PS/2 Mod. 30	12/12/86	26
PS/2 Mod. 30	02/05/87	26
PS/1	12/01/89	44

System Description	*ROM BIOS Date*	*Maximum Usable Type*
PS/2 Mod. 30 286	08/25/88	37
PS/2 Mod. 30 286	06/28/89	37
PS/2 Mod. 50	02/13/87	32
PS/2 Mod. 50Z	01/28/88	33
PS/2 Mod. 50Z	04/18/88	33
PS/2 Mod. 55SX	11/02/88	33
PS/2 Mod. 60	02/13/87	32
PS/2 Mod. P70 386 20 Mhz	01/18/89	33
PS/2 Mod. 70 386 16 Mhz	01/29/88	33
PS/2 Mod. 70 386 16 Mhz	04/11/88	33
PS/2 Mod. 70 386 16 Mhz	12/15/89	33
PS/2 Mod. 70 386 20 Mhz	01/29/88	33
PS/2 Mod. 70 386 20 Mhz	04/11/88	33
PS/2 Mod. 70 386 20 Mhz	12/15/89	33
PS/2 Mod. 70 386 25 Mhz	06/08/88	33
PS/2 Mod. 70 386 25 Mhz	02/20/89	33
PS/2 Mod. 70 486 25 Mhz	12/01/89	33
PS/2 Mod. 80 16 Mhz	03/30/87	32
PS/2 Mod. 80 20 Mhz	10/07/87	32
PS/2 Mod. 80 25 Mhz	11/21/89	33

Note: Type 15 is reserved in all systems. XT-class systems do not have hard disk support available (shown as N/A on this chart) in the motherboard BIOS. Support instead resides on the controller and varies by controller make and model.

C

Sector Formats

The tables in this appendix give technical information regarding sector formats, which may be useful to you in your data recovery efforts.

MFM Disk Sector Format

Table C.1 lists a typical MFM disk sector format.

Table C.1
Typical MFM Disk Sector Format

Bytes	*Name*	*Description*
16	Post index gap	All 4Eh, at track beginning after index mark
Sector data format; repeated 17 times for an MFM encoded track		
13	ID VFO lock	All 00h to sync the VFO for the ID
1	Sync byte	A1h to notify controller that data follows
1	Address mark	FEh defining that ID field data follows

continues

Table C.1 *(continued)*

Bytes	*Name*	*Description*
2	Cylinder number	A value defining actuator position
1	Head number	A value defining the head selected
1	Sector number	A value defining the sector
2	CRC	Cyclic redundancy check to verify ID data
3	Write turn-on gap	00h written by format to isolate ID from data
13	Data sync VFO lock	All 00h to sync the VFO for the data
1	Sync byte	A1h to notify controller that data follows
1	Address mark	F8h defining that user data field follows
512	Data	The area for user data
2	CRC	Cyclic redundancy check to verify data
3	Write turn-off gap	00h written by data update to isolate data
15	Inter-record gap	All 00h as a buffer for speed variation
693	Pre index gap	All 4Eh, at track end before index mark
571	Total bytes per sector	
512	Usable bytes per sector	
10,416	Total bytes per track	
8,704	Usable bytes per track	

Master/Extended Partition Boot Sector Table Format

Besides the short piece of program code in the master partition boot sector, the four-entry partition table is important. If the information in the table is corrupted, you cannot access information on disk. The format for this table and the offsets for the values contained within are listed in table C.2. You may be able to use this information to edit a corrupted table and restore it to working order.

Table C.2
Master/Extended Partition Boot Sector Table Format
Partition Table Entry #1

Offset	*Length*	*Description*
1BEh 446	1 byte	Boot indicator byte (80h = active, else 00h)
1BFh 447	1 byte	Starting head (or side) of partition
1C0h 448	16 bits	Starting cylinder (10) and sector (6)
1C2h 450	1 byte	System indicator byte
1C3h 451	1 byte	Ending head (or side) of partition
1C4h 452	16 bits	Ending cylinder (10) and sector (6)
1C6h 454	1 dword	Relative sector offset of partition
1CAh 458	1 dword	Total number of sectors in partition

Partition Table Entry #2

Offset	*Length*	*Description*
1CEh 462	1 byte	Boot indicator byte (80h = active, else 00h)
1CFh 463	1 byte	Starting head (or side) of partition
1D0h 464	16 bits	Starting cylinder (10) and sector (6)
1D2h 466	1 byte	System indicator byte
1D3h 467	1 byte	Ending head (or side) of partition

continues

Partition Table Entry #2 *(continued)*

Offset	*Length*	*Description*
1D4h 468	16 bits	Ending cylinder (10) and sector (6)
1D6h 470	1 dword	Relative sector offset of partition
1DAh 474	1 dword	Total number of sectors in partition

Partition Table Entry #3

Offset	*Length*	*Description*
1DEh 478	1 byte	Boot indicator byte (80h = active, else 00h)
1DFh 479	1 byte	Starting head (or side) of partition
1E0h 480	16 bits	Starting cylinder (10) and sector (6)
1E2h 482	1 byte	System indicator byte
1E3h 483	1 byte	Ending head (or side) of partition
1E4h 484	16 bits	Ending cylinder (10) and sector (6)
1E6h 486	1 dword	Relative sector offset of partition
1EAh 490	1 dword	Total number of sectors in partition

Partition Table Entry #4

Offset	*Length*	*Description*
1EEh 494	1 byte	Boot indicator byte (80h = active, else 00h)
1EFh 495	1 byte	Starting head (or side) of partition
1F0h 496	16 bits	Starting cylinder (10) and sector (6)
1F2h 498	1 byte	System indicator byte
1F3h 499	1 byte	Ending head (or side) of partition
1F4h 500	16 bits	Ending cylinder (10) and sector (6)
1F6h 502	1 dword	Relative sector offset of partition
1FAh 506	1 dword	Total number of sectors in partition

Signature Bytes

Offset	*Length*	*Description*
1FEh 510	2 bytes	Boot sector signature (55AAh)

Note: A "word" equals two bytes read in reverse order, and a "dword" equals two "words" read in reverse order.

Partition Table Cylinder and Sector Field Format

The boot indicator byte must contain 00h for a nonbootable partition or 80h for a bootable partition. Only one partition can be marked as bootable at a time. Table C.3 shows the partition table cylinder and sector field format.

Table C.3
Partition Table Cylinder and Sector Field Format

	Cyl #	*Sector #*	*Cylinder #*
Bit #	F E	D C B A 9 8	7 6 5 4 3 2 1 0
Bit Value	C C	S S S S S S	C C C C C C C C

Partition Table System Indicator Byte Values

The system indicator field contains an indicator of the operating system that "owns" the partition. Table C.4 lists the partition table system indicator byte values.

Table C.4
Partition Table System Indicator Byte Values

Value	*Description*
00h	No partition allocated in this entry
01h	Primary DOS, 12-bit FAT (partition < 16M)
04h	Primary DOS, 16-bit FAT (16M <= partition <= 32M)
05h	Extended DOS (points to next primary partition)
06h	Primary DOS, 16-bit FAT (partition > 32M)
07h	OS/2 HPFS partition
02h	MS-XENIX partition
03h	MS-XENIX user partition
08h	AIX file system partition
09h	AIX boot partition
50h	Ontrack Disk Manager read-only partition
51h	Ontrack Disk Manager read/write partition
56h	Golden Bow Vfeature partition
61h	Storage Dimensions Speedstor partition
63h	IBM 386/ix or UNIX System V/386 partition
64h	Novell NetWare partition
75h	IBM PCIX partition
DBh	Digital Research concurrent DOS/CPM-86 partition
F2h	Some OEM's DOS 3.2+ second partition
FFh	UNIX bad block table partition

Generic Hard Disk Master Partition Boot Sector

Figure C.1 shows a generic hard disk master partition boot sector, or MPBS. You can use this information to restore a damaged master partition boot sector program, because the program shown here functions for all DOS versions and most system configurations.

```
Generic Hard Disk Master Partition Boot Sector (MPBS):

Hexadecimal Byte Values                                          ASCII Text
       0  1  2  3  4  5  6  7  8  9  A  B  C  D  E  F            0123456789ABCDEF
===============================================================================
000   FA 33 C0 8E D0 BC 00 7C-8B F4 50 07 50 1F FB FC            .3.....|..P.P...
010   BF 00 06 B9 00 01 F2 A5-EA 1D 06 00 00 BE BE 07            ................
020   B3 04 80 3C 80 74 0E 80-3C 00 75 1C 83 C6 10 FE            ...<.t..<.u.....
030   CB 75 EF CD 18 8B 14 8B-4C 02 8B EE 83 C6 10 FE            .u......L.......
040   CB 74 1A 80 3C 00 74 F4-BE 8B 06 AC 3C 00 74 0B            .t..<.t.....<.t.
050   56 BB 07 00 B4 0E CD 10-5E EB F0 EB FE BF 05 00            V.......^.......
060   BB 00 7C B8 01 02 57 CD-13 5F 73 0C 33 C0 CD 13            ..|...W.._s.3...
070   4F 75 ED BE A3 06 EB D3-BE C2 06 BF FE 7D 81 3D            Ou...........}.=
080   55 AA 75 C7 8B F5 EA 00-7C 00 00 49 6E 76 61 6C            U.u.....|..Inval
090   69 64 20 70 61 72 74 69-74 69 6F 6E 20 74 61 62            id partition tab
0A0   6C 65 00 45 72 72 6F 72-20 6C 6F 61 64 69 6E 67            le.Error loading
0B0   20 6F 70 65 72 61 74 69-6E 67 20 73 79 73 74 65             operating syste
0C0   6D 00 4D 69 73 73 69 6E-67 20 6F 70 65 72 61 74            m.Missing operat
0D0   69 6E 67 20 73 79 73 74-65 6D 00 00 00 00 00 00            ing system......
0E0   00 00 00 00 00 00 00 00-00 00 00 00 00 00 00 00            ................
0F0   00 00 00 00 00 00 00 00-00 00 00 00 00 00 00 00            ................
100   00 00 00 00 00 00 00 00-00 00 00 00 00 00 00 00            ................
110   00 00 00 00 00 00 00 00-00 00 00 00 00 00 00 00            ................
120   00 00 00 00 00 00 00 00-00 00 00 00 00 00 00 00            ................
130   00 00 00 00 00 00 00 00-00 00 00 00 00 00 00 00            ................
140   00 00 00 00 00 00 00 00-00 00 00 00 00 00 00 00            ................
150   00 00 00 00 00 00 00 00-00 00 00 00 00 00 00 00            ................
160   00 00 00 00 00 00 00 00-00 00 00 00 00 00 00 00            ................
170   00 00 00 00 00 00 00 00-00 00 00 00 00 00 00 00            ................
180   00 00 00 00 00 00 00 00-00 00 00 00 00 00 00 00            ................
190   00 00 00 00 00 00 00 00-00 00 00 00 00 00 00 00            ................
1A0   00 00 00 00 00 00 00 00-00 00 00 00 00 00 00 00            ................
1B0   00 00 00 00 00 00 00 00-00 00 00 00 00 00 ≡1 ≡1            ..............≡≡
1C0   ≡1 ≡1 ≡1 ≡1 ≡1 ≡1 ≡1 ≡1-≡1 ≡1 ≡1 ≡1 ≡1 ≡1 ≡2 ≡2            ≡≡≡≡≡≡≡≡≡≡≡≡≡≡≡≡
1D0   ≡2 ≡2 ≡2 ≡2 ≡2 ≡2 ≡2 ≡2-≡2 ≡2 ≡2 ≡2 ≡2 ≡2 ≡3 ≡3            ≡≡≡≡≡≡≡≡≡≡≡≡≡≡≡≡
1E0   ≡3 ≡3 ≡3 ≡3 ≡3 ≡3 ≡3 ≡3-≡3 ≡3 ≡3 ≡3 ≡3 ≡3 ≡4 ≡4            ≡≡≡≡≡≡≡≡≡≡≡≡≡≡≡≡
1F0   ≡4 ≡4 ≡4 ≡4 ≡4 ≡4 ≡4 ≡4-≡4 ≡4 ≡4 ≡4 ≡4 ≡4 55 AA            ≡≡≡≡≡≡≡≡≡≡≡≡≡≡U.

NOTE: "≡1" through "≡4" indicate the locations of each of the
four partition table entries, whose values will differ from disk
to disk.
```

Fig. C.1. A generic hard disk master partition boot sector.

DOS Volume Boot Sector Format

Table C.5 lists the DOS volume boot (DVB) sector format.

Table C.5
DOS Volume Boot Sector Format

Offset Hex	Dec	Field Length	Description
00h	0	3 bytes	Jump instruction to boot program code
03h	3	8 bytes	OEM name and DOS version (“IBM 4.0”)
0Bh	11	1 word	Bytes/sector (usually 512)

continues

Table C.5 *(continued)*

Offset Hex	*Dec*	*Field Length*	*Description*
0Dh	13	1 byte	Sectors/cluster (must be a power of 2)
0Eh	14	1 word	Reserved sectors (boot sectors—usually 1)
10h	16	1 byte	FAT copies (usually 2)
11h	17	1 word	Maximum root directory entries (usually 512)
13h	19	1 word	Total sectors (if partition <= 32M, else 0)
15h	21	1 byte	Media descriptor byte (F8h for hard disks)
16h	22	1 word	Sectors/FAT
18h	24	1 word	Sectors/track
1Ah	26	1 word	Number of heads
1Ch	28	1 dword	Hidden sectors (if partition <= 32M, 1 word only)
The following information is for DOS 4.0 and later versions, else 00h:			
20h	32	1 dword	Total sectors (if partition > 32M, else 0)
24h	36	1 byte	Physical drive number (00h=floppy, 80h=hard disk)
25h	37	1 byte	Reserved (00h)
26h	38	1 byte	Extended boot record signature (29h)
27h	39	1 dword	Volume serial number
2Bh	43	11 bytes	Volume label ("NO NAME " stored if no label)
36h	54	8 bytes	File system ID ("FAT12 " or "FAT16 ")
The following information applies to all DOS versions:			
3Eh	62	450 bytes	Boot program code
1FEh	510	2 bytes	Signature bytes (55AAh)

Note: A "word" is two bytes read in reverse order, and a "dword" is two "words" read in reverse order.

DOS 3.3 Generic Volume Boot Sector Program

Figure C.2 shows an example of a DOS 3.3 generic volume boot sector program. You can use this information to restore a damaged DOS 3.3 volume boot sector program.

```
DOS 3.30 Generic Volume Boot Sector:

Hexadecimal Byte Values                                  ASCII Text
      0  1  2  3  4  5  6  7  8  9  A  B  C  D  E  F     0123456789ABCDEF
=============================================================================
000   EB 34 90 49 42 4D 20 20-33 2E 33 == == == == ==    .4.IBM  3.3=====
010   == == == == == == == ==-== == == == == == 00 00    ==============..
020   00 00 00 00 00 00 00 00-00 00 00 00 00 00 00 12    ................
030   00 00 00 00 01 00 FA 33-C0 8E D0 BC 00 7C 16 07    .......3.....|..
040   BB 78 00 36 C5 37 1E 56-16 53 BF 2B 7C B9 0B 00    .x.6.7.V.S.+|...
050   FC AC 26 80 3D 00 74 03-26 8A 05 AA 8A C4 E2 F1    ..&.=.t.&.......
060   06 1F 89 47 02 C7 07 2B-7C FB CD 13 72 67 A0 10    ...G...+|...rg..
070   7C 98 F7 26 16 7C 03 06-1C 7C 03 06 0E 7C A3 3F    |..&.|...|...|.?
080   7C A3 37 7C B8 20 00 F7-26 11 7C 8B 1E 0B 7C 03    |.7|.  ..&.|...|.
090   C3 48 F7 F3 01 06 37 7C-BB 00 05 A1 3F 7C E8 9F    .H....7|....?|..
0A0   00 B8 01 02 E8 B3 00 72-19 8B FB B9 0B 00 BE D6    .......r........
0B0   7D F3 A6 75 0D 8D 7F 20-BE E1 7D B9 0B 00 F3 A6    }..u... ..}.....
0C0   74 18 BE 77 7D E8 6A 00-32 E4 CD 16 5E 1F 8F 04    t..w}.j.2...^...
0D0   8F 44 02 CD 19 BE C0 7D-EB EB A1 1C 05 33 D2 F7    .D.....}.....3..
0E0   36 0B 7C FE C0 A2 3C 7C-A1 37 7C A3 3D 7C BB 00    6.|...<|.7|.=|..
0F0   07 A1 37 7C E8 49 00 A1-18 7C 2A 06 3B 7C 40 38    ..7|.I...|*.;|@8
100   06 3C 7C 73 03 A0 3C 7C-50 E8 4E 00 58 72 C6 28    .<|s..<|P.N.Xr.(
110   06 3C 7C 74 0C 01 06 37-7C F7 26 0B 7C 03 D8 EB    .<|t...7|.&.|...
120   D0 8A 2E 15 7C 8A 16 FD-7D 8B 1E 3D 7C EA 00 00    ....|...}..=|...
130   70 00 AC 0A C0 74 22 B4-0E BB 07 00 CD 10 EB F2    p....t".........
140   33 D2 F7 36 18 7C FE C2-88 16 3B 7C 33 D2 F7 36    3..6.|....;|3..6
150   1A 7C 88 16 2A 7C A3 39-7C C3 B4 02 8B 16 39 7C    .|..*|.9|.....9|
160   B1 06 D2 E6 0A 36 3B 7C-8B CA 86 E9 8A 16 FD 7D    .....6;|.......}
170   8A 36 2A 7C CD 13 C3 0D-0A 4E 6F 6E 2D 53 79 73    .6*|.....Non-Sys
180   74 65 6D 20 64 69 73 6B-20 6F 72 20 64 69 73 6B    tem disk or disk
190   20 65 72 72 6F 72 0D 0A-52 65 70 6C 61 63 65 20     error..Replace
1A0   61 6E 64 20 73 74 72 69-6B 65 20 61 6E 79 20 6B    and strike any k
1B0   65 79 20 77 68 65 6E 20-72 65 61 64 79 0D 0A 00    ey when ready...
1C0   0D 0A 44 69 73 6B 20 42-6F 6F 74 20 66 61 69 6C    ..Disk Boot fail
1D0   75 72 65 0D 0A 00 49 42-4D 42 49 4F 20 20 43 4F    ure...IBMBIO  CO
1E0   4D 49 42 4D 44 4F 53 20-20 43 4F 4D 00 00 00 00    MIBMDOS  COM....
1F0   00 00 00 00 00 00 00 00-00 00 00 00 00 00 55 AA    ..............U.

     "==" values indicate the area occupied by the Disk Parameter
Block, which will differ in actual values from disk to disk.
```

Fig. C.2. *A DOS 3.3 generic volume boot sector program.*

DOS 4.xx Generic Volume Boot Sector Program

Figure C.3 shows an example of a DOS 4.xx generic volume boot sector program. You can use this information to restore a damaged DOS 4.xx volume boot sector program.

```
DOS 4.xx Generic Volume Boot Sector:

Hexadecimal Byte Values                                           ASCII Text
       0  1  2  3  4  5  6  7  8  9  A  B  C  D  E  F             0123456789ABCDEF
-----------------------------------------------------------------------------------
000    EB 3C 90 49 42 4D 20 20-34 2E 30 == == == == ==            .<.IBM  4.0=====
010    == == == == == == == ==-== == == == == == == ==            ================
020    == == == == == == == ==-== == == == == == == ==            ================
030    == == == == == == == ==-== == == == == == FA 33            ==============.3
040    C0 8E D0 BC 00 7C 16 07-BB 78 00 36 C5 37 1E 56            .....|...x.6.7.V
050    16 53 BF 3E 7C B9 0B 00-FC F3 A4 06 1F C6 45 FE            .S.>|.........E.
060    0F 8B 0E 18 7C 88 4D F9-89 47 02 C7 07 3E 7C FB            ....|.M..G...>|.
070    CD 13 72 7C 33 C0 39 06-13 7C 74 08 8B 0E 13 7C            ..r|3.9..|t....|
080    89 0E 20 7C A0 10 7C F7-26 16 7C 03 06 1C 7C 13            .. |..|.&.|...|.
090    16 1E 7C 03 06 0E 7C 83-D2 00 A3 50 7C 89 16 52            ..|...|....P|..R
0A0    7C A3 49 7C 89 16 4B 7C-B8 20 00 F7 26 11 7C 8B            |.I|..K|. ..&.|.
0B0    1E 0B 7C 03 C3 48 F7 F3-01 06 49 7C 83 16 4B 7C            ..|..H....I|..K|
0C0    00 BB 00 05 8B 16 52 7C-A1 50 7C E8 87 00 72 20            ......R|.P|...r
0D0    B0 01 E8 A1 00 72 19 8B-FB B9 0B 00 BE DB 7D F3            .....r.........}.
0E0    A6 75 0D 8D 7F 20 BE E6-7D B9 0B 00 F3 A6 74 18            .u... ..}.....t.
0F0    BE 93 7D E8 51 00 32 E4-CD 16 5E 1F 8F 04 8F 44            ..}.Q.2...^....D
100    02 CD 19 58 58 58 EB E8-BB 00 07 B9 03 00 A1 49            ...XXX.........I
110    7C 8B 16 4B 7C 50 52 51-E8 3A 00 72 E6 B0 01 E8            |..K|PRQ.:.r....
120    54 00 59 5A 58 72 C9 05-01 00 83 D2 00 03 1E 0B            T.YZXr..........
130    7C E2 E2 8A 2E 15 7C 8A-16 24 7C 8B 1E 49 7C A1            |.....|..$|..I|.
140    4B 7C EA 00 00 70 00 AC-0A C0 74 29 B4 0E BB 07            K|...p....t)....
150    00 CD 10 EB F2 3B 16 18-7C 73 19 F7 36 18 7C FE            .....;..|s..6.|.
160    C2 88 16 4F 7C 33 D2 F7-36 1A 7C 88 16 25 7C A3            ...O|3..6.|..%|.
170    4D 7C F8 C3 F9 C3 B4 02-8B 16 4D 7C B1 06 D2 E6            M|........M|....
180    0A 36 4F 7C 8B CA 86 E9-8A 16 24 7C 8A 36 25 7C            .6O|......$|.6%|
190    CD 13 C3 0D 0A 4E 6F 6E-2D 53 79 73 74 65 6D 20            .....Non-System
1A0    64 69 73 6B 20 6F 72 20-64 69 73 6B 20 65 72 72            disk or disk err
1B0    6F 72 0D 0A 52 65 70 6C-61 63 65 20 61 6E 64 20            or..Replace and
1C0    70 72 65 73 73 20 61 6E-79 20 6B 65 79 20 77 68            press any key wh
1D0    65 6E 20 72 65 61 64 79-0D 0A 00 49 42 4D 42 49            en ready...IBMBI
1E0    4F 20 20 43 4F 4D 49 42-4D 44 4F 53 20 20 43 4F            O  COMIBMDOS  CO
1F0    4D 00 00 00 00 00 00 00-00 00 00 00 00 00 55 AA            M.............U.

     "==" values indicate the area occupied by the Disk Parameter
Block, which will differ in actual values from disk to disk.
```

Fig. C.3. *A DOS 4.xx generic volume boot sector program.*

DOS 5.xx Generic Volume Boot Sector Program

Figure C.4 shows an example of a DOS 5.xx generic volume boot sector program. You can use this information to restore a damaged DOS 5.xx volume boot sector program.

```
DOS 5.xx Generic Volume Boot Sector:

Hexadecimal Byte Values                                    ASCII Text
      0  1  2  3  4  5  6  7  8  9  A  B  C  D  E  F       0123456789ABCDEF
================================================================================
000  EB 3C 90 49 42 4D 20 20-34 2E 30 == == == == ==      .<.IBM  5.0=====
010  == == == == == == == ==-== == == == == == == ==      ================
020  == == == == == == == ==-== == == == == == == ==      ================
030  == == == == == == == ==-== == == == == == FA 33      ==============.3
040  C0 8E D0 BC 00 7C 16 07-BB 78 00 36 C5 37 1E 56      .....|...x.6.7.V
050  16 53 BF 3E 7C B9 0B 00-FC F3 A4 06 1F C6 45 FE      .S.>|.........E.
060  0F 8B 0E 18 7C 88 4D F9-89 47 02 C7 07 3E 7C FB      ....|.M..G...>|.
070  CD 13 72 7C 33 C0 39 06-13 7C 74 08 8B 0E 13 7C      ..r|3.9..|t....|
080  89 0E 20 7C A0 10 7C F7-26 16 7C 03 06 1C 7C 13      .. |..|.&.|...|.
090  16 1E 7C 03 06 0E 7C 83-D2 00 A3 50 7C 89 16 52      ..|...|....P|..R
0A0  7C A3 49 7C 89 16 4B 7C-B8 20 00 F7 26 11 7C 8B      |.I|..K|. ..&.|.
0B0  1E 0B 7C 03 C3 48 F7 F3-01 06 49 7C 83 16 4B 7C      ..|..H....I|..K|
0C0  00 BB 00 05 8B 16 52 7C-A1 50 7C E8 87 00 72 20      ......R|.P|...r
0D0  B0 01 E8 A1 00 72 19 8B-FB B9 0B 00 BE DB 7D F3      .....r.........}.
0E0  A6 75 0D 8D 7F 20 BE E6-7D B9 0B 00 F3 A6 74 18      .u... ..}.....t.
0F0  BE 93 7D E8 51 00 32 E4-CD 16 5E 1F 8F 04 8F 44      ..}.Q.2...'....D
100  02 CD 19 58 58 58 EB E8-BB 00 07 B9 03 00 A1 49      ...XXX.........I
110  7C 8B 16 4B 7C 50 52 51-E8 3A 00 72 E6 B0 01 E8      |..K|PRQ.:.r....
120  54 00 59 5A 58 72 C9 05-01 00 83 D2 00 03 1E 0B      T.YZXr..........
130  7C E2 E2 8A 2E 15 7C 8A-16 24 7C 8B 1E 49 7C A1      |.....|..$|..I|.
140  4B 7C EA 00 00 70 00 AC-0A C0 74 29 B4 0E BB 07      K|...p....t)....
150  00 CD 10 EB F2 3B 16 18-7C 73 19 F7 36 18 7C FE      .....;..|s..6.|.
160  C2 88 16 4F 7C 33 D2 F7-36 1A 7C 88 16 25 7C A3      ...O|3..6.|..%|.
170  4D 7C F8 C3 F9 C3 B4 02-8B 16 4D 7C B1 06 D2 E6      M|.........M|....
180  0A 36 4F 7C 8B CA 86 E9-8A 16 24 7C 8A 36 25 7C      .6O|......$|.6%|
190  CD 13 C3 0D 0A 4E 6F 6E-2D 53 79 73 74 65 6D 20      .....Non-System
1A0  64 69 73 6B 20 6F 72 20-64 69 73 6B 20 65 72 72      disk or disk err
1B0  6F 72 0D 0A 52 65 70 6C-61 63 65 20 61 6E 64 20      or..Replace and
1C0  70 72 65 73 73 20 61 6E-79 20 6B 65 79 20 77 68      press any key wh
1D0  65 6E 20 72 65 61 64 79-0D 0A 00 49 42 4D 42 49      en ready...IBMBI
1E0  4F 20 20 43 4F 4D 49 42-4D 44 4F 53 20 20 43 4F      O  COMIBMDOS  CO
1F0  4D 00 00 00 00 00 00 00-00 00 00 00 00 00 55 AA      M.............U.

     "==" values indicate the area occupied by the Disk Parameter
Block, which will differ in actual values from disk to disk.
```

Fig. C.4. *A DOS 5.xx generic volume boot sector.*

DOS Structure Formats

This section examines the DOS directory structure and format, DOS directory file attribute byte format, and file time and date creation maps.

DOS Directory Structure and Format

DOS directory entries are 32 bytes long and in the format shown it table C.6.

Table C.6
DOS Directory Format

Offset Hex	*Dec*	*Field Length*	*Description*
00h	0	8 bytes	File name
08h	8	3 bytes	File extension
0Bh	11	1 byte	File attributes
0Ch	12	10 bytes	Reserved
16h	22	1 word	Time of creation
18h	24	1 word	Date of creation
1Ah	26	1 word	Starting cluster
1Ch	28	1 dword	Size in bytes

Note: File names and extensions are left-aligned and padded with blanks. The first byte of the file name indicates the file status as follows:

00h	Entry is never used; entries past this point not searched.
05h	First character of file name is actually E5h.
E5h	File has been erased.
2Eh	Entry is a directory. If the second byte is also 2Eh, the cluster field contains the cluster number of parent directory (0000h if the parent is the root).

DOS Directory File Attribute Byte Format

Table C.7 lists the DOS directory file attribute byte.

Table C.7
DOS Directory File Attribute Byte

Bit Positions *7 6 5 4 3 2 1 0*	*Hex Value*	*Description*
0 0 0 0 0 0 0 1	01h	Read-only file
0 0 0 0 0 0 1 0	02h	Hidden file
0 0 0 0 0 1 0 0	04h	System file
0 0 0 0 1 0 0 0	08h	Volume label
0 0 0 1 0 0 0 0	10h	Subdirectory
0 0 1 0 0 0 0 0	20h	Archive (updated since backup)
0 1 0 0 0 0 0 0	40h	Reserved
1 0 0 0 0 0 0 0	80h	Reserved

The following examples illustrate the use of the file attribute byte:

0 0 1 0 0 0 0 1	21h	Read only, archive
0 0 1 1 0 0 1 0	32h	Hidden, subdirectory, archive
0 0 1 0 0 1 1 1	27h	Read only, hidden, system, archive

File Time of Creation

This word contains the time when the file was created or last updated. The time is mapped in binary to the bits, as shown in figure C.5.

```
<----- Offset 23-------------><------ Offset 22----------->
15 14 13 12 11 | 10  9  8  7  6  5 | 4  3  2  1  0
 H  H  H  H  H |  M  M  M  M  M  M | s  s  s  s  s
  hours 0-23   |   minutes 0-59    | No. 2-sec units
```

Fig. C.5. File time of creation map.

File Date of Creation

This word contains the date when the file was created or last updated. The date is mapped in binary to the bits, as shown in figure C.6.

```
<------ Offset 25 -------><------ Offset 24 ------->
15 14 13 12 11 10  9 |  8  7  6  5 |  4  3  2  1  0
 Y  Y  Y  Y  Y  Y  Y |  M  M  M  M |  D  D  D  D  D
 0-119 (1980-2099)   | Month 1-12  |   Day 1-31
```

Fig. C.6. File date of creation map.

DOS Disk Boot Sector and FAT ID Bytes (Media Descriptor)

Table C.8 lists the volume boot sector and FAT media descriptor bytes.

Table C.8
Volume Boot Sector and FAT Media Descriptor Bytes

Disk Type	*Hard Disk*	*Floppy Disks*						
Disk size (in.)	-	3 1/2	3 1/2	5 1/4	5 1/4	5 1/4	5 1/4	5 1/4
Disk capacity (K)	-	1440	720	1200	180	360	160	320
Media descriptor byte	F8h	F0h	F9h	F9h	FCh	FDh	FEh	FFh
Sides (heads)	-	2	2	2	1	2	1	2
Tracks/side	-	80	80	80	40	40	40	40
Sectors/track	-	18	9	15	9	9	8	8
Bytes/sector	-	512	512	512	512	512	512	512

Note: Beginning with DOS 2.0, the function of these boot sector or FAT ID bytes has been replaced by the volume boot sector disk parameter block.

Numeric entries in a FAT may be any of the following:

(0)000	Unused cluster (available).
(F)FF0-(F)FF6	Reserved cluster (not available).
(F)FF7	Bad cluster (not available).
(F)FF8-(F)FFF	Last cluster in a particular file.
(0)002-(F)FEF	Any value in this range indicates that the cluster is in use by a file, and the number itself indicates the next cluster occupied by this file.

Numeric entries usually used in a FAT are as follows:

(0)000	Unused cluster (available).
(F)FF7	Bad cluster (not available).
(F)FFF	Last cluster in a particular file.
(0)002-(F)FEF	Any value in this range indicates that this cluster is in use by a file, and the number itself indicates the next cluster occupied by this file.

Note that a 16-bit FAT uses the full four-digit hex number but a 12-bit FAT uses only the three-digit portion minus the leading digit in the parentheses.

Floppy and Hard Disk Default Cluster Sizes

Table C.9 lists the DOS default cluster/allocation unit sizes.

Table C.9
DOS Default Cluster/Allocation Unit Sizes

Disk or Volume Size	*Cluster/Allocation Unit Size*	*FAT Type*
5 1/4-inch/360K	2 sectors or 1,024 bytes	12-bit
5 1/4-inch/1.2M	1 sector or 512 bytes	12-bit
3 1/2-inch/720K	2 sectors or 1,024 bytes	12-bit
3 1/2-inch/1.44M	1 sector or 512 bytes	12-bit
0M < volume < 16M	8 sectors or 4,096 bytes	12-bit
16M ≤ volume ≤ 128M	4 sectors or 2,048 bytes	16-bit
128M < volume ≤ 256M	8 sectors or 4,096 bytes	16-bit
256M < volume ≤ 512M	16 sectors or 8,192 bytes	16-bit
512M < volume ≤ 1,024M	32 sectors or 16,384 bytes	16-bit
1,024M < volume ≤ 2,048M	64 sectors or 32,768 bytes	16-bit

Note that K equals 1,024 bytes and M equals 1,048,576 bytes.

D

Disk Maps

Floppy Disk Drive Maps

Table D.1 lists the DOS floppy disk layout parameters.

Table D.1
Floppy Disk Parameters

	Current Formats				*Obsolete Formats*		
Disk size (in.)	5 1/4	5 1/4	3 1/2	3 1/2	5 1/4	5 1/4	5 1/4
Disk capacity (K)	360	1200	720	1440	160	180	320
Media descriptor byte	FDh	F9h	F9h	F0h	FEh	FCh	FFh
Sides (heads)	2	2	2	2	1	1	2
Tracks/side	40	80	80	80	40	40	40
Sectors/track	9	15	9	18	8	9	8
Bytes/sector	512	512	512	512	512	512	512
Sectors/cluster	2	1	2	1	1	1	2
Boot sector size	1	1	1	1	1	1	1

continues

Table D.1 *(continued)*

	Current Formats				*Obsolete Formats*		
FAT size	2	7	3	9	1	2	1
Number of FATs	2	2	2	2	2	2	2
Root directory size	7	14	7	14	4	4	7
Maximum root entries	112	224	112	224	64	64	112
Total sectors/disk	720	2400	1440	2880	320	360	640
Total available sectors	708	2371	1426	2847	313	351	630
Total available clusters	354	2371	713	2847	313	351	315

Figure D.1 shows the drive map for floppy disks of type 01 (360K) formatted under MS-DOS as follows:

Drive type:	5 1/4-inch double-density 360K floppy
Drive geometry:	40 cylinders, 2 heads, 9 sectors/track
DOS version:	IBM or MS-DOS 2.0 or later
DVB:	Cylinder 0, head 0, sector 1; DOS sector 0
FAT #1:	Sectors 1-2; 2 sectors long
FAT #2:	Sectors 3-4; 2 sectors long
Root directory:	Sectors 5-11; 7 sectors long (112 entries)
Data area:	Sectors 12-719; clusters 2-355
Cluster size:	2 sectors (1,024 bytes)

Notes:

DVB = DOS volume boot sector
FAT = file allocation table

```
        BIOS Sector # (INT 13h)
Cyl Hd   1      2      3      4      5      6      7      8      9
 0  0 | DVB  |   FAT #1    |   FAT #2    | ROOT DIR (112 Entries;-->  |
      |  0   |  1   |  2   |  3   |  4   |  5   |  6   |  7   |  8   | <-DOS
    1 | <-- 7 Sectors)     | Cluster  2  | Cluster  3  | Cluster  4  |   Sector #
      |  9   |  10  |  11  | 12   -  13  | 14   -  15  | 16   -  17  | (INT 25/26h)
 1  0 | Cluster  5  | Cluster  6  | Cluster  7  | Cluster  8  | Clus-| <-Cluster #
      | 18   -  19  | 20   -  21  | 22   -  23  | 24   -  25  |  26  |   (INT 21h)
    1 |-ter 9| Cluster 10  | Cluster 11  | Cluster 12  | Cluster 13  |
      |  27  | 28   -  29  | 30   -  31  | 32   -  33  | 34   -  35  |

  . The rest of the disk follows the same Cluster/Sector pattern .

39  0 | Cluster 347 | Cluster 348 | Cluster 349 | Cluster 350 |Clust-|
      | 702  -  703 | 704  -  705 | 706  -  707 | 708  -  709 |  710 |
    1 |  351 | Cluster 352 | Cluster 353 | Cluster 354 | Cluster 355 |
      |  711 | 712  -  713 | 714  -  715 | 716  -  717 | 718  -  719 |
```

***Fig. D.1.** Disk map for 5.25-inch 360K floppy disk.*

Figure D.2 shows the drive map for floppy disks of type 02 (1.2M) formatted under MS-DOS as follows:

Drive type:	5 1/4-inch high-density 1.2M floppy
Drive geometry:	80 cylinders, 2 heads, 15 sectors/track
DOS version:	IBM or MS-DOS 3.0 or later (through 5.x)
DVB:	Cylinder 0, head 0, sector 1; DOS sector 0
FAT #1:	Sectors 1-7; 7 sectors long
FAT #2:	Sectors 8-14; 7 sectors long
Root directory:	Sectors 15-28; 14 sectors long (224 entries)
Data area:	Sectors 29-2399; clusters 2-2372
Cluster size:	1 sector (512 bytes)

Notes:

DVB = DOS volume boot sector
FAT = file allocation table

BIOS Sector # (INT 13h)

Cyl	Hd	1	2	3	4	5	6	7	8	9	10	11	12	13	14	15	
0	0	DVB	← FAT #1 (7 Sectors, 1-7) →							← FAT #2 (7 Sectors, 8-14) →							
		0	1	2	3	4	5	6	7	8	9	10	11	12	13	14	←DOS Sector # (INT 25/26h)
	1	← ROOT DIRECTORY (224 Entries; 14 Sectors, 15-28) →														2	
		15	16	17	18	19	20	21	22	23	24	25	26	27	28	29	
1	0	3 30	4 31	5 32	6 33	7 34	8 35	9 36	10 37	11 38	12 39	13 40	14 41	15 42	16 43	17 44	←Cluster # (INT 21h)
	1	18 45	19 46	20 47	21 48	22 49	23 50	24 51	25 52	26 53	27 54	28 55	29 56	30 57	31 58	32 59	
		The remainder of the disk follows the same Cluster/Sector pattern.															
79	0	2343 2370	2344 2371	2345 2372	2346 2373	2347 2374	2348 2375	2349 2376	2350 2377	2351 2378	2352 2379	2353 2380	2354 2381	2355 2382	2356 2383	2357 2384	
	1	2358 2385	2359 2386	2360 2387	2361 2388	2362 2389	2363 2390	2364 2391	2365 2392	2366 2393	2367 2394	2368 2395	2369 2396	2370 2397	2371 2398	2372 2399	

Fig. D.2. *Disk map for 5.25-inch 1.2M floppy disk.*

Figure D.3 shows the drive map for floppy disks of type 03 (720K) formatted under MS-DOS as follows:

Drive type:	3 1/2-inch double-density 720K floppy
Drive geometry:	80 cylinders, 2 heads, 9 sectors/track
DOS version:	IBM or MS-DOS 3.2 or later
DVB:	Cylinder 0, head 0, sector 1; DOS sector 0
FAT #1:	Sectors 1-3; 3 sectors long
FAT #2:	Sectors 4-6; 3 sectors long
Root directory:	Sectors 7-13; 7 sectors long (112 entries)
Data area:	Sectors 14-1439; clusters 2-714
Cluster size:	2 sectors (1,024 bytes)

Notes:

DVB = DOS volume boot sector
FAT = file allocation table

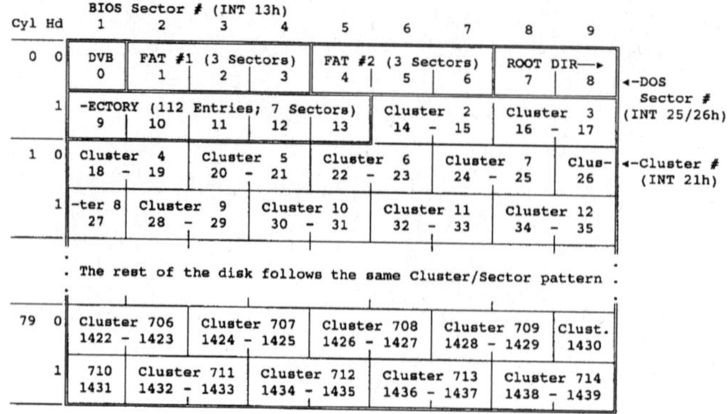

Fig. D.3. Disk map for 3.5-inch 720K floppy disk.

Figure D.4 shows the drive map for floppy disks of type 04 (1.44M) formatted under MS-DOS as follows:

Drive type:	3 1/2-inch high-density 1.44M floppy
Drive geometry:	80 cylinders, 2 heads, 18 sectors/track
DOS version:	IBM or MS-DOS 3.3 or later
DVB:	Cylinder 0, head 0, sector 1; DOS sector 0
FAT #1:	Sectors 1-9; 9 sectors long
FAT #2:	Sectors 10-18; 9 sectors long
Root directory:	Sectors 19-32; 14 sectors long (224 entries)
Data area:	Sectors 33-2879; clusters 2-2848
Cluster size:	1 sector (512 bytes)

Notes:

DVB = DOS volume boot sector
FAT = file allocation table

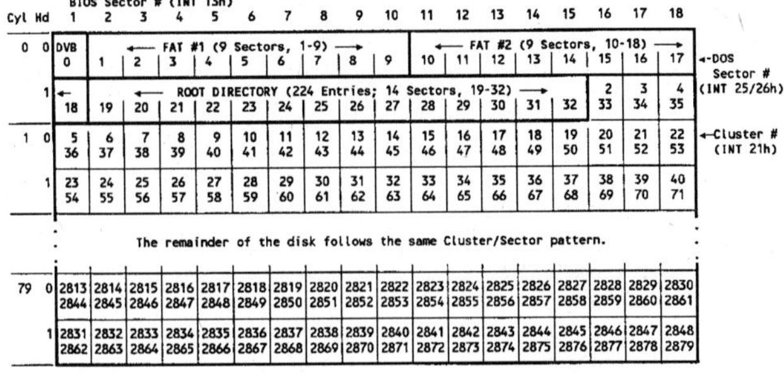

Cyl	Hd	1	2	3	4	5	6	7	8	9	10	11	12	13	14	15	16	17	18	
		BIOS Sector # (INT 13h)																		
0	0	DVB 0	← FAT #1 (9 Sectors, 1-9) → 1	2	3	4	5	6	7	8	9	← FAT #2 (9 Sectors, 10-18) → 10	11	12	13	14	15	16	17	←DOS Sector # (INT 25/26h)
	1	← 18	← ROOT DIRECTORY (224 Entries; 14 Sectors, 19-32) → 19	20	21	22	23	24	25	26	27	28	29	30	31	32	2 33	3 34	4 35	
1	0	5 36	6 37	7 38	8 39	9 40	10 41	11 42	12 43	13 44	14 45	15 46	16 47	17 48	18 49	19 50	20 51	21 52	22 53	←Cluster # (INT 21h)
	1	23 54	24 55	25 56	26 57	27 58	28 59	29 60	30 61	31 62	32 63	33 64	34 65	35 66	36 67	37 68	38 69	39 70	40 71	
		The remainder of the disk follows the same Cluster/Sector pattern.																		
79	0	2813 2844	2814 2845	2815 2846	2816 2847	2817 2848	2818 2849	2819 2850	2820 2851	2821 2852	2822 2853	2823 2854	2824 2855	2825 2856	2826 2857	2827 2858	2828 2859	2829 2860	2830 2861	
	1	2831 2862	2832 2863	2833 2864	2834 2865	2835 2866	2836 2867	2837 2868	2838 2869	2839 2870	2840 2871	2841 2872	2842 2873	2843 2874	2844 2875	2845 2876	2846 2877	2847 2878	2848 2879	

Fig. D.4. Disk map for 3.5-inch 1.44M floppy disk.

Hard Disk Drive Maps

Figure D.5 shows the disk map for a typical 10M hard drive (DOS 2.x) partitioned as a single MS-DOS volume as follows:

Drive type:	1, 23, 25, or 29 (IBM BIOS)
Drive geometry:	306 cylinders, 4 heads, 17 sectors/track (ST-506/412 MFM)
Drive capacity:	10.65 million bytes, or 10.16M
DOS version:	IBM or MS-DOS 2.0 or later
Hidden sectors:	1 (FDISK 2.x) including master partition boot sector
DVB:	Cylinder 0, head 0, sector 2; DOS sector 0
FAT #1:	Sectors 1-8; 8 sectors long
FAT #2:	Sectors 9-16; 8 sectors long
Root directory:	Sectors 17-48; 32 sectors long
Data area:	Sectors 49-20,736; clusters 2-2587
Cluster size:	8 sectors (4,096 bytes)

Notes:

MPB = master partition boot sector
DVB = DOS volume boot sector
FAT = file allocation table

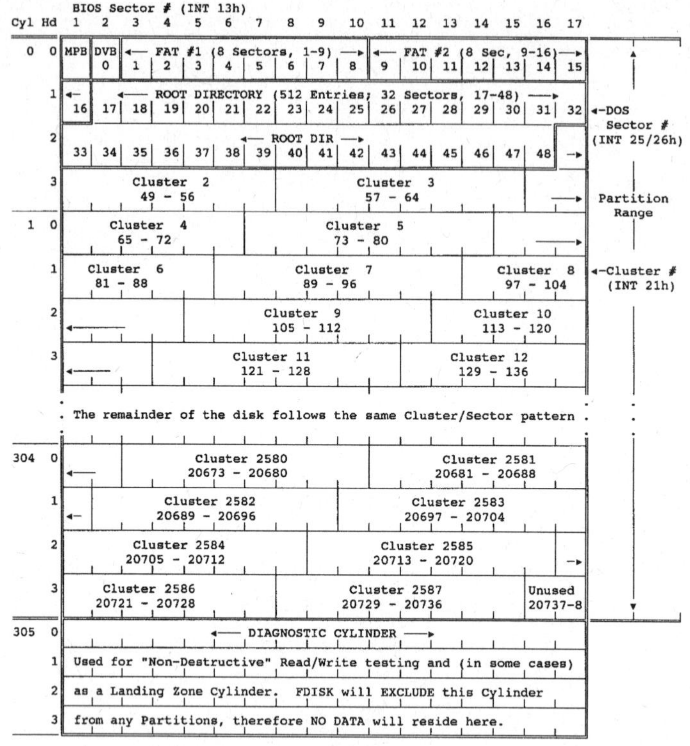

Fig. D.5. Disk map for a typical 10M hard drive (DOS 2.x).

Figure D.6 shows the disk map for a standard 10M hard disk (DOS 3.x or later) partitioned as a single MS-DOS volume as follows:

Drive type:	1, 23, 25, or 29 (IBM BIOS)
Drive geometry:	306 cylinders, 4 heads, 17 sectors/track (ST-506/412 MFM)
Drive capacity:	10.65 million bytes, or 10.16M
DOS version:	IBM or MS-DOS 2.0 or later
Hidden sectors:	17 (FDISK 3.0 or later) including master partition boot sector
DVB:	Cylinder 0, head 1, sector 1; DOS sector 0
FAT #1:	Sectors 1-8; 8 sectors long
FAT #2:	Sectors 9-16; 8 sectors long
Root directory:	Sectors 17-48; 32 sectors long
Data area:	Sectors 49-20,720; clusters 2-2585
Cluster size:	8 sectors (4,096 bytes)

Notes:

MPB = master partition boot sector
DVB = DOS volume boot sector
FAT = file allocation table

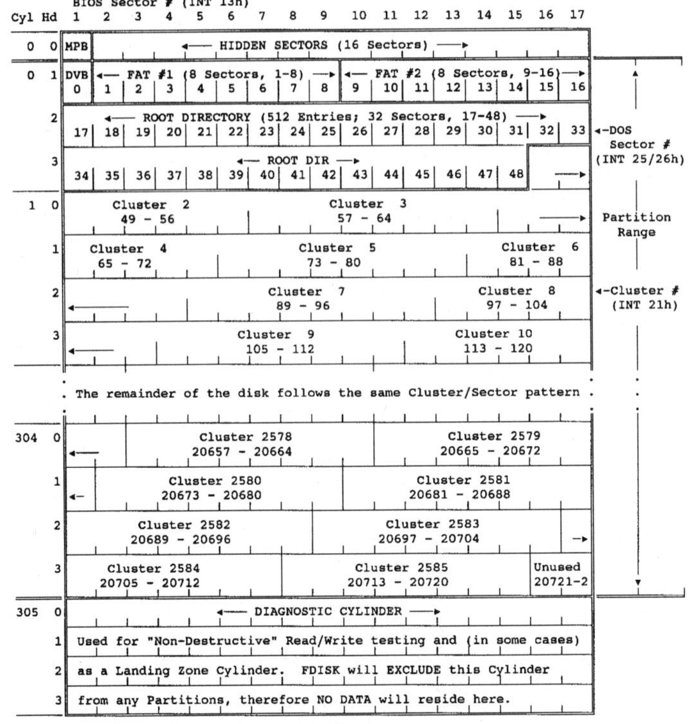

Fig. D.6. *Disk map for a standard 10M hard disk (DOS 3.x or later).*

Figure D.7 shows the disk map for a standard 20M hard disk (DOS 3.x or later) partitioned as a single MS-DOS volume as follows:

Drive type:	2 or 6 (IBM BIOS)
Drive geometry:	615 cylinders, 4 heads, 17 sectors/track (ST-506/412 MFM)
Drive capacity:	21.41 million bytes, or 20.42M
DOS version:	IBM or MS-DOS 3.0 or later
Hidden sectors:	17 including master partition boot sector
DVB:	Cylinder 0, head 1, sector 1; DOS sector 0
FAT #1:	Sectors 1-41; 41 sectors long
FAT #2:	Sectors 42-82; 41 sectors long
Root directory:	Sectors 83-114; 32 sectors long
Data area:	Sectors 115-41,734; clusters 2-10,406
Cluster size:	4 sectors (2,048 bytes)

Notes:

MPB = master partition boot sector
DVB = DOS volume boot sector
FAT = file allocation table

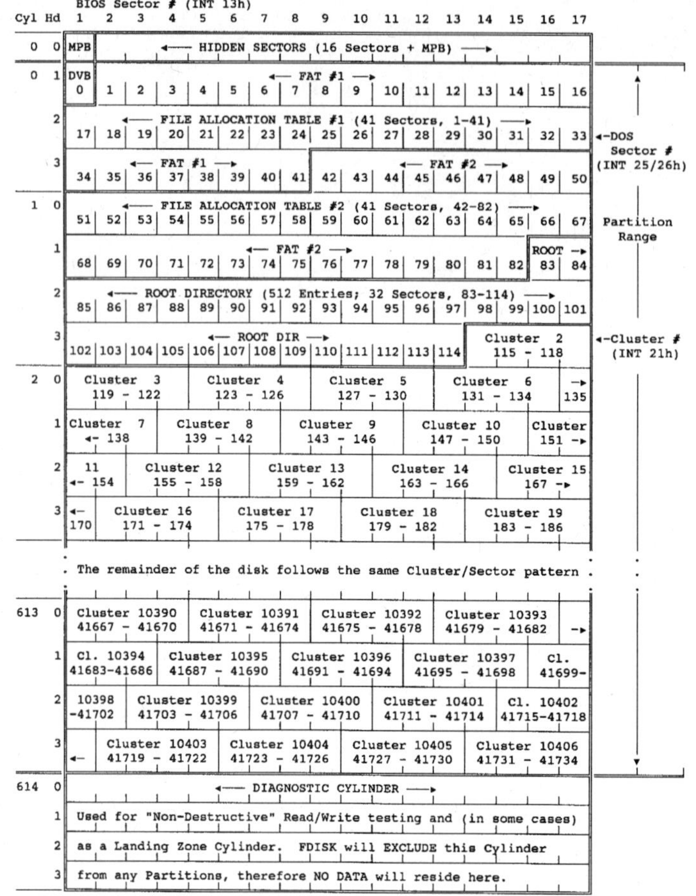

***Fig. D.7.** Disk map for a standard 20M hard disk (DOS 3.x or later).*

Figure D.8 shows the disk map for a standard 30M hard disk (DOS 3.x or later) partitioned as a single MS-DOS volume as follows:

Drive type:	8, 20, or 22 (IBM BIOS)
Drive geometry:	733 cylinders, 5 heads, 17 sectors/track (ST-506/412 MFM)
Drive capacity:	31.90 million bytes, or 30.42M
DOS version:	IBM or MS-DOS 3.0 or later
Hidden sectors:	17 including master partition boot sector
DVB:	Cylinder 0, head 1, sector 1; DOS sector 0
FAT #1:	Sectors 1-61; 61 sectors long
FAT #2:	Sectors 62-122; 61 sectors long

Root directory:	Sectors 123-154; 32 sectors long
Data area:	Sectors 155-62,202; clusters 2-15,513
Cluster size:	4 sectors (2,048 bytes)

Notes:

MPB = master partition boot sector
DVB = DOS volume boot sector
FAT = file allocation table

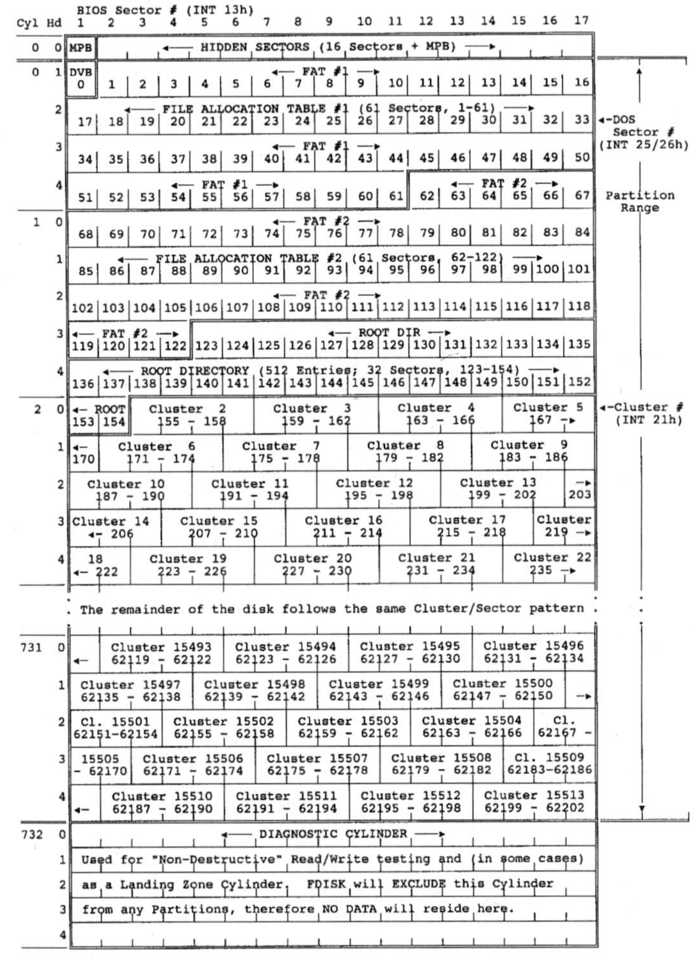

***Fig. D.8.** Disk map for standard 30M hard disk (DOS 3.x or later).*

ASCII and Extended ASCII Codes

This appendix presents the ASCII, Extended ASCII, and Extended-Function ASCII codes. In the tables, a ^ represents the Control (Ctrl) key. For example, ^C represents Ctrl-C.

ASCII Codes

The codes for the American Standard Code for Information Interchange (ASCII) are presented in the following table:

Decimal	*Hex*	*Octal*	*Binary*	*Graphic Character*	*ASCII Meaning*
0	0	0	00000000		^@ NUL (null)
1	1	1	00000001	☺	^A SOH (start-of-header)
2	2	2	00000010	●	^B STX (start-of-transmission)
3	3	3	00000011	♥	^C ETX (end-of-transmission)
4	4	4	00000100	♦	^D EOT (end-of-text)
5	5	5	00000101	♣	^E ENQ (enquiry)
6	6	6	00000110	♠	^F ACK (acknowledge)
7	7	7	00000111	•	^G BEL (bell)
8	8	10	00001000	◘	^H BS (backspace)
9	9	11	00001001	○	^I HT (horizontal tab)
10	A	12	00001010	◙	^J LF (line feed - also ^Enter)
11	B	13	00001011	♂	^K VT (vertical tab)
12	C	14	00001100	♀	^L FF (form feed)
13	D	15	00001101	♪	^M CR (carriage return)
14	E	16	00001110	♫	^N SO

Decimal	Hex	Octal	Binary	Graphic Character	ASCII Meaning
15	F	17	00001111	☼	^O SI
16	10	20	00010000	►	^P DLE
17	11	21	00010001	◄	^Q DC1
18	12	22	00010010	↕	^R DC2
19	13	23	00010011	‼	^S DC3
20	14	24	00010100	¶	^T DC4
21	15	25	00010101	§	^U NAK
22	16	26	00010110	▬	^V SYN
23	17	27	00010111	↨	^W ETB
24	18	30	00011000	↑	^X CAN (cancel)
25	19	31	00011001	↓	^Y EM
26	1A	32	00011010	→	^Z SUB (also end-of-file)
27	1B	33	00011011	←	^[ESC (Escape)
28	1C	34	00011100	∟	^\ FS (field separator)
29	1D	35	00011101	↔	^] GS
30	1E	36	00011110	▲	^^ RS (record separator)
31	1F	37	00011111	▼	^_ US
32	20	40	00100000		Space
33	21	41	00100001	!	!
34	22	42	00100010	"	"
35	23	43	00100011	#	#
36	24	44	00100100	$	$
37	25	45	00100101	%	%
38	26	46	00100110	&	&
39	27	47	00100111	'	'
40	28	50	00101000	(	(
41	29	51	00101001	)	)
42	2A	52	00101010	*	*
43	2B	53	00101011	+	+
44	2C	54	00101100	,	,
45	2D	55	00101101	–	–
46	2E	56	00101110	.	.
47	2F	57	00101111	/	/
48	30	60	00110000	0	0
49	31	61	00110001	1	1
50	32	62	00110010	2	2
51	33	63	00110011	3	3
52	34	64	00110100	4	4
53	35	65	00110101	5	5
54	36	66	00110110	6	6
55	37	67	00110111	7	7
56	38	70	00111000	8	8
57	39	71	00111001	9	9
58	3A	72	00111010	:	:
59	3B	73	00111011	;	;
60	3C	74	00111100	<	<
61	3D	75	00111101	=	=
62	3E	76	00111110	>	>
63	3F	77	00111111	?	?
64	40	100	01000000	@	@
65	41	101	01000001	A	A
66	42	102	01000010	B	B

Decimal	Hex	Octal	Binary	Graphic Character	ASCII Meaning
67	43	103	01000011	C	C
68	44	104	01000100	D	D
69	45	105	01000101	E	E
70	46	106	01000110	F	F
71	47	107	01000111	G	G
72	48	110	01001000	H	H
73	49	111	01001001	I	I
74	4A	112	01001010	J	J
75	4B	113	01001011	K	K
76	4C	114	01001100	L	L
77	4D	115	01001101	M	M
78	4E	116	01001110	N	N
79	4F	117	01001111	O	O
80	50	120	01010000	P	P
81	51	121	01010001	Q	Q
82	52	122	01010010	R	R
83	53	123	01010011	S	S
84	54	124	01010100	T	T
85	55	125	01010101	U	U
86	56	126	01010110	V	V
87	57	127	01010111	W	W
88	58	130	01011000	X	X
89	59	131	01011001	Y	Y
90	5A	132	01011010	Z	Z
91	5B	133	01011011	[	[
92	5C	134	01011100	\	\
93	5D	135	01011101	]	]
94	5E	136	01011110	^	^
95	5F	137	01011111	_	_
96	60	140	01100000	'	'
97	61	141	01100001	a	a
98	62	142	01100010	b	b
99	63	143	01100011	c	c
100	64	144	01100100	d	d
101	65	145	01100101	e	e
102	66	146	01100110	f	f
103	67	147	01100111	g	g
104	68	150	01101000	h	h
105	69	151	01101001	i	i
106	6A	152	01101010	j	j
107	6B	153	01101011	k	k
108	6C	154	01101100	l	l
109	6D	155	01101101	m	m
110	6E	156	01101110	n	n
111	6F	157	01101111	o	o
112	70	160	01110000	p	p
113	71	161	01110001	q	q
114	72	162	01110010	r	r
115	73	163	01110011	s	s
116	74	164	01110100	t	t
117	75	165	01110101	u	u
118	76	166	01110110	v	v

Decimal	*Hex*	*Octal*	*Binary*	*Graphic Character*	
119	77	167	01110111	w	w
120	78	170	01111000	x	x
121	79	171	01111001	y	y
122	7A	172	01111010	z	z
123	7B	173	01111011	{	{
124	7C	174	01111100	|	|
125	7D	175	01111101	}	}
126	7E	176	01111110	~	~
127	7F	177	01111111	Δ	Del
128	80	200	10000000	Ç	
129	81	201	10000001	ü	
130	82	202	10000010	é	
131	83	203	10000011	â	
132	84	204	10000100	ä	
133	85	205	10000101	à	
134	86	206	10000110	å	
135	87	207	10000111	ç	
136	88	210	10001000	ê	
137	89	211	10001001	ë	
138	8A	212	10001010	è	
139	8B	213	10001011	ï	
140	8C	214	10001100	î	
141	8D	215	10001101	ì	
142	8E	216	10001110	Ä	
143	8F	217	10001111	Å	
144	90	220	10010000	É	
145	91	221	10010001	æ	
146	92	222	10010010	Æ	
147	93	223	10010011	ô	
148	94	224	10010100	ö	
149	95	225	10010101	ò	
150	96	226	10010110	û	
151	97	227	10010111	ù	
152	98	230	10011000	ÿ	
153	99	231	10011001	Ö	
154	9A	232	10011010	Ü	
155	9B	233	10011011	¢	
156	9C	234	10011100	£	
157	9D	235	10011101	¥	
158	9E	236	10011110	₧	
159	9F	237	10011111	ƒ	
160	A0	240	10100000	á	
161	A1	241	10100001	í	
162	A2	242	10100010	ó	
163	A3	243	10100011	ú	
164	A4	244	10100100	ñ	
165	A5	245	10100101	Ñ	
166	A6	246	10100110	ª	
167	A7	247	10100111	º	
168	A8	250	10101000	¿	
169	A9	251	10101001	⌐	

Decimal	*Hex*	*Octal*	*Binary*	*Graphic Character*
170	AA	252	10101010	¬
171	AB	253	10101011	½
172	AC	254	10101100	¼
173	AD	255	10101101	¡
174	AE	256	10101110	«
175	AF	257	10101111	»
176	B0	260	10110000	░
177	B1	261	10110001	▒
178	B2	262	10110010	▓
179	B3	263	10110011	│
180	B4	264	10110100	┤
181	B5	265	10110101	╡
182	B6	266	10110110	╢
183	B7	267	10110111	╖
184	B8	270	10111000	╕
185	B9	271	10111001	╣
186	BA	272	10111010	║
187	BB	273	10111011	╗
188	BC	274	10111100	╝
189	BD	275	10111101	╜
190	BE	276	10111110	╛
191	BF	277	10111111	┐
192	C0	300	11000000	└
193	C1	301	11000001	┴
194	C2	302	11000010	┬
195	C3	303	11000011	├
196	C4	304	11000100	─
197	C5	305	11000101	┼
198	C6	306	11000110	╞
199	C7	307	11000111	╟
200	C8	310	11001000	╚
201	C9	311	11001001	╔
202	CA	312	11001010	╩
203	CB	313	11001011	╦
204	CC	314	11001100	╠
205	CD	315	11001101	═
206	CE	316	11001110	╬
207	CF	317	11001111	╧
208	D0	320	11010000	╨
209	D1	321	11010001	╤
210	D2	322	11010010	╥
211	D3	323	11010011	╙
212	D4	324	11010100	╘
213	D5	325	11010101	╒
214	D6	326	11010110	╓
215	D7	327	11010111	╫
216	D8	330	11011000	╪
217	D9	331	11011001	┘
218	DA	332	11011010	┌
219	DB	333	11011011	█

Decimal	*Hex*	*Octal*	*Binary*	*Graphic Character*
220	DC	334	11011100	▄
221	DD	335	11011101	▌
222	DE	336	11011110	▐
223	DF	337	11011111	▀
224	E0	340	11100000	α
225	E1	341	11100001	β
226	E2	342	11100010	Γ
227	E3	343	11100011	π
228	E4	344	11100100	Σ
229	E5	345	11100101	σ
230	E6	346	11100110	µ
231	E7	347	11100111	τ
232	E8	350	11101000	Φ
233	E9	351	11101001	Θ
234	EA	352	11101010	Ω
235	EB	353	11101011	δ
236	EC	354	11101100	∞
237	ED	355	11101101	φ
238	EE	356	11101110	ε
239	EF	357	11101111	∩
240	F0	360	11110000	≡
241	F1	361	11110001	±
242	F2	362	11110010	≥
243	F3	363	11110011	≤
244	F4	364	11110100	⌠
245	F5	365	11110101	⌡
246	F6	366	11110110	÷
247	F7	367	11110111	≈
248	F8	370	11111000	°
249	F9	371	11111001	∙
250	FA	372	11111010	·
251	FB	373	11111011	√
252	FC	374	11111100	^{n}
253	FD	375	11111101	^{2}
254	FE	376	11111110	■
255	FF	377	11111111	

Extended ASCII Keyboard Codes

Certain keys cannot be represented by the standard ASCII codes. To represent the codes, a two-character sequence is used. The first character is always an ASCII NUL (0). The second character and its translation are listed in the following table. Some codes expand to multikeystroke characters.

If an asterisk (*) appears in the column Enhanced Only, the sequence is available only on the Enhanced Keyboards (101- and 102-key keyboards).

Enhanced Only	*Decimal Meaning*	*Hex*	*Octal*	*Binary*	*Extended ASCII*
*	1	01	001	00000001	Alt-Esc
	3	03	003	00000011	Null (null character)
*	14	0E	016	00001110	Alt-Backspace
	15	0F	017	00001111	Shift-Tab (back-tab)
	16	10	020	00010000	Alt-Q
	17	11	021	00010001	Alt-W
	18	12	022	00010010	Alt-E
	19	13	023	00010011	Alt-R
	20	14	024	00010100	Alt-T
	21	15	025	00010101	Alt-Y
	22	16	026	00010110	Alt-U
	23	17	027	00010111	Alt-I
	24	18	030	00011000	Alt-O
	25	19	031	00011001	Alt-P
*	26	1A	032	00011010	Alt-[
*	27	1B	033	00011011	Alt-]
*	28	1C	034	00011100	Alt-Enter
	30	1E	036	00011110	Alt-A
	31	1F	037	00011111	Alt-S
	32	20	040	00100000	Alt-D
	33	21	041	00100001	Alt-F
	34	22	042	00100010	Alt-G
	35	23	043	00100011	Alt-H
	36	24	044	00100100	Alt-J
	37	25	045	00100101	Alt-K
	38	26	046	00100110	Alt-L
*	39	27	047	00100111	Alt-;
*	40	28	050	00101000	Alt-’
*	41	29	051	00101001	Alt-'
*	43	2B	053	00101011	Alt-\
	44	2C	054	00101100	Alt-Z
	45	2D	055	00101101	Alt-X
	46	2E	056	00101110	Alt-C
	47	2F	057	00101111	Alt-V
	48	30	060	00110000	Alt-B
	49	31	061	00110001	Alt-N
	50	32	062	00110010	Alt-M
*	51	33	063	00110011	Alt-,
*	52	34	064	00110100	Alt-.

Enhanced Only	*Decimal Meaning*	*Hex*	*Octal*	*Binary*	*Extended ASCII*
*	53	35	065	00110101	Alt-/
*	55	37	067	00110111	Alt-* (keypad)
	57	39	071	00111001	Alt-space bar
	59	3B	073	00111011	F1
	60	3C	074	00111100	F2
	61	3D	075	00111101	F3
	62	3E	076	00111110	F4
	63	3F	077	00111111	F5
	64	40	100	01000000	F6
	65	41	101	01000001	F7
	66	42	102	01000010	F8
	67	43	103	01000011	F9
	68	44	104	01000100	F10
	71	47	107	01000111	Home
	72	48	110	01001000	↑
	73	49	111	01001001	PgUp
	74	4A	112	01001010	Alt-Ω(keypad)
	75	4B	113	01001011	←
	76	4C	114	01001100	Shift-5 (keypad)
	77	4D	115	01001101	«
	78	4E	116	01001110	Alt-+ (keypad)
	79	4F	117	01001111	End
*	80	50	120	01010000	»
*	81	51	121	01010001	PgDn
*	82	52	122	01010010	Ins (Insert)
	83	53	123	01010011	Del (Delete)
	84	54	124	01010100	Shift-F1
	85	55	125	01010101	Shift-F2
	86	56	126	01010110	Shift-F3
	87	57	127	01010111	Shift-F4
	88	58	130	01011000	Shift-F5
	89	59	131	01011001	Shift-F6
	90	5A	132	01011010	Shift-F7
	91	5B	133	01011011	Shift-F8
	92	5C	134	01011100	Shift-F9
	93	5D	135	01011101	Shift-F10
	94	5E	136	01011110	Ctrl-F1
	95	5F	137	01011111	Ctrl-F2
	96	60	140	01100000	Ctrl-F3
	97	61	141	01100001	Ctrl-F4
	98	62	142	01100010	Ctrl-F5

Enhanced Only	*Decimal Meaning*	*Hex*	*Octal*	*Binary*	*Extended ASCII*
	99	63	143	01100011	Ctrl-F6
	100	64	144	01100100	Ctrl-F7
	101	65	145	01100101	Ctrl-F8
	102	66	146	01100110	Ctrl-F9
	103	67	147	01100111	Ctrl-F10
	104	68	150	01101000	Alt-F1
	105	69	151	01101001	Alt-F2
	106	6A	152	01101010	Alt-F3
	107	6B	153	01101011	Alt-F4
	108	6C	154	01101100	Alt-F5
	109	6D	155	01101101	Alt-F6
	110	6E	156	01101110	Alt-F7
	111	6F	157	01101111	Alt-F8
	112	70	160	01110000	Alt-F9
	113	71	161	01110001	Alt-F10
	114	72	162	01110010	Ctrl-PrtSc
	115	73	163	01110011	Ctrl-←
	116	74	164	01110100	Ctrl-→
	117	75	165	01110101	Ctrl-End
	118	76	166	01110110	Ctrl-PgDn
	119	77	167	01110111	Ctrl-Home
	120	78	170	01111000	Alt-1 (keyboard)
	121	79	171	01111001	Alt-2 (keyboard)
	122	7A	172	01111010	Alt-3 (keyboard)
	123	7B	173	01111011	Alt-4 (keyboard)
	124	7C	174	01111100	Alt-5 (keyboard)
	125	7D	175	01111101	Alt-6 (keyboard)
	126	7E	176	01111110	Alt-7 (keyboard)
	127	7F	177	01111111	Alt-8 (keyboard)
	128	80	200	10000000	Alt-9 (keyboard)
	129	81	201	10000001	Alt-0 (keyboard)
	130	82	202	10000010	Alt--(keyboard)
	131	83	203	10000011	Alt-= (keyboard)
	132	84	204	10000100	Ctrl-PgUp
*	133	85	205	10000101	F11
*	134	86	206	10000110	F12
*	135	87	207	10000111	Shift-F11
*	136	88	210	10001000	Shift-F12
*	137	89	211	10001001	Ctrl-F11
*	138	8A	212	10001010	Ctrl-F12
*	139	8B	213	10001011	Alt-F11

Enhanced Only	*Decimal Meaning*	*Hex*	*Octal*	*Binary*	*Extended ASCII*
*	140	8C	214	10001100	Alt-F12
	141	8D	215	10001101	Ctrl-↑/8 (keypad)
	142	8E	216	10001110	Ctrl-–(keypad)
	143	8F	217	10001111	Ctrl-5 (keypad)
	144	90	220	10010000	Ctrl-+ (keypad)
	145	91	221	10010001	Ctrl-↓/2 (keypad)
	146	92	222	10010010	Ctrl-Ins/0 (keypad)
	147	93	223	10010011	Ctrl-Del/. (keypad)
	148	94	224	10010100	Ctrl-Tab
*	149	95	225	10010101	Ctrl-/ (keypad)
*	150	96	226	10010110	Ctrl-* (keypad)
*	151	97	227	10010111	Alt-Home
*	152	98	230	10011000	Alt-↓
*	153	99	231	10011001	Alt-Page Up
*	155	9B	233	10011011	Alt-←
*	157	9D	235	10011101	Alt-→
*	159	9F	237	10011111	Alt-End
*	160	A0	240	10100000	Alt-↑
*	161	A1	241	10100001	Alt-Page Down
*	162	A2	242	10100010	Alt-Insert
*	163	A3	243	10100011	Alt-Delete
*	164	A4	244	10100100	Alt-/ (keypad)
*	165	A5	245	10100101	Alt-Tab
*	166	A6	256	10100110	Alt-Enter (keypad)

Extended Function ASCII Codes

The following extended codes are available only with the Enhanced Keyboards (101- and 102-key keyboards); the codes are available for key reassignment only with DOS 4.0 and later. The keys include the six-key editing pad and the four-key cursor-control pad. To reassign these keys, you must include the DEVICE=ANSI.SYS /X command in CONFIG.SYS or issue the enable extended function codes escape sequence (Esc[1q). All extended codes are prefixed by 224 decimal (E0 hex).

Decimal Meaning	*Hex*	*Octal*	*Binary*	*Extended ASCII*
71	47	107	01000111	Home
72	48	110	01001000	↑
73	49	111	01001001	Page Up
75	4B	113	01001011	←
77	4D	115	01001101	→
79	4F	117	01001111	End
80	50	120	01010000	↓
81	51	121	01010001	Page Down
82	52	122	01010010	Insert
83	53	123	01010011	Delete
115	73	163	01110011	Ctrl-←
116	74	164	01110100	Ctrl-→
117	75	165	01110101	Ctrl-End
118	76	166	01110110	Ctrl-Page Down
119	77	167	01110111	Ctrl-Home
132	84	204	10000100	Ctrl-Page Up
141	8D	215	10001101	Ctrl-↑
145	91	221	10010001	Ctrl-↓
146	92	222	10010010	Ctrl-Insert
147	93	223	10010011	Ctrl-Delete

Figure E.1 shows the extended ASCII line drawing characters.

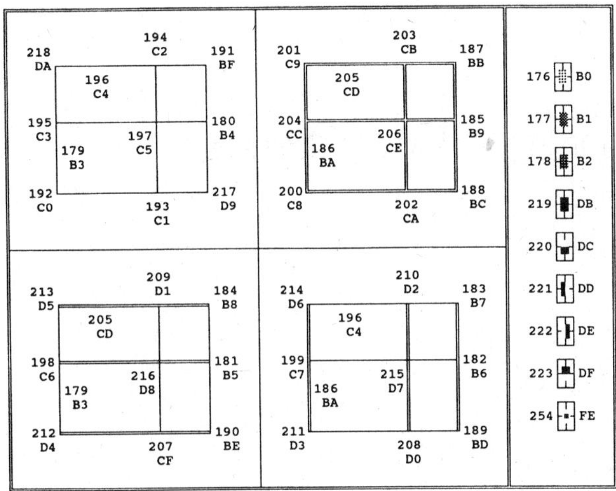

Fig. E.1. Extended ASCII line drawing characters.

F

Memory Maps

Figures F.1 and F.2 show the 16M map for an AT system in protected mode. Figure F.1 shows where the real-mode addressable memory ends. Figure F.2 shows where extended memory picks up. An 80286 or later system running in protected mode is required to address memory beyond the 1M boundary. The 8086 and 8088 cannot run in protected mode and therefore cannot access memory beyond the 1M boundary.

In the figures, the following symbols are used:

. = Program accessible memory

v = Video RAM

a = Adapter board (special-purpose) ROM and RAM

r = Motherboard ROM BIOS

b = IBM ROM (cassette) BASIC

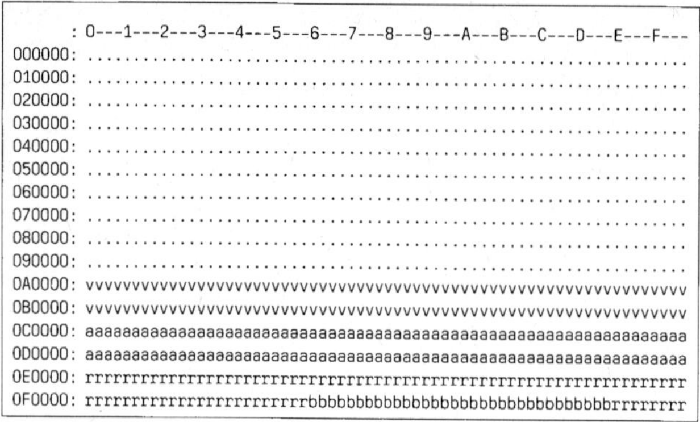

```
      : 0---1---2---3---4---5---6---7---8---9---A---B---C---D---E---F---
000000: ................................................................
010000: ................................................................
020000: ................................................................
030000: ................................................................
040000: ................................................................
050000: ................................................................
060000: ................................................................
070000: ................................................................
080000: ................................................................
090000: ................................................................
0A0000: vvvvvvvvvvvvvvvvvvvvvvvvvvvvvvvvvvvvvvvvvvvvvvvvvvvvvvvvvvvvvvvv
0B0000: vvvvvvvvvvvvvvvvvvvvvvvvvvvvvvvvvvvvvvvvvvvvvvvvvvvvvvvvvvvvvvvv
0C0000: aaaaaaaaaaaaaaaaaaaaaaaaaaaaaaaaaaaaaaaaaaaaaaaaaaaaaaaaaaaaaaaa
0D0000: aaaaaaaaaaaaaaaaaaaaaaaaaaaaaaaaaaaaaaaaaaaaaaaaaaaaaaaaaaaaaaaa
0E0000: rrrrrrrrrrrrrrrrrrrrrrrrrrrrrrrrrrrrrrrrrrrrrrrrrrrrrrrrrrrrrrrr
0F0000: rrrrrrrrrrrrrrrrrrrrrrrrbbbbbbbbbbbbbbbbbbbbbbbbbbbbbbbbbrrrrrrr
```

Fig. F.1. *IBM 16M memory map to the point where real-mode addressable memory ends.*

```
      : 0---1---2---3---4---5---6---7---8---9---A---B---C---D---E---F---
100000: ................................................................
110000: ................................................................
120000: ................................................................
130000: ................................................................
140000: ................................................................

        \
        /
        \

A large break occurs

        \
        /
        \

E80000: ................................................................
E90000: ................................................................
EA0000: ................................................................
EB0000: ................................................................
EC0000: ................................................................
ED0000: ................................................................
EE0000: ................................................................
EF0000: ................................................................
      : 0---1---2---3---4---5---6---7---8---9---A---B---C---D---E---F---
F00000: ................................................................
F10000: ................................................................
F20000: ................................................................
F30000: ................................................................
F40000: ................................................................
F50000: ................................................................
F60000: ................................................................
F70000: ................................................................
F80000: ................................................................
F90000: ................................................................
FA0000: ................................................................
FB0000: ................................................................
FC0000: ................................................................
FD0000: ................................................................
FE0000: rrrrrrrrrrrrrrrrrrrrrrrrrrrrrrrrrrrrrrrrrrrrrrrrrrrrrrrrrrrrrrrr
FF0000: rrrrrrrrrrrrrrrrrrrrrrrrbbbbbbbbbbbbbbbbbbbbbbbbbbbbbbbbbrrrrrrr
```

Fig. F.2. *IBM 16M memory map where extended memory picks up.*

Note the duplicate of the ROM BIOS at the end of the 16th megabyte. The memory in these last two segments is a mirror image of what is in the last two segments of the first megabyte. This duplicate ROM BIOS is required by the 80286 and later processors to provide for switching between real and protected mode.

Figure F.3 shows the logical locations and relationships among conventional, extended, and expanded memory. Notice that only the conventional and extended memory locations are directly addressable by the processor. The expanded memory can be accessed through a small window in the conventional memory space.

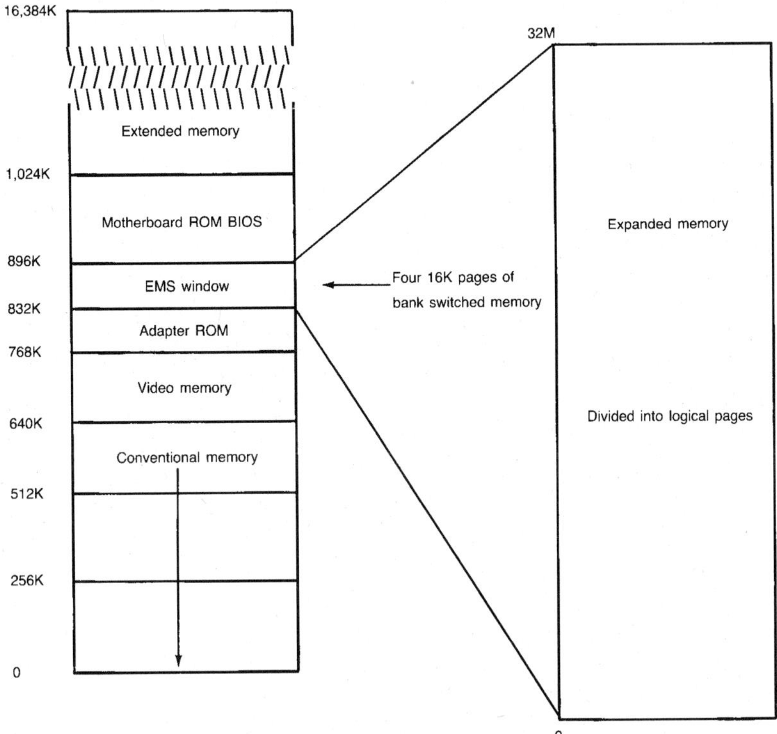

Fig. F.3. Memory location.

Index

Symbols

A

C

D

E

F

J-K

L

M

Q

R

T

U

V

W

X-Z

Computer Books From Que Mean PC Performance!

Spreadsheets

2-3 Database Techniques $29.95
2-3 Graphics Techniques $24.95
2-3 Macro Library, 3rd Edition $39.95
2-3 Release 2.2 Business Applications . . . $39.95
2-3 Release 2.2 PC Tutor $39.95
2-3 Release 2.2 QueCards $19.95
2-3 Release 2.2 Quick Reference . . . . . . $ 8.95
2-3 Release 2.2 QuickStart, 2nd Edition . . . $19.95
2-3 Release 2.2 Workbook and Disk $29.95
2-3 Release 3 Business Applications $39.95
2-3 Release 3 Workbook and Disk $29.95
2-3 Release 3.1 Quick Reference . . . . . . $ 8.95
2-3 Release 3.1 QuickStart, 2nd Edition . . . $19.95
2-3 Tips, Tricks, and Traps, 3rd Edition . . . $24.95
cel Business Applications: IBM Version . . $39.95
cel Quick Reference . . . . $ 8.95
cel QuickStart $19.95
cel Tips, Tricks, and Traps $22.95
ing 1-2-3/G $29.95
ing 1-2-3, Special Edition $27.95
ing 1-2-3 Release 2.2, Special Edition . . . $27.95
ing 1-2-3 Release 3.1, 2nd Edition $29.95
ing Excel: IBM Version $29.95
ing Lotus Spreadsheet for DeskMate $22.95
ing Quattro Pro $24.95
ing SuperCalc5, 2nd Edition $29.95

Databases

ASE III Plus Handbook, 2nd Edition $24.95
ASE III Plus Tips, Tricks, and Traps $24.95
ASE III Plus Workbook and Disk $29.95
ASE IV Applications Library, 2nd Edition . $39.95
ASE IV Programming Techniques $24.95
ASE IV Quick Reference . . . . $ 8.95
ASE IV QuickStart $19.95
ASE IV Tips, Tricks,and Traps, 2nd Edition. $24.95
ASE IV Workbook and Disk $29.95
ing Clipper $24.95
ing DataEase $24.95
ing dBASE IV $27.95
ing Paradox 3 . . . . $24.95
ing R:BASE $29.95
ing Reflex, 2nd Edition $24.95
ing SQL $29.95

Business Applications

ways Quick Reference . . . . $ 8.95
roduction to Business Software $14.95
roduction to Personal Computers $19.95
tus Add-in Toolkit Guide $29.95
rton Utilities Quick Reference . . . . $ 8.95
Tools Quick Reference, 2nd Edition . . . . $ 8.95
&A Quick Reference . . . . $ 8.95
e's Computer User's Dictionary . . . . . . $ 9.95
e's Wizard Book . . . . $ 9.95
icken Quick Reference . . . . $ 8.95
artWare Tips, Tricks, and Traps
2nd Edition $24.95
ing Computers in Business $22.95
ing DacEasy, 2nd Edition $24.95
ing Enable/OA $29.95
ing Harvard Project Manager $24.95
ing Managing Your Money, 2nd Edition . . $19.95
ing Microsoft Works: IBM Version $22.95
ing Norton Utilities $24.95
Using PC Tools Deluxe $24.95
Using Peachtree $27.95
Using PFS: First Choice $22.95
Using PROCOMM PLUS $19.95
Using Q&A, 2nd Edition $23.95
Using Quicken: IBM Version, 2nd Edition . . $19.95
Using Smart $22.95
Using SmartWare II $29.95
Using Symphony, Special Edition $29.95
Using Time Line $24.95
Using TimeSlips $24.95

CAD

AutoCAD Quick Reference . . . . $ 8.95
AutoCAD Sourcebook 1991 . . . . $27.95
Using AutoCAD, 3rd Edition $29.95
Using Generic CADD $24.95

Word Processing

Microsoft Word 5 Quick Reference . . . . . . $ 8.95
Using DisplayWrite 4, 2nd Edition $24.95
Using LetterPerfect $22.95
Using Microsoft Word 5.5: IBM Version,
2nd Edition $24.95
Using MultiMate $24.95
Using Professional Write $22.95
Using Word for Windows $24.95
Using WordPerfect 5 . . . . $27.95
Using WordPerfect 5.1, Special Edition . . . $27.95
Using WordStar, 3rd Edition $27.95
WordPerfect PC Tutor $39.95
WordPerfect Power Pack $39.95
WordPerfect Quick Reference . . . . $ 8.95
WordPerfect QuickStart $19.95
WordPerfect 5 Workbook and Disk $29.95
WordPerfect 5.1 Quick Reference . . . . . . $ 8.95
WordPerfect 5.1 QuickStart $19.95
WordPerfect 5.1 Tips, Tricks, and Traps . . . $24.95
WordPerfect 5.1 Workbook and Disk $29.95

Hardware/Systems

DOS Tips, Tricks, and Traps $24.95
DOS Workbook and Disk, 2nd Edition $29.95
Fastback Quick Reference . . . . $ 8.95
Hard Disk Quick Reference . . . . $ 8.95
MS-DOS PC Tutor $39.95
MS-DOS Power Pack $39.95
MS-DOS Quick Reference . . . . $ 8.95
MS-DOS QuickStart, 2nd Edition $19.95
MS-DOS User's Guide, Special Edition . . . $29.95
Networking Personal Computers, 3rd Edition $24.95
The Printer Bible $29.95
Que's PC Buyer's Guide $12.95
Understanding UNIX: A Conceptual Guide,
2nd Edition $21.95
Upgrading and Repairing PCs $29.95
Using DOS $22.95
Using Microsoft Windows 3, 2nd Edition . . $24.95
Using Novell NetWare $29.95
Using OS/2 . . . . $29.95
Using PC DOS, 3rd Edition $24.95
Using Prodigy $19.95
Using UNIX $29.95
Using Your Hard Disk $29.95
Windows 3 Quick Reference . . . . $ 8.95

Desktop Publishing/Graphics

CorelDRAW Quick Reference . . . . $ 8.95
Harvard Graphics Quick Reference . . . . . . $ 8.95
Using Animator $24.95
Using DrawPerfect $24.95
Using Harvard Graphics, 2nd Edition $24.95
Using Freelance Plus $24.95
Using PageMaker: IBM Version, 2nd Edition . $24.95
Using PFS: First Publisher, 2nd Edition $24.95
Using Ventura Publisher, 2nd Edition $24.95

Macintosh/Apple II

AppleWorks QuickStart $19.95
The Big Mac Book, 2nd Edition $29.95
Excel QuickStart $19.95
The Little Mac Book . . . . $ 9.95
Que's Macintosh Multimedia Handbook . . . $24.95
Using AppleWorks, 3rd Edition $24.95
Using Excel: Macintosh Version $24.95
Using FileMaker $24.95
Using MacDraw $24.95
Using MacroMind Director $29.95
Using MacWrite $24.95
Using Microsoft Word 4: Macintosh Version . $24.95
Using Microsoft Works: Macintosh Version,
2nd Edition $24.95
Using PageMaker: Macinsoth Version,
2nd Edition $24.95

Programming/Technical

Assembly Language Quick Reference . . . . . $ 8.95
C Programmer' sToolkit $39.95
C Quick Reference . . . . $ 8.95
DOS and BIOS Functions Quick Reference . . $ 8.95
DOS Programmer's Reference, 2nd Edition . . $29.95
Network Programming in C $49.95
Oracle Programmer's Guide $29.95
QuickBASIC Advanced Techniques $24.95
Quick C Programmer's Guide $29.95
Turbo Pascal Advanced Techniques $24.95
Turbo Pascal Quick Reference . . . . $ 8.95
UNIX Programmer's Quick Reference . . . . $ 8.95
UNIX Programmer's Reference $29.95
UNIX Shell Commands Quick Reference . . . $ 8.95
Using Assembly Language, 2nd Edition $29.95
Using BASIC $24.95
Using C $29.95
Using QuickBASIC 4 . . . . $24.95
Using Turbo Pascal $29.95

For More Information,
Call Toll Free!

1-800-428-5331

All prices and titles subject to change without notice. Non-U.S. prices may be higher. Printed in the U.S.A.

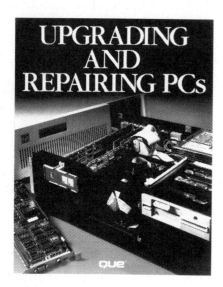

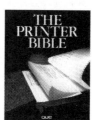

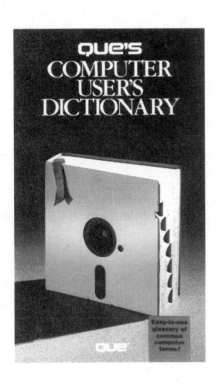

Find It Fast With Que's Quick References!

Que's Quick References are the compact, easy-to-use guides to essential application information. Written for all users, Quick References include vital command information under easy-to-find alphabetical listings. Quick References are a must for anyone who needs command information fast!

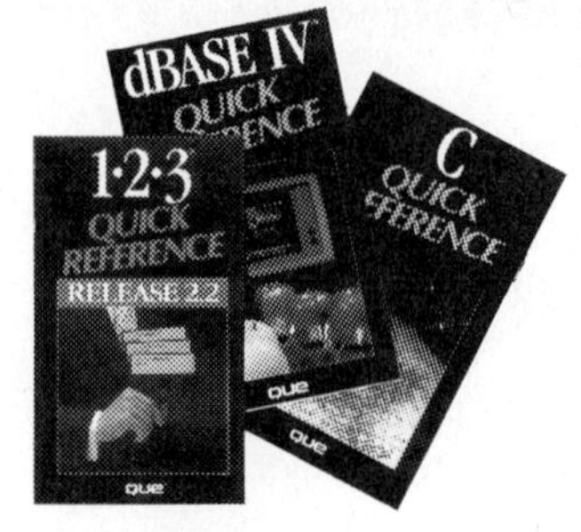

1-2-3 for DOS Release 2.3 Quick Reference
Release 2.3
Order #1352 **$9.95 USA**
0-88022-725-7, 160 pp., 4 3/4 x 8

1-2-3 Release 3.1 Quick Reference
Releases 3 & 3.1
Order #1267 **$8.95 USA**
0-88022-656-0, 160 pp., 4 3/4 x 8

Allways Quick Reference
Version 1.0
Order #1193 **$8.95 USA**
0-88022-605-6, 160 pp., 4 3/4 x 8

Assembly Language Quick Reference
IBM Version
Order #934 **$8.95 USA**
0-88022-428-2, 160 pp., 4 3/4 x 8

AutoCAD Quick Reference, 2nd Edition
Releases 10 & 11
Order #1217 **$8.95 USA**
0-88022-622-6, 160 pp., 4 3/4 x 8

Batch File and Macros Quick Reference
Through DOS 5.0
Order #1311 **$9.95 USA**
0-88022-699-4, 160 pp., 4 3/4 x 8

C Quick Reference
IBM Version
Order #868 **$8.95 USA**
0-88022-372-3, 160 pp., 4 3/4 x 8

CorelDRAW Quick Reference
Through Version 1.2
Order #1186 **$8.95 USA**
0-88022-597-1, 160 pp., 4 3/4 x 8

dBASE IV Quick Reference
Version 1.0
Order #867 **$8.95 USA**
0-88022-371-5, 160 pp., 4 3/4 x 8

DOS and BIOS Functions Quick Reference
Version 4
Order #932 **$8.95 USA**
0-88022-426-6, 160 pp., 4 3/4 x 8

Excel Quick Reference
Version 2.1
Order #1023 **$8.95 USA**
0-88022-473-8, 160 pp., 4 3/4 x 8

Fastback Quick Reference
Version 2.1
Order # 1260 **$8.95 USA**
0-88022-650-1, 160 pp., 4 3/4 x 8

Hard Disk Quick Reference
Through DOS 4.01
Order #974 **$8.95 USA**
0-88022-443-6, 160 pp., 4 3/4 x 8

Harvard Graphics Quick Reference
Version 2.3
Order #1084 **$8.95 USA**
0-88022-538-6, 160 pp., 4 3/4 x 8

Laplink Quick Reference
Laplink III
Order #1314 **$9.95 USA**
0-88022-702-8, 160 pp., 4 3/4 x 8

Microsoft Word 5 Quick Reference
Version 5.5
Order #976 **$8.95 USA**
0-80822-444-4, 160 pp., 4 3/4 x 8

Microsoft Works Quick Reference
Through IBM Version 2.0
Order #1306 **$9.95 USA**
0-88022-694-3, 160 pp., 4 3/4 x 8

MS-DOS 5 Quick Reference
Version 5.0
Order #1256 **$9.95 USA**
0-88022-646-3, 160 pp., 4 3/4 x 8

MS-DOS Quick Reference
Through Version 3.3
Order #865 **$8.95 USA**
0-88022-369-3, 160 pp., 4 3/4 x 8

Norton Utilities Quick Reference
Norton Utilities 5 & Norton Commander 3
Order #1053 **$8.95 USA**
0-88022-508-4, 160 pp., 4 3/4 x 8

PC Tools Quick Reference, 2nd Edition
Through Version 6.0
Order #1185 **$8.95 USA**
0-88022-596-3, 160 pp., 4 3/4 x 8

Q&A Quick Reference
Versions 2, 3, & 4
Order #1165 **$8.95 USA**
0-88022-581-5, 160 pp., 4 3/4 x 8

Quattro Pro Quick Reference
Through Version 2.0
Order #1304 **$8.95 USA**
0-88022-692-7, 160 pp., 4 3/4 x 8

Quicken Quick Reference
IBM Through Version 4
Order #1187 **$8.95 USA**
0-88022-598-X, 160 pp., 4 3/4 x 8

Turbo Pascal Quick Reference
Version 5
Order #935 **$8.95 USA**
0-88022-429-0, 160 pp., 4 3/4 x 8

UNIX Programmer's Quick Reference
AT&T System V, Release 3
Order #1081 **$8.95 USA**
0-88022-535-1, 160 pp., 4 3/4 x 8

UNIX Shell Commands Quick Reference
AT&T System V, Releases 3 & 4
Order #1147 **$8.95 USA**
0-88022-572-6, 160 pp., 4 3/4 x 8

Windows 3 Quick Reference
Version 3
Order #1230 **$8.95 USA**
0-88022-631-5, 160 pp., 4 3/4 x 8

WordPerfect 5.1 Quick Reference
WordPerfect 5.1
Order #1158 **$8.95 USA**
0-88022-576-9, 160 pp., 4 3/4 x 8

WordPerfect Quick Reference
WordPerfect 5
Order #866 **$8.95 USA**
0-88022-370-7, 160 pp., 4 3/4 x 8

To Order, Call:
(800) 428-5331 OR (317) 573-2510

NO POSTAGE
NECESSARY
IF MAILED
IN THE
UNITED STATES

BUSINESS REPLY MAIL
First Class Permit No. 9918 Indianapolis, IN

Postage will be paid by addressee

11711 N. College
Carmel, IN 46032

NO POSTAGE
NECESSARY
IF MAILED
IN THE
UNITED STATES

BUSINESS REPLY MAIL
First Class Permit No. 9918 Indianapolis, IN

Postage will be paid by addressee

11711 N. College
Carmel, IN 46032